Transatlantic Bondage

SUNY series, Afro-Latinx Futures
——————
Vanessa K. Valdés, editor

Transatlantic Bondage

Slavery and Freedom in Spain,
Santo Domingo, and Puerto Rico

Edited by
LISSETTE ACOSTA CORNIEL

Cover art: *The Gulf Stream*, Winslow Homer
© Catharine Lorillard Wolfe Collection, Wolfe Fund, 1906/The Metropolitan Museum of Art.

Published by State University of New York Press, Albany

© 2024 State University of New York

All rights reserved

Printed in the United States of America

No part of this book may be used or reproduced in any manner whatsoever without written permission. No part of this book may be stored in a retrieval system or transmitted in any form or by any means including electronic, electrostatic, magnetic tape, mechanical, photocopying, recording, or otherwise without the prior permission in writing of the publisher.

For information, contact State University of New York Press, Albany, NY
www.sunypress.edu

Library of Congress Cataloging-in-Publication Data

Name: Acosta Corniel, Lissette, 1977– editor.
Title: Transatlantic bondage : slavery and society in Spain, Hispaniola, and Puerto Rico / edited by Lissette Acosta Corniel.
Description: Albany, NY : State University of New York, [2024] | Series: SUNY series, Afro-Latinx futures | Includes bibliographical references and index.
Identifiers: LCCN 2023045135 | ISBN 9781438497938 (hardcover : alk. paper) | ISBN 9781438497945 (ebook) | ISBN 9781438497921 (pbk. : alk. paper)
Subjects: LCSH: Slavery—Spain—History. | Slavery—Hispaniola—History. | Slavery—Puerto Rico—History. | Enslaved persons—Spain—History. | Enslaved persons—Hispaniola—History. | Enslaved persons—Puerto Rico—History.
Classification: LCC HT1216 .T736 2024 | DDC 306.3/6209171246—dc23/eng/20240224
LC record available at https://lccn.loc.gov/2023045135

10 9 8 7 6 5 4 3 2 1

*In memory of
Gwendolyn Midlo Hall,
Joseph C. Dorsey,
and David M. Stark*

Contents

ACKNOWLEDGMENTS ix

INTRODUCTION 1
    Lissette Acosta Corniel

CHAPTER 1
Spanish Slave Legislation: From Slavery to Abolition in Spain
and the Americas 27
    Aurelia Martín Casares

CHAPTER 2
Legislation and Slavery from a Local Perspective: Slaves in the
Municipal Ordinances of Extremadura, 1500–1800 49
    Rocío Periáñez Gómez

CHAPTER 3
Slavery and the Pursuit of Freedom in Sixteenth-Century
Santo Domingo 73
    Richard Lee Turits

CHAPTER 4
African Slavery and Laws in La Española: The Beginnings of
Modern Colonization in the Americas (1520s–1540s) 103
    Anthony R. Stevens-Acevedo

CHAPTER 5
Black Women in Sixteenth-Century Santo Domingo: Free,
Enslaved, Founders, and Explorers 137
    Lissette Acosta Corniel

CHAPTER 6
Transgressing Social, Gender, and Sexual Norms in Colonial
Santo Domingo (1716–1719) 165
   Jacqueline Jiménez Polanco

CHAPTER 7
Fostering a Sense of Community in Seventeenth-Century
Puerto Rico: The Godparenthood of Enslaved Infants, Children,
and Adults in San Juan, 1672–1706 187
   David M. Stark

CHAPTER 8
A Tradition of Contraband: Secreting and Silencing the
Illegal Importation and Exploitation of Enslaved Africans in
Spanish Colonial Puerto Rico 229
   Jorge L. Chinea

CONTRIBUTORS 275

INDEX 279

Acknowledgments

This project originated from a symposium titled "Colonial Slave Legislations and Slavery in the Americas," sponsored by the CUNY Dominican Studies Institute (CUNY DSI), the Afro-Latin American Research Institute at Harvard University (ALARI), and the Black Studies Program at the City College of New York in 2014, during my postdoc at the CUNY DSI. After the exchange, immediately as we were getting up from our seats, Ana Lucia Araujo suggested that we consider the idea of developing the topics discussed into a book. Ana's seed grew to be this book, that we hope develops into many branches through scholars looking to write more about slavery in Spain, Santo Domingo, and Puerto Rico.

This book would not have become a reality without the support of the CUNY DSI and its staff, especially its director, Dr. Ramona Hernández, and its chief librarian, Prof. Sarah Aponte. I owe a lifetime debt to Prof. Aponte; assistant librarian Jhensen Ortiz; assistant archivist Jessy Pérez; accountant, Greysi Peralta; and research Assistant, Priscilla Mejía. I am indebted to the contributors for trusting the vision of the project, for the insightful exchanges, and for their patience. Some of the original contributors to this book include the late Gwendolyn Midlo Hall (2022) and Joseph C. Dorsey (2023). Joe read and listened to me many times on the phone as I read the first drafts of the introduction. He was so generous with his time and his knowledge, and I am fortunate to have benefited from being around when he laughed and danced. Joe loved to dance. Gwen and I spent a lot of time together in her apartment in East Lansing, Michigan. We even took a road trip once to surprise Joe Dorsey in Indiana. She later welcomed me in her home in Guanajuato, Mexico, where we worked on the final touches of the introduction, but the condition was that we had to have margaritas and how could I say no to Gwen? She was also very generous with her time, was feisty about her ideas, and guarded junior scholars like a mom. I am also thankful to her son Haywood Hall for allowing us to visit Gwen to the end. David M. Stark (2023) joined the project in 2019. From the beginning, David and I connected. We began to exchange ideas about his chapter on godparenthood in Puerto Rico. We then remembered that we had met at the Spanish Caribbean Conference, in Santo Domingo, that I co-coordinated for CUNY DSI in 2011. He was organized and committed to his work. Even as his illness progressed, he continued to work. David was especially respectful of my time and work, and I will forever be thankful.

In the Dominican Republic, my friends made everything happen for me during my writing time there. Ana Geraldo provided a quiet space for me to write, nourished me with delicious meals, and graced me with her understanding of what it means to have to be alone and write. Victor Martínez Rojas, my brother from other parents, and Samuel Lluveres (Boli) made sure I had everything I needed. Carlos Rodríguez Almaguer and Danay López saved me when I could not format the first drafts of the book. *Les agradezco tanto*. Natalia González, Quisqueya Lora Hugui, Pablo Mella, S.J., and Any Lafontaine are my rapid dial when I need to discuss any reference related to Dominican history. I admire them and enjoy the complicity so much. I also would like to thank Rudy Berihuete and Violeta Quezada for being ready to assist when needed. Nato, Tere, Gertrudis, and Popi in Río San Juan have never said no. *Lo que significan para mí no me alcanza ponerlo aquí*. In Cuba, Barbara Danzie León has been my human finding-aid, *gracias*. In Spain, José Luis Belmonte Postigo is one of the best and most generous scholars I have met, *gracias por todo*.

In the U.S., at the Borough of Manhattan Community College, I am thankful to Guerda Baucicaut and Raquel Whitmeyer from our library. Thank you for assisting me with so many requests. Our department's office assistant Rob de Anthony was ready and able when I had to compile data for my chapter, as he learned Spanish in the process. Ana Daniels, our department's administrative assistant, is God sent. The Summer Writing Accountability Team (SWAT 2021), Judith M. Anderson, Rigoberto Andino, Monica Foust, Prithi Kanakamedala, Shirley Leyro, RaShelle Peck, Kersha Smith, Anika Thrower, and Linta Varghese, held me accountable even when at moments I thought it was not going to happen. I am also very thankful for the course release time granted to work on this book. Anne Green, at Southeast Missouri State University, assisted me with compiling sources. At Dartmouth College, Keiselim A. Montás provided generous comments that improved my translation of Chapter 2. *Gracias Keisy por tu tiempo, cariño y amistad.* Elizabeth Zimmer, my on-call editor, I am so thankful for you. My heartfelt gratitude goes to Sarah Aponte and Anthony Stevens-Acevedo for being my 911, whether it was to ask about a source or to vent. I really do not know what I would have done without you two. Librarian, Jesús Alonso-Regalado at SUNY Albany, *eres lo máximo.*

I would like to express my sincere gratitude to the series editor, Vanessa K. Valdés, for believing that this was an important project. Thank you to acquisitions editor Rebecca Colesworthy, and the SUNY Press team that I worked with—Julia Cosacchi, John Britch, Susan Geraghty, Laura Glen, and Aimee Harrison. Rebecca, I would not have survived this process without your patience, suggestions, and good vibes. Jesse Tisch, thank you for going above and beyond during the indexing process. Thank you to the two anonymous readers for their generous comments and suggestions, which greatly improved the final version of the manuscript. I am especially thankful to David Wheat, one of those anonymous readers who later revealed his identity to me and whose references and continued feedback improved the final version of this book.

I am grateful for James Louis-Charles, who has been deprived of my time and company during the final stages of working on the manuscript. Thank you for your words of encouragement, support, love, patience, and for adapting to the insane process of writing and publishing. *Mèsi anpil cheri.*

To get all of this done, I operated on three engines: (1) my mentor, Colbert I. Nepaulsingh; (2) my immediate family—and yes, my family knows and is okay with the fact that Nepaulsingh is number 1; and (3) my community. Professor Nepaulsingh and his wife Marla Henríquez Nepaulsingh have been there in immeasurable ways. Two for one. I still cannot believe it. How did I get that lucky ticket? *Gracias* profe, for reading early versions of this project. My family, Sunilda Corniel, Moisés Rodríguez, Scarlet Bosque (Nani), and Eli Miguel Mercado have shielded me with their love, understanding, and support, including Penky, our rescued dog. Eli and Mami have been my research assistants since the beginning. Eli has been there since I was writing papers, and Mami has been the low-key content editor of all my work. Mami, *tu sabiduría me da luz. Tío Miguelito Corniel, tú has sido mi norte desde niña.*

My community, a village of family and friends who have become family is unwaveringly loyal, and for that I will forever be thankful. You, the *constantes*, uplift me.

Introduction

Lissette Acosta Corniel

This book attempts to highlight Santo Domingo[1] and Puerto Rico in the history of Atlantic slavery. New World slavery as it is conventionally understood—as a field of study—has not had to negotiate for space in scholarship, being that it has been widely addressed. In fact, it is considered one of the most important events in the world, not only because of its level of inhumane actions and consequences, but because more and more research about slavery has been produced through the years. Still, archival documents and gaps in scholarship show us that there is more to know about the first free and enslaved Blacks brought to the Americas. This study refers to Blacks who arrived by force, and, by contrast, free Blacks who requested licenses from the Spanish Crown to travel to the newly conquered colonies or obtained their freedom after arrival.[2] In this context, this book examines Africans and their descendants from various perspectives, starting with their history in Spain and foregrounding Santo Domingo and Puerto Rico. It aims to, first, suggest new areas of study in relation to the presence of free and enslaved black Africans—largely sub-Saharan Africans—in the Americas and their relation to Spain as the purveyor of Black slavery in the Western Hemisphere; second, it presents the islands of the Spanish Caribbean as a key component of the formation of Black identities and Black societies in the Americas, as well as ongoing, though shrinking, representations of the Black presence in Spain itself. And third, it contributes to the existing knowledge that emphasizes the Spanish Caribbean as a pivotal area of sociocultural, sociopolitical, and socioeconomic study in relation to Atlantic studies. Thus, to study Black people in the Spanish Caribbean, we look at their earlier presence in the history of Spain. The chapters in this collection consider first their life experiences as Afro-Iberians and second the extent to which there were transfers of these experiences to the Americas. To that end, while a growing number of scholars have published extensively on the topic in the last few decades, the interest in Blacks and slavery in Spain emerged in the early to the mid-twentieth century.[3] Scholars began the great and complex task of archival investigation, in order to unearth the history of Blacks in Spain, thereby situating the country as one of the receivers of the largest diasporic experience in the Western Hemisphere.

Blacks in Spain

To begin our understanding of "Afro-Spain," the works of Vicenta Cortés and Antonio Domínguez Ortiz rank among the first to be consulted.[4] One of the main problems for most scholars in Iberian Studies—writing about slavery in Spain—was to explain the difference between captive, servant, and slave in the Middle Ages. While these categories of servitude limited the civil liberties of certain individuals and groups, each formation occurred for different reasons, and each required a distinct process in the pursuit of freedom.[5] There were also people from various backgrounds who experienced enslavement in Spain. Though reasons for enslavement varied—for example, some were captured in war or presented as payment of debt, others were enslaved because of religious belief—these reasons gradually disappeared. In their place came "race-based" bondage. José Cortés López argues that it is generally said that "the colonization of the Americas was the cause of African slavery and its commerce."[6] López's assertion is only partly true. Prior to Spain's colonization of the Americas, Blacks were preferred in Spain over other slaves such as those from the Middle East and the Canary Islands. For instance, the gradual descent of Black people from human to slave status based on race can be seen soon after the colonization of the Canary Islands, when the Spanish Crown prohibited the enslavement of Indigenous Canarians, also called Guanches, who were considered captives as a result of Spain's takeover of their archipelago. Soon after, compulsory Black labor began to replace Guanche labor.[7] However, the presence of Black slaves in Spain precedes the colonization of the Canary Islands. For example, there is mention of

Blacks as early as the seventh and eighth centuries, when Black slaves were brought into Spain when it was under Muslim rule.[8] Further, two Black slaves—ethnic group not specified—were found in Valencia in 1350 and in 1419. Also, in Valencia, four Black slaves were identified as Mandinka, a large, far-flung West African ethnic group.[9]

Blacks in Spanish Renaissance Literature

While history has noted the physical presence of Blacks in Spain in the Renaissance period, perhaps it would be fitting to mention that Blacks also had a presence in literature, as in the case of the novel, *Lazarillo de Tormes*, published anonymously in Spain in 1554. The anonymity of the author has been blamed on the novel's content of strong racial affirmation related to what was going on in Spain at the time. The novel has been both praised and criticized for exposing Blacks and for the way race was made a central theme in the novel. The author presents Blacks in Spain beyond the idea of subalternism by creating a Black stepfather as one of the main characters, as if this ought to have been the norm in society at the time. On the other hand, Lazarillo, the main character and stepson, shares his shocking experience with readers as he tries to define and relate what he knows as good and bad, namely, Black and white, and how he struggles with this binary.[10]

Also in literature, several years later, we find Blacks in Miguel de Cervantes Saavedra's *Ingenious Gentleman, Don Quixote de la Mancha*, first published in 1605, and also in Cervantes Saavedra's short story, "El Celoso extremeño" or "The Jealous Extremaduran," published in 1613. In *Don Quixote*, we find a suddenly motivated Sancho Panza who shares his entrepreneurship plan of selling Black slaves so that he may live well-off from its profits, as he intends to turn the Black slaves white and yellow, meaning into silver and gold earnings.[11] A few years after publishing *Don Quixote*, Cervantes published a volume of short stories in 1613, including the story of "El Celoso extremeño," about the misfortune of a young girl who marries an older man. In this story, we find three Black characters—two female slaves, one whose name is Guiomar—and a male slave named Luis. While Luis is not the main character, it is his role that leads the story to its climax. Guiomar keeps readers abreast of social racial issues of the time through one of her lines, "Me black stays, whites go," when her mistress orders her to stay behind as the watchperson while the other white slaves are asked to go with the mistress.[12] Finally, and discussed mainly in contemporary works, we find Juan Latino, a former slave who became a professor of Latin at the University of Granada when it was almost impossible for slaves to learn how to read and write.[13]

Treatment of Enslaved Blacks in Spain

Raúl González Arévalo explains that "for the most part, slaves were considered a legal object and rarely a legal subject."[14] A case in which a slave would be deemed a legal subject as opposed to an object would be when the slave was purchasing his or her freedom. The condition of slaves as objects was emphasized in wills and dowries. Victor José Romero Martín studied the legal condition of the enslaved after the death of their enslavers by looking at wills in Córdoba in the second half of the sixteenth century. He found that for the most part the enslaved experienced one of the following: "continued to be enslaved under a new person, freedom, or freedom under temporary or financial conditions (or, in some cases, both simultaneously)."[15] The author describes the difficult process of obtaining information on the enslaved being that for the most part, the wills did not include a lot of details about them. The reason was simple. Details about the enslaved were relevant at the time of sale and not at the time of manumission.[16] The details on the bill of sale were important because the enslaved constituted financial gain for their owners. González Arévalo also explains that once it had been established that slaves were no more than a product, the question to be raised was what type of product they were. And, according to the author, "the physical descriptions in the proof of purchase as well as the possible defects, have served to compare the process of slave trading to that of cattle trading, producing the animalization of a person, until the latter became part of the human cattle constituted by the slave population.[17] This dehumanizing experience lived by Blacks in Spain transferred to the Americas. A similar skin-branding trend can be seen with the enslaved Black taken to the Indies.[18]

Described as more primitive and organic than other slaves, Blacks lacked the knowledge of the new land, the people, and the customs. A few Middle Easterners, but far more so North Africans, Moroccans above all, for example, are described as being more industrious and knowledgeable of the territory to which they were being introduced in Spain.[19] For this reason, it is important to make the distinction between Moors and Blacks. While the term *Moor* was later applied to black Africans, it was first used to refer to descendants of Arabs in the Iberian Peninsula. A similar distinction is made by the Spanish Crown in 1501, in an ordinance that prohibits the entrance of Moors—Moor also meant any Moroccan or practicing Muslim—converts, and non-Christianized blacks.[20] There is, however, one case where a Moor is described specifically as "a black Moor" in 1459, in the small city of Rodrigo in the province of Salamanca.[21] Subsequently, in sixteenth-century Spain, Black was used interchangeably to mean slave, and as the Black enslaved population increased so did the term.[22]

Whereas the number of Black slaves in Spain was nowhere near that of those in the Americas, over 6,000 Black slaves lived in sixteenth-century Seville among a population of approximately 87,538 residents. Most middle-class families owned at least one slave.[23] Though not such a high number as in Seville, Black slaves in Málaga amounted to approximately 400 between 1487 and 1538.[24] There were also enslaved Blacks in Valencia, Granada, and Cádiz, and their origin varied.[25] To that end, most of the Blacks brought to Spain came mainly from Guinea, Guinea-Bissau, Congo, Cape Verde, São Tomé, Sierra Leone, and Senegal, and some of their ethnicities included Wolofs or Jelofes, Mandinka, Bantu, and Carabalí (the name given to all slaves from southeast Nigeria).[26]

Hispaniola (Santo Domingo) and Puerto Rico

Enslaved Blacks from all of the groups above, in addition to others, were also taken to the Indies. For example, David Wheat explains that various ethnonyms and toponyms such as "Caçanga," "Banon," "Folupo," "Biafara," "Nalu," "Bioho," "Bran," and "Zape" can be found in state and church records for the Spanish Caribbean.[27] In 1605 in Santo Domingo, in an inventory of the properties belonging to Captain Agüero Bardecí, we find two females and one male slave belonging to the ethnic group Bran, and another female slave from the Arada group. The Bran are said to have come from what is today Guinea-Bissau.[28] The Arada, which could also be a spelling variation of the ethnic group Arará, are said to be from today's Republic of Benin. While Ararás's tradition can be found in several of the early colonies such as Santo Domingo, Puerto Rico, Cuba, and Haiti, it is in Haiti where the Ararás left their greatest cultural mark. Slavery escapees from Saint-Domingue settled near the capital city of Santo Domingo, calling their maroon community San Lorenzo de los Minas. The place still exists today and its population is still predominantly Black.

Gwendolyn Midlo Hall wrote about the possible origin of the maroons who founded and settled in San Lorenzo de los Minas and explains that Mina came to be used as short for Elmina to refer to the trading port built by the Portuguese in fifteenth-century present-day Ghana.[29] Building on Midlo Hall's work, Robin Law posits that "On the Gold Coast itself, when "Mina" was used in an ethnic sense, its basic meaning was people from Elmina specifically, as opposed to other communities in the region. But outside the Gold Coast, the name came to have a more inclusive meaning, referring to persons from the Gold Coast in general."[30] Law explains that the meaning of the term *Mina* is not in question, given that its name was given by the Portuguese to refer to gold mining.[31] Robin Law does argue, however, that "Minas" was not an African ethnic group but rather a toponym and product of European slave trading, first initiated by the Portuguese and expanded by Spain in the Americas.

In this setting, Spain set out to introduce human trafficking as a capitalist industry in its colonies, taking Blacks first to Hispaniola through the port of Santo Domingo, then Puerto Rico, followed by Cuba and the rest of the Caribbean islands—as well as Mexico, Peru, and what became the lower southwestern U.S. In Hispaniola, the first enslaved Blacks were taken in 1503, to work the gold mines alongside the enslaved Taino Indigenous population. The population of the island's Tainos soon began to decline as a result of the harsh labor imposed and new diseases brought by the Europeans. The need for enslaved Blacks, en masse, increased across the Caribbean as Spain's colonizing agenda expanded. Once established also in Puerto Rico and Cuba, the Spanish Crown moved to legalize the trafficking of Black Africans to the Americas through what they called *Asiento*. The *Asiento* is a type of business trading license that first took effect in 1518, making Santo Domingo the most important city, serving as the main conduit to transport goods, and most importantly, enslaved Blacks who would replace the dying Indigenous population.

The first two founded colonies of the Americas, Hispaniola (specifically the Dominican Republic, which shares the island with Haiti) and Puerto Rico, are often portrayed as distant cousins of the wealthy and lavish viceroyalty centers—and the often equally rich subterritoria-cum-juridicial divisions, the Audiencias of Mexico and Peru. Thus, historically, Hispaniola and Puerto Rico, which along with Cuba form the Spanish Caribbean, have been either grouped within Latin American history or separated only to highlight specific events that continue to dominate Spanish Caribbean scholarship. For instance, in the Dominican Republic, the European invasion and treatment of the Taino Arawaks, nationalism, the era of dictator Rafael Leonidas Trujillo, as well as the civil war shortly after the assassination of Trujillo, race, identity, and anti-Haitianism seem to preoccupy research much more than the topic of slavery. In Puerto Rico, while much has been written about slavery, the themes of the Spanish American War, nationalism, and Puerto Rico's political status and relations with the United States seem to take the lead in research interest.

For these reasons, this book's underlying themes of freedom and law contribute to the conversation about the lived experiences of free and enslaved Africans who sought to be part of a classist, dehumanizing society that later also added racial discrimination. The first two chapters in this anthology examine slavery and law in Spain from the medieval period to the eighteenth century. Intentionally, four of the chapters focus on slavery in Hispaniola and the part of the island that later became Santo Domingo and whose history regarding slavery waits to be freed from the archives. Equally important, the remaining two chapters are an indication of the wealth of research opportunities about slavery in Puerto Rico, and contribute to the already existing and growing scholarship in the island produced in Spanish.[32]

In the words of Dixa Ramírez, Hispaniola, for instance, is the navel of the hemisphere given its geographic location.[33] However, scholars have not been preoccupied with properly situating early slavery on the island, specifically, by simply calling the location Hispaniola, followed by a brief comment about the African presence in the island.[34] In the interim, readers lose centuries of the history of the enslavement of Black Africans in the first European settlement of the Americas (1492–1697).[35]

Additionally, the lack of consistency in properly situating the history of Hispaniola, referring to it with various names, has contributed—in a way—to what Dixa Ramírez calls "ghosting." The author explains that "persistent misnaming of either or both sides of the island in various fields of scholarship and over the two centuries has compounded archival erasure or miscategorization.[36] An example is Frank Tannenbaum's citation of Henry Brougham's work, *An Inquiry into the Colonial Policy of the European Powers*. Citing Brougham, Tannenbaum says that the French brought over 29,000 slaves to Santo Domingo in 1788, whereas Brougham refers to the place as St. Domingo.[37] Both are referring to the French colony of Saint Domingue, today Haiti. Another example is George W. Brown's "The Origins of Abolition in Santo Domingo," published in the *Journal of Negro History*, in 1992. Noting the title of this article, the reader is inclined to think that they will read about one of the two slavery abolitions in Santo Domingo, the one by Toussaint Louverture (1801) or the one by Jean Pierre Boyer (1822), but in fact, the article is about Saint Domingue and not Santo Domingo. It is fair to say that residents in Spain, Santo Domingo or the island might have contributed to the misnaming errors. Many times colonists would request travel licenses to Santo Domingo, as if this was the name of the island. However, historians have had the tools to correct that. An example of this case is the annexation of the Dominican Republic to Spain in 1861 after the former had obtained its independence in 1844. Anne Eller explains how the newly arrived Spanish soldiers questioned what they should call their new post: Santo Domingo, La Española, or Haiti.[38] While the political events that led to the island being divided and given the same name in different languages may lead to confusion, it is no sound excuse to continue to misname them and also "ghost" Santo Domingo in the scholarship.

This is the main reason why the book centers on Hispaniola under Spanish control and Puerto Rico, because more attention has been given to other areas tied to transatlantic slavery, such as Saint Domingue, Cuba, Brazil, and the U.S. This work is also a small act of rebellion against the scholarship. Laurent Dubois and Richard Lee Turits refer to the Caribbean as a centerpiece, land that was "contested in struggles for autonomy or wealth."[39] Nonetheless, parts of that Caribbean centerpiece have not been properly included in its interconnectedness in the scholarship of Caribbean slavery.

We do not know enough about the process or about the individual experiences of the free and enslaved population of Hispaniola before and after the French began to slowly invade the western side of the island, until they formed their own colony and made Saint Domingue their most prominent colony. As a result, the success of the French—in the seventeenth and eighteenth centuries—as a world economy locus because of their high sugar production by means of enslaving Black people, has yielded more attention to the scholarship of Atlantic Slavery. Contrary to the focus of many scholarly works, sugar cane and black African slaves were first introduced to Santo Domingo—what became the Spanish side of the island of Hispaniola—and not to Saint-Domingue, present day Haiti, initially also a Spanish colony.[40] Giusti Cordero contends that "in all, perhaps the major expression of the plantation/provision division of labor in the Caribbean is Hispaniola, an island whose overall position in Caribbean history is rarely discussed."[41] It seems as if Blacks became an imaginary people on the Spanish side of the island and in history—a neglect that David Wheat addresses by stating that "Africans' roles as de facto colonists in the early Spanish Caribbean challenge two long-standing assumptions: first, that a large-scale, export-oriented sugar industry was the intrinsic destiny of all Caribbean colonies and, second, that slavery was primarily important for colonies oriented toward extraction or exploitation, rather than settlement."[42] The topic of Blacks during the first 300 years of social development in Santo Domingo is disregarded over new modern discourses—that is, identity, nationalism, and a compartmentalized history of economy in the country that does not focus on Blacks, whether free or enslaved. Very few Dominican scholars—and other scholars who have settled in the country, preoccupied with the topic—began to address African history in Santo Domingo. But because their publications are in Spanish and very few have been translated into other languages, their contribution to the historical literature is limited.[43] Other international scholars have written about slavery in Santo Domingo or included/mentioned Santo Domingo in their research.[44]

Puerto Rico is not the exception. While the topic of slavery in Puerto Rico has been carefully studied, Jorge L. Chinea points out that when compared to the other islands that partook in the Transatlantic slave trade, Puerto Rico does not rank among the top in scholarship about slavery. Chinea posits that the reason could be because Puerto Rico did not join the sugar boom until the late eighteenth century.[45] Luis A. Figueroa contends that "although [sugar production] never matched Cuba's dominant share of the world sugar market, Puerto Rico developed into the second-largest producer of sugar in the Western Hemisphere."[46] After conducting field work in 1948 Puerto Rico, Sidney Mintz explains how "[he] felt as if we were on an island, floating in a sea of cane."[47] While one cannot say the same about Puerto Rico today, given the decline in its sugar production, the different skin shades of the island's people are directly connected to the sweet sugar cane and the bitter life lived by the enslaved African who, as in Puerto, were also taken to the rest of the Americas. Presumably believed to have first arrived in Puerto Rico in 1509, Blacks were taken there to work the gold mines, but when Spaniards did not obtain the amount of gold desired, they switched to sugar production. Thus, by 1523, the first sugar mill was built in the city of Añasco, known then as the plains of San German, and Blacks constituted the manpower for this new venture.[48] Studies show that in the 1530s there was a large presence of enslaved Africans in Puerto Rico.[49] The ethnicities of the Blacks taken to Puerto Rico include "jelofes, berbesí, bíafara, bañol, biocho, zape, lucumí, manicongo, angola, terranova, mandinga, and brama.⁵⁰ And in this fashion, similar to Hispaniola, cane sugar became the driver of the labor force in Puerto Rico, with women included among its newly arrived inhabitants. In 1540, Juana Villasante was registered as a sugar mill owner in San German. She received a license to bring fifteen enslaved Blacks after twenty of her slaves died from illness.⁵¹ And so, as in Santo Domingo, Puerto Rico received a share of the human profit being brought into the Americas in the sixteenth century.

Though slavery had lost its momentum in Puerto Rico by the seventeenth century as a result of a decline in sugar production, revenues from slave trade licenses amounted to 9.6 percent of the island's total commercial profit between 1606 and 1629. This number is relatively high considering that intercolonial commerce revenues reached only 5 percent. In this sense, on many occasions, slave commerce was the main source of financial support for the smallest of the Spanish Caribbean colonies.⁵² Nonetheless, whether undergoing a thriving or declining economy, the fact is that enslaved Blacks were present in Puerto Rico. In the eighteenth century, for instance, the island saw an increase in cattle-ranching and coffee farms, both operated by Black slaves. In 1790, there were 380 slaves and 865 free Blacks and mulattos, compared to 523 whites in the city of Río Piedras.⁵³ Also, slaves in Puerto Rico worked in the domestic sector as house slaves, in addition to working the sugar mills, cattle ranches, and coffee farms. Slave owners also reported owning slaves who worked as shoemakers, cooks, bakers, and launderers.⁵⁴ Furthermore, in the nineteenth century, the various professions reported in the 1846 census of San Juan exemplify the role of Blacks in Puerto Rico and the Americas, in general, beyond the plantation economy.

Unfortunately, their presence has been unequivocally linked to what many call a stale century in Puerto Rico in relation to the production of sugar. This takes us to another important objective in this book: to focus on the enslaved and free Africans and not only on sugar or the production of sugar. One can imagine that the reason for the lack of work—outside of the Dominican Republic—about slavery in Santo Domingo must be for the same reason referenced by Jorge L. Chinea earlier about the sugar boom taking off in Puerto Rico in the late eighteenth century. Sugar production in Hispaniola did not take off as it did in other colonies. Nonetheless, sugar production, like the human trafficking of enslaved Africans, started in Santo Domingo. Sugar should not have been the main focus of slavery from the beginning—it should have been the enslavement and trafficking of African people. A case in point is Verene A. Shepherd's book *Slavery without Sugar: Diversity in Caribbean Economy and Society since the 17th Century*. While the edited volume does not include a chapter about Santo Domingo—it does include one on Puerto Rico—it discusses slavery in other contexts beyond the production of sugar.[55]

For instance, many of the enslaved in Puerto Rico had a different vision other than to spend the rest of their lives in the plantations. They looked to Haiti and Santo Domingo as their north—places where, according to an enslaved man quoted by Benjamin Nistal Moret in 1826, "black men wore epaulets."[56] Haiti and Santo Domingo were places beyond the ocean but close to their vision of freedom. Moret also explains how in 1831, Andrés Melinton escaped the Carcel Real in Manatí, west of San Juan, Puerto Rico, despite missing one leg.[57] Although we are citing only one case, it is important to point out that Andres Melinton was not intimidated by his physical limitations or by the laws established in 1826 by the governor of Puerto Rico to further control the lives of the enslaved. Unlike the Real Cédula of 1789 by Charles IV, which applied to all of Spain's colonies, the rules of 1826 Puerto Rico only applied to Puerto Rico.[58] In Santo Domingo, despite the many laws created to control their behavior, the enslaved began to resist at the moment of their arrival. And when the enslaved escaped to the mountains, they roamed around *como chivos sin ley*, a common phrase in the Dominican Republic that translates as "goats without law" or "goats without rules." The phrase is also used to refer to people who break the law or simply circumvent the system under the pretext that others who are supposed to follow the law break it as well. Andrés Melinton *was a chivo sin ley*.

The diversity of the research, in topic and period, in this edited work gives life to the experience of free and enslaved Blacks in Spain and the colonies of Santo Domingo and Puerto Rico. Chapter 1 provides an overview of slavery and laws in Spain by tracing slavery to Roman Hispania, the Greek-Roman period, Visigothic Hispania, Muslim, and, finally, Catholic Spain. Chapter 1 also addresses the issue of lack of memory or knowledge about the topic of slavery among people in present-day Spain. Chapter 2 examines the local laws of Extremadura—which are managed by the municipalities—and zeros in on the life of free and enslaved Blacks on a microlevel, discussing how these laws sought to control black bodies and the spaces in which they moved. Some of these laws in Extremadura also applied to whites who may want to help Blacks. Chapter 3 highlights

Santo Domingo as the first slave society. Richard Lee Turits contends that "those held in chains on the island reached into the tens of thousands by the mid-1500s, and Santo Domingo became a pivotal crossroads in the early modern Atlantic. . . . Santo Domingo thus initiated a trajectory of racial and plantation slavery whose contours would shape the course of history in the Americas overall" (2).

Through the meticulous study of Rodrigo López's freedom suit in 1522, Chapter 3 also becomes a window into López's life as a free Black man who was sold into slavery six times after having been granted his freedom. Suitably, and in an attempt to follow a sequential order of events, Chapter 4 offers a detailed analysis of the slave laws of Santo Domingo from 1522 to 1545, created after the slave rebellion of 1521. Similar to the local laws of Extremadura discussed in Chapter 2, the slave laws of Santo Domingo not only controlled the lives of the enslaved, but also the lives of those with any intentions of providing any assistance to enslaved people, thus also controlling the enslaved population by creating laws that controlled the free Black and white population. Chapter 5 explores the lives of free Black women who ventured into traveling to Hispaniola from the early years of the Spanish Conquest, as well as free Black women who established themselves as entrepreneurs in the early decades of the seventeenth century. Free women of color entrepreneurship existed freely throughout the region. Not only were free women of color asking for travel licenses from Seville to the Indies, but those who were already settled seemed to be thriving.[59] The topic of free Black women is expanded in chapter 6 by examining the trial documents that serve as evidence to the experiences of four women who defied social norms in early-eighteenth-century Santo Domingo.[60] Both Chapters 5 and 6 explore an area of much-needed expansion in the scholarship about Black women in the first place of settlement for Blacks in the Americas.

In the last two chapters we move to the colony of Puerto Rico. In Chapter 7, where we read about community building, race, and class, and the religious practice of baptizing in late-seventeenth-century Puerto Rico, where both enslaved adults and infants are baptized, a testament to slave population growth through reproduction. Chapter 7 also serves as reference for cultural rituals practiced today in many of the former colonies. Chapter 8 highlights contraband slave trade in mid-nineteenth-century Puerto Rico, through a revision of the *Majesty*, the slave ship that arrived in Puerto Rico in 1859, believed to have been operated by U.S. and Cuban merchants.

The organization of *Transatlantic Bondage* invites readers to learn about the experiences of free and enslaved Africans in Spain, Hispaniola, and Puerto Rico during a span of almost 400 years. The essays presented cover a myriad of interconnected topics that can be further developed to continue to contribute to the historical legacy of slavery in Spain, but especially in Santo Domingo and Puerto Rico.

Notes

1. The island was called Ayiti by its natives the Taino Arawaks, and La Española after the European invasion. Subsequently, its name or how it was known continued to change in the next 300-plus years. The book title intentionally refers to slavery in Santo Domingo and not Hispaniola, to draw attention to Santo Domingo as a slave-holding society and not just French Saint Domingue, which was and still is part of Hispaniola. The book highlights slavery in Santo Domingo during the periods that it was under Spanish control—first called Hispaniola (in its English translation) and Santo Domingo after the island was split with France. The chapter will refer to Saint-Domingue as the French colony and Haiti, as an independent country. A chronology of the name changes is discussed in note 36.

2. AGI, Contratación, 5536, L. 1, F. 225 (4). In this document, Catalina, a free Black (*horra*) woman from Seville, requests a license for her and her son Diego to travel to the Indies in 1513. This and most of the colonial manuscripts cited in this introduction are part of the CUNY Dominican Studies Institute collection of documents pertaining to the First Blacks of the Americas, www.firstblacks.org, manuscript no. 013.

3. See Aurelia Martín Casares, *La esclavitud en la Granda del siglo XVI: género, raza y religión* (Granada, Spain: Universidad de Granada, 2000); Raúl González Arévalo, *La esclavitud en Málaga a fines de la Edad Media* (Jaén, Spain: Universidad de Jaén, 2006); Rocío Periañez Gómez, *Negros, mulatos y blancos: los esclavos en Extremadura durante la edad moderna* (Badajoz, Spain: Diputación de Badajoz, 2010); Reyes Fernández Durán. *La corona española y el tráfico de negros: del monopolio al libre comercio* (Madrid, Spain: Editorial del Economista, 2011); Arturo Morgado García, *Una metrópoli esclavista: el Cádiz de la modernidad* (Granada, Spain: Universidad de Granada, 2013).

4. See Vicenta Cortés, *La esclavitud en Valencia durante el reinado de los Reyes Católicos (1479-1516)* (Valencia, Spain: Excmo Ayuntamiento de Valencia, 1964) and Antonio Domínguez Ortiz, *La esclavitud en Castilla durante la edad moderna* (Madrid, Spain: Consejo Superior de Investigaciones Científicas, 1952).

5. Domínguez Ortiz, *Esclavitud en Castilla durante*, 25-31.

6. See José Cortés López, *Los orígenes de la esclavitud negra en España* (Madrid, Spain: Mundo Negro, 1982), 27.

7. Cortés López, *Orígenes de la esclavitud negra*, 23.

8. See Lee Anne Durham, *The History of the Blacks, the Jews, and the Moors in Spain* (Madrid. Spain: Plaza Mayor, 1975), 15.

9. Durham, *History of the Blacks*, 24–26.

10. See Mauricio Carrera, "El negro Zaide: la crítica del racismo en "El Lazarillo de Tormes," *Revista de la Universidad de México* 600-1 (2001): 13–19.

11. For this information, I used the following version of *Don Quijote*, Miguel de Cervantes, *Don Quijote de la Mancha* (Madrid, Spain: Alfaguara, 2004), 295–96.

12. See Miguel de Cervantes de Saavedra, *El zeloso extremeño* (Madrid, Spain: Imprenta del Colegio de Sordo-Mudos, 1843).

13. See Aurelia Martín Casares, *Juan Latino: talento y destino* (Granada, Spain: Universidad de Granada, 2016).

14. See Raúl González Arévalo, *La esclavitud en Málaga a fines de la Edad Media* (Jaén, Spain: Universidad de Jaén, 2006), 45.

15. Víctor José Romero Martín, "La situación jurídica del esclavo tras la muerte del dueño. Los testamentos tras la muerte de Felipe II (1556-1598)," in *Tratas, esclavitudes y mestizajes. Una historia conectada, siglos XV–XVIII*, eds. Rafael M. Pérez García, Manuel F. Fernández Chaves, and Eduardo França Paiva (Seville, Spain: Universidad de Sevilla, 2020), 256.

16. Romero Martín, "Situación jurídica del esclavo," 255.

17. Romero Martín, "Situación jurídica del esclavo," 45.

18. AGI Justicia 103-A, arrivada de nao con cargamento de esclavos a Santo Domingo/Ship arrival with merchandise to Santo Domingo. A similar skin-branding trend can be seen with the enslaved Black taken to the Indies.

In a Portuguese ship that anchored in Santo Domingo in 1555, the auction reads, "first of all, ninety-seven black slaves adult men and women and children and one female slave who was so skinny that she had nothing but bones, and who we could not keep," AGI, Escribanía de Cámara, 1-A, F. 577R. In another Portuguese ship that arrived with slaves to Santo Domingo in 1572, we find the description of a "male slave from Angola branded with the letters FR on his right arm and with a large opened wound in his leg."

19. Cortés Alonso, *La esclavitud en Valencia*, 58.

20. AGI, Indiferente, 418, L.1, F. 39R–42R.

21. Cortés López, *Orígenes de la esclavitud negra*, 24. The author explains that this was perhaps the case of a fugitive slave; Cortés Alonso, 63, poses that in cases where slaves were identified as Black Moors, it could be as a result of Blacks who had been bought by Moors and converted into their faith. Therefore, a racial and religious distinction was made.

22. In *La esclavitud en la Granada del siglo XVI*, 145, Martín Casares explains that the major problem in this case was not the fact that slave and Black were used synonymously in quotidian life, but also in legal documents where Black automatically implied slave.

23. See Reyes Fernández Durán, *La corona española y el tráfico de negros: del monopolio al libre comercio* (Madrid, Spain: El Economista, 2011), 20. According to the author there was no middle-class family that did not own one or many slaves.

24. González Arévalo, *Esclavitud en Málaga*, 101.

25. Cortés Alonso, 60; Martín Casares, *La esclavitud en la Granda del siglo XVI*, 144; Morgado García, *Metrópoli esclavista: el Cádiz*, 21–22.

26. Martín Casares, *La esclavitud en la Granda del siglo XVI*, 151; Morgado García, *Metrópoli esclavista: el Cádiz*, 101.

27. David Wheat, *Atlantic Africa and the Spanish Caribbean, 1570–1640* (Chapel Hill: University of North Carolina Press, 2016), 26.

28. AGI, Escribanía 3-A. F. 308V; see also Gwendolyn Midlo Hall, *Slavery and African Ethnicities in the Americas: Restoring the Links* (Chapel Hill: University of North Carolina Press, 2009), 88–89.

29. Midlo Hall, *Slavery and African Ethnicities*, 117.

30. Robin Law, "Ethnicities of Enslaved Africans in the Diaspora: On the Meanings of 'Mina' (Again)," *History in Africa* 32 (2005): 251.

31. Law, "Ethnicities of Enslaved Africans," 248.

32. For instance, Javier Alemán Iglesias offers new information about the labor contracts imposed on the newly freed Blacks in Puerto Rico, after the abolition of slavery from 1873 to 1876. Alemán Iglesias describes the inconsistency in style and information included in the contracts around the island and expands on the three mains patterns he found, which are explained in his work "De esclavo a liberto: los contratos de jornales en Puerto Rico, 1873–1876," in *Visiones transversales de Puerto Rico y el Caribe*, ed. Félix Huertas and Beatriz Cruz (San Juan, PR: Universidad Ana G. Méndez, 2020), 71–89.

33. Dixa Ramírez, Introduction, *Colonial Phantoms: Belonging and Refusal in the Dominican Americas, from the 19th Century to the Present* (New York: New York University Press, 2018), 9.

34. The aim is to highlight that the scholarship on slavery in the Americas is too brief when discussing the initial years of slavery and too often dismisses the importance of Santo Domingo in the history of slavery.

35. The first enslaved Blacks arrived to Santo Domingo in 1503, to work the gold mines as per request of Governor Nicholas de Ovando who arrived in 1502.

36. Dixa Ramírez, Introduction, 9. See also, George W. Brown, "The Origins of Abolition in Santo Domingo," *Journal of Negro History* 7, no. 4 (October 1992): 365–76. According to Elissa L. Lister, Dominicans refer to the Hispanic side of the island as Quisqueya and claim that this is the name that was given by the Tainos to the eastern side of the island. However, there is no sound evidence leading to the veracity of this history. Elissa L. Lister, "Lo indígena "dominicano": ideología y representación," in *Narrar el Caribe: Visiones históricas de la región*, ed. Laura Muñoz (Mexico City: Instituto de Investigaciones Dr. José María Luis Mora, 2019), ebook. On the other hand, some historians cite colonial chronicler Peter Martyr,

who was said to have heard the Tainos call the island Quisqueya. For a reference on Martyr, see Carl Ortwin Sauer, *The Early Spanish Main* (Berkeley: University of California Press, 1966), 45. The name Quisqueya also appears in a 1583 map in Laurence Bergreen's book, *Columbus: The Four Voyages* (204); however, the author does not provide a source for the map. Based on his research, Pedro Luis San Miguel explains that the name Quisqueya was another geographical mistake by Chritopher Columbus, who was looking to get to "Guisay, Quinsay o Quisay." See his excellent chapter "La importancia de llamarse República Dominicana O por qué nombrarse de otra forma que no sea Haití," in *Crear la nación: Los nombres de los países de América Latina*, ed. José Carlos Chiaramonte, Carlos Marichal, and Aimer Granados (Buenos Aires, Argentina: Editorial Sudamericana, 2008), 268. Here is a summary of the island's naming in chronological order: Prior to 1492, Ayiti and Quisqueya. From 1492 to 1498, La Española. 1498 to 1697, it was called La Española and Santo Domingo, interchangeably. From 1697 to 1801, the western side of the island then becomes a colony of France, and they call it French Saint Domingue. The Spaniards continued to call the eastern side Spanish Santo Domingo. The Haitian Revolution also takes place in 1791, and the newly free Blacks prepared to command their land. 1795 to 1804, the entire island is technically French Saint Domingue, because of the Treaty of Basel between France and Spain, where Spain ceded Spanish Santo Domingo to the French. There could be some ambivalence as to the name in 1801, because Haitian Revolution leader Toussaint Louverture crossed over to Spanish Santo Domingo, free the enslaved, and instituted a new constitution. 1802, Spanish Santo Domingo was invaded by the French who reestablished slavery and wanted to take back Saint Domingue. In 1804, Haitian Revolution leader Jean Jacques Dessalines gave Saint Domingue its native name back, Ayiti (Haiti), and in 1805, Haitian leaders Henri Christophe and Jean Jacques Dessalines united in a failed attempt to defeat and expel the French from Spanish Santo Domingo, in what is known as the Beheading of Moca or Degüello de Moca, where hundreds of French supporters were massacred. In 1808, the Spaniards took back Spanish Santo Domingo from the French, in the Battle of Palo Hincado. According to sociologist, Franklin Franco, the Spaniards were able to expel the French army from Spanish Santo Domingo because of military aid received from the English and Haitian leaders Alexander Petion and Henri Christophe (75–76). In 1821, citizens of Spanish Santo Domingo invited Haitian President Jean Pierre Boyer to go to Santo Domingo and abolish slavery, although many from the upper class rejected this idea and preferred being part of Simon Bolivar's plan to establish Gran Colombia composed of several Latin American and Caribbean countries. This invitation is known in Dominican history as the Haitian Invasion of 1822. Thus, the entire island was then Haiti but known as the Republic of Haiti on the west side and the Republic of Spanish Haiti on the east side, until 1844 when a group of citizens agreed that they wanted sovereignty and to achieve what Haiti had done earlier. It is also worth noting that after the Dominican independence Haiti attempted several failed invasions to stop Dominicans from giving their country back to enslaving powers such as France, Britain, Spain, and the United States, including the big Battle of the Number, where both armies destroyed cities on both sides in 1849. After obtaining their independence and becoming the Dominican Republic—named after the Dominican order—the newly established republic became Spanish Santo Domingo again in 1861, when its president Pedro Santana gave the newly established republic back to Spain. But in 1863, those who still wanted an independent republic sought out and received help from Haiti to assist in the restoration of the republic, which became again the Dominican Republic in 1965, after a two-year war with the Spanish soldiers. A suggestion could be to refer to the island as Ayiti when referring to it in pre-Columbian times; Hispaniola when referring to the entire island until 1697; Santo Domingo, when referring to the main city and to the Spanish colony between, 1697–1801 and 1809–1822; Haiti from 1822 to 1844; República Dominicana in 1844–1861; Spanish Santo Domingo, 1861–1865; and Dominican Republic from 1865 to the present.

37. Frank Tannenbaum, *Slave and Citizen* (Boston, MA: Beacon Press, 1946), 33. See also, Henry Brougham, *An Inquiry into the Colonial Policy of the European Powers*, vol. I (Edinburgh, UK; London: E. Balfour, Manners, and Miller, 1803), 530–31. Also, in *The Black Jacobins: Toussaint L'Overture and the San Domingo Revolution*, C. L. R. James correctly refers to the island as Haiti (with its modern name), as he explains that Columbus landed in the island of Ayiti, what the Tainos called the island, but wrongfully refers to Saint-Domingue as San Domingo.

38. Anne Eller, *We Dream Together: Dominican Independence, Haiti and the Fight for Caribbean Freedom* (Durham, NC, and London: Duke University Press, 2016), 88.

39. See Laurent Dubois and Richard Lee Turits, Introduction to *Freedom Roots: Histories of the Caribbean*, Chapel Hill: University of North Carolina Press, 2020), 1.

40. Charles Verlinden explains that Columbus first brought sugar cane to Ayiti called Española in 1493. See Charles Verlinden, *The Beginnings of Modern Colonization*, translated by Yvonne Freccero (Ithaca, NY: Cornell University Press, 1970), 22. The main idea here is to highlight the fact that more focus has been given to Saint-Domingue as a slave-owning society, while Santo Domingo remains understudied in terms of its slave-owning history.

41. See, Juan Giustti Cordero, "Beyond Sugar Revolutions: Rethinking the Spanish Caribbean in the Seventeenth and Eighteenth Centuries," in *Empirical Futures: Anthropologists and Historians Engage the Work of Sidney W. Mintz*, ed. George Baca et al. (Chapel Hill: University of North Carolina Press, 2009), 59–83.

42. See, David Wheat, *Atlantic Africa and the Spanish Caribbean, 1570–1640* (Chapel Hill: Omohundro Institute and University of North Carolina Press, 2018), 8.

43. See, Fray Cipriano de Utrera. "La condición social de los negros en época colonial." *Eme Eme: Estudios Dominicanos* 3, no. 17 (1975): 43–59. This piece by

Fray Cipriano de Utrera was published in 1975; however, the transcript is from a presentation given by Utrera in Puerto Plata in 1920. For the history of Blacks in Santo Domingo, Carlos Larrazabal Blanco published *Los negros y la esclavitud en Santo Domingo*, Dominican Republic: J. D. Postigo, 1967. Building on Blanco's work, Franklin J. Franco writes, *Los negros, los mulatos y la nación dominicana* (Santo Domingo, Dominican Republic: Editora Nacional, 1969), plugging the idea of Blackness in the country's nation building. This title is now available in English as part of the CUNY Dominican Studies Institute's Classic Knowledge in Dominican Studies as *Blacks, Mulattos, and the Dominican Nation*, translated by Patricia Mason (New York: Routledge, 2015). Subsequently, other major works ensued. See, for example, Carlos Esteban Deive, *Vodú y magia en Santo Domingo* (Santo Domingo, Dominican Republic: Museo del Hombre Dominicano, 1979). Also by Deive, *La Esclavitud del negro en Santo Domingo* (Santo Domingo, Dominican Republic: Museo del Hombre Dominicano, 1980), along with *Los Guerrilleros negros: esclavos fugitivos y cimarrones en Santo Domingo* (Santo Domingo, Dominican Republic: Fundación Cultural Dominicana, 1989) and F. Moya Pons, *Después de Colón: trabajo, sociedad y política en la economía del oro* (Madrid, Spain: Alianza Editorial, 1987). See also, Pedro Encarnación Jiménez, *Los negros esclavos en la historia Bayona, Manoguayabo y otros poblados* (Santo Domingo, Dominican Republic: Editora Alfa y Omega, 1993). Carlos Andújar published *La Presencia negra en Santo Domingo* (Santo Domingo, Dominican Republic: Ediciones UAPA, 1997). A translated version of Andújar's work was published in 2012 by Michigan State University Press under the title *The African Presence in Santo Domingo*, translated by Rosa María Andújar. Another great contribution has been a volume supported by UNESCO, *La ruta del esclavo* (Santo Domingo, Dominican Republic: Editora Buho, 2006). The book by Quisqueya Lora Hugui is a must, *Transición de la esclavitud al trabajo libre en Santo Domingo: el caso de Higüey* (Santo Domingo, Dominican Republic: Academia Dominicana de la Historia, 2012). Perhaps one of the most important books on slavery in Santo Domingo and the everyday life of both free and enslaved Blacks in eighteenth-century Santo Domingo is Raymundo González's seminal work, *De esclavos a campesinos: Vida rural en Santo Domingo colonial* (Santo Domingo, Dominican Republic: Archivo General de la Nación, 2011). Last, one of Carlos Esteban Deive's latest work is *¿Y tu abuela dónde está?: el negro en la historia y la cultura dominicanas* (Santo Domingo, Dominican Republic: Editora Nacional, 2013), the translation of the title is *And Where Is Your Grandmother?* A question directed primarily to the white and mulatto Dominican elite who do not recognize their African ancestry. Other works published by Dominican scholars in the diaspora and which address blackness include, Ginetta E. B. Candelario, *Black behind the Ears: Dominican Racial Identity from Museum to Beauty Shops* (Durham, NC, and London: Duke University Press, 2007); also, April J. Mayes, *The Mulatto Nation: Class, Race, and Dominican National Identity* (Gainesville: University Press of Florida, 2014);

Lorgia García-Peña, *The Borders of Dominicanidad: Race, Nation, and Archives of Contradictions* (Durham, NC, and London: Duke University Press, 2016) and Edward Paulino's, *Dividing Hispaniola: The Dominican Republic's Border Campaign against Haiti (1930–1961)* (Pittsburgh, PA: University of Pittsburgh Press, 2016).

44. Such is the case of Richard Lee Turits, "Freedom in el Monte: From Slaves to Independent Peasants in Colonial Santo Domingo," which is the first chapter in Turits's seminal work, *Foundations of Despotism: Peasants, the Trujillo Regime, and Modernity in Dominican History* (Standford, CA: Standford University Press, 2004); Michael A. Gómez, *Black Crescent: The Experience and Legacy of African Muslims in the Americas* (New York: Cambridge University Press, 2005), 3; Jane Landers and Barry Robinson, *Slaves, Subjects, and Subversives: Blacks in Colonial Latin America* (Albuquerque: University of New Mexico Press, 2006); and Jane Landers, "Cimarrón Ethnicity and Cultural Adaptation in the Spanish Domains of the Circum-Caribbean, 1503–1763," in *Identity in the Shadow of Slavery*, ed. Paul E. Lovejoy (London; New York: Continuum, 2000), 30–54; Lynn Guitar, "Boiling It Down: Slavery on the First Commercial Sugarcane Ingenios in the Americas (Hispaniola, 1530–45)," in *Slaves, Subjects, and Subversives: Blacks in Colonial Latin America*, eds. Jane Landers and Barry M. Robinson (Albuquerque: University of New Mexico Press, 2006), 39–82. Jose Luis Belmonte Postigo has written several chapters and articles about slavery in Santo Domingo. Selected works include "Sobre esclavitud y otras formas de dominio: Gradaciones de libertad y estatus social en Santo Domingo a fines del periodo colonial," in *Gente de color entre esclavos: Calidades raciales, esclavitud y ciudadanía en el Gran Caribe*, eds., José Antonio Piqueras Arenas and Imilcy Balboa Navarro (Granada, Comares, 2019), 159–78; "Esclavitud y Status Social en Santo Domingo y Puerto Rico Durante la Diáspora de la Revolución Haitiana," in *Formas de Liberdade. Gratidão, Condicionalidade e Incertezas no Mundo Escravista Nas Americas*, eds., Jonis Freire and María Verónica Secreto (Rio de Janeiro, Brazil: MAUAD, 2018), 71–102. The last three contributions by Postigo included in this reference list are particularly important for the argument being made in this volume, because they highlight slavery in seventeenth- and eighteenth-century Santo Domingo, and show that slavery was important there, as it was in other colonies; they are must-reads for the multilingual scholars who write about Atlantic slavery and slavery in the Spanish Caribbean. See "De cómo generar la costumbre articula derechos: Esclavos en Santo Domingo a fines del tiempo colonial," in *Afroamérica: Espacios e identidades*, eds., Javier Laviña Gómez and Ricardo Piqueras Céspedes (Barcelona, Spain: Icaria, 2013), 65–92; "No obedecen a nadie, sino cada uno gobierna a su familia," Etnicidad y política en la reducción del maniel de Bahoruco, 1785–1795," *Almanack* (2015): 813–40; and "Bajo el negro velo de la ilegalidad: Un análisis del mercado de esclavos dominicano 1746–1821," *Nuevo Mundo, Mundos Nuevos* (2016). Other important contributions include Ida Altman, "Key to the Indies: Port Towns in the Spanish Caribbean: 1493–1550," *The Americas* 74, no. 1

(January 2017): 5–26, and "Marriage, Family, and Ethnicity in the Early Spanish Caribbean," *William and Mary Quarterly* 70, no. 2 (2013): 225–50. David Wheat's *Atlantic Africa and the Spanish Caribbean, 1570–1640* (Chapel Hill: University of North Carolina Press, 2018), addresses slavery in early Santo Domingo, and it also discusses free Black women in early-seventeenth-century Santo Domingo in chapter 4, "Nharas and Morenas Horras," 142–80. Ana Ozuna, "Rebellion and Anti-colonial Struggle in Hispaniola," *Journal of Pan African Studies*. 11, no. 7 (May 2018): 77–95, contributes to the history of antislavery resistance in Santo Domingo. Juan José Ponce-Vazquéz and his book *Islanders and Empire: Smuggling and Political Defiance in Hispaniola, 1580–1690* (Cambridge, UK: Cambridge University Press, 2020), is a major contribution to the scholarship about colonial Hispaniola. Also, see his article, "Unequal Partners in Crime," *Slavery and Abolition* 37, no. 4 (2016): 704–23. Some of the latest international scholarship also includes Consuelo Naranjo Orovio's "Entre la historia y la ficción: terror y orden en Santo Domingo, siglo XIX," in *Esclavitud y legado afrodescendiente en el trópico*, eds., J. A. Piqueras and I. Balboa (Valencia, Spain: Biblioteca Historia Social, 2020), 65–87; *Los márgenes de la esclavitud: resistencia, control y abolición en el Caribe y América Latina*, Consuelo Naranjo Orovio (ed.) (Madrid, Spain: Dykinson, 2021), especially the chapters, "Discriminación racial contra negros y mulatos en Santo Domingo en la época colonial" by Amadeo Julián, "Esclavitud, reformas constitucionales y transformación de los procesos jurídicos de Puerto Rico (1800–1873)," by Gerardo Carlo-Altieri, and, Archipiélago de esclavos: trabajo forzado y seguridad pública en Puerto Rico, 1800–1850," by Consuelo Narango Orovio; and, Consuelo Naranjo Orovio y Miguel Ángel Puig-Samper (Eds.), *Color, raza y racialización en América y el Caribe* (Madrid, Spain: Editorial Los Libros de la Catarata, 2022), especially the chapters "Ciudadanía y trabajo: Debtes en torno a la supresión de la libreta de jornaleros en Puerto rico," by María del Carmen Baerga and "La armonía racial puertorriqueña: De Adolfina Villanueva a Alma Yariela Crus," by Bárbara I. Abadía-Rexach.

45. See Jorge L. Chinea, "Slavery and Child Trafficking in Puerto Rico at the Closing of the African Slave Trade: The Young Captives of the Slaver Majesty, 1859–1865," *Revista Brasileira do Caribe*17, no. 32, Janeiro-Junho (2016): 59–98; about slavery in sixteenth-century Puerto Rico, Elsa Gelpi Batiz titles her book *Siglo en Blanco: Estudio de la economía azucarera en el Puerto Rico del siglo XVI (1540–1612)*. A possible translation for Gelpi Batiz's work could be the forgotten century. An adequate title given Puerto Rico's isolation in the historiography of slavery in the Americas.

46. Luis A. Figueroa, *Sugar, Slavery, and Freedom in Nineteenth-Century Puerto Rico* (Chapel Hill: University of North Carolina Press, 2005), 49.

47. See Sidney Mintz. *Sweetness and Power: The Place of Sugar in Modern History* (New York: Penguin Books, 1986), Introduction, xvii–xviii.

48. See, Luis, M. Soler, *Historia de la esclavitud negra en Puerto Rico* (Río Piedras, PR: Editorial Universitaria Universidad de Puerto Rico, 1970), 28, 45.

49. See Rigoberto Andino's dissertation, *Coffee, Sugar, Enslaved Labor and the Social Production of Space: Slavery in the Municipality of 1872 Mayaguez, Puerto Rico*, n.p., Binghamton University, 2019. The author compares the works of Fernandez Mendez, Silvestrini and Luque de Sanchez in their varying estimates of the enslaved African population in Puerto Rico between 1501 and1530. Fernandez Mendez estimates, 1,503; Silvestrini and Luque de Sanchez list an enslaved population of 2,264, and the Trans-Atlantic Slave Trade Database (TASTD, Emory University) shows 1,575.

50. See Elsa Gelpí Baíz, *Siglo en blanco: estudio de la economía azucarera en el Puerto rico del siglo XVI (1540–1612)* (San Juan, PR: Editorial de la Universidad de Puerto Rico, 2000), 17. For Black slaves in Puerto Rico, see also, Joseph C. Dorsey. *Slave Traffic in the Age of Abolition: Puerto Rico, West Africa, and the non-Hispanic Caribbean, 1815–1859* (Gainesville: University Press of Florida, 2003).

51. Gelpí Baíz, *Siglo en blanco*, 20.

52. See, Enriqueta Vila Vilar, *Historia de Puerto Rico (1600–1650)* (Seville, Spain: Escuela de Estudios Hispano-Americanos, 1974), 227.

53. See, Fernando Picó. *Al filo del poder* (San Juan, PR: Editorial de la Universidad de Puerto Rico, 1993), 108.

54. See Mariano Negrón Portillo and Raúl Mayo Santana, *La esclavitud urbana en San Juan: estudio del registro de esclavos de 1872: primera parte* (Río Piedras, PR: Centro de Investigaciones Sociales, Universidad de Puerto Rico, 1992), 69.

55. See Evelyn Powell Jennings, "Enslavement in Colonial Havana, 1763–1790," in *Slavery without Sugar: Diversity in Caribbean Economy and Society Since the 17th Century*, ed., Verene A. Shepherd (Gainesville: University Press of Florida, 2002), 152–82. Powell Jennings breaks away from the trend in scholarship, at the time, of writing about sugar in relation to slavery in Cuba. The author pays homage to the hundreds of enslaved Africans who were exploited in other types of forced labor.

56. Benjamin Nistal Moret, *Esclavos prófugos y cimarrones, Puerto Rico, 1770–1870* (Río Piedras, PR: Editorial de la Universidad de Puerto Rico, 1984), 207.

57. Moret, *Esclavos prófugos y cimarrones*, 65.

58. Guillermo Baralt explains that these laws were created to limit even more the space in which slaves could move. Some of these restrictions included that slaves from another plantation could not visit each other. Also, that slaves should engage in celebrations only during allotted holidays and from 3:00 p.m. to sunset as stipulated in articles 1, 2, and 3 of the Laws of 1826, Puerto Rico. See Guillermo A. Baralt, *Esclavos rebeldes: conspiraciones y sublevaciones de esclavos en Puerto Rico (1795–1873)* (Río Piedras, PR: Ediciones Huracán, 1981), 68–69.

59. Wheat, *Atlantic Africa and the Spanish Caribbean*, 148–49.

60. For a similar study on trial transcripts see Heather Rachelle White "Between the Devil and the Inquisition: African Slaves and the Witcraft Trials in Cartagena de Indies," *North Star: A Journal of African American Religious History* 8, no. 2 (Spring 2005): 1–15.

Bibliography

Primary Sources

Archivo General de Indias (AGI) Contratación, 5536, L. 1, F. 225 (4).
AGI, Justicia 103-A, "Arrivada de nao con cargamento de esclavos a Santo Domingo."
AGI, Escribanía de Cámara, 1-A, F. 577R.
AGI, Escribanía 3-A. F. 308V.
AGI, Indiferente, 418, L.1, F. 39R–42R.

Secondary Sources

Alemán Iglesias, Javier. "De esclavo a liberto: los contratos de jornales en Puerto Rico, 1873–1876." In *Visiones transversales de Puerto Rico y el Caribe*, edited by Félix Huertas and Beatriz Cruz, 71–89. San Juan, PR: Universidad Ana G. Méndez, 2020.
Altman, Ida. "Key to the Indies: Port Towns in the Spanish Caribbean: 1493–1550." *The Americas* 74, no. 1 (January 2017): 5–26.
———. "Marriage, Family, and Ethnicity in the Early Spanish Caribbean." *William and Mary Quarterly* 70, no. 2 (2013): 225–50.
Andino, Rodrigo. "Coffee, Sugar, Enslaved Labor and the Social Production of Space: Slavery in the Municipality of 1872 Mayaguez, Puerto Rico." PhD diss., Binghamton University, 2019.
Baralt, Guillermo. *Esclavos rebeldes: conspiraciones y sublevaciones de esclavos en Puerto Rico (1795–1873)*. Río Piedras, PR: Ediciones Huracán, 1981.
Belmonte Postigo, José Luis. "Sobre esclavitud y otras formas de dominio: Gradaciones de libertad y estatus social en Santo Domingo a fines del periodo colonial." In *Gente de color entre esclavos. Calidades raciales, esclavitud y ciudadanía en el Gran Caribe*, edited by José A Piqueras Arenas and Imilcy Balboa Navarro, 159–78. Granada, Spain: Comares, 2019.
———. "Esclavitud y Estatus Social en Santo Domingo y Puerto Rico Durante la Diáspora de la Revolución Haitiana." In *Formas de Liberdade. Gratidão, Condicionalidade e Incertezas no Mundo Escravista Nas Americas*, edited by Jonis Freire and María Verónica Secreto, 71–102. Rio de Janeiro, Brazil: MAUAD, 2018.
———. "Bajo el negro velo de la ilegalidad. un análisis del mercado de esclavos dominicano 1746–1821," *Nuevo Mundo Mundos Nuevos* [En ligne], Débats, mis en ligne le 07 juillet 2016. DOI: https://doi.org/10.4000/nuevomundo.69478.
———. "No obedecen a nadie, sino cada uno gobierna a su familia": Etnicidad y política en la reducción del maniel de Bahoruco, 1785–1795.

Almanack 11 (September–December 2015): 813–40. DOI: https://doi.org/10.1590/2236-463320151113.

———. "De cómo generar la costumbre articula derechos: Esclavos en Santo Domingo a fines del tiempo colonial." In *Afroamérica. Espacios e identidades*, edited by Javier Lavina and Ricardo Piqueras Céspedes, 65–92. Barcelona, Spain: Icaria, 2013.

Bergreen, Laurence. *Columbus: The Four Voyages*. New York: Viking, 2011.

Brougham, Henry. *An Inquiry into the Colonial Policy of the European Powers, Vol. I*. Edinburgh, London, E. Balfour, Manners, and Miller, 1803.

Brown, George W. "The Origins of Abolition in Santo Domingo." *Journal of Negro History* 7, no. 4 (1922): 365–76.Candelario, Ginetta E. B. *Black behind the Ears: Dominican Racial Identity from Museum to Beauty Shops*. Durham, NC, and London: Duke University Press, 2007.

Carrera, Mauricio. *El negro Zaide: la crítica del racismo en "El Lazarillo de Tormes."* Revista de la Universidad de México 600–1 (2001): 13–19.

Chinea, Jorge L. "Slavery and Child Trafficking in Puerto Rico at the Closing of the African Slave Trade: The Young Captives of the Slaver Majesty, 1859–1865." *Revista Brasileira do Caribe* 17, no. 32 (January–June 2016): 59–98.

Cipriano de Utrera, Fray. "La condición social de los negros en época colonial." *Eme Eme: Estudios Dominicanos* 3, no. 17 (1975): 43–59.

Comisión Nacional Dominicana de la Ruta del Esclavo. *La ruta del esclavo*. Santo Domingo, Dominican Republic: Editora Buho, 2006.

Cortes, Lopez, José. *Los orígenes de la esclavitud negra en España*. Madrid, Spain: Mundo Negro, 1982.

Cortés Alonso, Vicenta. *La esclavitud en Valencia durante el reinado de los Reyes Católicos (1479–1516)*. Valencia, Spain: Excmo Ayuntamiento de Valencia, 1964.

De Cervantes, Miguel. *Don Quijote de la Mancha*. Madrid, Spain: Alfaguara, 2004.

Domínguez Ortiz, Antonio. *La esclavitud en Castilla durante la edad moderna*. Madrid, Spain: Consejo Superior de Investigaciones Científicas, 1952.

Deive, Carlos Esteban. *¿Y tu abuela dónde está?: el negro en la historia y la cultura dominicanas*. Santo Domingo, Dominican Republic: Editora Nacional, 2013.

———. *Los Guerrilleros negros: esclavos fugitivos y cimarrones en Santo Domingo*. Santo Domingo, Dominican Republic: Fundación Cultural Dominicana, 1989.

———. *La Esclavitud del negro en Santo Domingo*. Santo Domingo, Dominican Republic: Museo del Hombre Dominicano, 1980.

———. *Vodú y magia en Santo Domingo*. Santo Domingo, Dominican Republic: Museo del Hombre Dominicano, 1979.

Dorsey, Joseph C. *Slave Traffic in the Age of Abolition: Puerto Rico, West Africa, and the Non-Hispanic Caribbean, 1815–1859*. Gainesville: University Press of Florida, 2003.

Dubois, Laurent, and Richard Lee Turtis. *Freedom Roots: Histories of the Caribbean*. Chapel Hill: University of North Carolina Press, 2020.

Durham, Lee Anne. *The History of the Blacks, the Jews, and the Moors in Spain*. Madrid, Spain: Plaza Mayor, 1975.
Eller, Anne. *We Dream Together: Dominican Independence, Haiti and the Fight for Caribbean Freedom*. Durham, NC, and London: Duke University Press, 2016.
Encarnación Jiménez, Pedro. *Los negros esclavos en la historia Bayona, Manoguayabo y otros poblados*. Santo Domingo, Dominican Republic: Editora Alfa y Omega, 1993.
Fernández Durán, Reyes. *La corona española y el tráfico de negros: del monopolio al libre comercio*. Madrid, Spain: El Economista, 2011.
Figueroa, Luis A. *Sugar, Slavery, and Freedom in Nineteenth-Century Puerto Rico*. Chapel Hill: University of North Carolina Press, 2005.
Franco Pichardo, Franklin J. *Blacks Mulattos, and the Dominican Nation*. Translated by Patricia Mason. New York: Routledge, 2015.
GarcíaPena, Lorgia. *The Borders of Dominicanidad: Race, Nation, and Archives of Contradictions*. Durham, NC, and London: Duke University Press, 2016.
Gelpí Baíz, Elsa. *Siglo en blanco: estudio de la economía azucarera en el Puerto Rico del siglo XVI (1540–1612)*. San Juan, PR: Edición de la Universidad. de Puerto Rico, 2000.
Giustti, Cordero, Juan. "Beyond Sugar Revolutions: Rethinking the Spanish Caribbean in the Seventeenth and Eighteenth Centuries." In *Empirical Futures: Anthropologists and Historians Engage the Work of Sidney W. Mintz*, edited by George Baca, Aisha Khan, and Stephan Palmié. Chapel Hill: University of North Carolina Press, 2009.
Gomez, Michael A. *Black Crescent: The Experience and Legacy of African Muslims in the Americas*. New York: Cambridge University Press, 2005.
González Arévalo, Raúl. *La esclavitud en málaga a fines de la Edad Media*. Jaén, Spain: Universidad de Jaén, 2006.
Guitar, Lynn. "Boiling It Down: Slavery on the First Commercial Sugarcane Ingenios in the Americas (Hispaniola, 1530–45)." In *Slaves, Subjects, and Subversives: Blacks in Colonial Latin America*, edited by Jane Landers and Barry M. Robinson, 39–82. Albuquerque: University of New Mexico Press, 2006.
Hamilton Johnson, Harry. *The Negro in the New World*. New York: Macmillan, 1910.
James, C. L. R. *The Black Jacobins: Toussaint L'Ouverture and the San Domingo Revolution*. London: Penguin Books, 2001.
Landers, Jane, and Barry Robinson. *Slaves, Subjects, and Subversives: Blacks in Colonial Latin America*. Albuquerque: University of New Mexico Press, 2006.
———. "Cimarrón Ethnicity and Cultural Adaptation in the Spanish Domains of the Circum-Caribbean, 1503–1763." In *Identity in the shadow of slavery*, edited by Paul E. Lovejoy. London; New York: 2000.
Larrazabal Blanco, Carlos. *Los negros y la esclavitud en Santo Domingo*. Santo Domingo, Dominican Republic: J. D. Postigo, 1967.
Law, Robin. "Ethnicities of Enslaved Africans in the Diaspora: On the Meanings of "Mina" (Again)." *History in Africa* 32 (2005): 247–67.

Lister, Elissa L. "Lo indígena "dominicano" ideología y representación." In *Narrar el Caribe: Visiones históricas de la región*, edited by Laura Muñoz. Mexico City: Instituto de Investigaciones Dr. José María Luis Mora, 2019. Ebook.

Lora Hugui, Quisqueya. *Transición de la esclavitud al trabajo libre en Santo Domingo: el caso de Higüey*. Santo Domingo, Dominican Republic: Academia Dominicana de la Historia, 2012.

Martin Casares, Aurelia. *La esclavitud en la Granda del siglo XVI: género, raza y religión*. Granada, Spain: Universidad de Granada, 2000.

———. *Juan Latino: talento y destino*. Granada, Spain: Universidad de Granada, 2016.

Mayes, April. *The Mulatto Nation: Class, Race, and Dominican National Identity*. Gainesville: University Press of Florida, 2014.

Mayo Santana, Raul, and Negrón Portillo, Mariano. *La esclavitud urbana en San Juan: estudio del registro de esclavos de 1872: primera parte*. Río Piedras, PR: Centro de Investigaciones Sociales, Universidad de Puerto Rico, 1992.

Midlo Hall, Gwendolyn. *Slavery and African Ethnicities in the Americas: Restoring the Links*. Chapel Hill: University of North Carolina Press, 2009.

Mintz, Sidney. *Sweetness and Power: The Place of Sugar in Modern History*. New York: Penguin, 1986.

Morgado García, Arturo. *Una metrópoli esclavista: el Cádiz de la modernidad*. Granada, Spain: Universidad de Granada, 2013.Moya Pons, F. *Después de Colón: trabajo, sociedad y política en la economía del oro*. Madrid, Spain: Alianza Editorial, 1987.

Naranjo Orovio, Consuelo. "Entre la historia y la ficción: terror y orden en Santo Domingo, siglo XIX." In *Esclavitud y legado afrodescendiente en el trópico*, edited by J. A. Piqueras and I. Balboa, 65–87. Valencia, Biblioteca Historia Social, 2020.

———. *Los márgenes de la esclavitud: resistencia, control y abolición en el Caribe y América Latina*. Madrid, Spain: Dykinson, 2021.

———. *Color, raza y racialización en América y el Caribe*. Madrid, Spain: Editorial Los Libros de la Catarata, 2022.

Nistal Moret, Benjamin. *Esclavos prófugos y cimarrones, Puerto Rico, 1770–1870*. Río Piedras, PR: Editorial de la Universidad de Puerto Rico, 1984.

Ozuna, Ana. "Rebellion and Anti-colonial Struggle in Hispaniola." *Africology: The Journal of Pan-African Studies* 11, no. 7 (May 2018): 77–95.

Paulino, Edward. *Dividing Hispaniola: The Dominican Republic's Border Campaign against Haiti (1930–1961)*. Pittsburgh, PA: University of Pittsburgh Press, 2016.

Periañez Gómez, Rocío. *Negros, mulatos y blancos: los esclavos en Extremadura durante la edad moderna*. Spain: Diputación de Badajoz, 2010.

Pico, Fernando. *Al filo del poder*. San Juan, PR: Editorial de la Universidad de Puerto Rico, 1993.

Ponce-Vazquez, Juan José. *Islanders and Empire: Smuggling and Political Defiance in Hispaniola, 1580–1690*. Cambridge, UK: Cambridge University Press, 2020.
———. "Unequal Partners in Crime." *Slavery and Abolition* 37, no. 4 (2016): 704–23.
Powell Jennings, Evelyn. "Enslavement in Colonial Havana, 1763–1790." In *Slavery without Sugar: Diversity in Caribbean Economy and Society Since the 17th Century*, edited by Verene A. Shepherd, 152–82. Gainesville, Florida: University Press of Florida, 2002.
Ramírez, Dixa. *Colonial Phantoms: Belonging and Refusal in the Dominican Americas, from the 19th Century to the Present*. New York: New York University Press, 2018.
Sauer, Carl Ortwin. *The Early Spanish Main*. Berkeley: University of California Press, 1966.
San Miguel, Pedro Luis. "La importancia de llamarse República Dominicana O por qué nombrarse de otra forma que no sea Haití." In *Crear la nación. Los nombres de los países de América Latina*, edited by José Carlos Chiariamonte, Carlos Marichal and Aimer Granados, 257–71. Buenos Aires, Argentina: Editorial Sudamericana, 2008.
Soler, Luis M. *Historia de la esclavitud negra en Puerto Rico*. Río Piedras, PR: Editorial Universitaria Universidad de Puerto Rico, 1970.
Tannenbaum, Frank. *Slave and Citizen*. Boston, MA: Beacon Press, 1946.
Turits, Richard Lee. *Foundations of Despotism: Peasants, the Trujillo Regime, and Modernity in Dominican History*. Stanford, CA: Stanford University Press, 2004.
Verlinden, Charles. *The Beginnings of Modern Colonization*. Translated by Yvonne Freccero. Ithaca, NY: Cornell University Press, 1970.
Vila Vilar, Enriqueta. *Historia de Puerto Rico (1600–1650)*. Sevilla: Escuela de Estudios Hispano-Americanos, 1974.
Wheat, David. *Atlantic Africa and the Spanish Caribbean, 1570–1640*. Chapel Hill: Omohundro Institute and University of North Carolina Press, 2018.
White, Heather Rachelle. "Between the Devil and the Inquisition: African Slaves and the Witchcraft Trials in Cartagena de Indies," *North Star: A Journal of African American Religious History* 8, no. 2 (Spring 2005).

Chapter 1

Spanish Slave Legislation

From Slavery to Abolition in Spain and the Americas

Aurelia Martín Casares

Introduction

Slavery existed in the Iberian Peninsula since before Christ and continued to be present well into the nineteenth century, when it was abolished in the last Spanish colonies in the Caribbean and, some years later, in Portuguese Brazil. Originally, it was legislatively interpreted as a way of preserving the life of the prisoners of a "just war" against a foreign and infidel enemy. Obviously, this is a common past to most of Europe. It is also worth noting that slavery already existed in pre-Columbian America and precolonial Africa, prior to the arrival of Europeans, and that various countries in the Arab and Asian world kept slavery laws in force until the late twentieth century.

In any case, there is no doubt that slavery was part of Spanish legislative texts for at least two thousand years. Nevertheless, it is striking that in contemporary Spanish collective thinking the prevailing notion is that "there were no slaves in Spain." I have frequently heard this statement, which has been recited to me even by the keepers of historical records at places where I have worked searching for sources. In fact, most Spanish people are unaware that the stepfather in the novel *Lazarillo de Tormes* was a Black man from a slave background, even though this picaresque novel is a mandatory school read. Yet it is made clear in the first chapter, which bears the title "Lázaro Tells about His Life and Parents," where we can indeed read that his stepfather was of African descent and his brother was Afro-Spanish.

> So, with his visits and the relationship going right along, it happened that my mother gave me a pretty little black baby (brother), and I used to bounce it on my knee and help keep it warm. I remember one time when my black stepfather was playing with the little fellow, the child noticed that my mother and I were white but that my stepfather wasn't and he got scared. He ran to my mother and pointed his finger at him and said, "Mama, it's the bogeyman!" And my stepfather laughed: "You little son-of-a-bitch!"
>
> Even though I was still a young boy, I thought about the word my little brother had used, and I said to myself: How many people there must be in the world who run away from others when they don't see themselves!

Likewise, slavery is brought up several times in *El ingenioso hidalgo don Quijote de la Mancha*, particularly in the passages where Sancho Panza ponders the possibility of importing sub-Saharan slaves into Spain. "What is it to me if my vassals are black? What more have I to do than make a cargo of them and carry them to Spain, where I can sell them and get ready money for them, and with it buy some title or some office in which to live at ease all the days of my life?"

Moreover, Black people even came to be central characters in popular comedies of the Golden Age, such as *La Comedia Famosa de Juan Latino* by Diego Ximénez de Enciso. Actually, Juan Latino, a relevant figure in the Spanish Renaissance, was a slave of sub-Saharan origin from Granada.[1] His knowledge of Latin and his humanist education led him to become the *Magister Ionannen Latinum* (the master Juan Latino), professor of Latin at the University of Granada.[2] He was, furthermore, the first Afro-Spanish writer and the first Afro-European to publish a book of poems in a European language, namely, *Austrias Carmine*, dedicated to Don Juan de Austria and his role in the battle of Lepanto. In 1849, when slavery still existed in Cuba, George Ticknor described Juan Latino's work as one of the most extraordinary in the world, referring to its author as one of the most eminent intellectuals of sub-Saharan descent.[3] Later, Afro-Cuban historian Calixto C. Masso stated the following about Juan Latino: "He is the most remarkable of the Spanish blacks, and we qualify him as a source of pride for Spain and his race because his life is the soundest proof of the attitude of the people of Spanish origin regarding black people and the racial issue that in Spain, at the time, the human factor was more valued than the color of the skin."[4] And yet, his story is barely known.

In these pages, I could quote plenty of literary characters in Spanish literature, both main and secondary, who were actually not only slaves of sub-Saharan origin, but also converted Moors or North African Arabs, and even stories of Christian Spanish women captured by Muslims, but there is no space for that, nor is it the point of this chapter. Also, given the importance of the topic and to reach multilingual readers, multiple sections of this chapter are direct translations of earlier writings.[5] In any case, I will make a reference to the printed press to recall the fact that, in the eighteenth century, Madrid newspapers featured news about slaves using the following terms:

> On Jacometrenzo Street, at the Eagle Inn, or at Joseph Matías' bookshop, across from the steps to San Felipe el Real, a person can be found who wants to buy a black boy or girl aged 8, 10 or 12 at most.[6]

> Anyone interested in buying a 20-year-old black man who knows a little about cooking and horses, and also a nearly new carriage and a pair of mules, please enquire at the confectionery shop on Fuencarral Street, opposite San Pedro and San Pablo.[7]

These advertisements give us a good idea about how integrated slavery was in the everyday life of the Spanish people, and show us the harsh reality of its victims, who were kept nameless, completely anonymous, reduced to a skin color and in par with livestock. This clearly shows the imprint of slavery in the Iberian Peninsula and not only in the American colonies of the Empire.

Slave Legislation from the Romans to the Global Spanish Empire[8]

The enslavement of the Turdetani Iberians in Roman Hispania[9] was one of the cruelest to take place in the Iberian Peninsula. Historiography reveals that some Roman military leaders committed atrocities such as butchering or selling into slavery entire settlements that had negotiated truces with them.[10] In this vein, Seneca from Córdoba wrote "*Quot servi, tot hostes*"[11] (so many servants, so many enemies). In fact, in the Graeco-Roman world it was legally possible to enslave people in a war context, as was pointed out by Greek philosophers such as Heraclitus. The first Christian authors, such as Saint Ambrose in the fourth century and Saint Augustine in the fifth, also addressed "just war" in the same way, as a justification to enslave the vanquished, thus saving their lives.

Legislation on slavery in the Greco-Roman period inspired its subsequent codification in Visigothic Hispania, as was recorded in the seventh century in King Recesvinto's *Liber Iudiciorum*,[12] in which slaves appear in a good number of provisions that would later become the *Fuero juzgo*[13] in several territories of the Iberian Peninsula. In Muslim Spain, since the arrival of the Arabs in the year 711, and during the period of Al-Andalus, Sharia law was applied, namely the Islamic law that allowed the enslavement of infidels and consequently the enslavement of Spanish Christians and Black African Animists. In parallel, in medieval Christian Spain, and more specifically in the thirteenth century, slavery was codified in the so-called *Siete Partidas*,[14] a body of legislation developed under Alfonso X "the Wise" (*el Sabio*) and based on Roman laws and Spanish traditions. Specifically, the law that directly regulated slavery was Law I, Title XXI, of the fourth *Partida*, which states the following: "Servitude is a long-established custom by which men who were naturally free are made to serve under another man's orders, against the natural order. The term 'servant' comes from the Latin word *servare*, which means 'saving'. And this was established by the Emperors. Because previously, all prisoners were executed. But the Emperors decided that they should be spared and put to good use." The medieval *Siete Partidas* clearly established the reasons for which people could be enslaved, these being basically two: war and birth; namely, (1) for being captured in wartime as enemies of the faith, and (2) for being born to a slave mother, even if the father was a free man. This legislation was directly inherited from Roman law. However, the Romans also justified enslavement for cause of debt ("when one is free and allows himself to be sold"[15]), a practice that almost completely vanished in Renaissance Spain but was still preserved in the *Partidas*.

It was precisely during the Spanish Renaissance that the work of Aristotle was revisited with particular interest and specifically his definition of slavery, which put the emphasis on slavery by nature and the idea of property: "It is necessary to understand the word 'property' in the same way as the word 'part': the part is not only part of a whole, but also belongs in an absolute manner to something different to it. [. . .] He who by natural law does not belong to himself, but, notwithstanding his human condition, belongs to another man, is a slave by nature [. . .] he becomes a property, and as such is a completely individual instrument of use."[16]

Regarding Renaissance and modern legislation on slavery, several of the bodies of legislation enacted did not include a specific section on slavery, but nevertheless mentioned certain slavery-related situations. These were the *Ordenamiento de Montalvo* of 1484, the *Leyes de Toro* of 1505, the *Nueva Recopilación de Leyes del Reino* of 1566, and the *Novísima Recopilación de Leyes* of 1735. It is worth noting that all of these legislations point to the *Siete Partidas*, as a reference regarding the codification of causes for enslavement. Slaves were not only mentioned in these compendiums of laws, but also in the ordinances issued by local councils all over the Iberian Peninsula.

Meanwhile, a large number of decrees and specific laws were passed, which closed the loopholes in the aforementioned legislation, regulating, among other matters, the fiscal income for the Crown (taxes such as *alcabala*, or sales tax, and *almojarifazgo*, or import-export duty, among others), the price of slaves in America, or the evolution of taxes on the slave trade. These decrees also addressed matters such as the relationship with the various companies that had the monopoly on the trade of slaves of sub-Saharan descent with Spanish America, namely, the Compañía de Guinea de Francia, and subsequently, the Compañía del Asiento de Inglaterra. It is relevant to note that, as early as 1604, a Royal document was issued regarding the expected relationship between the viceroys and royal officials in the Indias (i.e., the Americas) and the Compañía Real de Guinea, established in France and entrusted with the introduction of Black slaves into Spanish America.

But possibly one of the most controversial of these specific laws was the Pragmática y declaración sobre los moriscos esclavos que fueron tomados en el reyno de Granada, passed by King Felipe II in 1572. This law allowed the enslavement of the Morisco people, despite having been baptized and therefore being de facto Christians.[17] Precisely the biggest problem faced by Felipe II was the feasibility of enslaving the Moriscos, as they had been converted to Christianity and were, furthermore, also subjects of the Spanish Crown.

To all these bodies of legislation, decrees, and specific laws produced in the Iberian Peninsula, with the goal of regulating slavery in Spain, must be added all the colonial laws issued to achieve the same result in the Americas. I am referring, for instance, to the *Código Negro Carolino* (17843) of Santo Domingo, which was a copy of the previous *Código Negro Francés* (1685).[18] To these, we can add the references to slaves that appear in broader legislative texts issued exclusively for the American colonies from the sixteenth century onward, such as the *Leyes de Burgos* of 1512, the *Nuevas Leyes* of 1542, or the *Recopilación de Leyes de Indias* of 1680, among others.

Once the complex world of Spanish slavery-related legislation has been outlined, I consider that the main concerns of Spanish rulers and legislators and, indeed, those that resulted in a considerable number of laws on slavery dealings, were the following: (1) "just war" as a justification for enslavement, (2) the regulation of North African slavery in the Mediterranean, (3) the ban on the enslavement of Native Americans and the control of the ethnic-religious origins of the slave population transported to America, (4) the regulation of the introduction of black African slaves into America through the European companies that held the monopoly on the slave trade, (5) the prevention and repression of slave uprisings, (6) the regulation of the fiscal and tax aspects of the slave trade, and (7) the regulation of the long process of abolition.

As this is a subject that deserves being dealt with in greater length than these pages would allow, I will limit myself to addressing some of the laws related to the aforementioned topics in a synthesized way.

"Just War" as a Legitimate Justification for Enslavement

Regarding this topic, it is worth noting that the Spaniards clashed against the Muslim conquerors in direct armed conflict during the Medieval period, later confronted the Morisco rebels from the Kingdom of Granada, and were at the same time fighting the North Africans or *berberiscos*[19] in the Mediterranean. All these conflicts justified Arab-Muslim slavery in legal terms as an effect of "just war." Besides, Christian Spaniards were also enslaved by Spanish Muslims, North Africans, and the Turks.

However, the enslavement of Black Africans was in fact a commercially driven form of enslavement, as opposed to a war-motivated one. As such, it did not fit with the legal principles by which an individual could be taken prisoner, as outlined in the *Siete Partidas*. In fact, the enslavement of Black Africans was accepted because of the existing belief that, prior to the actual commercial transaction, a "just war" had taken place between the various ethnic groups that made up the Black African kingdoms of the early modern period, whose leaders would have, in turn, sold the human bounty to the Europeans. In fact, Spanish moralists were fully aware that the purchase of Black Africans rekindled the internal conflicts between the different sub-Saharan ethnic groups. Indeed, Dominican theologian Tomás de Mercado, in chapter XXI of his work *Suma de Tratos y Contratos*, of 1571, pointed out that these moralists were well aware of the legal irregularities that took place regarding the enslavement of black Africans, as can be clearly appreciated in the following passage:

> It is common knowledge that in rescuing and transporting the blacks from their lands to here or the Americas, two thousand tricks are used, a thousand robberies are carried out and a thousand evil deeds committed [. . .] To the first title of "just war" can be added the fact that they are all, or almost all, unjust. As they [the blacks] are barbarians, they are moved not by reason but by passion, and do not question their rights. Furthermore, as the Portuguese and the Spaniards pay well for black slaves even in times of peace, they hunt each other down like deer, moved by greed, and they fight each other and have it as custom to capture each other in the bushes, where they often go hunting or gathering firewood for their dwellings. In such a way, many are taken captive against any justice.[20]

As we can see here, Tomás de Mercado considered that both the Portuguese and the Spaniards promoted internal wars among the African people so as to benefit from the trade of unfairly enslaved prisoners. However, Mercado himself also stated that, in sixteenth-century western sub-Saharan Africa, freedom was taken away for no legitimate reason, such as petty crime, misdemeanor, or falling out of favor with the local leader. In fact, he wrote that the same thing that would merely get a subject expelled from the Royal Court in Spain was sufficient justification in Guinea for the enslavement of individuals, and possibly of their whole families. The ease with which sub-Saharan people captured and enslaved each other, according to Mercado, was further boosted by the unscrupulousness of Spanish slave traders.

> Apart from the injustices and thefts they [the sub-Saharans] inflict on each other, myriad other wrongdoings happen in those places, by which the Spaniards fooled them and finally brought them as slaves to the harbors, attired in rattles, hats, beads and other paraphernalia, where they stealthily made them board the ships, and set sail unto the high seas. Although in past times there was much greater corruption in all this, it is now very much corrected, not only for reason of the blacks getting wittier through experience, but also by reason of the laws passed and rigorously enforced by the King of Portugal.[21]

Another Spanish moralist, Bartolomé de Albornoz, wrote that it was not the slave owner's responsibility to investigate the circumstances of these Africans' capture and enslavement, as their sale was legal in Spain.[22] Thus, he did what many slave owners and most rulers were already doing: look the other way.

The Regulation of North African Slavery in the Mediterranean

Another important matter, clearly reflected in Spanish legislation, was the regulation of slavery in the Mediterranean. Generally speaking, North Africans captured in the Mediterranean were regarded as candidates for enslavement, except during the occasional temporary truce periods negotiated with North African rulers.[23] Throughout the early modern period, there even were times when slave traders were exempted from the royal tax on the capture and sale of North African slaves. In 1724, for instance, a decree was issued granting "all ship-owners from the Mediterranean coast the free use and sale of the Moors (i.e., North Africans) they might capture, without having to pay the levy of the *quinto*" (this being the transaction tax, equivalent to a fifth of the sale price, otherwise applied to the rest of the slave trade).[24] At the same time, it was legal to capture Spaniards to either sell them as slaves in North Africa or keep them captive in Algiers or any other North African city until their families eventually paid the ransom set by the Arab-Moslem authorities. It is worth noting that there were already many sub-Saharan slaves in North Africa, which meant that asking for a ransom for captive Spaniards was often more profitable than selling them into slavery, in a market already saturated with black African labor. Due to this, the religious orders of the Mercedarians and the

Trinitarians devoted a great part of their work to the rescue of Spanish Christians held captive in North Africa.

The Ban on the Enslavement of Native Americans and the Control of the Ethno-Religious Background of the Slave Population Transported to the Americas

Another of the substantial concerns, reflected in the legislation of the time on slavery in the Hispanic world, was the ban on the enslavement of Native Americans. In 1541, it was formally forbidden for Spaniards to buy "Indian" slaves from the landlords or indigenous authorities of the Peruvian provinces. The text of this Royal Provision stated that it was common practice for Native Americans "to enslave each other for very light reasons," as can be appreciated in the following passage:

> Don Carlos & c. By which we are informed that because it is permitted for Spaniards gone to conquer and populate the province of Perú to rescue and purchase from the landlords and authorities and other persons indigenous to the country the Indians that are their vassals and slaves, the situation has gone to such excess that many slaves have been taken that are not decently treated, and are forced to excessive work and many other hardships: from which, apart from the great embarrassment that comes from it unto our Holy Catholic Faith and the diminishing of their lives, these Indians suffer injustice and aggravation in the way that they are enslaved by these notables: because it is known to us the ease with which they enslave their servants, which is for very light reasons. And in meaning to address this in order to stop this inconvenience from taking place, seen and debated in our Council of the Indies, it was agreed that we would send this letter, and we saw to it. By which we forbid and command that from the day this provision is made public in the city of the Kings of that province, under no circumstance, directly or indirectly, shall any Spaniard from these Kingdoms dare rescue or purchase from those landlords, notables or other native persons who are peaceful subjects of the Crown, any Indian that they may have in their service; and if anyone challenges this, he will lose his

> ownership and the slaves be set free to do as they please, and the buyer will lose whatever sum he paid [. . .].[25]

The text highlights the lawmakers' awareness of the fact that Spaniards had bought numerous natives from Peruvian leaders and noblemen and that those natives were being used as slaves, forced to work endlessly. All of this led the Spanish Crown, under this specific decree, to forbid its citizens from buying slaves from the local landlords and to consider any slaves found in this situation as free persons. However, the enslavement of Native Americans was allowed in certain specific cases, when it was considered a consequence of a "just war." This was, for instance, the case of the rebel "Indians" of Venezuela and Cabo de Vela, who could be captured for having rebelled against the Spaniards, according to a law enacted in 1530.[26] Likewise, it was decreed that the Indians from the Chilean War (1608) could be enslaved as they had "killed many members of the clergy and also Governor Martín García de Loyola and many of his vassals, and taken others captive."[27] As can be seen, the very few cases in which the enslavement of Native Americans was allowed were related to specific situations in which a direct conflict took place, a situation regarded as a "just war" by the Spaniards.

At the same time as the enslavement of Native Americans was being banned, laws were enacted to control the origin of the slaves transported to colonial Spanish America. Specifically, it was constantly forbidden to transport North Africans and converted Muslims to the Americas, so as to "contain the spread of the faith of Mohammad." All of this can be clearly appreciated by observing the licenses granted by the Crown for the introduction of slaves into America, which were mandatory for all slave owners upon boarding ship in Spain to the American colonies.

Overall, it can be safely stated that there were marked differences in the way of legislation on Black Africans compared to Native Americans. The general tendency was to try to attract the latter, as King Felipe said, "by peaceful means" with a view to evangelizing them; by contrast, in the case of Black Africans, no "concern for their souls" was shown except in a few personal initiatives, such as that of Jesuit priest Alonso de Sandoval, who welcomed slaves from Africa upon their arrival in Cartagena de Indias, taking care of their baptism. In fact, only Black slaves who converted to Catholicism could be set free in eighteenth-century Dutch and British colonies.

In this respect, it could be assumed that the attitude toward Native Americans of Queen Isabel I, Bartolomé de las Casas, and other Spanish moralists led to the freedom of those natives and to the increase in Black African slavery in America. Indeed, Black African slave labor played an essential part in the development of colonial America, particularly on the Spanish colonial side, since on the Portuguese side there was no liberation of the native Brazilians.

The Regulation of the Introduction of Enslaved Black Africans into the Americas

It must be mentioned that, early in the Spanish Renaissance, sub-Saharans were known as "Ethiopians" as opposed to "blacks," in a clear reference to Ethiopia, a much-respected civilization at the time, represented by King Balthazar in the Adoration of Christ by the Three Kings. However, as the centuries passed and slavery ties deepened, sub-Saharans were increasingly reduced to being called "Blacks," with an exclusively biological connotation, which concealed their African cultural background and became a synonym for "slave," particularly in the seventeenth and eighteenth centuries, when trade with the Americas significantly intensified.

In any case, as previously underscored, the introduction of Black Africans into Spanish colonial America was always carried out through the European (not Spanish) companies that monopolized trans-Atlantic trade. This trade also entailed the enactment of a set of laws concerning these companies. In fact, in 1604 there already was a Royal decree on the obligations of viceroys and government officials in the American colonies in their dealings with the Compañía Real de Guinea, established in France, which had the monopoly on the introduction of Black African slaves into America.[28] Subsequently, in 1713, the *Assiento ajustado entre las dos majestades católica y británica sobre encargarse la compañía de Inglaterra de la Introducción de esclavos negros en la América Española* took place. This was an agreement between King Felipe V of Spain and Queen Anne Stuart of England that stated the following: "By which having reached the termination of the agreement with the *Compañía real de Guinea*, established in France, on the introduction of black slaves into the Indies, and given the wish of the Queen of England and the Company of England on her behalf to enter into this relationship [. . .] They commit to introduce 144,000 blacks of both sexes and all ages, that is, 4,800 blacks per year for 30 years."[29] As can clearly be observed in this sample fragment, the Queen of England was committing to introduce almost 5,000 Black African slaves yearly into the Spanish colonies. However, notwithstanding all the legislation regarding the introduction of Black Africans into America by the French and English, the slave trade—and hence the enslavement of Black Africans—was never fully justified or permitted by Spanish legislation, as it did not originate in "just war," as previously pointed out. This may explain the absence of Spanish companies involved in the slave trade, as it went against the law to enslave any individuals that were not directly captured in a war context.

The Prevention and Repression of Slave Uprisings

Another prevailing topic in Spanish legislation on slavery was the prevention and repression of slave uprisings. Generally speaking, this legislation was essentially concerned with the American context and aimed to ensure that slaves would not leave their living quarters after curfew, that they would always settle with Spanish owners, that they would not be armed, that nobody would purchase anything from them, and so on. It also regulated the punishment for rebels and runaways, who could be marked by iron or even castrated. Most certainly because of this, the blacksmith's house was also known as the runaway house in Spain.

Yet another matter addressed by legislation was the prevention of the phenomenon of the so-called *esclavos cortados* (cut slaves), who were slaves rented out in a more open regime; Felipe III attempted to ban this in 1619, invalidating permission to rent out their work. The Spanish Crown considered slaves who were put to work by their owners outside their owner's domain, even if they gave their earnings to their owners, to be enjoying a status of semifreedom judged pernicious to the Kingdom.

It must also be noted that marriages between slaves were perfectly legal in Spain, and even marriages between slaves and free citizens. There are numerous cases of marriages between slaves and freed slaves or free citizens, most of them preserved in the records of church registries. An example of this was the marriage of Juan Latino and Ana de Carleval, a free white woman.

The Regulation of Taxes
and the Fiscal Aspects of the Slave Trade

Regarding this issue, most of the legislation focused on trans-Atlantic trade and referred to the regulation of the Crown's fiscal income but also to the market price of enslaved people. In 1556, for instance, a Royal Decree was issued setting a maximum price for the "sale of blacks in the Americas."[30] The price was limited to 100 ducats in Isla Española, San Juan, Cuba, and the rest of the islands, and 110 ducats in the provinces of Tierra Firme, Cartagena, Santa Marta, Venezuela, Cabo de Vela, Honduras, and Guatemala. The price limit was 120 ducats in Nicaragua and Nueva España, 140 in the New Kingdom of Granada and Popayan, 150 in Peru and Río de la Plata, and 180 ducats in Chile. However, five years later, in 1561, this Royal Decree was revoked, thus allowing the sale of "Blacks" at any price, most certainly due to market pressure.[31]

In any case, it is worth ending this topic with the original text of the Royal Decree, as it gives a clear view of the prevailing mind-set regarding the introduction of slave labor and the great economic impact of Black African slavery on colonial production methods.

> Don Felipe: Having been informed of the shortage of farmers and laborers in our Indies, Islands and Tierra Firme of the Ocean Sea, it is necessary for the Spaniards who there reside to use blacks, in their farms and estates as in other ventures, and as the need is high in those parts, those who trade in slaves ask for an excessive price, and each day the price rises more, for which, were we not to remedy the situation, the farms of those places would collapse and the sugar mills would be deserted and the mines would not benefit; and for it all to remain and improve, it would be wise to set the value of these blacks, giving moderate leeway to the traders and other sellers; and wanting to provide for this, seen and agreed by the members of our Council of the Indies and with the King's blessing, it was agreed that we would set this letter, and we saw to it. By which we command that the blacks from Santo Tomé and Guinea who are taken to our Indies, Islands and Tierra Firme of the Ocean Sea and Southern Sea, from the day this letter is made public in the city of Seville, cannot be sold for a higher price than this, in the islands of Española, San Juan and Cuba and the other islands of our said Indies, 100 ducats apiece; and in the provinces of Tierra Firme, Cartagena, Santa Marta, Venezuela, Cabo de la Vela, Honduras and Guatemala, 110 ducats; in the provinces of Nicaragua and New Spain, 120 ducats; in the provinces of Perú and Río de la Plata, 150 ducats; in the New Kingdom of Granada and Popayan, 140 ducats; in

the provinces of Chile, 180 ducats; and the blacks who originate from Cabo Verde can be sold in the Islands and aforementioned provinces for 20 ducats more apiece and not more.

The Regulation of the Long Process of Abolition

Finally, abolitionist laws arrived to the Spanish courts, starting with the Ley Moret of 1870, which freed the children of slave mothers and was followed by a series of consecutively issued partial abolition decrees, and concluding with the abolition of slavery in Puerto Rico (1873) and Cuba (1886).

Nevertheless, regarding abolitionism, it is worth noting that it was a social movement that began in Europe, had close ties to Protestantism and specifically the Quakers, and subsequently spread to the United States and the Hispanic world. It is true that Spain joined the eighteenth-century abolitionist movement later than other countries. Yet, it is also a fact that the intellectual world was receptive to the idea and that the Spanish people also accepted it, which did not happen in other non-European historical contexts, in which slavery remained legal until well into the twentieth century. In fact, Spain produced great abolitionist figures, such as Emilio Castelar, Isidoro de Antillón, Clara Campoamor, Rafael María de Labra, and more. Furthermore, abolitionism was closely linked to the suffragist movement and the struggle for female vote. In fact, a considerable proportion of the antislavery movement was made up of women, under the lead of the writer Gertrudis Gómez de Avellaneda.

It is difficult to pinpoint the origins of abolitionism in Spain, as it would imply going back to the first thinkers who denounced the mistreatment of slaves or otherwise raised awareness about this issue, which would be no easy task. In any case, abolitionism (in the Aristotelian sense of stopping individuals from being the "property" of others) became established in the sixteenth century, with the ban on the enslavement of Native Americans. Queen Isabel I "the Catholic" specifically mentioned the freedom of the natives in her 1505 will. Subsequently, a provision was issued in 1528, "which commands that none of the indigenous people of New Spain can be enslaved or branded";[32] another law was issued in 1530, directed to the courts of Santo Domingo and México and the governors and other authorities of the American colonies, stating that Native Americans could not be enslaved ("by cause of just war, ransom, purchase or barter, under penalty of the loss of the owner's possessions").[33] Likewise, Carlos V enacted several decrees in the *Leyes Nuevas* of 1542–1553, in which he banned the possession of American natives as slaves. I am referring, for instance, to the Royal Provision, which stated that "under no cause of war, or any other, may a native be enslaved; and they should be treated as subjects of the Crown," and "the courts should set the natives free whenever the owner fails to produce legitimate ownership titles."[34] Moreover, a number of decrees on abolition or "On the freedom of the natives" quickly succeeded each other. In the case of Native Americans, it is particularly striking that even "just war" enslavement was abolished, as it was still considered legal in Spain. This fact is explicitly brought to light in the laws of 1542, which point out that "no one may enslave the natives, not even if they are captured in just war, nor sell them to another person."[35]

Meanwhile, early modern thinkers such as Tomás de Mercado, Alonso de Sandoval, Juan Márquez or Enrique Villalobos questioned the way Black African slave trade was conducted, but still accepted slavery as such. However, in the seventeenth century, abolitionist voices began to appear calling for the liberation of Black Africans, going beyond the condemnation of the inhuman practices of the trade. One of these voices was Francisco José de Jaca, who wrote a little-known text titled *Resolución sobre la libertad de los negros*.[36] Another one was Epifanio de Moirans, who wrote a text in 1684 titled *Siervos libres o justa defensa de la libertad natural de los esclavos*.[37] Subsequently, slavery was progressively abolished by a series of laws enacted in the second half of the nineteenth century, which, as mentioned earlier, led to its final abolition in the various countries that constituted the Hispanic world, the last ones to do so being Puerto Rico (1873) and Cuba (1886).

Regarding contemporary Spain, it would be fitting to question whether slavery was really abolished once and for all in a legislative context, or if the new forms of contemporary slavery brought on by globalization highlight the fact that freedom and personal integrity were not sufficiently regulated in the legislation over the last two centuries. There is little doubt that, in contemporary Europe, attempts to stem modern forms of slavery are being made using legal texts, which in turn put pressure on nation-states through national and international legislation; all this is highly effective, as laws hold the power to change the world. Yet, there are also nongovernment organizations that are fighting for the rights of people who live in comparable situations of freedom deprivation, although obviously not symmetrical to historical slavery. Some examples are women exploited by the international sex trade, among whom there are many Nigerians who live in Spain. Furthermore, women and children have always suffered most in these situations due to their extreme vulnerability and, unfortunately, this is still so.

It is a fact that Europe and Spain progressed steadily toward the development of the Charter of the Rights of Man, which later came to be known as Human Rights due to the pressure from women's collectives. In this regard, there are many opinions pointing to a regression within the framework of human rights in Europe that could well be caused by a lack of interest from nation-states in identifying and penalizing modern slavery situations driven by globalization. However, I believe that slavery should be placed in its specific historical and global context, and it must not be forgotten that today there are traditional slavery situations that were never revoked in social practice, as happens in Sudan, Thailand, India, or certain Persian Gulf countries, to name a few.

In any case, it is clear that people caught in unfavorable socioeconomic situations and additionally subjected to cultural discrimination are still susceptible to being "enslaved," not only in Spain but in any other country. In fact, the exploitation of other human beings has not entirely disappeared from the world, despite legislation and abolitionist movements that have fought and continue to fight for personal freedom, because unfortunately profit seems to prevail on personal integrity. Thus, in my opinion, it seems that slavery remains dormant until the social and legislative context enables it to resurface through gaps or loopholes.

Notes

Excerpts from this chapter are direct translations originally published in "De la esclavitud al abolicionismo en la historia de España: legislación, guerrajusta y discursos," in Esclavitud, mestizaje y abolicionismo en los mundos hispánicos," ed. Aurelia Martín Casares (Granada, Spain: University of Granada, 2015), 307–29.

    1. Aurelia Martín Casares, *Juan Latino: Talento y destino* (Granada, Spain: Universidad de Granada, 2016). I am planning to publish soon an English translation of this biography, as it includes extensive unpublished data and shows Juan Latino in a different light.

    2. In April 2016, the University of Granada's Juan Latino Permanent Seminar for Studies on Slavery and Abolitionism, of which I am honored to be the director, was created. We keep three of his original works, as well as various historic documents that bear witness to his time at our university.

3. "Is not only one of the rarest books in the world, but is one of the most remarkable illustrations of the intellectual faculties and possible accomplishments of the African race," George Ticknor, *History of Spanish Literature* (New York: Harper & Brothers, 1849), 582.

4. Calixto C. Masó, *Juan Latino: gloria de España y de su raza* (Chicago: Northeastern Illinois University, 1972), 18.

5. See, for example, "De la esclavitud al abolicionismo en la historia de España: legislación, guerra justa y discursos," in *Esclavitud, mestizaje y abolicionismo en los mundos hispánicos*, ed. Aurelia Martín Casares (University of Granada, 2015), 307–29.

6. *Diario Noticioso, Curioso, Erudito y Comercial Público y Económico*, April 1, 1758.

7. *Diario Noticioso, Curioso, Erudito y Comercial Público y Económico*, October 21, 1765. The advertisement ran again on October 19 and 21.

8. I have addressed aspects related to slavery legislation in several previous publications: Aurelia Martín Casares, "El pensamiento político, la Corona y la Iglesia frente a la esclavitud," in *La esclavitud en la Granada del siglo XVI: género, raza y religión*(Granada, Spain: Universidad de Granada, 2000), 65–90; Aurelia Martín Casares, "Domestic Service in Spain: Legislation, Gender and Social Practice," in *Domestic Service and the Formation of the European Identity (16th–21st centuries)*, ed. Antoinette Fauve-Chamoux (Oxford, UK: Peter Lang, 2004), 189–211; and Aurelia Martín Casares and Margarita García Barranco, "Legislation on Free Soil in 19th Century Spain, the Case of the Slave Rufino and Its Consequences (1858–1879)," in *Free Soil in the Atlantic World*, ed. Sue Peabody and Keila Grinberg (New York: Routledge, 2015), 131–46.

9. The Romans started to use the name "Hispania" to refer to the territory previously known as Iberia.

10. Antonio Domínguez Ortíz, *España, tres milenios de historia* (Madrid, Spain: Marcial Pons, 2000), 19.

11. Seneca. *Epistulae morales ad Lucilium* 48, 5.

12. *El libro de los juicios (Liber Iudiciorum)* (Madrid, Spain: Agencia Estatal Boletín Oficial del Estado, 2015). Preliminary study by Rafael Ramis, Latin text with Spanish translation.

13. *Fuero juzgo*, BN, Mss/5774 (between 1401 and 1525).

14. In the Spanish medieval kingdoms, slavery was the norm. As an example, in 1238, in the Kingdom of Valencia, the Parliament enacted a law on the donation of slaves. Libro VIII. Ru. VIII. I. Sobre las donaciones. "Sobre la donación o libramientos de esclavos y bienes mediante carta. Disposición por la que si alguno comprase esclavos u otros bienes con carta, y los donase o librase en razón de donación o venta a otra persona, tenga ello tanto valor como si se hubiese librado la posesión de aquellos siervos o bienes vendidos al segundo beneficiario." Cortes de Valencia, *En l'any de Nostre Senyor mil docents trentahuyt, nou dies a*

la entrada de octubre pres lo senyor en Jacme, per la Gracia de Deu, Rey d'Arago, la ciutat de Valencia, 1238 (Madrid, Spain: Biblioteca Nacional, I/1312[1], fol. 62r).

15. Cuarta Partida, título XXI, ley II.

16. Aristotle, *Politics,* book I, chapter 2: "On slavery."

17. Aurelia Martín Casares, "La esclavitud por guerra: la rebelión de los moriscos," in *La esclavitud en la Granada del siglo XVI: Género, raza y religión* (Granada, Spain: Editorial Universidad de Granada, 2000), 173-92.

18. Manuel Lucena Salmoral, *Los códigos negros de la América española* (Alcalá de Henares: UNESCO, 1996); Manuel Lucena Salmoral, *Regulación de la esclavitud negra en las colonias de América Española (1503-1886). Documentos para su estudio* (Murcia, Spain: Universidad de Murcia y Universidad de Alcalá, 2005).

19. *Berberisco* was the term used to define the inhabitants of North Africa, whether they be Arab or truly Berber. This was due to the name of the territory, known at the time as *Berbería,* or "Barbary Coast."

20. Tomás De Mercado, *Suma de tratos y contratos,* in *Biblioteca de autores españoles. Obras escogidas de filósofos,* ed. Nicolás Sánchez Albornoz (Madrid: Atlas, [1571] 1953), 277.

21. De Mercado, *Suma de tratos y contratos.*

22. "¿Qué se yo si el esclavo cautivado fue justamente captivado?" (How can I know if the slave was rightfully captured?), wondered Bartolomé de Albornoz in *De la esclavitud, Biblioteca de Autores Españoles: Obras escogidas de filósofos* (Madrid, Spain: Atlas, 1953), 232.

23. Aurelia Martín Casares, "Berbería. La toma de ciudades, el corso y las cabalgadas," in "La esclavitud en la Granada del siglo XVI: género, raza y religión" (Granada, Spain: Universidad de Granada, 2000), 161-73.

24. Real Resolución que establece el libre uso y venta de moros que apresasen los corsistas. June 7, 1724. Archivo de la Corona de Aragón. Chancillería, vol. 11, fol. 50.

25. *Provisión por la que se prohíbe que los españoles puedan rescatar o comprar de los caciques de las provincias del Perú indio alguno por esclavo u otra manera.* Biblioteca Nacional, HAi/1706 (IV), 367. HA, HAi, and VC accompanying references from the BN (National Library) are internal library codes

26. BN, HA/38374, 91-97.

27. BN, HAi/3129, 215-216.

28. *Real cédula acerca de lo que han de observar los virreyes y oficiales reales en Indias con relación a la Compañía Real de Guinea establecida en Francia a cuyo cargo está la introducción de esclavos negros en América.* December 23, 1604. Real Academia de la Historia (henceforth RAH), 9/1753, 48r-48v.

29. RAH, 9/1756, 138r-138v.

30. *Real cédula sobre la tasa del precio y de cómo se han de vender los negros en las Indias.* BN, HA/68926, 247-49.

31. *Revocación de las Reales Provisiones que están dadas sobre la tasa de los negros que se llevan a las Indias para que los puedan vender a cualquier precio.* Archivo General de Indias, Sevilla, Contratación, Leg. 5091, September 9, 1561.

32. BN, AHI/19317 (9), no. 120, 434–37.

33. BN, HA/48134, 65r–66r. *Provisión dirigida a la Audiencias de Santo Domingo y México y a los Gobernadores, Corregidores, Alcaldes Mayores y demás Justicias de las Indias, por la que se ordena que en adelante no se pueda cautivar o hacer esclavos a los indios, ya sea por guerra justa, rescate, compra o trueque, so pena de la pérdida de sus bienes al que fuere hallado que tiene indios como esclavos.*

34. BN, VC 1831/1, 10.

35. BN, HAi/1706 (IV), 368–69.

36. F. De Jaca, [1682]. *Resolución sobre la libertad de los negros y sus originarios, en estado de paganos y después ya cristianos* (Madrid, Spain: CSIC, 2002).

37. Epifanio De Moirans, *Siervos libres o justa defensa de la libertad natural de los esclavos* (Madrid, Spain: CSIC, [1684] 2007).

Bibliography

BN = Biblioteca Nacional/National Library

Albornoz Bartolomé de. *De la esclavitud, Biblioteca de Autores Españoles: Obras escogidas de filósofos*. Madrid, Spain: Atlas, 1953.
Aristotle. *Politics*, book I, chapter 2: "On slavery."
BN, HA/38374, 91–97.
BN, HAi/3129, 215–16.
BN, AHI/19317 (9), no. 120, 434–37.
BN, HA/48134, 65r–66r.
BN, VC 1831/1, 10.
BN, HAi/1706 (IV), 368–69.
De Jaca, F. *Resolución sobre la libertad de los negros y sus originarios, en estado de paganos y después ya cristiano*. Madrid, Spain: CSIC, (1682) 2002.
De Moirans, Epifanio. *Siervos libres o justa defensa de la libertad natural de los esclavos*. Madrid, Spain: CSIC, (1684) 2007.
De Mercado, Tomás. "Suma de tratos y contratos," in *Biblioteca de autores españoles: Obras escogidas de filósofos*, edited by Nicolás Sánchez Albornoz. Madrid, Spain: Atlas, (1571) 1953.
Diario Noticioso, Curioso, Erudito y Comercial Público y Económico, October 21, 1765.
———, April 1, 1758.
Domínguez Ortíz, Antonio. *España, tres milenios de historia*. Madrid, Spain: Marcial Pons, 2000.

El libro de los juicios (Liber Iudiciorum). Preliminary study by Rafael Ramis, Latin text with Spanish translation. Madrid, Spain: Agencia Estatal Boletín Oficial del Estado, 2015.

Fuero juzgo, BN, Mss/5774 (between 1401 and 1525).

Lucena Salmoral, Manuel. *Regulación de la esclavitud negra en las colonias de América Española (1503–1886): Documentos para su estudio*. Murcia, Spain: Universidad de Murcia y Universidad de Alcalá, 2005.

———. *Los códigos negros de la América española*. Alcalá de Henares, Spain: UNESCO, 1996.

Martín Casares, Aurelia. *Juan Latino: Talento y destino*. Granada, Spain: Universidad de Granada, 2016.

———. "Domestic Service in Spain: Legislation, Gender and Social Practice." In *Domestic Service and the Formation of the European Identity (16th–21st Centuries)*, edited by Antoinette Fauve-Chamoux, 189–211. Oxford, UK: Peter Lang, 2004.

———. "La esclavitud por guerra: la rebelión de los moriscos." In *La esclavitud en la Granada del siglo XVI: Género, raza y religión*. Granada, Spain: Editorial Universidad de Granada, 2000.

———. "El pensamiento político, la Corona y la Iglesia frente a la esclavitud." In *La esclavitud en la Granada del siglo XVI: género, raza y religión*. Granada, Spain: Universidad de Granada, 2000.

———. "Berbería. La toma de ciudades, el corso y las cabalgadas." In *La esclavitud en la Granada del siglo XVI: género, raza y religión*. Granada, Spain: Universidad de Granada, 2000.

Martín Casares, Aurelia, and Margarita García Barranco. "Legislation on Free Soil in 19th Century Spain, the Case of the Slave Rufino and its Consequences (1858–1879)." In *Free Soil in the Atlantic World*, edited by Sue Peabody and Keila Grinberg, 131–46. New York: Routledge, 2015.

Masó Calixto C. *Juan Latino: gloria de España y de su raza*. Chicago: Northeastern Illinois University, 1972.

Provisión por la que se prohíbe que los españoles puedan rescatar o comprar de los caciques de las provincias del Perú indio alguno por esclavo u otra manera. Biblioteca Nacional, HAi/1706 (IV), 367.

Real Academia de la Historia (RAH), 9/1753, 48r–48v. *Real cédula acerca de lo que han de observar los virreyes y oficiales reales en Indias con relación a la Compañía Real de Guinea establecida en Francia a cuyo cargo está la introducción de esclavos negros en América*. December 23, 1604.

———. 9/1756, 138r–38v.

Ramis, Rafael. *El libro de los juicios (Liber Iudiciorum)*. Madrid, Spain: Agencia Estatal Boletín Oficial del Estado, 2015.

Real Resolución que establece el libre uso y venta de moros que apresasen los corsistas. June 7, 1724. Archivo de la Corona de Aragón. *Chancillería*, vol. 11, fol. 50.

Real cédula sobre la tasa del precio y de cómo se han de vender los negros en las Indias. BN, HA/68926, 247–49.

Revocación de las Reales Provisiones que están dadas sobre la tasa de los negros que se llevan a las Indias para que los puedan vender a cualquier precio. Archivo General de Indias, Seville, Contratación, Leg. 5091. September 15, 1561.

Seneca. *Epistulae morales ad Lucilium* 48, 5.

Ticknor, George. *History of Spanish Literature.* New York: Harper & Brothers, 1849.

Valencia, Cortes de. *En l'any de Nostre Senyor mil docents trentahuyt, nou dies a la entrada de octubre pres lo senyor en Jacme, per la Gracia de Deu, Rey d'Arago, la ciutat de Valencia,* 1238. Madrid, Spain: Biblioteca Nacional, I/1312(1), fol. 62r.

Chapter 2

Legislation and Slavery from a Local Perspective
Slaves in the Municipal Ordinances
of Extremadura, 1500–1800

Rocío Periáñez Gómez

In Castille, during the Modern Age, the concern for the regulation of matters related to slaves did not have a significant development as related to general affairs. In fact, it seems that all, or at least what was deemed most significant, had been settled long ago, and there was no need to bring anything substantially new to what had already been done. Except for exact mentions in the *Nueva Recopilación* or the *Novísima Recopilación*, dealing with very specific aspects,[1] any controversy needing resolution would use as point of reference the contents of *Las Siete Partidas*, written no less than 300 years before. It is surprising to see how laws within *Las Partidas* were used in the eighteenth century in judicial cases where slaves were involved, even when many of these provisions had become obsolete and the state had adapted new formulas more in line with the new circumstances.

However, despite the lack of developments in regard to the grounds on which slavery was based, that is, means of liberation or the "rights" of slaves,[2] we can find—at a more particular level—laws or measures that locally affected slaves, specifically, laws affecting the slave population living in localities where municipal ordinances or resolutions dictated by the municipalities' councils were adopted.

There is no doubt about the interest that the study of municipal ordinances has gained in recent years, the acquisition of knowledge about the organization and development of municipalities, their forms of government, their local history, and even environmental studies. Yet, at least specifically, the study of slavery has barely been addressed.[3] In actuality, it has been a resource unexploited by historians for the production of knowledge about such institutions. Researchers have mainly relied on other sources such as notarial or parochial records from which serial data can be obtained to address issues such as slave trade, the release of people held in slavery, or the demographic evolution of the slaves. However, the information provided by municipal laws—mainly qualitative—complements the "traditional" sources and helps clarify and qualify certain aspects of slavery that are less known due to the nature of the documents usually employed. In this setting, municipal laws allow us to get closer to society's perception of the slave population. Through these laws, we come into contact with aspects of slavery such as labor in various forms, and, at times, they show us the problems or most frequent concerns generated by the presence of slaves within the community. However, we must be cautious when using ordinances as a source of information, given that the nature of their creation is to correct and punish deviant behavior.

The aim of this chapter is to show the value of municipal ordinances for gaining knowledge about slavery through the analysis of some of these legislative compilations, which were developed in Extremadura during the modern period and contain references to the slave population. It is necessary, therefore, to provide some details on the geographical and chronological context of our study, as well as some of the sources of documentation used. As for the physical space that forms the framework of our work, we must say that the significance of Extremadura will be acknowledged, given its background as having been a territory under the Crown of Castile and marked by its border position with the Kingdom of Portugal. The border will be both a place of exchange—especially in regard to the traffic of slaves—and a scenario for conflict. During the modern age, the institution of slavery was fully settled in the area. However, there were differences between the north of Extremadura and south bordering Andalusia. In the north, the presence of slaves was more limited, and linked to densely populated areas, as well as to the elites who wield political, economic, and social power. In the borders of Andalusia, slavery found major growth as it existed well into the eighteenth century. The slaves who lived in Extremadura were a diverse group in terms of origin. Among them we can find Berbers, Turks, sub-Saharan Africans, and slaves born in Portugal and Extremadura, although the presence of Black slaves who were provided through trade by the Portuguese from its African colonies was predominant.[4]

In regard to municipal ordinances, we have analyzed twenty of them written in the cities of Cáceres, Zafra, Llerena, Los Santos de Maimona, Villalba, Almendralejo, Fregenal of Sierra, and Valderde de Llerena within the region of Extremadura between the sixteenth and eighteenth centuries.[5] This study has found that the majority of references to slaves are related to the sixteenth century. There are two possible explanations for this: first, most of the ordinances correspond to the sixteenth-century period,[6] which enjoyed a stage of splendor in regard to ordinances in Castile;[7] second, because slavery experienced a boom in the Iberian Peninsula,[8] and in particular in Extremadura, during the sixteenth century and into the early decades of the seventeenth century.[9] Although there was a resurgence of drafting ordinances in the eighteenth century, slavery in Extremadura became a residual phenomenon; therefore, we only find minimal references to slaves in ordinances produced in the eighteenth century.[10]

Among the ordinances consulted we can distinguish, first, those that devote a specific title to slaves. Such is the case of the ordinances of Cáceres 1569, containing the "Ordinances of black men and women."[11] Also, most importantly, those of Zafra 1528, given that they developed more extensive rules intended for the slave population in Title XIX: "*De los esclavos.*" And second, also in Zafra, those with varied measures of control which include rules that make references to slaves.

In our analysis, we will deal with different aspects that allow us to structure the work: controlling conduct, limitation of activities and repression of vices, ending with the penalties imposed. At the same time, this study will compare legislations that, in relation to the slaves, were issued at the same time by the municipal authorities of other towns in the peninsula and beyond, in order to draw parallels and contrasts between what was happening in Extremadura and in other parts of the Spanish monarchy.

Controlling Conduct

One of the concerns of the civic authorities reflected in municipal ordinances and agreements is the control of the slave population at various levels. This includes issues regarding safety, morality, any activities performed by the slaves, and habits. The rules were dictated in order to solve problems that were or had been present in earlier times, that is to say, they were the response to events that had been raised in the community and that according to the town's people and authorities had to be solved. However, it is important to note that many times ordinances were written as preventive measures, allowing for the opportunity to adopt norms previously established somewhere else. This would contribute to existing prejudices against the slave population and the notion that the enslaved people had certain tendencies that had to be repressed.

In regard to safety, the measures taken generally focused on avoiding the concentration of slaves in various spaces, walking around at odd times, especially at night, or carrying weapons. Large congregations of slaves caused misgivings and concerns for the authorities. As result, the rules issued in different cities and towns aimed at preventing these assemblies, as was the case of Seville[12] and Murcia, where they were forbidden to get together during holidays and roam the streets at night. For instance, the ordinance states that "because and as a result of blacks slaves walking around so freely and exempt in this city of Murcia, they commit many robberies and there are other issues that arise among them such as getting wounded or killed."[13] It seems that this type of legislation was more common in urban environments, perhaps not so much because there existed a larger number of slaves, but because it was more difficult to control them in these areas than it was in smaller and medium-size locations. In the case of Extremadura, we found that in the ordinances of Zafra, the first measure aimed specifically at slaves expressed, "first of all, that no male or female slaves of any owner in this city gather for their ceremonies or eating activities and if so they shall be whipped publicly fifty times."[14]

Although slaves were forbidden to get together, which may indicate the concern of the authorities about such concentrations of people, there are no other norms in the ordinances of this villa that are present in other places, as we shall see later. This evidences the existence of conflict in relation to the slave population living in it. Therefore, we think that the purpose of establishing the norms goes beyond issues concerning safety. However, the gatherings among the enslaved populations that occurred during the daytime were not as threatening as those that occurred at night. According to the ordinances, supported by the darkness of the night, slaves went around in the dark committing multiple crimes difficult to contain. Hence the existence of rules which were adopted in Llerena, where the slave population deserved to be mentioned in several of its municipal ordinances of 1632, in relation to the insecurity caused by the slaves' meetings and their performances. Ordinance CXLVIII, "That no slave goes out at night," states the following:

> Given the disarray that exists within the enslaved of this Villa, who wonder around in groups at night, and it seems that there are many issues, and robberies of chickens and other things, which bring much harm to the Villa, and to the neighbors and residents of the Villa. And to address this, it was ordered and commanded that any slaves walking more than one found in the said Villa after nightfall be taken to prison and placed inside the dungeon and not be released without trial.[15]

And, reiterating the supposed threats caused by slaves going out at night, we find ordinance CLXXXII: "that slaves do not carry arms at night," which is expressed as the following:

> We order and command that no slave may carry arms at night unless said slave is accompanying his/her master, after the prayers, or face losing said arms and spend a night in jails, standing up in a cell. And any slave who goes out after the curfew, would lose the arms and would end up in jail standing in a cell; and that the jailer would release such slave without rights to his master, the day after, and that the slave shall not carry arms during the day without the company of his master. And if the slave loses the arms, must be put in prison for that night and sleep standing. And any slave who is out after hours and again loses his/her arms and sleeps standing in prison; and whom the correction officer lets go the next day who was imprisoned without rights and who during the day does not carry arms without his/her master.[16]

In this case the regulation focuses on the nocturnal activities of slaves giving rise to growing insecurity among the population, given that the dark conditions allowed said slaves the opportunity to commit criminal acts, mainly thefts, but also possible aggressions. Hence, the restrictions on carrying weapons; however, as the ordinance points out, they were allowed to carry arms as long as they were accompanied by their owners.

Despite the proliferation of such measures in Castilian territory, these laws were not as marked as they later were in the Americas, where the issue became more serious as there was a higher concentration of slaves and there existed a greater fear of riots staged by slaves. There was also the fear of slaves escaping from their owners, as it can be learned from the first legal measures toward the slave population in the New World, as well as the ordinances of the Audiencias and councils of the cities of Santo Domingo, Cubagua, Veracruz, or Quito.[17] Along with punishing the "criminal acts" of slaves, some municipal ordinances seemed to be designed to control their moral behavior, which in the case cited below refers to the to the idea of promiscuity often attributed to slaves. The rules of Zafra ordered the following:

> And that anyone who has a male or female slave allows for them to have sexual relations with other slaves and if they did and the owner was to find out, the latter must marry them within a month or sell them so that they may no longer own them. The owner would also receive a fine one thousand maravedís and the slave one hundred lashes.
>
> And that no resident of the villa who owns a female slave or female slaves allows that a male slave belonging to another resident whether from this villa or another, mates with a female slave or female slaves they own. And those who know about it and allow it should receive a penalty of one thousand maravedís and the female slave one hundred lashes.[18]

It is noteworthy to point out that, although the standards refer to slaves, the responsibility for compliance rests on the owners. The offense penalizes both the owner and the slave. The solution to end the aforementioned illicit relations among slaves was to legitimize the union of slaves through marriage or a final separation by selling them. As for the second measure mentioned above, in addition to showing the apparent permissiveness showed by the owners through this type of behavior, perhaps because of the benefits they could get from the female slaves by increasing their wealth with children born to slaves who inherited the condition of their mothers, it also denotes the concern of municipal authorities to end some immoral habits that seemed to have been fairly widespread. To this we must add the pragmatic character of the ordinance in order to avoid future litigation between the owners of the slaves, on the property of the children that slaves could generate as a result of these relationships.

The attempt to avoid unlawful conduct rests behind the following provision found in ordinances of Llerena regarding women's customs of going out to fetch water or to wash clothes.

Because many married women, young ones and honest and slaves and other people have the need to go fetch water and go to the springs to wash clothes and other things they need, and because as a result of many young men and slaves and other suspicious people who go to see them and talk to them while the women are in the springs, and her parents stop sending the women there to avoid inconveniences and issues that are normally addressed by the town hall, and issues of honesty that take place. Given the above, it was ordered and commanded that no one should go to the water fountain la Pellejera and other water springs.[19]

But the guarding of moral norms may be present in other ordinances from the Zafra ordinances cited before: the prohibition of slaves meeting to cook meals and hold ceremonies. It is possible that during these meetings the enslaved people showed behavior that was frowned on by the authorities. The literature of the Golden Age informs us of blacks' interest toward music and dance. The writings of moralists show criticism of certain slaves' dances that were characterized by its sensuality and eroticism;[20] perhaps in the ceremonies mentioned, slaves performed dances that were deemed inappropriate.

The Limitation of Activities

On many occasions, we find references in the ordinances that speak of some of the activities performed by slaves. This allows us to learn about some of the tasks slaves performed for their owners. As for Extremadura, although we are certain of slaves' participation in the artisan sector, we did not find ordinances that restrict slaves from taking part in said odd jobs. Different from other areas such as Seville, where in 1527, it was prohibited for linen weavers to train their slaves. This was different from the case of Granada, where ordinances titled "Ordinances for the Arts and the Skill of Weaving" stipulated that no slave should learn to weave. The same applied in the ordinances of Ronda, in the region of Andalucía, Spain, regarding slaves working with silk.[21]

The activities most frequently cited in the ordinances of Extremadura refer to low-skilled work related to farming. And in fact, these are not rules designed exclusively for the slave population, given that the ordinances say these low-skilled jobs are also performed by free men and women. In this setting, the statutes of Valverde de Llerena of 1554 express: "As such we order and command that anyone, resident or child of a resident, or adolescent or male and female slave who cuts wood in the meadows of this council and any other place in Carrasco, big or small, for plowing or for any other thing should pay the penalty."[22] References to slaves are found in the statutes of Fregenal de la Sierra in 1668, about the crops grown in the countryside and the wineries that seek to protect themselves from the cattle that go into the fields and damage the crops. The latter is an indication that slaves took part in this type of labor. In this case, we can cite for example ordinance 18, "About no one going to or sending another person to search the wineries until the council provides its license," which states,

> We order and command that no person despite their status or condition, goes to or send their children, servants, or slaves to look for left overs in the wineries until they receive a license from the council, in order to avoid the much damage that is usually caused while going to get the said remains before the end of the grape harvest in all the wineries. The penalty for any person who shows up in the wineries to get left overs without the license from the Council shall be, for each violation, a fine of two hundred maravedís split in four parts as it is indicated in the Ordinances in this title.[23]

Another type of work, apparently commonly performed by slaves in southern Extremadura, was selling the firewood they collected, a practice that drew suspicion on the slaves as contained in the ordinances of Zafra.

> And that many slaves who bring wood home to their masters as well as to sell it before they arrive at their master's home or in the market where they go to sell the wood, they sell part of it and take advantage of it and steal it and hide it from their masters. We order and command that no one buys from a slave part of the wood that they carry and whomever buys, must buy the entire load and if people buy it each time should face the penalty of two hundred maravedís.[24]

It is clear that slaves were selling some of the wood without permission from the owners in order to earn their own money. Also, illegal sales carried out by slaves were not limited to selling wood, and therefore these rules were found in Caceres.

> That no one be smart enough to buy or exchange anything with a male or female slave nor receive from them or some of them anything to hold and anyone who did from now on would pay as penalty the value of the item purchased or exchanged or received or hold or pawned with more than two times the value so that the value of the item maybe split for the owner and the master who holds it and the value raised at two times half may go to the accused and the other half for the council and as such that the penalty that justice requires may not be removed this was publicly announced in the public market of this villa.[25]

However, we would like to point out that the ordinance does not address the slaves, but free people who are ordered to not purchase or keep goods provided by the slaves since they cannot trust the origin of objects obtained from the slaves. It is presumed that slaves obtain the items from stealing from their masters or other people. The attribution to slaves as thieves was based in the mentality of the time as manifested more or less explicitly in local norms.[26] Another defect commonly attributed to enslaved people was that of being "huidores" or fugitives, which explains the existence of certain rules such as this one in Llerena.

> That no resident or visitor of this villa give any donkeys or any other animals to slaves to carry wood and if they would give it to them, and something happened for lending the animals, it is their responsibility: and the said slaves, nor their owners be forced to explain about the donkeys, or any other issue, nor pay the fine, unless it could not be proved that the slave owner received money, or paid, and allowed it, and sent his/her slave, to take animals and monies, or charged money for the donkeys carried by his/her slave.[27]

In the above ordinance, in addition to exempting owners from liability for fraudulent acts committed by their slaves, it was mainly to prevent slaves from having the chance to steal from their masters by keeping some of the profits from their own work, which legally did not belong to them. To this we must add that it was also about preventing the slaves from having access to means, such as animals, which could facilitate their escape.

The Repression of Vice

The extension of the idea that slaves, for the sake of being slaves, were carriers of a number of flaws and defects, is reflected in the municipal bylaws not only in Extremadura, but in general, in all the Hispanic world. In addition to being considered thieves and fugitives, as already mentioned, one of the vices slaves were most frequently accused of was of being drunks. Actually, the three vices were interrelated, although explained in a rather simplified form; the problem was presented in the following form: the slave stole to buy alcohol and fled to avoid punishment for robbery.

Perhaps for that reason, one of the major concerns of the authorities was to prevent slaves from access to alcohol. At least that is what emerges from the fact that laws to prevent slaves from entering taverns and inns and purchasing wine are the most widespread throughout the Castilian and American territory. José Luis Cortés explains that slaves were prohibited from entering taverns in Valladolid, as well as in Murcia. In these two places, the prohibition focuses on Sundays and holidays.[28] In Málaga in 1529, bar owners were prohibited from giving drinks to slaves, "because of the many inconveniences that it caused."[29] The same prohibition can be found across the ocean in ordinances such as the one found in the city of Cubagua in 1537, in Cartagena de Indias in 1558 and 1573, and those of Quito in 1568.[30]

Extremadura was no exception in implementing similar rules, being the one with the most recurrence from the north to the south in the region. This is what we find in the ordinances of Zafra, Cáceres, Llerena, and Los Santos de Maimona. We also find it in the many agreements adopted by the council in various municipalities, such as Jerez de los Caballeros or Trujillo.[31]

The interest shown in slaves not having access to alcohol is linked to the alleged criminal and disruptive behavior that sought to be avoided. Specifically, the agreement of the council of Jerez of February 21, 1521, stated that, "because there are many white and black slaves, and they are welcomed in many taverns and houses where they are given food and drink, which causes a lot noise and robberies done by them, which are followed by other inconveniences in drinking and causing other concerns."[32] As mentioned before, theft was often associated with the vice of drinking, as it was understood that the slaves obtained money or goods illegally, given their slave status, and as such could not have any property. The council argued that drunkenness led to fights and public disturbances.

These measures changed and added more control depending on the location and time. Thus, the prohibition of giving wine to the slaves also added not to feed them, welcome them, or receive clothing in exchange for a drink. It also includes gambling. As an example, we can point to another of the agreements adopted by the council of Jerez de los Caballeros, on December 17, 1543.

> That any person who sells wine does not allow or give wine to any male or female slave nor allow them to drink in the tavern, so that when they went for wine for their masters, they should receive it, and in the same way, no bartender nor waiter in the taverns nor bars allow female slaves nor any other person gambles in the tavern or bar in any gambling game. And for each time that it could be proved a violation, they pay the penalty of three *reales*, half for the person who reports it and half for the justice or official who oversee the sentence.[33]

Similarly, although the previous order does not specify what kind of games slaves participated in, the ordinance of Villalba in 1549 specifically cites the card games and bets: "And that no one may give food or water to a slave and also does not allow card games in their house even if it is in small amounts so the penalty of six maravedís for each time that allowed that a slave gambled or ate or drank in their home."[34]

From the content in the regulations, we can deduce that slaves received support from people who bought supposedly stolen merchandise, who would provide liquor and food with the money it was assumed slaves obtained illegally. The ordinance also leads us to think that the people referenced in the regulations allowed slaves to stay in their homes, thus becoming participants and covering up for the slaves' wrongdoings. This must be one of the reasons why the authorities aimed at preventing it, as is shown in ordinance CCLXXXI in Llerena. The latter is titled, "Do not take in slaves in any home," and it states the following:

> For many slaves of this Villa commit a lot of robberies and crimes in this said Villa at night and during the day which they dare to commit, as a result of having lodging in many of the homes of other slaves and free female slaves, and of other

houses of tavern owners and poor people, who welcome them and take them in their homes. To remedy this, we agree and mandate, that from now on no slave or free female slave, or other resident of this Villa dare to take in their home at night, or during the day any slave nor female slave nor feed them, or give them drinks even if they bring you food and drinks, nor sleep in your house, so the penalty of that one found or it became known after investigation of having accepted during the day, or night, or allowed them to eat, sleep any slave or female slave in their home, that for the same case obtain the penalty of six hundred maravedís, split into thirds, in the said form; and in addition to this is exiled from this Villa and their terms and jurisdiction for one year following, and do not break, so penalty that for the first time is given 100 lashes and double exile, and for the second be exiled permanently.[35]

Penalties

As for the sanctions imposed for violating the rules, they vary depending on whether the offenders are free or slaves. As we have seen, some of the ordinances were created to penalize free people generally by having to pay fines. However, when the punishment was intended for slaves, the sanctions could fall on the owners or on the slaves. For example, in the town of Los Santos de Maimona, it is expressed that the owner is expressly responsible for paying the fine in the same way that a father should take responsibility for his child and a boss for an employee: "And that when any young man who runs errands violates a rule, just as short as of other things, leaving the master the young man or his possessions as credit or discontinuing the young man's earnings, being free and if not free, be forced to the penalty made by his employee, and if it were son or slave, that the father be forced to the penalty and the master as well."[36] However, it seems that the fact that some penalties were imposed on the masters and not on the slaves, drove slaves to contravene the rules knowing they would not be punished. The latter is seen in the ordinances of Zafra as they address the issue of slaves.

> And because in many of the laws of our ordinances there are given fines generally for free men as well as for slaves and since

said penalties are to be paid by the slave owners slaves are not afraid to be fined we order and mandate that when any slave is involved in any of the violation that the owner may choose to pay the fine or that his slave be given 50 lashes publicly in the villa and the owner be obliged to hand in the slave to the justice system so that the punishment of 50 lashes is executed and if not hand in the slave within three days or be obliged to comply and pay the said fine so there is no place in the fines that in this title are found against the slaves owners because in this case we order that the slave owners are obliged to pay to the fines against them precisely.[37]

As we have seen in some of the ordinances previously cited, in Llerena the penalties for slaves used to be for them to go to prison. However, the ordinances also show that there were specific distinctions based on whether a person was free or a slave. For instance,

that any man found after sunset, if he was free, that he pay the fine of two *reales*, one real for the council and one real for the witness, and that he may be at the prison the same night; and if he was a slave, that he pay the same fine and if his owner wanted to give the slave twenty lashes in the prison and not pay the two *reales*, that is his choice, that the slave spent the night in prison the same night he is captured.[38]

The same discrimination can be seen in the ordinances of Almendralejo, where there are no "specific" laws for slaves, yet the fines are concretely established. Thus, it is stated in Title VIII, based on "The waters from the Wells and water tights of this villa. First law of the penalty incurred for those who enter the wells to bathe in the waters of the wells."

We order and mandate that any person who went in and bathed in any of the wells of this villa must pay the penalty of four hundred maravedís every time that is caught or is found in any of the bathing paths of the said wells and spent thirty days in prison and if it was a slave be given one hundred lashes in public and if it was a free person and did not have means to pay that spent double the amount of days in prison with the cuffs assigned by the mayors.[39]

A similar way to address the issue is found in the title "Of the wineries," ordinance 6, "against those who enter the wineries," and also in the title "Of the vegetable gardens," ordinance 2, "against those who enter the vegetable gardens belonging to others." These ordinances offer different penalties for both free people and slaves, but slaves' sanctions remained fines that must be paid by their owners. However, owners also had the following option: "And it was a slave and his owner and master did not want to pay for him, that he may be taken to prison and given inside of it fifty lashes."[40] It is known that corporal punishment, particularly lashing, constitute the most widespread way to punish slaves, and owners could choose between paying the fine or having the slave whipped.

Conclusion

The existence of municipal ordinances aimed directly at slaves or that allude to them exposes the need to monitor some of the particular issues affecting the life of the community in regard to the presence of the slave minority within the population. The basic concerns that led to dictating the rules relating to the slaves were twofold: (1) the maintaining of order and safety and (2) guarding morality. Both can be linked to the existing pejorative view about slaves, who were seen as quarrelsome individuals, promiscuous, thieves, and drunks. Hence the rules are directed to suppress, prevent, and control alleged deviations from this group.

Although we often find ordinances that refer to specific problems being raised in the town or city where they are drafted, in most cases we can observe, with minor distinctions, the repetition of similar measures in different places. This leads us to question to what extent the ordinances responded to the real behavior of the slaves or whether the regulations were derived from preconceived ideas about Blacks. There is no doubt that in the common mentality slaves, were considered to be vile and this marked the conduct of the free people and above all, the authorities regarding this minority.

Notes

This chapter was originally written in Spanish by the author and translated by Lissette Acosta Corniel.

1. Arturo Morgado takes a look at this "modern" law in his book *Una metrópoli esclavista. El Cádiz de la modernidad* (Granada, Spain: Universidad de Granada, 2013), 25–28.

2. When we talk about "rights" we refer, for example, to marriage even without the permission of their owners or to plead for their freedom and to have legal assistance to protect or defend their interest as it was collected in Las Partidas. José Luis Cortés López, *La esclavitud negra en la España peninsular del siglo XVI* (Salamanca, Spain: Universidad de Salamanca, 1989), 82–86.

3. There are exceptions, for example, for America: Manuel Lucena Salmoral, *Regulación de la esclavitud negra en las colonias de América Española (1503-1886): Documentos para su estudio* (Madrid, Spain: Universidad de Alcalá and Universidad de Murcia, 2005) or Manuel Lucena Salmoral, *Los Códigos Negros de la América española* (Madrid, Spain: Ediciones Unesco andUniversidad de Alcalá, 1996). However, such studies are not so common for Spain, although we can quote the work of Raúl González Arévalo, "Ordenanzas municipales y trabajo esclavo en la Corona de Castilla (siglos XV–XVI)," in *Schiavitù e servaggio nell'ecomomia europea secc, XI–XVIII* (Florence, Italy: Firenze University Press, 2014), 431–64, the recent edited: "Esclavitud y normativa ciudadana. Dinámicas sociales de integración y exclusión en las ordenanzas municipales de la corona de Castilla, siglos XV–XVI)," in *Ser y vivir esclavo. Identidad, aculturación y agency (mundos Mediterráneos y atlánticos, siglos XIII–XVIII)* (Madrid: Casa Velázquez, 2021), 223–40 and the work of Rocío Periáñez Gómez, "Esclavitud y poderes públicos. Esclavos en las ordenanzas extremeñas: el caso de Zafra," *Cuadernos de Çafra* II (2004): 157–71.

4. Rocío Periáñez Gómez, *Negros, mulatos y blancos: los esclavos en Extremadura durante la Edad Moderna* (Badajoz, Spain: Diputación de Badajoz, 2010).

5. The consultation of these ordinances was made directly, as in the case of the ordinances of Caceres or Llerena, in the respective Municipal Archives of these locations, or Zafra, at the Centro de Estudios Extremeños based in Badajoz. Others have had access through the publications that have made them available in journals and monographs. Finally, we should highlight the work being done through the digitization of historical documents in the archives, which serves to make such sources available to researchers. The manuscript of the Ordinances of Almendralejo, which is in the National Library, can be accessed through the Hispanic digital library (http://www.bne.es/es/Catalogos/BibliotecaDigitalHispanica/Inicio/index.html) or different ordinances, such as the Sierra Fregenal or Valverde de Llerena available on the website of the Council of Badajoz (http://www.dip-badajoz.es/cultura/archivo/index.php?seleccion=_digital).

6. Although some of the documents consulted were released later, we know that its approval was made in the sixteenth century. For example, those of Llerena, which were confirmed in 1632, but its wording is from the time of Philip II.

7. Miguel Ángel Ladero Quesada, "Las ordenanzas locales: Siglos XIII al XVIII," *En la España Medieval* 21 (1998): 307.

8. Antonio Domínguez Ortiz, in his pioneering article on slavery in Castilla, noted that the boom period of the institution of slavery was framed between the sixteenth century and the first half of the seventeenth century, and that its decline was seen since the early eighteenth century. Although the expansion of studies in the subject of slavery have allowed for the qualification of this periodization at the regional level, you can say it was the general trend in Castilian territory. Antonio Domínguez Ortiz, "La esclavitud en Castilla durante la Edad Moderna," in *La esclavitud en Castilla durante la Edad Moderna y otros estudios de marginados*, Granada, Spain: Comares, 2003: 31–32.

9. Rocío Periáñez Gómez, *Negros, mulatos y blancos*, 57–73.

10. Ordinances to which we have access for the eighteenth-century only, Llerena, 1708 contains references to slaves. Archivo Histórico Municipal de Llerena, *Gobierno municipal*, leg. 542/81 1.1. The total absence of references to slaves in the ordinances of cities like Badajoz or Jerez de los Caballeros is striking, despite accounts indicating that these cities had a prominent slave population in the modern age, which would influence other documents later. *Ordenanzas de la M.N. y M.L. Ciudad de Badajoz* (Madrid, Spain: Oficina de Antonio Sanz, 1767). Feliciano Correa Gamero, Genaro González Carballo, and Antonio Carrasco García, *Los jerezanos del siglo XVIII: las ordenanzas municipales de Xerez de los Caballeros de 1758* (Badajoz, Spain: Menfis Editores, 1994).

11. "Ordenanza de los negros e las negras."

12. Alfonso Franco Silva, *La esclavitud en Sevilla y su tierra a fines de la Edad Media* (Seville, Spain: Diputación Provincial, 1979), 216.

13. Ángel-Luis Molina Molina, "Contribución al estudio de la esclavitud en Murcia a fines de la Edad Media (1475–1516), Murguetana 53 (1978): 115. "*Por quanto e cabsa de andar tan sueltos y exentos los esclavos negros en esta çibdad de Murçia, fazen muchos furtos y entre ellos otros acaesçen muchas quistiones y heridas y muertes.*"

14. Since these ordinances have been published with an introductory study by Angel Bernal Estevez, when we mention them we will refer to this publication. Ángel Bernal Estévez, "La vida cotidiana en Zafra a principios del siglo XVI: Las ordenanzas municipales de 1528," *Cuadernos de Çafra* III (2005): 295. "*Primeramente que ningunos esclavos ni esclavas de vecinos desta villa se ayunten a hazer sus çerimonias ni comidas so pena de cada çinquenta açotes dados públicamente.*"

15. Archivo Histórico Municipal de Llerena, *Gobierno municipal*, leg. 542/81 1.1. *Ordenanzas de la ciudad de Llerena.* "Esclavos no anden de noche."

> Iten, vista la dicha desorden que ay en los esclavos desta Villa, que andan en quadrillas de noche, e aun remanece que ay muchas quistiones, e hurtos de gallinas e otras cosas, de que a la Villa viene

mucho daño, e a los vezinos e moradores della. E por la cuitar, ordenaron, e mandaron, que qualesquier esclavos que se hallaren, que anduvieren por la dicha Villa después de anochecido que anduvieren juntos de más de uno solo, que los lleven a la cárcel los que ansí hallaren juntos, y los echen en el cepo, e de allí no sean sueltos sin mandamiento de la justicia.

16. Archivo Histórico Municipal de Llerena, *Gobierno municipal*. "*Otrosi ordenamos, e mandamos, que ningún esclavo trayga armas de noche, sino fuere acompañando a su amo de noche, después de la Oración, so pena de avellas perdido; e duerma aquella noche en la cárcel de pies en el cepo. E qualquier esclavo que anduviere después de la Queda, pierda ansí mismo las armas, y fuera de pies en el cepo; e que el carcelero suelte otro día el esclavo que tuviere preso sin derechos; e que de día no la trayga sin su amo.*"
17. Manuel Lucena Salmoral, *Regulación de la esclavitud*, 13–42.
18. Ángel Bernal Estévez, "La vida cotidiana en Zafra," 295.

Iten que ninguna persona que tenga esclavo o esclava en sus casa consientan que tengan ayuntamiento carnal los dichos esclavos y si la tubieren y lo supieren sus dueños dentro de un mes los casen o vendan al uno dellos para que salgan de su poder so pena de mill maravedís al señor del esclavo o esclava y al esclavo den çient açotes.

Iten que ninguna persona vecino desta villa que tenga esclava o esclavas en su casa consienta que esclavo de otro vecino ni de fuera de la villa tenga ayuntamiento carnal con la esclava o esclavas que en su casa tuviere y el que lo supiere y lo consentiere incurra en pena de mil maravedís y el esclava pena de çient açotes.

19. Archivo Histórico Municipal de Llerena, *Gobierno municipal*, leg. 542/81 1.1. *Ordenanzas de la ciudad de Llerena*, Ordenanza CXLIX.

Otrosi, por quanto muchas mugeres casadas, donzellas e moças honestas y esclavas y otras personas, tienen necesidad de yr a la fuente por agua e a los arroyos a lavar paños e otras cosas que an menester, e por causa de muchos moços y esclavos y otras personas sospechosas, que las van a ver, e hablar a las fuentes, e arroyos, e dexan yr e sus padres e señores las dexan de embiar, por evitar los inconvinientes e quistiones que del ayuntamiento de las dichas gentes se suele seguir, e los inconvinientes que para la honestidad se recrecen. Por ende ordenaron e mandaron que ninguno sea osado de yr a la fuente la Pellejera e Arroyos.

20. Aurelia Martín Casares, *La esclavitud en la Granada del siglo XVI* (Granada, Spain: Universidad, 2000), 422–24.

21. Raúl González Arévalo, "Ordenanzas municipales," 447.

22. Archivo Municipal de Valverde de Llerena. *Expedientes de normas municipales*. 1.1.01/28.6.2. f. 2v. Similarly, ordinances 4 and 5 refer to free Blacks: "*Otrosí que qualquiera persona, veçino o hijo de veçino o moço o moça o esclabo o esclaba que traxere de la dicha dehesa del conçejo deste dicho lugar haze de leña siendo de matas pardas que se entren de carrasco o mesto o alcornoque o coscoxa o azebuche siendo tomado cargado o pagar cargar*"; "*Otrosí que qualquiera persona veçino deste dicho lugar o de otra parte cualquiera que sea o hijo suyo, o moço, esclavo o moços o hijos, o esclabas que traxeren carga de leña de la dicha dehesa del conçejo*," Archivo Municipal de Valverde, *Expedientes de normas municipales*, fs. 3v y4.

23. Archivo Municipal de Fregenal de la Sierra, *Fondo Histórico General*, caja, 1. That slaves were employed in the vineyards also is reflected in the Ordinances of Barcarrota. Tomás Pérez Martín, "Las ordenanzas de Villanueva de Barcarrota confirmadas por Felipe II," *Revista de Estudios Extremeños* LXVIII, (2012): 378.

> *Ytem se ordena y manda que ninguna persona de qualquiera estado o condición que sea, baya ni embie a sus hijos, criados o esclavos a cojer rebuscos de las viñas hasta tanto que por el concejo sea dada licencia, para evitar los grandes daños que suelen causar de ir a coger los dichos rebuscos antes de aber acavado de vendimiar todas las viñas, so pena que qualquiera persona que fuere o imbiare antes que el Concejo dé la dicha licencia pague por cada vez que fuere a coger los rebuscos doscientos maravedís repartidos en quartas partes como se contiene en las Ordenanzas porcima antes de este título.*

24. Ángel Bernal Estévez. "La vida cotidiana en Zafra," 295.

> *Yten que muchos esclavos de los que traen leña así para casa de sus señores como para vender antes que lleguen a casa de sus señores o a la plaça donde an de vender la leña venden alguna parte della y se aprovechan dello y lo hurtan y encubren a sus señores ordenamos y mandamos que ninguna persona compre de ningún esclavo parte de la leña que traxere y el que lo hubiere de comprar compre la carga entera y si de otra manera la compraren por cada vez incurran en pena de doscientos maravedís.*

25. Archivo Histórico Municipal de Cáceres, *Ordenanzas municipales de Cáceres*, 1569, f. 357v. Not just in Caceres, but also in Zafra (Ángel Bernal Estévez, "La vida cotidiana en Zafra," 295).

Que nynguna persona sea osada de comprar ni trocar cosa alguna de esclavo y de esclava ny de resçibir dellos ny de alguno dellos cosa alguna dada ny en guarda e qualquier que lo hiziere de aquí adelante yncurra en pena de pagar el valor de la cosa que comprare o trocare o resçibiere o dada en guarda o enpeño con más el dos tanto lo qual se reparta en esta manera el valor de la cosa para el dueño o señor de la cosa e el dos tanto la mytad para el acusador e la mytad para el conçejo e que por esto no se le quite la pena que el derecho ympide lo qual fue pregonado públicamente en la plaça pública desta villa.

26. At the meeting of the council of Murcia on January 30, 1478, it was said: "*porque los esclavos que hay en esta çibdat son muy grandes ladrones, de manera que por no tener pena fazen muy grandes furtos*," citado por Ángel Luis Molina Molina, "Contribución al estudio de la esclavitud," 114.

27. Archivo Histórico Municipal de Llerena, *Gobierno municipal*, leg. 542/81 1.1., *Ordenanzas de la ciudad de Llerena* . . . , CXLVI: *Que no se den a esclavos asnos para traer leña*. Also in Zafra: "*Iten que ninguna persona dé azémila, ni mula ni asno ni otra bestia a ningún esclavo para que trayga leña a medias ni por dinero ni en otra manera sin sabiduría y voluntad del señor del esclavo y el que de otra manera diere alguna bestia a algún esclavo para traer leña por cada vez incurra en pena de trescientos maravedís.*" Ángel Bernal Estévez, "La vida cotidiana en Zafra," 295.

28. José Luis Cortés López, *La esclavitud negra*, 90.

29. Quoted by Raúl González Arévalo, "Esclavitud y normativa ciudadana," 234.

30. Manuel Lucena Salmoral, *Regulación de la esclavitud*, 37, 69–70 y 74.

31. Ángel Bernal Estévez, "La vida cotidiana en Zafra," 295; Archivo Histórico Municipal de Cáceres, *Ordenanzas municipales de Cáceres*, 1569, fs. 357v-358; Archivo Histórico Municipal de Llerena, *Gobierno municipal*, leg. 542/81 1.1., *Ordenanzas de la ciudad de Llerena* . . . , CXLVII: *Que no den vino a los esclavos*; Arcadio Guerra. "Ordenanzas municipales de Felipe II a Los Santos de Maimona," *Revista de Estudios Extremeños*, VIII (1952): 518. Ordenanza 47; Archivo Municipal de Jerez de los Caballeros, *Acuerdos del cabildo*, H.A.a. 2/2, s.f. (23 de enero de 1528). The measure, we assume that unfulfilled, repeated in subsequent years. Archivo Municipal de Trujillo, *Libro de acuerdos* (1519–1521), leg.14, f.217v. (18-1-1521) y *Libro de acuerdos* (1551–1557), leg. 28 (1), f. 130 (21-3-1552).

32. Archivo Municipal de Jerez de los Caballeros, *Acuerdos del cabildo*, H.A.a. 1/1, f. 179 (21-2-1521). "*Que porque en esta villa ay muchos esclavos blancos y negros y en muchas tavernas y casas los acogen dándoles de comer y bever a cabsa de lo qual se hazen muchos ruidos y ladronizos por ellos y se siguen otros inconvenientes enbeviéndose y haziéndose desconciertos.*"

33. Archivo Municipal de Jerez de los Caballeros, *Acuerdos del cabildo*, H.A.a. 2/10, f. 74. In 1583 ordinances of the town of Los Santos de Maimona include the following:

> Item que cualquiera persona que jugare dineros a cualquier juego con cualquier esclavo de vecino de esta villa o le comprare trigo, cebada, centeno u otra cualquier cosa, paque de pena doscientos maravedís, y si fuere hombre de veinte años arriba, pague la pena al doblo y si lo tomaren de noche jugando, pague la pena al doblo, que son cuatrocientos y ochocientos maravedís y pierda los maravedís que le ganaren y los que les dieren por cualquier cosa, todo lo cual sea la mitad para el denunciador y la otra mitad para el dueño del esclavo.

Arcadio Guerra, "Ordenanzas municipales de Felipe II a Los Santos de Maimona," *Revista de Estudios Extremeños* LXXX (1952): 527. Ordinance 92.

34. Isabel María Pérez González. "Ordenanzas de Villalba," *Revista de Estudios Extremeños* XXXV no. 2 (1979): 262. "*Yten que ninguna persona de a comer ni beber en su casa a esclavo alguno ni consienta que en su casa juegue a los naipes aunque sea en poca cantidad so pena de seys maravedís por cada vez que consintiere que esclavo juegue o coma o beba en su casa.*"

35. Archivo Histórico Municipal de Llerena, *Gobierno municipal*, leg. 542/81 1.1. *Ordenanzas de la ciudad de Llerena*.

> Por quanto muchos esclavos desta Villa hazen muchos hurtos e delitos en esta dicha Villa de noche y de dia lo qual se atreven a hazer, a causa de tener como tienen, recogimiento de muchas casas de esclavos, y esclavas horras, e de oras casas de taberneros y personas pobres, que los resceptan e acojen en su casa. Para remedio desto acordamos, e mandamos, que de aquí adelante ningun esclavo, ni esclava horros, ni otro vecino desta dicha Villa sea osado de recibir en su casa de noche, ni de día a ningun esclavo ni esclava ni les dé de comer, ni de bever aunque ellos le lleven la comida, e bebida, ni duerman en sus casa, so pena que el que fuere hallado, o se supiere por pesquisa aver resceptado de día, o de noche, o dexare aver comido, o dormido algun esclavo, o esclava en su casa, que por el mismo caso incurran en pena de seyscientos maravedís, repartidos por tercios, por la forma susodicha; e que demás desto sea desterrado desta dicha Villa e sus términos e juridición por tiempo de un año primero siguiente, e no lo quebrante, so pena que por la primera vez le sean dados cien açotes y el destierro doblado, y por la segunda sea desterrado perpetuamente.

36. Arcadio Guerra, "Ordenanzas municipales de Felipe II," 527, ordinance 93.
37. Ángel Bernal Estévez, "La vida cotidiana en Zafra," 296.

Yten porque en muchas leyes desta nuestras ordenanzas ay puestas penas de dineros generalmente ansí para hombres libres como para esclavos y como las tales penas aya de pagar los señores de los esclavos no temen de incurrir en ellas los dichos esclavos ordenamos y mandamos que quando algún esclavo incurriere en alguna de las dichas pecuniarias sea en escogençia del señor pagar la pena del dinero o que den a su esclavo cincuenta açotes públicamente por la villa y el señor sea obligado a entregar a la justicia su esclavo para que se le execute la dicha pena de açotes y no lo entregando dentro de terçero día sea obligado a pagar y page la dicha pena lo qual no aya lugar en las penas pecuniarias que en este título están puestas contra los señores de los esclavos porque en este caso mandamos que los señores de los esclavos sean obligados a pagar las penas contra ellos puestas preçesamente.

38. Archivo Histórico Municipal de Llerena, *Gobierno municipal*, leg. 542/81 1.1. *Ordenanzas de la ciudad de Llerena*, Ordenanza CXLIX. . . . *que qualquier hombre que fuere tomado de la dicha hora en adelante hasta salido el sol, si fuere libre, que pague dos reales de pena, el un real para los propios del Concejo, y el otro real para el que lo acusare, y que esté la misma noche en la cárcel; y si fuere esclavo, que pague la misma pena y si el señor del tal esclavo quisiere, que le den veynte açotes en la cárcel y no pagar los dichos dos reales, que sea su escogencia, con que duerma el esclavo en la cárcel la misma noche que fuere tomado*

39. Biblioteca Nacional de España, MSS/9878, fs. 17v–18.

Ordenamos y mandamos que qualquier persona que se metiere o echare a vañar en qualquiera de los pozos de esta villa que cayga e incurra en pena de quatroçientos maravedís cada bez que fuere tomado o se hallare por qualquiera vía que se vaña en qualquier de los dichos pozos y que esté treinta días en la cárzel y si fuere esclavo que le den zien azotes públicamente y si fuere libre y no tuviere de qué pagar que esté los días doblados en la cárzel con las prisiones que los alcaldes que fueren mandaren

40. Both when entering the vineyards and orchards, punishment for slaves whose masters do not want to pay the fine would be fifty lashes. Biblioteca Nacional de España, MSS/9878, fs. 52–52v. and f. 54–54v.

Bibliography

Bernal Estévez, Ángel. "La vida cotidiana en Zafra a principios del siglo XVI: Las ordenanzas municipales de 1528." *Cuadernos de Çafra* III (2005): 211–341.
Correa Gamero, Feliciano, Antonio Carrasco García, and Genaro González Carballo. *Los jerezanos del siglo XVIII: las ordenanzas municipales de Xerez de los Caballeros de 1758*. Badajoz, Spain: Menfis Editores, 1994.
Cortés López, José Luis. *La esclavitud negra en la España peninsular del siglo XVI*. Salamanca, Spain: Universidad de Salamanca, 1989.
Domínguez Ortiz, Antonio. "La esclavitud en Castilla durante la Edad Moderna." In *La esclavitud en Castilla y otros estudios de marginados*. Granada, Spain: Comares, 2003.
Fernández-Daza Alvear, Carmen. "Las ordenanzas de Burguillos de 1551." *Revista de Estudios Extremeños* XLVI (1990): 361–71.
Franco Silva, Alfonso. *La esclavitud en Sevilla y su tierra a fines de la Edad Media*. Seville, Spain: Diputación Provincial, 1979.
González Arévalo, Raúl. "Ordenanzas municipales y trabajo esclavo en la Corona de Castilla (Siglos XV–XVI)." In Simoneta Cavaciocchi(ed.), *Schiavitù e servaggio nell'ecomomia europea secc, XI–XVIII (Serfdom and Slavery in the European Economy 11th–18th Centuries)*, 431–64. Florence, Italy: Firenze University Press, 2014, 431–64.
———. "Esclavitud y normativa ciudadana: Dinámicas sociales de integración y exclusión en las ordenanzas municipales de la Corona de Castilla (siglos XV–XVI)." *Ser y vivir esclavo. Identidad, aculturación y agency (mundos Mediterráneos y atlánticos, siglos XIII–XVIII)*. Madrid, Spain: Casa Velázquez, 2021, 223–40.
Guerra, Arcadio. "Ordenanzas municipales de Felipe II a Los Santos de Maimona," *Revista de Estudios Extremeños* VIII (1952): 495–534.
Ladero Quesada, Miguel Ángel. "Las ordenanzas locales: Siglos XIII al XVIII, *En la España Medieval* 21 (1998): 293–338.
Lucena Salmoral, Manuel. *Regulación de la esclavitud negra en las colonias de América Española (1503-1886): Documentos para su estudio*. Madrid, Spain: Universidad de Alcalá and Universidad de Murcia, 2005.
———. *Los Códigos Negros de la América española*. Madrid, Spain: Ediciones Unesco-Universidad de Alcalá, 1996.
Márquez Hidalgo, Francisco, and Valencia Rodríguez, Juan M. *Berlanga: Una villa extremeña del siglo XVI a través de dos documentos de la época: las Ordenanzas Municipales (1574-1577); Regla fundacional de la Hermandad de la Veracruz (1567)*. Badajoz, Spain: Diputación de Badajoz, 1993.
Martín Casares, Aurelia. *La esclavitud en la Granada del siglo XVI*. Granada, Spain: Universidad, 2000.

Molina Molina, Ángel Luis. "Contribución al estudio de la esclavitud en Murcia (1475–1516), *Murgetana* 53 (1978): 111–34.

Morgado García, Arturo. *Una metrópoli esclavista: El Cádiz de la modernidad.* Granada, Spain: Universidad de Granada, 2013.

Ordenanzas de la M.N. y M.L. ciudad de Badajoz. Madrid, Spain: Oficina de Antonio Sanz, 1767.

Pérez González, Isabel María. "Ordenanzas de Villalba," *Revista de Estudios Extremeños* XXXV (1979): 221–76.

Pérez Marín, Tomás. "Las ordenanzas municipales de Villanueva de Barcarrota confirmadas por Felipe II," *Revista de Estudios Extremeños* LXVIII (2012): 343–98.

Periáñez Gómez, Rocío. *Negros, mulatos y blancos: los esclavos en Extremadura durante la Edad Moderna.* Badajoz, Spain: Diputación de Badajoz, 2010.

———. "Esclavitud y poderes públicos: Esclavos en las ordenanzas municipales extremeñas: el caso de Zafra," *Cuadernos de Çafra* II (2004): 157–71.

Chapter 3

Slavery and the Pursuit of Freedom in Sixteenth-Century Santo Domingo

RICHARD LEE TURITS

On October 10, 1531, Rodrigo López appeared before the Audiencia of Santo Domingo, the ruling body and highest court for this first Spanish colony in the Americas. López, who was then enslaved, came to court to claim that he had the right to be free. "I Ruy [Rodrigo] López of black color [*de color negro*], free from all servitude appear before your majesty and say that I am . . . emancipated and free [*horro y libre*]," López testified. "Rodrigo de León, who is now in this city, is forcibly detaining me, saying that I am to be his slave and using me, while I owe him no servitude whatsoever." With this declaration, López petitioned the court to overturn a prior ruling rejecting a similar claim of wrongful enslavement that he had made several years earlier before a lower-court judge in Cubagua, an island off the coast of Venezuela, also colonized by Spain, where López and another putative owner were living at that time. Since then, López had been sold to León who had taken him to Santo Domingo. López would benefit from this, his at least fifth sale, which placed him in one of the administrative centers of Spain's new colonial empire as well as at the heart of an emerging Atlantic world of slavery. López benefited because there the Audiencia found that he should, in fact, be free.[1]

López's victory, one of the earliest freedom suits in the Americas, was the product of a remarkable series of events driven by the actions of people of African descent, enslaved and free, living in this new transatlantic world. That world was in part the product of a voracious demand for enslaved labor (then both African and indigenous American) among Spaniards in Santo Domingo during the first half of the sixteenth century. López's life and struggle for freedom offer glimpses into Santo Domingo's history as the first major plantation economy and slave society in the Americas. This history is little known and rarely studied, in part perhaps because Santo Domingo would later become the first major plantation economy and slave society to collapse, largely the result, it appears, of sustained resistance to slavery on the part of the enslaved.[2]

In the past, scholars of Latin America often assumed that Spanish colonists quickly abandoned the Caribbean for the bullion riches of Mexico and Peru, almost immediately after the conquest of these colonies, while many Caribbeanists have imagined that Barbados, colonized by the British in the mid-1600s, was the "first black slave society." Similarly, scholars of world history, such as Fernand Braudel, have portrayed major sugar production in the Caribbean as not beginning until the mid-seventeenth century.[3] Yet, in fact, more than a century earlier, European colonists had built the first major plantation economy and society made up mostly of enslaved people in the Americas when they initiated large-scale sugar production in Santo Domingo. The numbers of people held in chains on the island reached into the tens of thousands by the mid-1500s, and Santo Domingo became a pivotal crossroads in the early modern Atlantic. Hellish as the island was for the majority who were legally owned and controlled by others, this society of human property was an economic boon for the few, and the colonial elite was therefore ready to overlook the inferno they had created. Before the collapse of the sugar and ginger economies in the early seventeenth century, that inferno initiated a trajectory of racial slavery and plantation economies whose contours would shape the course of history in the Americas overall. Rodrigo López's life was immersed in these historical developments, the early African-Atlantic slave trade and the expansion of slavery to unprecedented dimensions in the lands the Spanish imperiously renamed the "New World."[4]

Slavery in Early Santo Domingo

Rodrigo López's story begins in Lisbon, where he was born into slavery and given the family name of the man who owned him, Ruy López. No doubt at the owner's behest, Rodrigo López was taught to read and write and thereby attained skills that were exceptional even for a free person at the time. This prepared him eventually to help administer Ruy López's cotton plantation on Cape Verde (a Portuguese colony near the shores of West Africa), where Ruy López had moved, and to work in his slave-trading operations there and on the nearby West African coast. Specifically, Rodrigo López oversaw the loading and readying of slave ships. At the end of 1522, Ruy López, then on his death bed, completed his will. In it he granted, upon his passing, freedom to Rodrigo López and Rodrigo's sister, Catalina, with the condition that Rodrigo continue to administer Ruy's businesses. This arrangement was to last for three years, after which Rodrigo was to sell his former owner's estate and pay off his debts. During those three years, Rodrigo would remain in a type of legal limbo between free and enslaved, under the custody of the executor of the will, but also himself running a major slave-trading operation. The will also left him fifteen thousand *maravedís*, a significant amount of money, and twenty-five *quintales* of cotton [*algodón sucio*] "with which to earn a living."[5]

Around 1525, with little time left to go before Rodrigo López was to receive his legal freedom, Ruy López's nephew, Cristóbal González, showed up at his uncle's estate and began trying to sell and to export people held there in bondage without permission to do so. Rodrigo López objected, he later recalled, and reported González's efforts to Ruy López's siblings in Lisbon. In frustration, González acted to remove Rodrigo López from the scene altogether. González directed López to meet a ship master, Juan Sombrero, at the port, supposedly to collect "some money and other things for a shipment [of slaves] that we were making from Guinea," López testified. Once López came on board, "the boatswain and those who were inside seized and shackled me and put me below deck," together with other enslaved persons.

Rodrigo López had gone to a slave ship as a quasi-free Black man participating in the slave trade, as, ironically, he had been required to do to meet the conditions for his own liberation. But there he ended up on the other end of the trade instead, kidnapped and sold to the ship's captain, Sombrero. Sombrero, in turn, soon sold Rodrigo López to Bartolomé Corral, the factor of another slave ship in Cape Verde on its way to Spanish America. This ship belonged to Antón López (no relation), and as soon as the ship landed in Cubagua, Antón paid Corral for Rodrigo.[6] When Rodrigo López protested that he was, in fact, a free man, Antón whipped him, presumably hoping that brutal punishment would quell Rodrigo's determination to claim his lawful liberty. Antón López, though, soon sold Rodrigo López again, this time to Juan de la Barrera, perhaps suspecting that Rodrigo's resistance would never cease and therefore deciding that he was too risky an asset to hold onto.[7]

It was at this point that López managed to have his case heard by the Cubagua authorities. Multiple witnesses testified on López's behalf. Nonetheless, on December 5, 1528, the judge declared that López's owner, Juan de la Barrera, had "shown what is sufficient for him to have won in this case," while, as a subsequent court recorded it, López had not "proven his liberty." Following the court's decision, Barrera sold his highly skilled but also challenging human property to another buyer, Alonso Díaz, who in turn sold him yet again, to Rodrigo de León. It was León who took López to Santo Domingo.[8]

López's new residence, a large island of mostly untamed woods roughly the size of Portugal, had only recently become home to dozens of large sugar plantations. Spanish conquerors initially made gold mining the main industry in this land that Columbus imperiously renamed *la isla Española* (Spanish Island) and that was soon also to be called Santo Domingo.[9] But by the late 1510s, mines were becoming less and less productive, even as the industry would continue on a smaller scale for decades.[10] As the bullion economy declined, European colonists expanded sugar production. They drew on the model of large plantations run on enslaved labor that the Spanish and Portuguese had initiated in the Canaries, Madeira, and São Tomé (all small islands, like Cape Verde, near the western shores of Africa). Sugar took off as did the importation of enslaved laborers. With only a modest-sized European population and vast indigenous communities, once perhaps in the hundreds of thousands, all but killed off by Spanish conquest and by germs they had no immunity to—or disappeared through procreation and integration with people of European or African origins—Santo Domingo was quickly transformed into a society in which most of the population were enslaved. Giant cattle ranches also expanded across large stretches of land, and these, too, relied on enslaved labor, as did the extant gold industry.[11]

The trajectory of slavery in the Americas launched in Santo Domingo would be unprecedented in terms of sheer numbers. The extensive importation of enslaved people to Santo Domingo from Europe had been formally approved by the Crown in 1501, nine years after the colony was established. As this trade to the Americas grew, Spain began issuing licenses to individuals to introduce a set number of enslaved persons into Spain's

American colonies over a specified period. These licenses were sometimes granted, but mostly sold. By the end of the 1510s, the numbers authorized in such licenses rose momentously. In 1518, the governor of Bressa (part of present-day France), Lorenzo de Gorrevod, was licensed to export 4,000 enslaved Africans to the Americas, a number far larger than any in the past. This license also allowed the import of slaves directly from West Africa without passing through the peninsula. Gorrevod's license was perhaps unprecedented in this regard, but soon slave ships traveling directly from Africa to the Caribbean would become the norm.[12] In addition to the many thousands of authorized slave imports, vast numbers of enslaved people were brought to Santo Domingo fraudulently and as contraband, using, for instance, the same license to bring even three times the authorized number or managing to use no license at all.[13]

Santo Domingo quickly became the motor and hub of the escalating African-Atlantic slave trade linking Europe, Africa, and the Caribbean. The fever pitch of that trade in the 1520s shaped the course of Rodrigo López's life. He was sold at least five times along the journey that ended for him in Santo Domingo, and there he was rented out to a sugar mill owner—even in the very moment that he was in court suing for his freedom. This all suggests the intensity of the demand for enslaved labor in Santo Domingo and the Greater Caribbean, and the profitability of the buying, selling, and renting of people overall. Most of those to whom López was sold following his first owner's death were themselves slave traders, as was Ruy López.

The commerce in which Rodrigo López was held captive was also developing in virtually unprecedented ways in terms of the demography of the enslaved, for slavery in the Americas would eventually be isolated to one group—people of African descent. This was in stark contrast to the multiple sources of slave labor during the early decades of the sixteenth century, when, above all, indigenous Americans made up a substantial portion of enslaved workers in Santo Domingo. After conquest, the island's indigenous inhabitants were divided up and forced to provide labor for a large part of the year to European colonists in the so-called *encomienda* (entrustment) system, before being permitted to return to their homes. But these local indigenous laborers, so long as they remained obedient subjects of the Crown, were not legally enslavable. At the same time, a vast deadly trade developed that involved Europeans enslaving and taking people from other parts of the Americas to Santo Domingo. Colonists fought and captured people on islands and in continental areas that Spanish authorities deemed to be "useless"—without precious metals and not, yet at least, sought as areas for active colonization—as well as in any areas where the local populations refused, or were depicted as refusing, Spanish sovereignty. Resistance to colonial rule or simply opportunistic accusations that certain populations were inherently bellicose and unamenable to foreign domination (people who were generally given the name "Caribs" or *Caníbales*) made them legal targets for enslavement as prisoners of "just war." Tens of thousands of people were ultimately captured, enslaved, and brought to Santo Domingo from the Bahamas, the Lesser Antilles, the northern coast of South America, Nicaragua, and other places in the Greater Caribbean. A large portion perished in transport or not long after their arrival as a result of starvation, dehydration, abuse, and disease.[14] Those who survived worked as gold miners, domestic laborers, and, especially during the sugar industry's early expansion, cane cutters, as well as on public works projects.[15] One of López's owners, Juan de la Barrera, was, in fact, primarily a trader in enslaved Indians, operating out of both Cubagua and Santo Domingo.

Across Spanish America in the early decades of the sixteenth century, there were a small number of slaves of European, Eurasian, and North African origins.[16] They had been forcibly brought to the Americas from Southern Europe, where prior to Columbus's landing in the Americas and even prior to the African-Atlantic slave trade, slaves of European, Eurasian, and North African descent described as "white" were a familiar part of Southern European society, especially in a number of important cities. In the early 1400s, nearly one in ten persons in the Spanish city of Valencia was owned by another person. Seville, Barcelona, and the island of Mallorca were also places with significant populations kept in bondage, as were Genoa and Palermo, where the enslaved made up, at various times, between 2 and 5 percent of these cities' residents. The detailed attention to slavery in Spain's thirteenth-century enumeration of legal principles, the *Siete Partidas*, indicates the continuous significance of this institution in Spain from the days of the Roman Empire.[17] The number of people in bondage was not close to the scale of slavery that would develop soon in Santo Domingo, but slavery was clearly a normal practice in late medieval Southern Europe.[18]

Enslaved laborers had flowed into Southern Europe in the late medieval period from diverse regions. This commerce in bound humans, particularly of Orthodox Christians, had been continually fed by wars and raids in Eastern Europe, the Caucasus, Russia, and neighboring areas around the Black Sea.[19] While this trade from the Black Sea region to Valencia and other parts of Spain prior to the African-Atlantic slave trade was substantial, probably the greater part of the bound population in the Catholic areas of Spain and Portugal was the product of Catholic raids and attacks on Muslim regions of the Iberian peninsula, as well as on neighboring islands, the North African coast, and ships at sea.[20]

Yet in the mid-fifteenth century, the traditional sources of enslaved laborers in Southern Europe began to dwindle. The vast expansion of the Ottoman Empire at this time produced a growing demand for slaves that diverted the Black Sea slave trade away from Southern Europe.[21] At the same time, the eight-century-long battles between Catholic and Muslim Iberians came largely to an end in the late 1400s—and thus, the supply of enslaved prisoners of war or captives from those battles—when Catholic hegemony was established over the entire peninsula.

The legacy of Southern Europe's highly diverse slave population in terms of geographical origins was still evident in the early-sixteenth-century Americas. In this period, the Spanish Crown issued hundreds of licenses to bring slaves described as "white" to Santo Domingo and elsewhere in Spanish America. For example, even in 1573, a license was granted to Captain Cepeda de Ayala to bring Martín Zayas, a "slave of white color," along with four Black slaves, to the Americas.[22] In the 1520s, slave codes in Santo Domingo made explicit reference to "white," "black," and other slaves (particularly native Canary Islanders), thus reflecting and anticipating slaves from diverse origins.[23] This legacy was perhaps evident even in Rodrigo López's case itself. The continual reference to him as "Rodrigo of black color" may reflect the fact that it was still imaginable that an enslaved person could also be "of white color."[24]

Yet the possibility of slaves "of white color" was, in practice, already remote in the Americas by the time López arrived in Santo Domingo. The dwindling of Southern Europe's traditional sources of enslaved people occurred almost simultaneously with Europeans, specifically the Portuguese, reaching sub-Saharan Africa by ship for the first time in the 1440s. Large numbers of enslaved people from this region had long been brought to the Mediterranean and elsewhere by North African traders crossing the Sahara. But now Europeans could exploit, divert, and augment this trade at a comparatively low cost. And they immediately began forcibly transporting enslaved people from sub-Saharan Africa—as many as eighty thousand persons, A. J. R. Russell-Wood calculated, "from the area between the Saharan littoral and Kongo in the half-century preceding Columbus's landfall in the Americas." The enslaved were shipped to Portugal and Spain, to their Atlantic-island possessions, and, subsequently in the sixteenth century, to Santo Domingo and other parts of the Americas.[25]

Also in the sixteenth century, the spread and consolidation of Spain's overseas empire led the Crown to limit more and more of those areas where the indigenous population could be enslaved. There were fewer places where Spain was still legally at war, and continuing enslavement in areas where Spanish rule was already established provoked indigenous resistance, flight, and rebellion. Restricting the enslavement of Indians to captives of legal wars in the increasingly small regions of ongoing conquest, though, could not be effectively enforced. That was surely one of the main reasons the Crown issued decrees in the 1530s and 1540s, rejecting altogether any new enslavement of free Indians, albeit with major exceptions continuing to be made in practice and law.[26] Although Spanish laws did not emancipate already enslaved indigenous people, in 1545 the Crown ordered that the reported 5,000 people native to the Americas held in bondage in Santo Domingo be freed unless the "possessor" could prove that the enslaved had been legally captured in the past. Few putative owners could produce such legal titles, so almost all of the enslaved Indians in the colony were freed, at least according to the law. Large numbers would, however, be kidnapped, exported, and sold in places in the Americas and Europe where Spanish slave laws either did not apply or were scarcely enforced. And others would continue to be held illegally in bondage in Santo Domingo.[27] Nonetheless, paired with the surely high mortality continuing among Indians on the island, the Crown's actions against indigenous enslavement meant that after the mid-1500s, bondage in Santo Domingo, de facto and de jure, became limited almost entirely to people of African descent—a racialization of slavery that would be continually repeated elsewhere in the Americas.[28]

Slavery and the Law

In the context of the growing equation of slavery with Blackness in Santo Domingo and so much of the Atlantic world, free people of African descent were especially vulnerable to illegal reenslavement, even if they had secured freedom through legal manumission. The proceedings and verdict in López's first case tried in Cubagua make clear how difficult it was to prove wrongful reenslavement and how the law favored de facto owners. Most of the witnesses in this case were Spanish and Portuguese sailors working on ships that traveled back and forth between Cape Verde and the Caribbean. Some testified that they had seen "Rodrigo López *de color negro*" in Cape Verde, and many remembered him being elegantly dressed. One recalled him with papers in his hand, indicating that he was literate. Another testified that a cobbler in Cape Verde had explained to him that López was a freed man, hence his refined manner. A sailor who traveled to Cubagua on the same ship as López testified that he heard people on board discussing the fact that López was being taken away by traders as if he were a slave, even though he had been a free man in Cape Verde. Another testified that Sombrero, the trader who first kidnapped López in Cape Verde, had shared with him that he (Sombrero) had purchased López from a Portuguese man (Cristóbal González) who had insisted that "he not leave the said Black in any land within the Portuguese empire." González stressed that López could read and write and therefore possessed the skills that he might employ in a legal battle with Sombrero over López's freedom. For that reason, López had to be taken away to Spanish America. The testimony strongly suggested that both González and Sombrero knew full well that López was free and that selling him as a slave was illegal. Nonetheless, López lost his case.[29]

Yet the law did not always play a merely nominal or farcical role in determining slave or free status in the early-sixteenth-century Spanish Empire. After arriving in Santo Domingo, López appealed his case to the Audiencia of Santo Domingo, and this time he won his freedom despite powerful opponents with a direct interest in his enslavement. During the proceedings, the court agreed to let León, the trader who brought López to Santo Domingo, lease López to Diego Caballero to work at his sugar mill. Caballero was a wealthy planter, accountant of the Royal Treasury, and former secretary of the Audiencia, thus one of the colony's more prominent and presumably influential figures. In less than a year, in November 1532, acting against the interests of Caballero and León—and in some ways slave owners in general—the Audiencia declared López free. León appealed to the *Consejo de Indias* in Spain during which time López remained free (following the payment of a bond). The Audiencia's ruling was sustained in 1535.[30]

It seems that López was successful on appeal because he did not rely this time on hearsay but rather on written documentary evidence. Rodrigo López obtained this evidence thanks to remarkable efforts at transatlantic collaboration and communication orchestrated by his sister, Catalina López, who had remained in Cape Verde. One can imagine her distress since Rodrigo's disappearance in 1525, likely suspecting that he had been illegally reenslaved. She was also apparently determined to locate and free him. Her efforts to do so may be what led to her encounter with Vicente Fernández, a sailor who had arrived in Cape Verde in 1530. He was coming from Cubagua, he informed Catalina, where he had seen Rodrigo being held as a slave. Fernández had, in fact, spotted Rodrigo on two occasions on a ship that passed close enough to Fernández's to be sure it was he. Fernández could not tell Catalina who was keeping Rodrigo in bondage, but at least she now had a small but solid lead.

Catalina next approached a judge in Cape Verde and obtained from him a notarized copy of Ruy López's will freeing her and her brother. She brought this document to the port of Ribeira Grande, where ships came from Spain to purchase enslaved Africans who would then be exported to the Caribbean. She searched there for someone on their way to Cubagua willing to carry the will to Rodrigo. To her and Rodrigo's improbable good fortune, she somehow encountered Bernaldino de Trepana [Trápana] Galiano, a sailor likely of Italian origin who had lived in Cape Verde and had known both Rodrigo López and Ruy López in the past. Trepana had even been with both Lópezes at Ruy's house, and upon Ruy's death, Trepana later recalled, "had heard it discussed publicly" that "said accountant," Ruy López, had freed Rodrigo López "of black color." Trepana agreed to help the two López siblings who had been freed by Ruy.[31]

Perhaps Catalina offered money to Trepana Galiano's to sign up for this mission, or perhaps he acted out of a personal sense of obligation to her, Rodrigo, or Ruy. The historical record does not disclose his reason. It does show, though, that Catalina López and Bernaldino Trepana Galiano managed somehow to get the notarized copy of Ruy López's will to Rodrigo in Santo Domingo, without anything akin to an address or known location, and without knowing at first that he had been taken to Santo Domingo from Cubagua. The document's journey took over one-and-a-half years, after which Rodrigo López finally had the written evidence he needed. He presented it to the judges of the Audiencia, who then declared that Rodrigo López was, in fact, a free man.[32]

Evidently notarized documents could not be discounted with ease. Were one to have one's manumission papers in order, Rodrigo López's case suggests, the odds were in favor of securing freedom. This should not be altogether surprising, given that freedom suits and securing one's liberty through manumission were already well-established Spanish legal processes that predated the African-Atlantic slave trade and the Spanish conquest of the Americas. Enslaved Africans in Spanish America had the same rights to sue for their freedom in court as had enslaved Africans, Russians, Muslim Iberians, and others in fifteenth-century Spain.[33] Although "[t]he naked brutality of slavery was often cloaked in a language of legal niceties" in fifteenth-century Valencia (Spain), writes Debra Blumenthal, "the respect given to due process and the consequent access to the kingdom's courts it afforded enslaved men and women is striking given the formal definition of slaves as the legally disenfranchised."[34] That noteworthy due process continued to prevail in the first years of Spanish colonization of the New World, it seems.

Of course, López's history equally manifests how tragically weak the law could be, despite a noteworthy degree of due process, in challenging illegal slaveholding. Spaniards kidnapping and illegally enslaving people, both African and indigenous American, was common.[35] Those hoping to sue for their freedom had to first reach Spanish judicial officials—no easy feat for most of the enslaved who ran the risk of brutal retaliation such as Rodrigo López had suffered by owners for attempting to contact local authorities. The enslaved would also presumably need to convince a judge that their case was plausible enough to be heard. Finally, the plaintiff had to prevail in terms of evidence, specifically written evidence. As in López's suit, in practice the burden of proof fell on the enslaved to demonstrate that they had been manumitted—at least if they had once been legally enslaved—rather than an alleged owner having to prove that the person they claimed to own was still legally a slave.[36] (The fact that, after 1545, Spain placed the burden of proof so firmly on the possessors of enslaved Indians in Santo Domingo reflected the Crown's commitment to ending the illegal enslavement of indigenous people in its colonies.)

It is noteworthy that Sombrero and González anticipated that taking López to the Americas could keep him at a safe distance from the law. González also apparently found partners in crime, who appear to have thought it unnecessary to be secretive about an illegal operation. This is suggested by the numerous sailors who reported overhearing conversations about López having been a freed man who was kidnapped and sold back into slavery. What those illegally enslaving and exporting López failed to consider, though, was how new forms of globalization produced by the African-Atlantic slave trade could also be exploited by people resisting slavery. Sailors crisscrossing the Atlantic linked ordinary people, as well as markets and empires, across three continents. Those sailors, too, included a perhaps significant number of free people of sub-Saharan African descent.[37]

It was the remarkable collaboration with sailors traveling between Cape Verde, Cubagua, and Santo Domingo that made it possible for Rodrigo and Catalina López to communicate and send across the Atlantic the papers necessary to secure his freedom. López's legal triumph is a testament, on the one hand, to the long-standing and uninterrupted laws, institutions, and practices of both slavery and manumission in Spanish history and, on the other, to the remarkable exploitation of those laws by African-descended people. The case also makes clear the powerful legal and commercial forces of slavery in Santo Domingo by 1530, and thus its important role in the emerging Atlantic world of slavery.

Slavery and Rebellion:
The Decline of Santo Domingo's Plantation Society

It is unclear whether Rodrigo López chose to remain in Santo Domingo after the conclusion of his suit in 1535. If he did, he would have witnessed both the economic rise and intense horrors of the colony's slave society. By the 1540s, Santo Domingo's enslaved population reached approximately 15,000 people, while the European population was a mere 5,000 or 6,000, according to estimates from the time. And the number of slaves would even rise subsequently, despite the dramatic ending here to indigenous American enslavement. Santo Domingo's sugar plantations averaged upward of 100 enslaved laborers, and some estates eventually reached multiple times that—large numbers for plantations at any point in world history.[38] Through the exploitation of the enslaved, the island's sugar industry took off. Annual sugar exports to Spain totaled around 1,400 tons in 1543. A great deal of sugar was also sold as contraband to European rivals, and some was marketed within the region. Altogether, available figures suggest that total production each year could be several times higher than sugar exports to Seville, historian Genaro Rodríguez Morel emphasizes. Santo Domingo's plantation economy was so dramatic for the time that the late-eighteenth-century Martinican-born scholar Moreau de St. Méry would recall it as "the prototype of all the sugar and slave colonies" that developed later in the Americas. The island's enslaved population did not, though, work just in the sugar industry. Many labored in other agricultural areas and on large ranches, making possible an impressive cattle industry that added greatly to the colony's wealth. Some forty to sixty thousand hides were sent to Spain each year. Also, a substantial part of the population owned by others was forced to work as servants and urban laborers, including some 2,000 in the capital alone. Also, many of those held in slavery mined ore from gold deposits that remained productive. Striking as the sugar economy was, it was not the colony's only important industry, nor did it encompass a large portion of the island's vast terrain.[39]

Yet Santo Domingo's wealth, its sugar plantations, and multiple thriving industries, rested on unstable as well as inhuman foundations. The law denied the vast majority their will, and that majority was forced to labor under intolerable conditions. The powerful resistance this almost inevitably produced was unstoppable, given the island's demographic and geographical—as well as political and economic—conditions. In particular, it was impossible for the state to put a stop to enslaved people's continual escape. The colonial state's repressive apparatus was nowhere near up to the task for an island as vast, mountainous, and wooded as Santo Domingo—almost two hundred times the size of Barbados, which 100 years later would become the next major plantation economy in the Caribbean. This geography created possibilities for people to escape, hide, and subsist on wildlife, including the then rapidly multiplying livestock brought from Europe. From the start, enslaved individuals fled and spread across the island's untamed woods and hills, often connecting there with Indian rebels. By the 1540s, the number of people who escaped their legal owners was estimated to be well into the thousands. At that time, many formed bands that went on the attack against the colony's slave owners, burning plantations and liberating many still in chains. Local authorities relied on regular militias and mercenaries to capture those who had fled from and revolted against slavery. But the costs of repression were high and inevitably hurt the economy's profitability. To pay for the state's ad hoc repressive apparatus, the government had to raise sales taxes on salt, sugar, leather, wheat, wine, and other products, which substantially increased prices and gave rise to widespread protests among the European settlers. And nonetheless, escape and rebellion continued to prevail.[40]

These long-standing challenges that Santo Domingo's sugar plantation owners and operators faced became insurmountable, it appears, in the late sixteenth century, when the high cost of resistance and flight by those being kept in slavery combined with escalating sugar competition from Brazil and elsewhere, and resultant downward pressures on global sugar prices.[41] Indeed, by the final decades of the 1500s, Santo Domingo's sugar industry had entered a cycle of decline from which it would never recover.[42] Spaniards in Santo Domingo sought to sustain their plantations and export agriculture by developing a new ginger economy and later, very briefly, cacao production. And ginger thrived for a number of decades. But like sugar, ginger and cacao production could not endure.[43] By the second half of the seventeenth century, Santo Domingo had a modest cattle economy only, coupled with food production—above all cassava.[44]

No one event or cause stands out as singularly responsible for the collapse of the Americas' first plantation economy.[45] But perhaps the most fundamental economic challenges faced by plantation owners were the result of the favorable conditions for escape and resistance by the enslaved. Slave resistance decreased productivity and profits, as did high taxes levied to support state campaigns to fight rebels and recapture escaped slaves. And these costs could not be sustained under more competitive market conditions.[46] By the mid-1600s, most erstwhile Dominican planters were living as modest cattle ranchers with limited wealth to import or purchase human property. Many Spaniards sold their slaves for needed cash, often to the enslaved themselves who found a variety of ways to earn and to secure funds to purchase their freedom from their owners. Most importantly, slave owners had ever fewer resources to prevent permanent flight by the enslaved. Although precise and complete population statistics are problematic for this period, records do show a profound demographic shift. The enslaved had composed most of society at the century's start. By the late 1600s, though, the largest part of the population were people who had escaped or been freed from slavery. And this new predominant population of refugees from bondage and their children were now living with substantial autonomy as independent peasants dispersed across the countryside, practicing itinerant agriculture, and hunting and raising wildlife on the open range. Soon major towns, too, were formed mostly by de facto free people of African descent.[47]

Even if Rodrigo López had decided to live out his days in Santo Domingo, he could not, alas, have lived long enough to see the land where he had proven his liberty against all odds become one where most people of African origin were free, and where free African descendants constituted the largest group in the colony. This free population experienced what was certainly a highly constrained freedom. The free African-descended majority in Santo Domingo was never legally equal to those who were increasingly identified over time as "Whites" (as opposed to "Christians"), as well as "Spaniards." To the contrary, free African descendants lived within an empire where slavery was legal and the legal racial hierarchy grew more elaborate over time. Already by the mid-1500s, the Crown had begun promulgating laws excluding free people of African descent—already then a significant population—from certain areas of commerce, numerous professions, bearing arms, and wearing fine clothes.[48] And, while varying over time, approximately 15 percent of society remained enslaved over the rest of the colonial period until Santo Domingo was annexed by Haiti in 1822, and slavery was immediately abolished.[49] At the same time, one can reasonably argue that free people of African descent constituted and reshaped the Dominican nation, countering Spanish racist hierarchies and expectations in postplantation Santo Domingo. Most of this nation, it appears, were those who escaped slavery and their progeny. But they were also descendants of manumitted slaves, including victors in freedom suits, such as Rodrigo López. One hundred and fifty years before slavery legally came to an end, most of the African-descended population in Santo Domingo had managed through resistance of all kinds to carve out an important measure of freedom.[50]

Notes

I am grateful to Magalis Leyva who helped to transcribe records from Rodrigo López's freedom suit. María de los Ángeles Meriño Fuentes and Aisnara Perera Díaz provided critical insights about the case, as well as paleographic assistance. Indeed, many ideas in this work developed in ongoing conversation with them. The chapter also benefited from Hannah Rosen's important interventions. Thanks as well to David Wheat for his generous comments.

This chapter is a substantially expanded and revised version of "Slavery and the Pursuit of Freedom in 16th-Century Santo Domingo," in *Oxford Research Encyclopedias: Latin American History*, ed. William H. Beezley (Oxford, UK: Oxford University Press, 2019), https://oxfordre.com/latinamericanhistory. It is republished with the permission of Oxford University Press.

1. "Ruy" here was either the scribe's mistake or conceivably a name Rodrigo López sometimes used. It was the given name of his first legal owner. "Rodrigo López, de color negro, natural de Lisboa, con Rodrigo de León, mercader residente en Santo Domingo, sobre la libertad de aquel," 1531–1535, Archivo General de Indias (AGI), Justicia, leg. 11, no. 4 (hereafter, "Rodrigo López").

2. For a full treatment of this history, see "An Enslaved New World: Slavery, Freedom, and the Making of Race in Santo Domingo (1492–1865) (unpublished manuscript)." On the definition of a "slave society" (versus "a society with slaves"), see Ira Berlin, *Many Thousands Gone: The First Two Centuries of Slavery in North America* (Cambridge, MA: Harvard University Press, 1998), 8–9; and Moses I. Finley, *Ancient Slavery* (New York: Viking, 1980), 79–80.

3. Hilary McD. Beckles, *The First Black Slave Society: Britain's "Barbarity Time" in Barbados, 1636-1876* (Kingston, Jamaica: University of the West Indies Press, 2016); and Fernand Braudel, *Capitalism and Material Life, 1400-1800* (New York: Harper and Row, 1973), 156. The history of sugar, slavery, and the major economic and social transformations in the sixteenth-century Spanish Caribbean is glaring by its absence in most synthetic treatments of early colonial Latin America, and the region is generally cast instead as a space primarily of early administrative experimentation. See, for example, Peter Bakewell, *A History of Latin America* (Oxford, UK: Blackwell Publishing, 2004), 78-95. An exception to this scholarly neglect is Sidney W. Mintz, *Sweetness and Power: The Place of Sugar in Modern History* (New York: Penguin Books, 1985), 32-33.

4. Columbus named the lands he stumbled upon "the Indies" to indicate that they were part of Asia. Leading European figures immediately realized, though, that Columbus was wrong and that instead he had landed in "places unknown" to Europeans, or a "new world," as Italian courtier Peter Martyr de Anglería wrote in 1493. Quoted in Hugh Thomas, *Rivers of Gold: The Rise of the Spanish Empire, from Columbus to Magellan* (New York: Random House, 2003), 107.

5. The value of 15,000 *maravedís* can be discerned from the fact that Rodrigo López would be sold for two-thirds that amount by Juan Sombrero (see "Rodrigo López"). In 1539, slave prices in Cape Verde varied between 12,000 and 15,000 *maravedís* (Valían de Forné et al. [Genovese merchants] versus the *Consejo de Santo Domingo*, 1539, AGI, Justicia 16). The exceptional education, administrative position, status, and ultimately inheritance Ruy López granted to his slave Rodrigo López was such that some scholars have speculated that Ruy might have been Rodrigo's father. This is certainly possible. However, there is no reference to it in the record of Rodrigo's case. And if this were true, Rodrigo might have mentioned it there to make the case that he had been freed still more plausible. There seems, in short, insufficient basis to draw conclusions about this question. Cf. Abraham L. Liddell, "Social Networks and the Formation of an African Atlantic: The Upper Guinea Coast, Cape Verde, and the Spanish Caribbean, 1450-1600 (PhD diss., Vanderbilt University, 2021), esp. 52, 56 (quotation), 57, 73-74, 79; Vicenta Cortés Alonso, "La liberación del esclavo," *Anuario de Estudios Americanos* 22 (1965): 540. Cortés Alonso adds the fact that Ruy López had no recognized children as further support for the speculation that he might have been Rodrigo's father.

6. Most likely Corral had been acting as an agent for Antón López.

7. "Rodrigo López." On Juan de la Barrera, see "Relación de los cargos que se hicieron de la pesquisa secreta contra Pedro de Herrera y los descargos que dio del tiempo que fue alcalde en la isla de Cubagua," 1533, AGI, Justicia, leg. 53-A. Cubagua was itself a major slave island at the time. Its then thriving pearl industry was driven initially by enslaved Indians from the greater Caribbean and, starting in the 1520s, a growing proportion of enslaved Africans. Those

enslaved were forced to dive deeply underwater to capture oysters, work that was perilous and sometimes fatal. Molly A. Warsh, "A Political Ecology in the Early Spanish Caribbean," *William and Mary Quarterly* 71, no. 4 (October 2014): 523–24, 541–46; Michael Perri, "'Ruined and Lost': Spanish Destruction of the Pearl Coast in the Early Sixteenth Century," *Environment and History* 15, no. 2 (May 2009): 132–37; Carlos Esteban Deive, *La Española y la esclavitud del Indio* (Santo Domingo, Dominican Republic: Fundación García Arévalo, 1995), 341, 389–91; and Julian Granberry, "Spanish Slave Trade in the Bahamas, 1509–1530: An Aspect of the Caribbean Pearl Industry (continued)," *Journal of the Bahamas Historical Society* 2 (October 1980): 15.

8. "Rodrigo López."

9. For examples from 1512 and 1576, see Vicente Rubio, *Indigenismo de ayer y de hoy* (Santo Domingo: Fundación García Arévalo, 2009), 67; and Vicente Rubio, *Cedulario de la isla de Santo Domingo*, vol. 1 (1492–1501 (Santo Domingo, Dominican Republic: Centro de Altos Estudios Humanísticos y del Idioma Español, 2007), 67.

10. Esteban Mira Caballos, "Otros sectores productivos y económicos," in *Historia general del pueblo dominicano*, vol. 1, ed. Genaro Rodríguez Morel (Santo Domingo, Dominican Republic: Academia Dominicana de la Historia, 2013), 426–27; and Frank Moya Pons, *El oro en la historia dominicana* (Santo Domingo, Dominican Republic: Academia Dominicana de la Historia, 2016).

11. Laurent Dubois and Richard Lee Turits, *Freedom Roots: Histories from the Caribbean* (Chapel Hill: University of North Carolina Press, 2019), 58–63; Frank Moya Pons, *History of the Caribbean* (Princeton, NJ: Markus Wiener, 2007), 7–11; Lynne A. Guitar, "Cultural Genesis: Relationships among Indians, Africans and Spaniards in Rural Hispaniola, First Half of the Sixteenth Century" (PhD diss., Vanderbilt University, 1998), 290–93; Stuart B. Schwartz, "Spaniards, *Pardos*, and the Missing Mestizos: Identities and Racial Categories in the Early Hispanic Caribbean," *New West Indian Guide* 71, no. 1/2 (1997): 5–19; and Kathleen Deagan and José María Cruxent, *Columbus's Outpost among the Taínos: Spain and America at La Isabela, 1493–1498* (New Haven, CT: Yale University Press, 2002), 219–22.

12. "Cédule du Gouverneur de Brésa," August 18, 1518, in Georges Scelle, *La traite négrière aux Indes de Castile, contrats et traités d'assiento: Étude de droit public et d'histoire diplomatique puisée aux sources originales et accompagnée de plusierus documents inédits*, vol. 1 (Paris: L. Larose & L. Tenin, 1906), 755; Thomas, *Rivers of Gold*, 413; Hugh Thomas, *The Slave Trade: The Story of the Atlantic Slave Trade, 1440–1870* (New York: Simon & Schuster, 1997), 102. Historians Marc Eagle and David Wheat document a slave ship from "Guinea" selling at least fifty-four people in San Juan in 1520 and 1521. Marc Eagle and David Wheat, "The Early Iberian Slave Trade to the Spanish Caribbean, 1500–1580," in *From the Galleons to the Highlands: Slave Trade Routes in the Spanish Americas*, ed. Alex Boruki, David Eltis, and David Wheat (Albuquerque: University of New Mexico Press,

2020), 51. Toby Green hypothesizes that some ships may have come directly from West Africa to Santo Domingo even before 1518, perhaps illegally. Toby Green, "Building Slavery in the Atlantic World: Atlantic Connections and the Changing Institution of Slavery in Cabo Verde, Fifteenth-Sixteenth Centuries," *Slavery and Abolition* 32, no. 2 (2011): 238. Note that Gorrevod was spelled in multiple ways.

13. Genaro Rodríguez Morel, *Orígenes de la economía de plantación de La Española* (Santo Domingo: Editora Nacional, 2012), 95–99, 111–17; Alejandro de la Fuente, *Havana and the Atlantic in the Sixteenth Century* (Chapel Hill: University of North Carolina Press, 2008), 35–37; Hugh Thomas, *The Slave Trade: The Story of the Atlantic Slave Trade, 1440–1870* (New York: Simon & Schuster, 1997), 98–102; and "A la sacra cesárea majestad, los oficiales reales de Santo Domingo Diego Caballero, Francisco Dávila y Juan de Pasamonte," Santo Domingo, June 17, 1535, AGI, Santo Domingo, leg. 74, R. 1; Marc Eagle, "The Early Slave Trade to Spanish America: Caribbean Pathways, 1530–1580," in *The Spanish Caribbean and the Atlantic World in the Long Sixteenth Century*, ed. Ida Altman and David Wheat (Lincoln: University of Nebraska Press, 2019), 140, 142, 155n14, 155n22.

14. Alonso de Zuazo, *juez de residencia*, to Guillermo de Chièvres, January 22, 1518, in Alonso de Zuazo and Rodrigo Martínez Baracs (ed.), *Cartas y memorias, 1511–1539* (Mexico City: Cien de México, 2000), 88; Esteban Mira Caballos, *El indio antillano: repartimiento, encomienda, y esclavitud (1492–1542)* (Seville: Editorial Muñoz-Moya, 1997), 285; Thomas, *Rivers of Gold*, 304; Deive, *La Española*, 150; Deagan and Cruxent, *Outpost*, 210; Deive, *La Española*, esp. 89–155; Jalil Sued-Badillo, "The Island Caribs: New Approaches to the Question of Ethnicity in the Early Colonial Caribbean," in *Wolves from the Sea: Readings in the Anthropology of the Native Caribbean*, ed. Neil L. Whitehead (Leiden, the Netherlands: KITLV Press, 1995), 67; and O. Nigel Bolland, "Colonization and Slavery in Central America," *Slavery & Abolition* 15, no. 2 (1994): esp. 13–15; Peter Hulme, *Colonial Encounters: Europe and the Native Caribbean, 1492–1797* (London: Methuen, 1986), 15; Erin Stone, "War and Rescate: The Sixteenth-Century Circum-Caribbean Indigenous Slave Trade," in *The Spanish Caribbean*, ed. Altman and Wheat.

15. Deive, *La Española*, 164–65, 388–89; and Rodríguez Morel, *Orígenes*, 129.

16. On slaves identified as "white" in the Americas, see below. Spaniards also took some slaves of Asian descent to the New World in the sixteenth and seventeenth centuries, in particular from Portuguese-controlled areas of India and from the Spanish-ruled Philippines. See Tatiana Seijas, *Asian Slaves in Colonial Mexico: From Chinos to Indians* (New York: Cambridge University Press, 2014), esp. 251. For one documented case in Cuba, see Alejandro de la Fuente, *Havana and the Atlantic in the Sixteenth Century* (Chapel Hill: University of North Carolina Press, 2008), 106. For examples of enslaved people from India in Spain and Spanish America already in the early sixteenth century, see AGI, Panama 235, L.7, F.61V–62R; and Thomas, *The Slave Trade*, 105.

17. For stipulations focused on slavery and freedom, see the *Las Siete Partidas del rey don Alfonso el Sabio, cotejadas con varios códices antiguos por la Real academia de la Historia*, vol. 3 (Madrid, Spain: La Imprenta Real, 1807), 4th *partida*, titles 21 and 22, 117–28.

18. Roser Salicrú i Lluch, "Slaves in the Professional and Family Life of Craftsmen in the Late Middle Ages," in *La famiglia nell'economia europea, secc. XIII-XVIII: atti della "Quarantesima settimana di studi," 6-10 Aprile 2008*, ed. Simonetta Cavaciocchi (Florence, Italy: Firenze University Press 2009), 325–26, 326n8; William D. Phillips Jr., *Slavery in Medieval and Early Modern Iberia* (Philadelphia: University of Pennsylvania Press, 2014), 24, 36–37, 61–62; Alfonso Franco Silva, *La esclavitud en Sevilla y su tierra a fines de la edad media* (Seville: Diputación Provincial de Sevilla, 1979), 47–51; Debra Blumenthal, *Enemies and Familiars: Slavery and Mastery in Fifteenth-Century Valencia* (Ithaca, NY: Cornell University Press, 2009), 1, 9, 9n1, 10, 20; Charles Verlinden, *L'esclavage dans l'europe médiévale* (Bruges, Belgium: De Tempel, 1955), 451–55, 748–49, passim; Sally McKee, "Domestic Slavery in Renaissance Italy," *Slavery and Abolition* 29, no. 3 (September 2008): 316; and Charles Verlinden, "Les origines coloniales de la civilization atlantique," *Cahiers d'Histoire Mondiale* 1, no. 2 (1953): 385.

19. On the importance of the Black Sea slave trade in the late medieval period, see: Blumenthal, *Enemies*, 1, 9–10; McKee, "Domestic Slavery," 308–11; Steven A. Epstein, *Speaking of Slavery: Color, Ethnicity, and Human Bondage in Italy* (Ithaca, NY: Cornell University Press, 2001); Bernard Lewis, *Race and Slavery in the Middle East: An Historical Enquiry* (New York: Oxford University Press, 1990), 11–15, 54–69; Iris Origo, "The Domestic Enemy: The Eastern Slaves in Tuscany in the Fourteenth and Fifteenth Centuries," *Speculum* 30, no. 3 (July 1955); Alan W. Fisher, "Muscovy and the Black Sea Trade," *Canadian-American Slavic Studies* 6, no. 4 (Winter 1972): 576–78; David Brion Davis, *Challenging the Boundaries of Slavery* (Cambridge, MA: Harvard University Press, 2003), 1721; Charles Verlinden, *The Beginnings of Modern Colonization* (Ithaca, NY: Cornell University Press, 1970), 2829; David Brion Davis, *Inhuman Bondage: The Rise and Fall of Slavery in the New World* (Oxford, UK: Oxford University Press, 2006), 82; Verlinden, "Les origines," 385; Jacques Heers, *Esclaves et domestiques au moyen-age dans le monde méditerranéen* (Paris: Fayard, 1981), 69–70; Henry and Renée Kahane, "Notes on the Linguistic History of 'Sclavus,'" in *Studi in onore di Ettore Lo Gatto e Giovanni Maver*, Collana di *Ricerche Slavistiche*, no. 1 (Rome: Sansoni, 1962), 349–53, 360; and Alice Rio, *Slavery after Rome, 500–1100* (Oxford, UK: Oxford University Press, 2017), 24, 29, 37, 40, 165–67. Scholars have shown that even in the 1600s, Orthodox Christian slaves from the Black Sea and from Greece could be found laboring on Spanish and other Western European galleys. See David Wheat, "Mediterranean Slavery, New World Transformations: Galley Slaves in the Spanish Caribbean, 1578–1635," *Slavery and Abolition* 31,

no. 3 (September 2010): 329–33; and Seymour Drescher, *Abolition: A History of Slavery and Antislavery* (Cambridge, UK: Cambridge University Press, 2009), 13.

20. Blumenthal, *Enemies*, 1, 9–10; and William D. Phillips, *Slavery in Medieval and Early Modern Iberia* (Philadelphia: University of Pennsylvania Press, 2014), chap. 2.

21. Halil Inalcik, *An Economic and Social History of the Ottoman Empire*, vol. 1, *1300–1600* (Cambridge, UK: Cambridge University Press, 1994), 274–85; and Alan W. Fisher, "Chattel Slavery in the Ottoman Empire," *Slavery and Abolition* 1, no. 1 (May 1980): 34–35.

22. Real cédula, April 8, 1573, AGI, Indiferente General 1968, leg. 19, folio 125. The author collected and counted licenses for "white" slaves from diverse records at the AGI.

23. Ordinances, Diego Colón, January 6, 1522, AGI, Patronato 295, Número 104, Anthony Stevens-Acevedo, *The Santo Domingo Slave Revolt of 1521 and the Slave Laws of 1522. Black Slavery and Black Resistance in the Early Colonial Americas* (New York: CUNY Dominican Studies Institute, 2019); Manuel Lucena Salmoral, *Leyes para esclavos: El ordenamiento jurídico sobre la condición, tratamiento, defensa y represión de los esclavos en las colonias de la América española*, in *Tres grandes cuestiones de la historia de Iberoamérica*, ed. José Andrés-Gallego (Madrid, Spain: Fundación MAPFRE TAVERA, 2005), 559–60, 587.

24. I capitalize "black" and "white" when the words refer to a fundamental social group and envisioned community related to shared descent, analogous to capitalizing what is generally understood today as "ethnicity." I do not capitalize "black" and "white" when they refer essentially to a specific appearance or lineage that is not a basis for such a community. Thus, my use of "white" will move from lower to upper case by the end of the sixteenth century, as its referent changes from at first an appearance to eventually a collective identity in a social sense, or from a "color" to a "race." See Turits, "An Enslaved New World," chaps. 1 and 2.

25. A. J. R. Russell-Wood, "Before Columbus: Portugal's African Prelude to the Middle Passage and Contribution to Discourse on Race and Slavery," in *Race, Discourse, and the Origin of the Americas: A New World View*, ed. Vera Lawrence Hyatt and Rex Nettleford (Washington, DC: Smithsonian Institution Press, 1995), 148–49; Phillips, *Slavery*, 22; and Verlinden, "Les origines," 385.

26. Richard Konetzke, *Colección de documentos para la historia de la formación social de Hispanoamérica, 1493–1810*, vol. 1 (Madrid, Spain: Consejo Superior de Investigaciones Científicas, 1953), 134–46, 215–18, 244–48, 291–92, 459–60, 531–32, 592–93, 626–28; real provisión, September 19, 1528, AGI, Indiferente General 421, L.13, F.375V–76R; real cédula, November 20, 1528, AGI, Patronato 275, Ramo 8, no. 6; Al Emperador del Obispo de Venezuela October 8, 1538 and "Al Emperador Licenciado Castañeda," Santo Domingo, July 22, 1539, Biblioteca Nacional José Martí de Cuba (BNJM), Manuscritos, Colección Morales,

tomo (T.) 81; Andrés Reséndez, *The Other Slavery: The Uncovered Story of Indian Enslavement in America* (Boston, MA: Houghton Mifflin Harcourt, 2016), 91, 122, and 132–48; Tatiana Seijas, *Asian Slaves in Colonial Mexico: From Chinos to Indians* (New York: Cambridge University Press, 2014), esp. 63, 109–16, 219, and 239–40; Nancy E. van Deusen, "Indios on the Move in the Sixteenth-Century Iberian World," *Journal of Global History* 10, no. 3 (November 2015), 387–88.

27. Real Cédula, April 24, 1545, AGI, Santo Domingo 868, leg. 2, folios 234–39; Deive, *La Española*, 355–68. Cf. Lynne Guitar, "Boiling It Down: Slavery on the First Commercial Sugarcane Ingenios in the Americas (Hispaniola, 1530–45)," in *Slaves, Subjects, and Subversives: Blacks in Colonial Latin America*, ed. Jane G. Landers and Barry M. Robinson (Albuquerque: University of New Mexico Press, 2006), 47–48.

28. Philip Morgan, "Caribbean Slavery," in *The Rise and Demise of Slavery and the Slave Trade in the Atlantic World*, ed. Philip Misevich and Kristin Mann (Rochester, NY: University of Rochester Press, 2016), 69–72; Brett Rushforth, *Bonds of Alliance: Indigenous and Atlantic Slaveries in New France* (Chapel Hill: University of North Carolina Press, 2012), esp. 355–57; and Stuart B. Schwartz, *Sugar Plantations in the Formation of Brazilian Society: Bahia, 1550–1835* (Cambridge, UK: Cambridge University Press, 1985), 65–72. Cf. Yuko Miki, "Slave and Citizen in Black and Red: Reconsidering the Intersection of African and Indigenous Slavery in Postcolonial Brazil," *Slavery & Abolition* 35, no. 1 (2014): 1–22.

29. "Rodrigo López."

30. "Rodrigo López." Caballero is identified as the Audiencia secretary in "Residencia que se tomó a los Licenciados Cristóbal Lebrón, Lucas Vázquez de Ayllón, Juan Ortiz de Matienzo, Marcelo de Villalobos, y Pedro León Oidores, y Fiscal de la Real Audiencia de Santo Domingo, por el Licenciado Gaspar de Espinosa Juez nombrado para este efecto," 1527, AGI, Justicia. leg. 50, no. 1.

31. "Rodrigo López." Trepana Galiano was presumably European, given that no racial identity was noted in the trial record. Cortés Alonso specifies further that "Trápana" was Sicilian, though does not state why—perhaps because of his surname. Cortés Alonso, "La liberación del esclavo," 27.

32. "Rodrigo López." Cf. Toby Green, "Building Slavery in the Atlantic World: Atlantic Connections and the Changing Institution of Slavery in Cabo Verde, Fifteenth-Sixteenth Centuries," *Slavery and Abolition* 32, no. 2 (2011): 236–40. Green's history and analysis of this case appear to be based on the first trial in Cubagua in 1528 and not Rodrigo López's subsequent successful appeal in Santo Domingo.

33. Blumenthal, *Enemies*, esp. 194–224.

34. Blumenthal, *Enemies*, 6.

35. On illegal kidnapping and enslavement of people indigenous to the Americas, see Al Emperador del Obispo de Venezuela, October 8, 1538 and "Al Emperador Licenciado Castañeda, Santo Domingo," July 22, 1539, BNJM,

Manuscritos, Colección Morales, T. 81; and Konetzke, *Colección*, vol. 1, 134–35, 145–46, 215–18, 244–48.

36. This seems to have been the case for those seen as having clearly been enslaved at one point, at least. Blumenthal's work on fifteenth-century Valencia (Spain), though, highlights the ways that, in theory, the burden fell instead on putative owners when attempting legally to enslave alleged captives in "just war" (or someone known to have once been free). "[B]efore a captive could legitimately be sold as a slave . . . he or she first had to be presented before the bailiff general, . . . the Crown official entrusted with investigating the legitimacy of all captures and collecting the Crown's cut of the booty." Blumenthal, *Enemies*, 20.

37. Toby Green, *The Rise of the Trans-Atlantic Slave Trade in Western Africa, 1300–1589* (Cambridge, UK: Cambridge University Press, 2012), 114; and Leo J. Garofolo, "The Shape of a Diaspora: The Movement of Afro-Iberians to Colonial Spanish America," in *Africans to Spanish America: Expanding the Diaspora*, ed. Sherwin K. Bryant, Rachel Sarah O'Toole, and Ben Vinson III (Urbana: University of Illinois Press, 2012), 40.

38. Report of Alonso de Ávila, *vecino* and *regidor* of the city of Santo Domingo, July 28, 1533, AGI, Justicia 12, no. 1, Ramo 2; Juan de Echagoian, "Relación de la isla Española enviada al Rey D. Felipe II por el Lic. Echagoian," *Boletín del Archivo General de la Nación* 4, no. 19 (1941), 446. On the date when Echagoian, former judge of the audiencia of Santo Domingo, wrote his report, 1568, see Cipriano de Utrera, *Santo Domingo: Dilucidaciones históricas*, vol. 1 (Santo Domingo, Dominican Republic: Imprenta de "Dios y Patria," 1927), 128–32. See also Rodríguez Morel, "El Sector Azucarero," 396–97; Rodríguez Morel, *Orígenes*, 189; Río Moreno, *Los inicios de la agricultura europea en el nuevo mundo*, 441.

39. Estimates for the total enslaved population in the mid- and late 1540s varied substantially, and this may in part be the result of the emancipation of some 5,000 enslaved people native to the Americas at that time. Al Emperador, Melchor de Castro, Escribano de Minas, Santo Domingo, July 25, 1543, BNJM, Manuscritos, Colección Morales, T. 81; Guitar, "Boiling It Down," 47–48; Rodríguez Morel, *Orígenes*, 55, 129–30, 209; Genaro Rodríguez Morel, "Esclavitud y vida rural en las plantaciones azucareras de Santo Domingo, Siglo XVI," *Anuario de Estudios Americanos* 49 (1992): 94, 99–100; Rodríguez Morel, "El sector azucarero," 395; Genaro Rodríguez Morel, "The Sugar Economy of Española in the Sixteenth Century," in *Tropical Babylons: Sugar and the Making of the Atlantic World*, ed. Stuart B. Schwartz (Chapel Hill: University of North Carolina Press, 2004), 103–4; M. L. E. Moreau de Saint-Méry, *A Topographical and Political Description of the Spanish Part of Saint-Domingo: Containing, General Observations on the Climate, Population and Productions; on the Character and Manners of the Inhabitants; with an Account of the Several Branches of the Government*, vol. 2, trans. William

Cobbett (Philadelphia, PA: printed by the author, 1798 [1796]), 99; Mira Caballos, "Otros sectores productivos y económicos," 436-39; Juan de Echagoian, "Relación de la isla española enviada al Rey D. Felipe II por el Lic. Echagoian," *Boletín del Archivo General de la Nación* 4, no. 19 (1941): 446; Memorial de Rodrigo Ribero, December 29, 1580, AGI, Santo Domingo 70, R.1, no. 10; Deive, *Los guerrilleros negros*, 43; and Deive, *La Española*, 353-56, 368.

    40. Rodríguez Morel, *Orígenes*, 118-28, 156-57; Carlos Esteban Deive, *Los guerrilleros negros: Esclavos fugitivos y cimarrones en Santo Domingo* (Santo Domingo, Dominican Republic: Fundación Cultural Dominicana, 1989), 43-67; and Moya Pons, *History*, 18-20.

    41. Stuart B. Schwartz, *Sugar Plantations in the Formation of Brazilian Society: Bahia, 1550-1835* (Cambridge, MA: Cambridge University Press, 1985), 16-19, 37, 165; Río Moreno, *Los inicios de la agricultura europea*, 438; Rodríguez Morel, *Orígenes*, 177; Fernando Ortiz, *Los negros esclavos* (Havana, Cuba: Editorial de Ciencias Sociales, 1996), 54.

    42. "Testimonio de los frutos de la isla española cargados para España desde el año de 1603 hasta el de 1607," January 2, 1608, in Incháustegui Cabral, *Reales cédulas y correspondencia*, vol. 3, 863; Juana Gil-Bermejo García, *La Española: Anotaciones históricas, 1600-1650* (Seville, Spain: Escuela de estudios hispano-americanos; 1983), 63-64, 63n23.

    43. Ginger plantations were sizable, but small relative to the extraordinary size of Santo Domingo's sixteenth-century sugar plantations. Antonio Osorio to the King, October 2, 1606, in Emilio Rodríguez Demorizi, *Relaciones históricas de Santo Domingo* (Santo Domingo, Dominican Republic: Editora Montalvo, 1945), vol. 2, esp. 425-28, 441-44; Justo del Río Moreno and Lorenzo E. López y Sebastián and, "El jengibre: Historia de un monocultivo caribeño del siglo XVI," *Revista complutense de historia de América* 18 (1992): 63-87; Bethany Aram, "Caribbean Ginger and Atlantic Trade, 1570-1648," *Journal of Global History* 10 (2015), 410-30; Mira Caballos, "Otros sectores productivos y económicos," 444-46; Gil-Bermejo García, *La Española*, 65-69; "Testimonio de los frutos de la isla española cargados para España desde el año de 1603 hasta el de 1607, in Incháustegui Cabral, *Reales cédulas y correspondencia*, vol. 3, 863; Genaro Rodríguez Morel, "El contrabando y la decadencia de las relaciones de producción esclavistas," in *Historia general del pueblo dominicano*, vol. 1, ed. Genaro Rodríguez Morel (Santo Domingo, Dominican Republic: Academia Dominicana de la Historia, 2013), 621; María Isabel Paredes Vera, "La decadencia de la población y de la economía de estancias hasta mediados del siglo XVII," in *Historia general del pueblo dominicano*, vol. 2, ed. Raymundo González de Peña (Santo Domingo, Dominican Republic: Academia Dominicana de la Historia, 2018), 95.

    44. Frank Moya Pons, *Historia colonial de Santo Domingo* (Santiago, Dominican Republic: Universidad Católica Madre y Maestra, 1974), 201, 205-10, 220.

45. For diverse hypotheses, see Rodríguez Morel, "El Sector Azucarero," 412–16; Justo Lucas del Río Moreno, *Los inicios de la agricultura europea en el Nuevo Mundo, 1492–1542* (Seville, Spain: Caja Rural de Sevilla, 1991), 360–61, 438–39; Stephan Palmié, "Toward Sugar and Slavery," in *The Caribbean: A History of the Region and Its People*, ed. Stephan Palmié and Francisco Scarano (Chicago, IL: University of Chicago Press, 2011), 137; Rodríguez Morel, *Orígenes*, 177; Rodríguez Morel, "Sugar Economy," 107–8; Moya Pons, *History*, 25.

46. Rodríguez Morel, *Orígenes*, 177; Rodríguez Morel, "Sugar Economy," 107–8; Schwartz, *Sugar Plantations*, esp. 16–19, 37, 66; Moya Pons, *History*, 24–25, 313n4; and Stephan Palmié, "Toward Sugar and Slavery," in *The Caribbean: A History of the Region and Its People*, ed. Stephan Palmié and Francisco Scarano (Chicago, IL: University of Chicago Press, 2011), 137.

47. Despite its limitations, a detailed population report by the Archbishop on Santo Domingo's cities, towns, and village in 1681 indicates that free African descendants were by far the largest demographic group in the colony and perhaps the majority already. Domingo Fernández Navarrete, "Relación de las ciudades, villas y lugares de la isla de Sancto Domingo y Española," April 30, 1681, in *Clío* (May–June 1934), 91–95. See Turits, "An Enslaved New World," chap. 3.

48. Wenceslao Nicolás Vega Boyrie, *Historia del derecho colonial dominicano* (Santo Domingo, Dominican Republic: Instituto Tecnológico de Santo Domingo, 1986), 95; Javier Malagón Barceló, *Código negro carolino (1784)* (Santo Domingo, Dominican Republic: Taller, 1974), 142–47; and Konetzke, *Colección*, vol. 1, for example, 290–91, 455, 611–12; de la Fuente, *Havana*, 180.

49. Larrazábal Blanco, *Los negros*, 183–84; Antonio Sánchez Valverde, *Idea del valor de la Isla Española* (Santo Domingo, Dominican Republic: Editora Nacional, 1971 [first published in 1785]), 169.

50. For another portrait of the post-plantation period, see David Wheat, *Atlantic Africa and the Spanish Caribbean, 1570–1640* (Chapel Hill: University of North Carolina Press, 2016).

Bibliography

Aram, Bethany. "Caribbean Ginger and Atlantic Trade, 1570–1648," *Journal of Global History* 10, no. 3 (2015): 410–30.

Bakewell, Peter. *A History of Latin America*. Oxford, UK: Blackwell, 2004.

Beckles, Hilary McD. *The First Black Slave Society: Britain's "Barbarity Time" in Barbados, 1636–1876*. Kingston, Jamaica: University of the West Indies Press, 2016.

Berlin, Ira. *Many Thousands Gone: The First Two Centuries of Slavery in North America*. Cambridge, MA: Harvard University Press, 1998.

Blumenthal, Debra. *Enemies and Familiars: Slavery and Mastery in Fifteenth-Century Valencia.* Ithaca, NY: Cornell University Press, 2009.
Bolland, Nigel. "Colonization and Slavery in Central America," *Slavery & Abolition* 15, no. 2 (1994): 11-25.
Braudel, Fernand. *Capitalism and Material Life, 1400-1800.* New York: Harper and Row, 1973.
"Cédule du Gouverneur de Brésa." August 18, 1518. In Georges Scelle, *La traite négrière aux Indes de Castile, contrats et traités d'assiento: Étude de droit public et d'histoire diplomatique puisée aux sources originales et accompagnée de plusierus documents inédits*, vol. 1. Paris: L. Larose & L. Tenin, 1906.
Davis, David Brion. *Inhuman Bondage: The Rise and Fall of Slavery in the New World.* Oxford, UK: Oxford University Press, 2006.
———. *Challenging the Boundaries of Slavery.* Cambridge, MA: Harvard University Press, 2003.
de la Fuente, Alejandro. *Havana and the Atlantic in the Sixteenth Century.* Chapel Hill: University of North Carolina Press, 2008.
Deagan, Kathleen, and José María Cruxent. *Columbus's Outpost among the Taínos: Spain and America at La Isabela, 1493-1498.* New Haven, CT: Yale University Press, 2002.
Deive, Carlos Esteban. *La Española y la esclavitud del Indio.* Santo Domingo, Dominican Republic: Fundación García Arévalo, 1995.
———. *Los guerrilleros negros: Esclavos fugitivos y cimarrones en Santo Domingo.* Santo Domingo, Dominican Republic: Fundación Cultural Dominicana, 1989.
Drescher, Seymour. *Abolition: A History of Slavery and Antislavery.* Cambridge, UK: Cambridge University Press, 2009.
Dubois, Laurent, and Richard Lee Turits. *Freedom Roots: Histories from the Caribbean.* Chapel Hill: University of North Carolina Press, 2019.
Echagoian, Juan de. "Relación de la isla Española enviada al Rey D. Felipe II por el Lic. Echagoian," *Boletín del Archivo General de la Nación* 4, no. 19 (1941), 446.
Eagle, Marc. "The Early Slave Trade to Spanish America: Caribbean Pathways, 1530-1580." In *The Spanish Caribbean and the Atlantic World in the Long Sixteenth Century*, edited by Ida Altman and David Wheat. Lincoln: University of Nebraska Press, 2019, 139-62.
Eagle, Marc, and David Wheat, "The Early Iberian Slave Trade to the Spanish Caribbean, 1500-1580." In *From the Galleons to the Highlands: Slave Trade Routes in the Spanish Americas*, edited by Alex Boruki, David Eltis, and David Wheat. Albuquerque: University of New Mexico Press, 2020, 47-72.
Epstein, Steven A. *Speaking of Slavery: Color, Ethnicity, and Human Bondage in Italy.* Ithaca, NY: Cornell University Press, 2001.

Fisher, Alan W. "Chattel Slavery in the Ottoman Empire." *Slavery and Abolition* 1, no. 1 (May 1980): 34–35.
Fisher, Alan W. "Muscovy and the Black Sea Trade." *Canadian-American Slavic Studies* 6, no. 4 (Winter 1972): 575–94.
Finley, Moses I. *Ancient Slavery*. New York: Viking, 1980.
Franco Silva, Alfonso. *La esclavitud en Sevilla y su tierra a fines de la edad media*. Seville: Diputación Provincial de Sevilla, 1979.
Garofolo, Leo J. "The Shape of a Diaspora: The Movement of Afro-Iberians to Colonial Spanish America." In *Africans to Spanish America: Expanding the Diaspora*, edited by Sherwin K. Bryant, Rachel Sarah O'Toole, and Ben Vinson III. Urbana: University of Illinois Press, 2012, 27–49.
Granberry, Julian. "Spanish Slave Trade in the Bahamas, 1509–1530: An Aspect of the Caribbean Pearl Industry (Continued)," *Journal of the Bahamas Historical Society* 2 (October 1980): 15–17.
Green, Toby. *The Rise of the Trans-Atlantic Slave Trade in Western Africa, 1300–1589*. Cambridge, UK: Cambridge University Press, 2012.
———. "Building Slavery in the Atlantic World: Atlantic Connections and the Changing Institution of Slavery in Cabo Verde, Fifteenth-Sixteenth Centuries." *Slavery and Abolition* 32, no. 2 (2011): 227–45.
Guitar, Lynne. "Boiling It Down: Slavery on the First Commercial Sugarcane Ingenios in the Americas (Hispaniola, 1530–45). In *Slaves, Subjects, and Subversives: Blacks in Colonial Latin America*, edited by Jane G. Landers and Barry M. Robinson. Albuquerque: University of New Mexico Press, 2006, 39–82.
Guitar, Lynne A. "Cultural Genesis: Relationships among Indians, Africans and Spaniards in Rural Hispaniola, First Half of the Sixteenth Century." PhD diss., Vanderbilt University, 1998.
Heers, Jacques. *Esclaves et domestiques au moyen-age dans le monde méditerranéen*. Paris: Fayard, 1981.
Hulme, Peter. *Colonial Encounters: Europe and the Native Caribbean, 1492–1797*. London: Methuen, 1986.
Inalcik, Halil. *An Economic and Social History of the Ottoman Empire*, vol. 1, *1300–1600*. Cambridge, UK: Cambridge University Press, 1994.
Kahane, Henry, and Renée. "Notes on the Linguistic History of 'Sclavus.'" In *Studi in onore di Ettore Lo Gatto e Giovanni Maver*, Collana di *Ricerche slavistiche*, no. 1. Rome: Sansoni, 1962.
Konetzke, Richard. *Colección de documentos para la historia de la formación social de Hispanoamérica, 1493–1810*, vol. 1. Madrid. Spain: Consejo Superior de Investigaciones Científicas, 1953.
Las Siete Partidas del rey don Alfonso el Sabio, cotejadas con varios códices antiguos por la Real Academia de la Historia, vol. 3. Madrid, Spain: La Imprenta Real, 1807.

Lewis, Bernard. *Race and Slavery in the Middle East: An Historical Enquiry*. New York: Oxford University Press, 1990.

Liddell, Abraham L. "Social Networks and the Formation of an African Atlantic: The Upper Guinea Coast, Cape Verde, and the Spanish Caribbean, 1450–1600." PhD diss., Vanderbilt University, 2021.

Lucena Salmoral, Manuel. *Leyes para esclavos: El ordenamiento jurídico sobre la condición, tratamiento, defensa y represión de los esclavos en las colonias de la América española*. In *Tres grandes cuestiones de la historia de Iberoamérica*, edited by José Andrés-Gallego. Madrid, Spain: Fundación MAPFRE TAVERA, 2005.

Malagón Barceló, Javier. *Código negro carolino (1784)*. Santo Domingo, Dominican Republic: Taller, 1974.

McKee, Sally. "Domestic Slavery in Renaissance Italy." *Slavery and Abolition* 29, no. 3 (September 2008), 305–26.

Miki, Yuko. "Slave and Citizen in Black and Red: Reconsidering the Intersection of African and Indigenous Slavery in Postcolonial Brazil." *Slavery & Abolition* 35, no. 1 (2014): 1–22.

Mintz, Sidney W. *Sweetness and Power: The Place of Sugar in Modern History*. New York: Penguin, 1985.

Mira Caballos, Esteban. "Otros sectores productivos y económicos." In *Historia general del pueblo dominicano*, vol. 1, edited by Genaro Rodríguez Morel. Santo Domingo, Dominican Republic: Academia Dominicana de la Historia, 2013.

———. *El indio antillano: repartimiento, encomienda, y esclavitud (1492–1542)*. Seville: Editorial Muñoz-Moya, 1997.

Morgan, Philip. "Caribbean Slavery." In *The Rise and Demise of Slavery and the Slave Trade in the Atlantic World*, edited by Philip Misevich and Kristin Mann. Rochester, NY: University of Rochester Press, 2016, 64–99.

Moya Pons, Frank. *El oro en la historia dominicana*. Santo Domingo, Dominican Republic: Academia Dominicana de la Historia, 2016.

———. *History of the Caribbean*. Princeton, NJ: Markus Wiener, 2007.

———. *Historia colonial de Santo Domingo*. Santiago, Dominican Republic: Universidad Católica Madre y Maestra, 1974.

Origo, Iris. "The Domestic Enemy: The Eastern Slaves in Tuscany in the Fourteenth and Fifteenth Centuries," *Speculum* 30, no. 3 (July 1955), 321–66.

Palmié, Stephan. "Toward Sugar and Slavery." In *The Caribbean: A History of the Region and Its People*, edited by Stephan Palmié and Francisco Scarano. Chicago, IL: University of Chicago Press, 2011, 131–48.

Paredes Vera, María Isabel. "La decadencia de la población y de la economía de estancias hasta mediados del siglo XVII." In *Historia general del pueblo dominicano*, vol. 2, edited by Raymundo González de Peña. Santo Domingo, Dominican Republic: Academia Dominicana de la Historia, 2018.

Perri, Michael "'Ruined and Lost': Spanish Destruction of the Pearl Coast in the Early Sixteenth Century," *Environment and History* 15, no. 2 (May 2009), 129–61.
Phillips Jr., William D. *Slavery in Medieval and Early Modern Iberia*. Philadelphia: University of Pennsylvania Press, 2014.
Reséndez, Andrés. *The Other Slavery: The Uncovered Story of Indian Enslavement in America*. Boston, MA: Houghton Mifflin Harcourt, 2016.
Rio, Alice. *Slavery after Rome, 500–1100*. Oxford, UK: Oxford University Press, 2017.
Río Moreno, Justo Lucas del. *Los inicios de la agricultura europea en el Nuevo Mundo, 1492–1542*. Seville, Spain: Caja Rural de Sevilla, 1991.
Río Moreno, Justo L. del, and Lorenzo E. López y Sebastián. "El jengibre: historia de un monocultivo caribeño del siglo XVI." *Revista complutense de historia de América* 18 (1992): 63–87.
Rodríguez Demorizi, Emilio. *Relaciones históricas de Santo Domingo*. Santo Domingo, Dominican Republic: Editora Montalvo, 1945.
Rodríguez Morel, Genaro. *Orígenes de la economía de plantación de La Española*. Santo Domingo, Dominican Republic: Editora Nacional, 2012.
———. "El contrabando y la decadencia de las relaciones de producción esclavistas." In *Historia general del pueblo dominicano*, vol. 1, edited by Genaro Rodríguez Morel. Santo Domingo, Dominican Republic: Academia Dominicana de la Historia, 2013.
———. "The Sugar Economy of Española in the Sixteenth Century." In *Tropical Babylons: Sugar and the Making of the Atlantic World*, edited by Stuart B. Schwartz. Chapel Hill: University of North Carolina Press, 2004, 85–114.
Rubio, Vicente. *Indigenismo de ayer y de hoy*. Santo Domingo, Dominican Republic: Fundación García Arévalo, 2009.
———. *Cedulario de la isla de Santo Domingo*, vol. 1 (1492–1501. Santo Domingo, Dominican Republic: Centro de Altos Estudios Humanísticos y del Idioma Español, 2007.
Russell-Wood, A. J. R. "Before Columbus: Portugal's African Prelude to the Middle Passage and Contribution to Discourse on Race and Slavery." In *Race, Discourse, and the Origin of the Americas: A New World View*, edited by Vera Lawrence Hyatt and Rex Nettleford. Washington, DC: Smithsonian Institution Press, 1995, 134–68.
Rushforth, Brett. *Bonds of Alliance: Indigenous and Atlantic Slaveries in New France*. Chapel Hill: University of North Carolina Press, 2012.
Saint-Méry, L. E. Moreau de M. *A Topographical and Political Description of the Spanish Part of Saint-Domingo: Containing, General Observations on the Climate, Population and Productions; on the Character and Manners of the Inhabitants; with an Account of the Several Branches of the Government*, vol. 2, translated by William Cobbett. Philadelphia: Printed by the author, 1798.
Salicrú i Lluch, Roser. "Slaves in the Professional and Family Life of Craftsmen in the Late Middle Ages." In *La famiglia nell'economia europea, secc. XIII–*

XVIII, atti della "Quarantesima settimana di studi," 6–10 Aprile 2008, edited by Simonetta Cavaciocchi. Florence. Italy: Firenze University Press, 2009.
Sánchez Valverde, Antonio. *Idea del valor de la isla Española*. Santo Domingo, Dominican Republic: Editora Nacional, 1947.
Schwartz, Stuart B. "Spaniards, *Pardos*, and the Missing Mestizos: Identities and Racial Categories in the Early Hispanic Caribbean." *New West Indian Guide* 71, no. 1/2 (1997): 5–19.
———. *Sugar Plantations in the Formation of Brazilian Society: Bahia, 1550–1835*. Cambridge, UK: Cambridge University Press, 1985.
Seijas, Tatiana. *Asian Slaves in Colonial Mexico: From Chinos to Indians*. New York: Cambridge University Press, 2014.
Stone, Erin. "War and Rescate: The Sixteenth-Century Circum-Caribbean Indigenous Slave Trade." In *The Spanish Caribbean and the Atlantic World in the Long Sixteenth Century*, edited by Ida Altman and David Wheat. Lincoln: University of Nebraska Press, 2019, 47–68.
Sued-Badillo, Jalil. "The Island Caribs: New Approaches to the Question of Ethnicity in the Early Colonial Caribbean." In *Wolves from the Sea: Readings in the Anthropology of the Native Caribbean*, edited by Neil L. Whitehead. Leiden, the Netherlands: KITLV Press, 1995, 61–89.
Thomas, Hugh. *Rivers of Gold: The Rise of the Spanish Empire, from Columbus to Magellan*. New York: Random House, 2003.
———. *The Slave Trade: The Story of the Atlantic Slave Trade, 1440–1870*. New York: Simon & Schuster, 1997.
Turits, Richard Lee. "An Enslaved New World: Slavery, Freedom, and the Making of Race in Santo Domingo (1492–1865)." Unpublished manuscript.
Utrera, Cipriano de. *Santo Domingo: Dilucidaciones históricas*, vol. 1. Santo Domingo, Dominican Republic: Imprenta de "Dios y Patria," 1927.
van Deusen, Nancy E. "Indios on the Move in the Sixteenth-Century Iberian World." *Journal of Global History* 10, no. 3 (November 2015), 387–409.
Vega Boyrie, Wenceslao Nicolás. *Historia del derecho colonial dominicano*. Santo Domingo, Dominican Republic: Instituto Tecnológico de Santo Domingo, 1986.
Verlinden, Charles. *The Beginnings of Modern Colonization*. Ithaca, NY: Cornell University Press, 1970.
———. *L'esclavage dans l'europe médiévale*. Bruges, Belgium: De Tempel, 1955.
———. "Les origines coloniales de la civilization atlantique." *Cahiers d'histoire mondiale* 1, no. 2 (1953).
Warsh, Molly A. "A Political Ecology in the Early Spanish Caribbean." *William and Mary Quarterly* 71, no. 4 (October 2014): 517–48.
Wheat, David. "Mediterranean Slavery, New World Transformations: Galley Slaves in the Spanish Caribbean, 1578–1635." *Slavery and Abolition* 31, no. 3 (September 2010): 327–44.

———. *Atlantic Africa and the Spanish Caribbean, 1570–1640*. Chapel Hill: University of North Carolina Press, 2016.

Zuazo, Alonso de and Rodrigo Martínez Baracs, eds., *Cartas y memorias, 1511–1539*. Mexico City: Cien de México, 2000.

Chapter 4

African Slavery and Laws in La Española

The Beginnings of Modern Colonization
in the Americas (1520s–1540s)

ANTHONY R. STEVENS-ACEVEDO

Introduction

La Española or Santo Domingo—also known as Hispaniola in English—was the cradle of Blackness, Black slavery, and Black fight against slavery in the modern, post-Columbian Americas.[1] There are indications that one settler of Black African ancestry accompanied Columbus in his first (1492) and/or second (1493) trip to the Americas.[2] There is direct archival evidence of the presence of Blacks in the colony since 1503. By 1518 the Black population was already larger than the European settlers' population, and by 1530 the number of Blacks had surpassed that of European settlers and aboriginals together. During the 1530s and 1540s, at the peak of the sugar-plantation economy of the colony, historians have estimated the Black constituency at between 12,000 and 30,000, versus a white European population of 5,000 and a rapidly dwindling Native population of 4,000 or less.[3] Consequently, these Black Africans and their offspring were the first instance of what David Wheat redefined in 2016 as a settler population of Black people working under the new Spanish empire.[4] And as the earliest enclave of Black enslavement in the continent in early modern times, La

Española was also the site where the first known laws were devised to control the enslaved and free Black population in the region.[5]

Though these early Black codes[6] have received some attention in Dominican historical scholarship, they have been much less studied by the historiography written in English. This is part of a still prevalent trend that in general has neglected considerably, until very recently, the peculiarities and impact of the first century of colonial social experience as it unfolded, both in La Española, in particular, as well as in the Spanish Caribbean, in general.[7]

This chapter contributes an initial shedding of light onto this very local topic by (1) calling the attention of early colonial Latin American and Caribbean scholars to the potential usefulness of these slave laws as historical sources, and (2) presenting provisional research results about the dynamics of the colonial experiment of Black slavery in the first permanent European colony of the Americas.[8]

As sources, these laws pose a variety of challenges to the understanding of both their regulatory purpose as well as the particular circumstances surrounding their specific processes of promulgation. One particular challenge is the considerable difference of the number and type of social issues related to the lives of enslaved people that each set of laws addresses. Another is that the laws do not always address the same items with the same degree of detail, and this might pose a limitation to the depth of our possible comparisons. Also, the dating of some of the laws is somewhat vague.[9]

Departing from a notion that laws are usually issued to stop or prevent certain social behaviors, an attempt has been made here to do a reading of these sixteenth-century laws of La Española as a means to identify which were some of the behaviors and actions by the enslaved Blacks that these ordinances were trying to stop or eradicate. In this commentary, priority is given to selected aspects of the lives of enslaved Black Africans of La Española as they are mentioned or implicitly alluded to in these ordinances. The intention has been for this observation to subsequently allow drawing cross-time comparisons with other slave legislations from other Caribbean and Latin American colonies and other historical periods or moments. This, in turn, could help us construct a more comprehensive and nuanced understanding of Black slavery as a human experience that unfolded and impacted many different geographical, social, ethnic, and chronological settings of the colonial world and era.

In addition, besides the evidence contained in the laws, when looked at through the lens of other types of nonnormative sources, the response by the enslaved population in La Española to these ordinances seems to have repeatedly challenged them. They resorted to frequent running away, openly rebelling against and attacking slave masters and colonists, as well as by forming maroon communities in certain remote mountainous and heavily forested areas of the colony that remained rather inaccessible to the colonial authorities of Santo Domingo. It was a resistance that, though in a limited way, still persisted even after slaves were brought before the colonial justice system. As late as the 1570s, there are testimonies of slaves fleeing on a regular basis from colonists' rural estates. There is also archival evidence that by the 1530s, they were presenting claims to freedom when encouraged by their colonist masters to enter Christian marriage, upholding freedom as an inherent status bestowed by this Christian sacrament. And finally, there is documentary proof from the 1540s that when Blacks and Natives were tried at the colonial tribunals as criminal defendants, they actively and consciously used key elements of the Spanish judicial system, such as appeals, to considerably delay probable harsh sentences that could entail their execution. Many of these appeals needed to be sent to the metropolis for resolution by a higher court, and took a long time to be resolved.[10]

Except for the analysis by Alejandro de la Fuente García of Cuban ordinances on slaves of the 1550s and 1560s, included in his *Havana and the Atlantic in the Sixteenth Century* (2008), and some comments by Emilio Roig de Leuchsenring in 1937 on the same legislation, we have not been able to find other scholarly works addressing the issue of early colonial legislation about enslaved Blacks.[11] As to the content of the said Havana ordinances, it shows some similarities to those of the Black codes produced in Santo Domingo, except that, at least until the 1570s, the harshness of the punishments prescribed for Black slaves in Cuba seems to have been lesser, with no mention of the death penalty.

La Española's Sixteenth-Century Slavery Laws as Historical Sources

Four legal codes and portions of codes devoted to the control of the enslaved Black population of La Española during the first half of the 1500s have survived into our time, issued in the years 1522,[12] 1528, 1535–1543, and 1544, respectively, and all of them approved by the Spanish Crown as late as 1547, with an additional one drafted somewhere between 1528 and 1531, but never promulgated.

The survival of these ordinances seems to be the result of a long-term preservation or archiving of old laws at the *Audiencia* of Santo Domingo, at least into the late 1780s. At this time they were reviewed, recompiled, and selectively incorporated into a new Black code draft under the title *Código negro carolino*. Whatever parts of the codes from the 1500s were not incorporated into the *Código negro* unfortunately seem to have disappeared. Except for the laws of 1522 and the draft of code of around 1528–1531, which were preserved separately in Spain's archives, the only source we have for the rest of sixteenth-century La Española's local legislation about Black people are the copies of ordinances attached to the manuscripts of the *Código negro* of the late 1700s.[13] We know of no other promulgation of ordinances about Black people in La Española during roughly two centuries after the 1500s, except for the *cédulas* and equivalent individual mandates stemming directly from the Crown and usually directed to its colonial officials.

The oldest preserved set of laws in the colonial Americas to regulate the enslaved Blacks were issued in Santo Domingo, in January of 1522, just a few days after the first known rebellion by enslaved Blacks. The rebellion occurred a few miles west of Santo Domingo, during the just concluded Christmas festivities of 1521.[14] For about a century, historians had been dating this earliest rebellion in 1522, due to an anachronistic reading of chronicler Gonzalo Fernández de Oviedo's narrative (1535) on the matter, in which the so-called nativity calendar was used, which considered December 25 as the beginning of every New Year. Since then, and not noticing the difference between Fernández de Oviedo's calendar and our contemporary one, historians had read the year of the rebellion to be 1522, that is, projecting our own contemporary calendar onto Fernández de Oviedo's dating, when in fact it was 1521, as per our calendar.

A second set of laws was issued just six years later, in 1528.[15] Until Carlos Esteban Deive published the Laws of 1522 in 1989 for the first time, the Laws of 1528 had been considered, in Dominican historical scholarship, as the first laws dealing with the control of enslaved Blacks in the Americas. The Laws of 1528 seem to have been motivated by a desire to introduce some limitations to abusive punishments committed by La Española's slaveholders that were perceived as potentially counterproductive for the overall stability of the slavery regime of the colony.[16]

A third set of ordinances was written in La Española around 1530, but never officially promulgated. These laws happen to reflect a particular concern for the preservation of the enslaved Black labor force of the colony, while trying to maintain it under severe control. These peculiar draft ordinances, whose manuscript is incomplete with only nine stipulations, show no explicit publication date and authorship. Curiously enough, they have been actually published in print since 1869, but, despite their exceptionality, this essay may be the first one to address them with some detail in the scholarship on early colonial Latin America and even in Dominican Studies for more than a century. Nonetheless, after thorough examination of both the published printed version and the archival manuscript, we think there is reasonable evidence in the content of the manuscript to trace the authorship to Governor-Bishop Sebastián Ramírez Fuenleal, who was in charge of the governorship of La Española between 1528 and 1531.[17]

Subsequent to these earliest set of laws of the post-1521 rebellion period, what has survived as loosely dated legislation on Black people in La Española is a series of more or less lengthy fragments and excerpts of ordinances targeted at the Black population and dating from the 1530s to the 1540s.[18] These seem to have been issued as updates of the earlier laws, to the extent that it would seem that thereafter, for almost two centuries, the colonial authorities of La Española may have not felt a need to embark in any systematic rewriting of laws on enslaved Blacks until late in the eighteenth century, when an ambitious new draft of ordinances was put together by the Audiencia of Santo Domingo following instructions from the Spanish Crown.[19]

When looked at as a legislative sequence, these ordinances pose a triple complexity that might explain the scant commentary published about them by historians so far. One has to do with the lack of an exact dating of some of them, which means it is not possible to determine which were issued earlier and which were issued later in the period. The other is the fragmented and incomplete condition of several of them, with extensive segments of the original clauses or prescriptive provisions missing.

A third complexity comes from the language of some segments of the text that might be hard for contemporary readers to grasp, either because: (1) mistakes may have been made in the handwritten copy from the eighteenth century (or earlier) of the original sixteenth-century manuscripts that may have possibly distorted the spelling and meaning, or (2) those segments may have had earlier original meanings, now lost, to which we so far have no access. Both circumstances in turn seem to be the result of two historical developments affecting these sources. One was the vanishing of the main repository or compilation of La Española's local colonial laws at some undetermined date after the 1760s. The other was the handling by colonial officials of La Española in the late 1760s of the only set of copies of the documents that ended up making it into our times. They seem to have kept only the partial and rather fragmented set that they felt were useful for their purposes as they, in response to an order from the Spanish Crown, worked in preparing a new general code to regulate Blacks in the Spanish empire. In preparing the code's draft known since then as *Código Negro Carolino*, the said colonial officials seem to have done an arbitrary selection of some of the old ordinances in which neither their original dates nor many of their original clauses were preserved.[20]

Some content analysis may be done of La Española's ordinances on Blacks of the sixteenth century that can give us at least an overall sense of aspects of the collective behavior of the colony's Black population (and especially, of Black runaway slaves) that were most worrisome to the colonial government officials and the Iberian colonists at large throughout the 1500s. The following is a selection of some of the most salient themes in the Black codes of the colony throughout half a century.

The Repression of Runaway Enslaved Blacks as a Political Priority

Both the 1522 and 1528 laws begin by alerting readers to the need for an immediate re-capturing of runaway slaves then on the loose in La Española to make them return "to the service of their masters." Interestingly, no provisions were included in these surviving colonial codes or fragments of codes of the early Spanish empire about the possibilities of the enslaved Blacks ever accessing freedom, despite the fact that all along the legally and socially sanctioned mechanism of manumission had existed in the territories and jurisdiction of the Castilian Crown since medieval times, including sixteenth-century La Española. These Black codes from La Española in the 1500s were strictly about slavery as a system in place and social life within that system, and when people with free status are cited in the text of the codes, it is always as rare elements whose mentioning is due to their condition as either beneficiaries of slavery or potential collaborators against it, and even in this latter case those mentioned tended to be free Blacks more than free whites: Iberians or people not explicitly labeled as Blacks.

A "Grace Period" for Running Away Conceded to Enslaved?

In the 1522 legislation, promulgated on January 6, just about a week after the 1521 Christmas rebellion, the slaves who were fugitive or in a state of flight at the promulgation of the code were given what seems to have been implicitly a "grace period" of twenty days subsequent to the proclamation of the laws to return to their masters, after which they would be punishable with some kind of physical harm. In the 1528 laws, issued on October 9 of that year, and to be applied from that date onward, the window may have remained the same or been reduced to fifteen days.[21] But when it comes to the punishment, the first set of laws imposed severance of a foot of the slave when captured after twenty days away, while the 1528 laws reduced it to 100 lashes and strapping with an iron ring of twenty pounds for an entire year. In case of an absence of twice as long (forty days), the 1522 laws condemned the slave to death by hanging, while the penalty under the 1528 laws was the severance of a foot, with execution imposed after a third fleeing of fifteen days, unless the slave were to return on his own volition before being captured.[22]

As to slaves who were to run away *after* the date of promulgation of the 1522 laws (January 6), there would be a window of ten days within which the slave could return under no punishment, yet beyond that lapse the punishment would be severance of a foot the first time, and hanging on the second instance, accompanied with some discretionary torture in case the captive runaway was deemed guilty of other crimes.[23]

Local Political Change and Updating of the Slave Laws

Interestingly enough, at the initial exordium-like explanatory part of both the 1522 and 1528 legislations, there is the explicit statement that each had been designed by joint input of the capital's city council's members as well as of the judges of the *Audiencia*, with jurisdiction over the entire colony, and keeping in mind prior ordinances.[24] In the case of the 1522 laws, the earlier ordinances mentioned, or alluded to, have not survived into our time. In the case of the 1528 laws, the prior ordinances—as per all existing evidence—were the 1522 laws. This immediately raises the question of to what extent we should look at La Española's 1528 legislative moment as one of re-adapting or "softening" of the rules by the local colonial elite vis-à-vis a sociopolitical reality among the enslaved that the elite perceived as no longer of the same dangerousness as in early 1522. By 1528, the fleeing of slaves was still being mentioned in government sources of La Española, but no reporting was done of violent uprising similar to that of Christmas of 1521.

Ethnically Based Differential Punishment for Runaways?

The 1528 ordinances incorporated for the first time—to the extent that we can compare to the prior "black code" of 1522—differential types of punishment against runaway enslaved Blacks based on whether they were *bozales* or ladinos, that is, based on whether they were known to have spent less than a year in La Española since their arrival (in which case they were considered *bozales*) or more than a year (when they would be expected to be enculturated enough in Spanish language and Christian religion as to be considered *ladinos*, the same category under which those native to or raised within Spanish culture were labeled).[25]

If *bozal* slaves fled on their own and not following a *ladino* who induced them, the 1528 ordinances state, the time-window for a non-punishable escape will be fifty days. Only when it is for more than fifty days, the same penalties decreed in ordinance 1 of the 1528 code were to apply. Conversely, the other non-*bozal* or *ladino* slaves were given twenty days from the issuing of these ordinances to return to their masters. After that, the penalty when caught would be the severance of a foot, and if captured after an additional twenty days being away, death by hanging.[26] This same differential punishment based on length or degree of enculturation appears again in the third set of ordinances of the next decade and a half (1535–1542 and 1545).[27]

In other words, this concept implied that, for the crime of fleeing the physical confines of enslavement, a less severe punishment—and therefore more tolerance—would be applied to those we may call, from our own contemporary perspective, "recently arrived" slaves, than to the more "seasoned" or creolized or Hispanicized slaves. It was a concept based on the argument that oftentimes the *bozal* escapees ran away not because of having committing a crime, but "because of" ("*por*") or coerced ("*impuestos*") by *ladino* slaves.[28]

Slave-Chasing Police

In both the 1522 and 1528 ordinances, a constable for Black slaves (often under the title of *fiel ejecutor*) is mentioned as an existing post already in place or as a post to be immediately created to lead the pursue of fugitive slaves in the island beyond Santo Domingo City. This official was bestowed with powers to exert vigilance throughout the countryside outside of Santo Domingo city, and to chase and forcefully detain runaway or wandering slaves, and even to judicially try them and punish them once captured, in some cases. Civilians were mandated and expected to follow them at any instance when the *ejecutor* may have needed to draft them on the spot to be part of a fugitive-chasing *cuadrilla* or gang, and penalties were established for those who refused to do so. Aside from the mandatorily drafted civilians, at times we find an entire triad of squads of four men (a total of twelve individuals) established in the laws to work permanently (or for as long as the leading colonial authorities deemed it necessary) in recapturing fugitive slaves and bringing them back to the forced-labor setting of their masters' estate or unit of production.[29]

A Slave-Policing Role or Prescribed Vigilantism for Civilians

Already in the 1522 ordinances, masters in general and overseers of slaves in farms and mines were ordered to denounce the fleeing of their slaves to the *fiel ejecutor* or *ejecutor* or constable-prosecutor of slaves that was about to be appointed in the island as per other provisions contained in this same set of laws, or to any of the other judicial officials of the colony after the tenth day. Violators would pay a fine and the proceeds would be used to finance the cost of enforcement. The *ejecutor* and the justice officials were charged with reporting on the matter to the colony's top authorities and enforcing these ordinances. Masters and their representatives were also mandated to play an active role in chasing and repressing slaves' flight as well.[30] The second and third provisions in the Ramírez Fuenleal ordinances of 1530 include the notion of civilians as covigilant of slaves, being subject to punishment (according to the fifth ordinance) if they are proven to have remained unresponsive to any crime or fault by a slave that they were deemed knowledgeable or witnesses of.[31]

Access to Weapons

Black slaves having access to weapons or utensils that could be used as weapons in La Española was a key theme in the ordinances issued by the colonial authorities during large part of the sixteenth century for the control of the enslaved population. The rebellion of Christmas of 1521 revealed that, given the chance, some slaves were perfectly capable of mounting a deadly uprising against the Spanish colonists, at least in the rural setting, and a number of maroon slave squads were able to generate a great degree of anxiety and fear with their assaults and attacks against settlers in different areas of the island-colony distant from Santo Domingo City, thanks to their use of weapons, even if as simple as sharpened wooden spears. The 1522 laws established that neither "blacks nor slaves" would be allowed to carry "offensive weapons" at any time "within a settlement or on the road," except for a palm-long knife. Violators would be penalized with the loss of the piece and a fine of six pesos of gold or fifty lashes; in a second instance, a foot would be cut off, and a third time, the slave would be auctioned off or a second foot will be cut off.[32] Slaves would have nine days from the date of the ordinances to give up all their weapons except the mentioned knives, otherwise the weapons would be confiscated and weapon-carrying slaves would have a foot cut off.[33] Slave masters and their representatives had three additional days after the first nine days from the date of the announcement of the ordinances to report any violation of this regulation to the executors, and if they did not, they would incur a fine of five *pesos de oro*.[34]

The eighth provision of the 1528 ordinances declared that all Black slaves were forbidden from carrying "offensive weapons," except for butchers and cowboys, who would be allowed to carry a hand-palm's length knife. The penalty for violation of the ordinance would be twelve *pesos* or instead 100 lashes while tied to the city's punishment pole. A second instance would be punished with a foot and hand cut off and a twenty-five-pound piece of iron attached. No Black slave whatsoever would be allowed to carry those weapons at all on Sundays and holidays.[35]

In governor Ramírez de Fuenleal's draft ordinances on Blacks of 1530, all slaves in general were forbidden from carrying any type of weapon beside a pointless knife of no more than a hand-palm in length, with the exception of cowboys when in the countryside working with (or moving from one place to another accompanying) cattle, in which case they could carry a spear or a *desjarretadera*, and cart drivers and *arrieros*, who were allowed to carry a regular dagger (*puñal*) while at work. Violators of the rule were to be punished with 100 lashes at the stake of Santo Domingo City the first time, and with 200 lashes and a hand nailed to the pole for two hours in future occasions (5th ordinance). The Black ordinances of 1543, in provision 17, ordered that no Blacks, either *ladinos* or *bozales*, were to carry weapons or have them at home, unless they were cattle ranchers, muleteers, or cowboys, or if their master had given them permission to do so. The punishment to violators would be the loss of the weapon and a payment of two *pesos*, otherwise 100 lashes and being shackled to a fifteen-pound iron during six months. Those with their master's permission would be allowed to carry a knife with no sharp point.[36]

Larceny

Stealing and robbing by Black slaves were two types of actions also condemned in La Española's Black codes of the 1500s. They are mentioned as factual behaviors incurred by enslaved Blacks in which reportedly free male and female Blacks of the city of Santo Domingo, some either owning or renting their own homes, performed a central role of collaboration. The laws therefore reflect the existence of a wide practice and network of mutual support between free and enslaved Blacks, in confrontation with the established norms and authorities around private property as a fundamental tenet of early colonial society in La Española.

On the other hand, it seems obvious as well that for some reason, as the decades went on during the 1500s, in the eyes of the colonial authorities, more and more the key factor in trying to control this larceny was the fact that the free Blacks of the city reportedly sheltered the robbers, rather than the Blacks who were accused of engaging in the stealing. Simultaneously, the penalties for this assistance given to the stealing seem to have become softer and softer. Altogether it would seem that these laws are indicating a social process in the city where the controls exerted over the Black population were weakening.

As per La Española's 1522 ordinances on Blacks and slaves, a slave proven to have incurred stealing was to be punished in very drastic terms. When convicted a first time for larceny, he would have a foot severed.

If convicted a second time, the punishment was death by hanging.[37] The 1535–1542 and 1545 ordinances on La Española's slaves, in their 9th ordinance, declare that since "many" Blacks wondered around in Santo Domingo City and within two leagues from the town and stole things and then passed the stolen goods on to have them sold in the city, any male or female Black who fed, gave to drink, or hid another "absent" Black in their dwelling or elsewhere would be punished with 200 lashes the first time, and with irons put on both feet the second time.[38] According to ordinance no. 8 of the 1535–1542 and 1545 ordinances on slaves, in Santo Domingo "many free black men and women" violated the existing ordinances by sheltering and hiding in their homes Black male and female slaves as well as Indians who stole "day and night." Thus, it was mandated that those "free blacks" did not host those slaves or their things. Otherwise, they were to be fined three *pesos* of gold the first time, and would be meted 100 lashes the second time, plus being forbidden to do trade in the city.[39]

Black Presence in Two Distinct Demographic Worlds: Rural and Urban

In passing, these sixteenth-century Black codes also provide us a sort of semidistant broad picture of what reveals itself to be an important aspect of the demographically dominant Black population in La Española during the first half of the 1500s: its vigorous, dual presence and living in two rather distinct human and economic environments: a rural setting that was home to the larger segments of the Black population, including a majority integrated by the enslaved individuals toiling in agricultural, livestock-tending, and mining activities; and an urban setting exemplified preeminently by the city of Santo Domingo where another, lesser segment of the Black population, formed by enslaved as well by free individuals, lived and worked as domestic slaves, renting themselves out and participating in restricted but still important ways in some aspects of the commercial economy.[40]

It would seem arguable, considering the traditional dominance, in the existing scholarship on the early colonial Black presence in La Española, of studies frequently focused on the plantation-centered, enslaved Black population, that the sets of ordinances about Black people of the 1500s may function as a firm reminder that the historiographical portrait of this population segment of early colonial La Española will not be complete and adequately balanced until many more studies of the colony's urban Blacks during the period studied here are produced.

Not only do the Black codes of sixteenth-century La Española remind us of this socioeconomic and residential duality of the Black inhabitants of the colony at the time. They also shed light on how interconnected the rural and the urban settings of the south-central region of the island were at the time, and more specifically the large rural hinterland surrounding the City of Santo Domingo, and the city proper itself, for the most part confined by walls. As some of the subsequent sections of this study will indicate, a lot of that interaction was embodied by a Black population that found a way to move back and forth on its own between the city and the most immediate countryside, especially during Sundays and holidays.[41]

Participation in the Market via Salaried Work

Already in La Española's 1522 ordinances on Blacks and slaves, there is open mentioning of some Blacks of Santo Domingo City engaging in salaried work done for people other than their masters in exchange for a portion of the earned salary being paid by the slave to his master or owner. It seems clear that then this hiring out of slaves was only allowed to "vecinos" or denizens of the city with full political rights, but the rule does not seem clear enough since it also indicates that owners of slaves will not be allowed to collect daily proceeds from their slaves.[42]

The 1528 laws on Black slaves plainly admit that in Santo Domingo City "there are many black slaves, mischievous, drunk and robbers who commit many larcenies and excesses, and with their daring encourage the other bad ones." Out of this concern, it was mandated that nobody would be allowed to rent out or have their slaves wander in search for paid work unless they had a license from the city council, after masters paid a deposit, and provided that, in the case of skilled slaves, the master was not expecting the slave to give him or her a daily pay.[43] This admission in a legislative document of the need by some denizens to rely on a specific type of financial arrangement with their slaves that would imply a cash income for the owner, seems to us another expression of what we have described as the broad social dilemma (economic need vs. social violence risk) that slavery represented for settlers and colonists of La Española in these decades of the 1500s.[44]

The theme reappears in the 1535–1542 and 1544 ordinances that stated that in Santo Domingo City "many male and female blacks wander around engaging in different jobs, agreements and contracts for a pay, and they settle with their masters and they [agree] to give them an amount per month or per week or per day, from which many inconveniences stem, especially that they do not acknowledge their masters, nor enter their houses, except only when they go to pay them [the masters] their salaries, from which little by little they [the slaves] keep gaining a kind of freedom," to which the ordinance responds with a total prohibition of this hiring out of the slaves by their masters, apparently except when these slave-master agreements are done under a license from the Santo Domingo city council.[45] This is reiterated in another short set of supplementary ordinances of May 1544.[46]

Participation in the Market via Selling Merchandises

The 1535–1542 and 1544 ordinances are the first ones to explicitly prohibit the engaging by *vecinos* of the city of Santo Domingo in any selling of wine or cloth to slaves, or in any selling or buying whatsoever with slaves altogether.[47] The theme appears more forcefully in the April 1544 ordinances, where it is clearly indicated that both male and female Black slaves are forbidden from selling items on the street except for firewood, water, stones, and soil carried by themselves. This regulation would be reissued shortly thereafter.[48] Regular trade, another ordinance openly declared, was to be left to "free men." Slaves were allowed to sell items made with their own hands (ropes, horse-riding equipment), but only if they sold them to their own masters, "so they do not learn that there may be other [buyer] better than their master, no matter how good he [the other] may be."[49]

Another ordinance reiterated separately the notion of slaves being only permitted to sell to their master, "so they do not learn that there is one better than their master," while adding that the slaves could only sell "countryside items" ("*cosas monteses*") and with the written permission from their masters or overseers. If the slave wanted to sell in Santo Domingo City, they had to have a permit given by the *fiel ejecutor* or other justice officials. From the same entry we learn that in fact there were a number of Blacks that "on holidays and Sundays" were already selling "some things" from countryside estates.[50]

Another set of Santo Domingo's ordinances on Blacks apparently from the same period stated that there were numbers of Black women (presumably free) doing a peddling on the streets that was suspect to be a conduit for goods stolen in areas outside the city by other Blacks of undetermined status, and per this understanding it was then mandated that female Black peddlers could only do the selling during daylight hours.[51]

Along a similar restrictive spirit, in the ordinances issued in April of 1544, it was determined that only three Black men would be allowed to sell all the grass to be sold in Santo Domingo, while two others would be permitted to sell wood at the main square. They could not sell anything else anywhere else. Four Black women were allowed to sell cattle guts at the meat store. Charcoal and water could be sold freely, but Blacks who did could not sell anything else. All these sales could only be done during daylight hours.[52] Sometimes a market or social weakness or challenge within the local colonial society would seem to open the door to some tolerance in the ordinances for some additional slave participation in the most modest ranks of the local economy, like in the case of the May 1544 ordinance that recognized the need for effective distribution of "fruits and vegetables" in Santo Domingo, where there were also "some poor widows and persons of their kind that live on the salary of their female black slaves." In response, the ordinance gave permission for forty female Black slaves to do exclusively the said selling, only at the public squares, during daylight and never engaging in any purchase.[53] The April 9, 1544 ordinances had established in more general terms that no Black was allowed to sell or buy to or from other Blacks or have a store, and that they would only be allowed to sell wood for fuel, grass, water, and coal.[54]

Restraints to Physical Mobility

In the 1522 laws, Blacks and slaves were prohibited from going from one farm to another on holidays, except if accompanied by a supervising person or carrying a license (3v). Slaves were prohibited from getting together in groups in the countryside (3v–4v). Additionally, there was a general prohibition of unshackling somebody else's slaves. Also, whoever unshackled the slave would be responsible for any conduct of the slave (3v). Slaves were mandated to stay within two *leguas* (about four kilometers) of their master's farm or home, unless they carried a written permit from their supervisor (4r). In the 1528 laws on Blacks, it is stated that when La

Española's slaves gathered in farms, sugar estates, and other places, they engaged in "dangerous conversations" that resulted in damages. To avoid such gatherings, these ordinances prohibited slaves to move from one estate to another without their masters or overseers or without written permission from them. The first instance of violation was to be punished with 100 lashes; the second with 200, to be delivered by the masters or persons in charge.

In governor Ramírez de Fuenleal's draft laws of 1530, all Black slaves, except when accompanied by their masters, are forbidden from riding horses, except for cowboy slaves and slaves in charge of oxen who are allowed to do so while within the premises of their job and not away from it. Any Spaniard who witnessed a violation of this norm without intervening or denouncing it to the authorities would be fined, and the accuser was to be rewarded (4th ordinance). As to mobility options in their daily lives, in Ramirez's ordinances slaves were totally prohibited from moving from place to place except when carrying a written permit doing so, which stated the destination and the duration, otherwise the slave could be apprehended and shackled and given to the judicial authorities. If civilians captured a fugitive slave, they would be compensated by the slave owner with payment, while if the slave had caused injury to somebody while on the loose, the owner would be put in jail in accordance with the existing laws. If the slave stopped by night at any place, he had to show the written permit to the person in charge, or otherwise be detained, punished, and incarcerated (6th ordinance).

Ramirez de Fuenleal's draft ordinances also imposed responsibilities of inspection and vigilance by overseers on slaves. Slave quarters (huts or *bohios*) had to be inspected every night by the overseers of each plantation or farm in search of outside slaves hidden by slaves of that plantation, and it was mandated that the outside slaves and their protectors both be delivered to the authorities for punishment, while overseers were to be fined, with one-third of the fine going to any accuser (7th ordinance). No slave was allowed to go from one estate (*ingenio or hacienda*) to another after dark. If the slave was caught doing so, the owner of the visited estate was mandated to immediately punish (or order the punishment of) the slave, notify the slave's owner to pick up the slave, or otherwise pay a fine, of which one-third would go to the accuser if there was one (8th ordinance).

The 1535–1542 and 1544 ordinances established that

> To prevent the wickedness and larceny reportedly committed in the city of Santo Domingo by slaves coming from other locations

on Sundays, Easter and holidays, it was recommended that this traveling be prohibited, except for *arriero* slaves involved in specific tasks ordered by their masters. Also, blacks were forbidden from having dogs at their homes, except if they were cowboys or shepherds and the dog was kept at a rural estate. In case they violated this rule, the ordinances authorized any "Spaniard" to kill their dog at will and the black slave owner and violator of the rule would suffer 50 lashes.[55]

The April 9, 1544, laws included an additional prohibition regarding the mobility of Black female slaves. None of them would be allowed to walk out of the city of Santo Domingo into the countryside to get any type of garden produce or natural item, and if they did, any free person was allowed to detain them and shackle them and would be entitled to be compensated with a payment by the slave's owner.[56] The norm seems to have been a measure to privilege the interest and status of one particular social sector of the free population ("poor widows") against competition by the enslaved Black women. It was mandated that the female Black slaves belonging to poor widows had to be issued a license that they had to carry on their persons, and if they did not, they would be punished with 100 lashes. All of which is clear indication the female Black slaves in Santo Domingo City were at the time actually trying to earn cash in the local market dynamics of the City of Santo Domingo through the selling of agricultural products.

Treatment and Punishment of Slaves by Slaveholders

The 1522 Santo Domingo's ordinances are possibly the earliest source on the use of punishment that went from whipping to severance of limbs to execution (by hanging or "cruel death"), as a central tool of the slavery-based economic and social order they implemented in the colony as they began to develop a plantation-centered economy. Yet the experience of the 1521 slave rebellion must have been also a factor in the degree of harshness the authorities were contemplating as retribution to slave resistance in this particular set of laws. Eight years later, when we know that there were still insurrections by Black slaves, the perception of confrontations by the enslaved may have changed somewhat. According to ordinance 22 of Santo Domingo's 1528 ordinances on Blacks, sometimes "black slaves uprise because of ill treatment, both in terms of what they eat as well as what they drink, as well as due to the excessive unjustified punishment they receive from the persons in charge of them." The ordinance went on to recommend that the new appointed official in charge of prosecuting crime by Black slaves (the *fiel ejecutor*) should look into cases of excessive punishment and determine when penalties or punishments of the slave owners were necessary.[57] Ordinance 23 reiterated the same notion, stating that one of the main bases of the safety and peace of the Black slaves was their treatment, and thus ordered that all masters must provide their slaves with at least pants and a large shirt and a blanket.[58] In the Ramírez de Fuenleal draft ordinances of 1530, the first normative provision listed is a call to the "good treatment" of the slaves by their masters, both in terms of the providing of food and clothing, as well as a condemnation of cruelty in the application of physical punishment as retribution for perceived bad behavior, in the form of beatings and severance of limbs and forms of violence causing permanent physical impairment. This prohibition of punishment in the form of loosely applied torture seems to constitute quite a departure from the harshness mandated in the text of the 1522 laws issued right after La Española's rebellion at Christmas in 1521. In the 1535–1542 and 1545 laws on Black slaves of La Española, ordinance 34 establishes that the captain-pursuer of runaway slaves is mandated to report to the *Audiencia* any cases known of excessive punishment, ill treatment, or undernourishment of slaves by masters, and must momentarily order whatever he deems adequate so they are "well treated." This seems enough reason to imagine that a number of La Española's slave masters at the time were indeed incurring these types of abuse or very similar to it, to the extent that the authorities felt the need to prohibit them explicitly.[59]

In the May 20, 1544, ordinances on Blacks of La Española, the *cepo* or pillory is again cited as the instrument to be used to punish any female Black slave found to be going from Santo Domingo City to the countryside "to collect any item, either wild or farmed."[60]

Yet physical violence exerted on the slaves did not eradicate their resistance in different manners during the sixteenth century in La Española. At some point, the colonists and the Spanish Crown seem to have wondered whether the exercise of punishment beyond a certain point of violence may have actually functioned as a fuel to resistance rather than a deterrent. One of the clearest moments when the slave repression dilemma became evident was in 1545, where we see Crown prince and future emperor Phillip expressing, in written orders sent to the colonial authorities of Santo Domingo, both the will to vigorously punish La Española's Black maroons and yet to deter the colony's slave masters from exerting "excessive" punishment that, in the eyes of the prince, would further encourage slave flight from forced-work sites.

Racialization of Enslaved Africans in the Text of the Ordinances

Another theme worth looking into in the laws on Black people produced by the small governing elite of La Española during the sixteenth century is the racialization of slavery. Usually, this refers to the ways in which the harshest forms of economic, social, and political subordination in colonial social life began to be predominantly or exclusively associated with the Black population of African descent in the Dominican early colonial society, and by extension in the Americas. One way of tracing this socio-racial issue is by following the semantic use of the words *negro* and *slave* in the text of the legislation. In 1991, Dominican historian Raymundo González, referring especially to the eighteenth century, began to point out how in colonial La Española's slavery, free Blacks still suffered social discrimination comparable to that of enslaved Blacks. This perspective on the impact of Dominican slavery was followed and reinstated for the first time in the English language scholarship in 2003[61] by historian Richard Turits, and more explicitly in 2009[62] by referring to the conflating of slavery and African descent in Spanish Santo Domingo before anywhere else in the colonial Americas. Commenting on the observations by Cuban historian Alejandro De la Fuente [63] in 2008 on Cuban laws of the second half of the sixteenth-century concerning Blacks, Turits described how "in Cuba, and still earlier in Spanish Santo Domingo, many modern forms of anti-black racism were consolidated," mentioning Cuban "new regulations and punishments that discriminated against both slaves and free persons of (full or partial) African descent"[64] and promoted (in De la Fuente's words) "the image that blackness was . . . inherently dishonorable."[65]

The title-like heading itself of the manuscript of the Santo Domingo Black code of 1522 already includes a racial generalization, "Copy of the ordinances on blacks," and the paragraph introducing the text of the existing copy refers to these laws as "ordinances related to the remedy and punishment of the blacks of this Española island."[66] Sometimes in these ordinances Blacks and slaves appear to be mentioned as differentiated groups, but the merging of race and status appears reiterated, for instance, when stating that "harsher" regulations were needed so that "the said Blacks and slaves be very coerced and controlled and had no forces or way to be able to uprise and coalesce."[67] Referring to the 1521 rebellion, the prelude to the laws states that "it has occurred that the Blacks and slaves that there are in this said island, without any fear and with devilish thoughts" had rebelled (fo. 1v, 23) and refers to the uprising as "the said uprising of the said Blacks" (fo. 1v, 24). Both "Blacks" and "slaves" are mentioned as different categories in the provision forbidding their carrying of "offensive weapons," either when in villages or roads, and even if accompanied by their masters.[68] A number of other diverse prohibitions contained in the ordinances explicitly refer to "Blacks and slaves" (ordinance VI, v, 25). Yet in a number of ordinances, we see an identification of Black and slave (ordinance X, fo. 4r, 26; XVI, fo. 6r, 27; XIX, fo. 7r, 28; XXII, fo. 7v, 28; XXII, fo. 7v, 29).

Like in the case of the 1522 Black code, the Santo Domingo 1528 ordinances "for the peace and security of the black slaves" (Utrera, *Historia: Militar de Santo Domingo*, vol. I, 202) also mention Blacks and slaves as different people and enslaved Blacks sometimes as "black slaves," sometimes as just "slaves," and sometimes just as "blacks," which again, seems to indicate an ideological association, in the minds of some or many Spanish settlers, of Blackness as a racial feature and enslavement as a social condition or status. It refers to "the fleeing by the blacks and slaves" (203–5; 207–9).

The draft of ordinances on Black slaves prepared around 1530 by La Española's Bishop-Governor Sebastián Ramírez de Fuenleal show multiple instances of this same overlapping of the notions of enslaved and Black. From the title at the top of the surviving manuscript, "Hordenanças de la horden que se a de tener en el tratamiento con los negros," it is clear that the general collective notion of "negros" (Blacks) is used to refer specifically to the enslaved Blacks[69] (ordinances 1 and 3–7). A racial differentiation with very specific consequences seems to be alluded to in ordinance 9, when it comes to the punishment recommended for "any slave or free black or whatever other person" accused of "hiding or holding at [their] homes male or female blacks that are running away from their masters," implicitly identifying or correlating once again Blacks as slaves. Punishment of 200 lashes is prescribed for the culprits if they are "captives" ("*cautivo*"), and half of the said amount in case they are "a male or female black or a male or female Indian," but no such physical torment whatsoever is mentioned or contemplated for the accused if he or she happened to be a "whatever other" or a white person. Finally, as to racial contents of these laws, it is also interesting that in recommending a functional structure of social control in the production units of La Española worked by slaves, ordinance 2 prescribes a clearly racially segmented hierarchy, ordering that in "any estates holding black slaves or Indians in their service, they are to have a white man as overseer or foreman." "All the blacks" ("*todos los negros*"), goes on to say ordinance 3, "do that which their masters impose on them" ("aquello en que sus amos les ynponen, eso hazen").

In the 1535–1542 and 1545 ordinances, there is ample use of the term "negro" with an evident meaning equivalent to "slave" from the first ordinance, which refers to the flight and crimes committed by "blacks, white and berberisco slaves," as if Blacks were understood to be slaves by definition. This may be an indication of an increased racialization of slavery as decades went by in sixteenth-century La Española (see, for instance, ordinances 7–9, 17, 22, 23, and 25).[70] The same thing happened in the "Ordinances that the City Council Submitted to the Audiencia," another one of the loose fragments of Black codes of the period, where ordinances 3, 4, 5, and 11 also use the terms "negro" and "negra" clearly to refer to an enslaved Black man or woman.[71]

On the Ordinances of April 9, 1544, promulgated on May 22, 1544, and of May 20, 1544, respectively, the words "negros" and "negras" are used to describe enslaved Black men and women, a meaning we can infer when in the same text they are referred to explicitly as, for instance, "male blacks belonging to the persons that the city may appoint" ("negros de las personas que la ciudad nombrare")[72] and "female blacks of poor and in-need widows" ("negras [. . .] de viudas pobres y necesitadas").[73]

Religious Indoctrination and Enculturation

The religious indoctrination of enslaved Africans was a concern of the Spanish Crown that was frequently mentioned in decrees and orders coming from the royal court in Spain to Santo Domingo during the 1500s. There were complaints about lack of attention by slaveholders to the provision of dedicated physical space and ritual utensils for the catechization of those in bondage in the documents issued by authorities, but these religious concerns do not seem to have ever triggered any drastic penalization for noncompliance in La Española. On the other hand, the Christianization of enslaved Africans in La Española during the sixteenth century seems to have generated locally a political dilemma for the colonization-enslavement imperial project similar to the exploitation-maintenance one posed by the intensive slavery system associated to the sugar-plantation economy. Catholic indoctrination and Spanish enculturation meant that *bozal* slaves would become *ladino* slaves. There is evidence that at least the promotion of marriage as a Christian ritual and status among the slaves led them to envision and demand what was a radical scenario: deserving and gaining freedom as a result of becoming Christian. This was an option that the Crown explicitly discarded, reaffirming and enforcing the legal and spiritual validity of being enslaved while Christian, that is, of a type of Christianization that did not entail freedom.

In the 1522 ordinances, the predominant thought about La Española's free Blacks and enslaved Blacks in relation to Christianity seems to have been that Blacks as non-Christians did not respect Christianity and represented a threat to the Christian Spanish settlers, who defined them as people "with devilish thoughts" who despised Christians and had "little fear of God" (1v).[74] And there was practically no mention whatsoever throughout the entire body of the 1528 ordinances about religion or their catechization as Christians, the focus being almost totally on the prevention and repression of slaves' flight and the implementation and financing of dedicated police squads to chase them.[75] And as it has been mentioned before, the ordinances of 1530 gave considerable attention to the catechization of enslaved Black Africans on its second prescription.

According to these ordinances, during the first six months of purchase, the masters will be obliged to teach the Spanish "vulgar" language to the slaves, as well as to baptize them and teach them the Christian doctrine. This because "all Blacks are by their own inclination friendly to becoming Christians and easy to convert," and even take pride in being Christians, so that many slaves are "good Christians and very devout and virtuous" (3rd ordinance). After the first six months of each slave being under the power of the master, if the master does not show evidence of having complied with this, a first fine of one-fourth of the value of the salve will be applied against him, another one of one-half of the value after the second instance, and the full value of the slave after the third term of noncompliance, with any accuser to receive one-third of the respective fine. If a slave is sold or bought before these obligations are met, both seller and buyer will be fined the said penalties (3rd ordinance). As to the ordinances on Blacks during the rest of the 1530s and the 1540s, issued in La Española, only the ordinances of 1535–1544 devote an extremely brief mention of the matter of catechization in ordinance 36, where it mandates the constable for Blacks to do what he can so the slaves "be instructed in the things of the faith."[76]

Solidarity with Fugitive Slaves as Social Resistance against Slavery

The fact that many of the slave codes issued in La Española throughout the first half of the 1500s contain provisions against both enslaved as well as nonenslaved individuals assisting fugitive slaves by providing them shelter, nourishment, alerts about constables pursuing them, help in getting rid of shackles, and other forms of aid seems a clear indication that these behaviors of support for Black people who were in violation of the colonial slavery laws were either (1) a social reality of La Española, (2) a suspected reality, or (3) an occurrence possible enough, in the minds of the colonial authorities, for the latter to try to prevent it with the type of retribution spelled out in the laws. It could be argued, though, that the reiteration of the same or very similar prohibitions in this regard in different subsequent ordinances throughout the decades, often accompanied in the text of the ordinances by statements pointing out or claiming that those assistive behaviors were a fact, seem to be evidence that the former was often the case.

Thus, rather than enumerating the ways in which practically all the existing Black codes of La Española of the 1500s describe, once and again, the same or very similar acts of collaboration with the runaway slaves, it may be more appropriate to point out some details that reveal particularly meaningful aspects of these actions. One would be the fact that at least for the urban setting of Santo Domingo in the 1530s and 1540s (as the 1535–1542 and 1545 ordinances point out), the hosting and hiding of stray slaves by other slaves is mentioned as the main source of slaves running away or marooning. This would seem to pinpoint a Black-to-Black solidarity as the backbone of this basic form of resistance against enslavement.[77]

These Black codes also considered that at least during some junctures of the period studied here, the social collaboration with the fugitive slaves of La Española (such as providing them refuge or alerts against the proximity of constables in their pursuit) could have happened across social class or status lines, as in the case of masters and overseers assisting slaves on the run, a collaboration explicitly prohibited by the 1522 ordinances.[78] In other instances, aside from this cross-class cooperation, the text of the laws points at a cross-ethnic one, such as the entry in the 1528 ordinances on Blacks that states any Spaniard who unshackles, unties, or lets lose any slave who is not his own will pay a fine and even get a flogging (this being the only case of physical punishment we have seen in all the ordinances contemplated for a European).[79] The assistance given to fugitive Black slaves occurred as well across gender lines and across territorial lines. On some occasions, the ordinances warn that either men or women helping runaways will be punished. On others, the text of the laws mentions slaves residing in the countryside being helped by individuals in urban settings such as Santo Domingo.

Conclusion

The ordinances or legal codes issued in La Española during the sixteenth century for the control of the enslaved Blacks deserve to be carefully studied. They are a window into what the Spanish colonists' official political mentality, expectations, and norms in regard to the enslaved Black population of the colony were, as well as into how the colony's Blacks responded to those norms and, implicitly, what they thought about them. In this essay, an effort has been made to highlight how these ordinances convey the ways in which the colonial authorities tried to control the enslaved Black population (and to some extent, Blacks in general) in La Española. It also shows some of the actions of resistance against, and challenges to, the colonial laws that the enslaved Blacks of this colony seem to have engaged in during this period.

After conducting a preliminary analysis of all the specific legal codes, sections, and fragments of codes on slaves from sixteenth-century La Española that have made it into our times, one purpose appears, pervasively and dominantly, in these legal texts. It is the repressive function of these laws, their deliberate aim of controlling and repressing the actions of and any imaginable resistance by the Black population of the colony. These laws were not only about the enslaved Black people of La Española, but also about the free Blacks. This author would argue that they also referred to non-Blacks, to the extent that, at any point, any of them may have felt inclined or tempted to engage in what the colonial authorities would have considered a form of collaboration with the resistance by the enslaved Black population. Out of twenty-seven law provisions we identified among the surviving pieces of ordinances designed to limit any potential freedom of the enslaved population, ten were specifically devoted to the chasing and the physical restraining of the slaves.

In sum, La Española's Black codes of the sixteenth century, beginning as early as 1522, seem to have been guided by a dominant intent to increase the physical and political control exerted over a Black population (enslaved and free) in general that was perceived as dangerous. This subjection was to be achieved by: severely restricting the freedom of movement of the Black population and the opportunities for group gathering and socializing of Blacks; a policing system to repress the fleeing of slaves via pursuit, capture, and punishment, including dismemberment and execution; designating several dedicated judicial officials to watch over the Black population; establishing a policing information system about slaves' escapes by mandating slave owners and overseers to report such escapes; forcing the Black population to stay indoors by night; encouraging the civilian population to act as vigilantes vis-à-vis the enslaved Black population; keeping a register of existing slaves within the colony to prevent the access to "offensive weapons" by Black people; limiting slaves' participation in the local market as merchants competing with the established free merchants; fine-tuning a differential-control strategy vis-à-vis the Black *ladino* and Black *bozal* population; preventing the communication among slaves and between slaves and nonslaves; and suppressing opportunities for solidarity or collaboration among slaves and between slaves and free people, by punishing any instances of assistance to and solidarity with fugitive slaves by either other slaves or free population. The legislation also mandated the devising of the material means to achieve the control and order sought, by establishing a local tax to be paid by slave owners to fund the chasing of fugitive slaves; and creating a separate coffer with its own accounting books to save and manage the fines collected from violators of the ordinance. In a few instances the wording of the legislation shows an intent of controlling and discouraging the "mistreatment" and abuse against enslaved Blacks by masters and overseers, but if we are to judge by the minimal attention given to the subject, it does not seem to have been a priority for those who promulgated these laws.

After the discussion in this chapter of these legal texts, it continues to seem evident that there is a need to further explore them—as well the entire array of judicial, fiscal, commercial, entrepreneurial, notarial, and more personal documents from sixteenth-century La Española that have made it into the surviving archives, regardless of how scant they may be in some cases. This broader diversity of sources provides us with more numerous sets of data with which to learn about and understand the lives of the enslaved Black people of La Española in the 1500s.

Notes

1. I am consciously vindicating here the title and inspiration of Silvio Torres-Saillant's *Introduction to Dominican Blackness*, the 1994 path-breaking seminal essay that called the attention of the English language scholarship to the need to reassess the role and the long-term impact of the Afro-Dominican cultural legacy that began in La Española in the 1490s.

2. *First Blacks in the Americas*, New York: CUNY Dominican Studies, doc. no. 071. Accessed on September 28, 2022 at http://firstblacks.org/en/manuscripts/fb-primary-071-manuscript/transcription/.

3. For a relatively recent update on the demographic estimates on sixteenth-century La Española, see Anthony Stevens-Acevedo, *Juan Rodriguez and the Beginnings of New York City*, New York: CUNY Dominican Studies Institute, 2013, graph. 1, 65.

4. David Wheat: *Atlantic Africa and the Spanish Caribbean, 1570–1640*. Chapel Hill: University of North Carolina Press, and Williamsburg: Omohundro Institute of Early American History and Culture, 2016.

5. Several versions of these ordinances have been preserved in more or less extensive, excerpted, or extracted fashions in the Archivo General de Indias in Seville, Archivo Histórico Nacional in Madrid, and Archivo Nacional de Cuba in Havana, most of them as copies made in the late eighteenth century. Not all of the versions have been published. For a complete list of the ordinances, see the "Works Cited" section of this essay.

6. I have used the notion of "Black code" or "Black laws" or "slave laws" throughout this chapter in a predominantly functional manner, rather than guided by any technical definition that jurists or lawyers may use in their profession. The implicit notion I have used here is that of a textually (and sometimes physically) subsequent group or series of laws addressing one common item, in this case the lives of Black people, mostly enslaved but sometimes including freed and free people as well. It is a "lato sensu" way of using the term ultimately focusing on the intention and the target population of those laws more than anything else.

7. For a rather comprehensive listing of the studies produced by English language scholars (and Dominican scholars) on the early colonial Black population of La Española, see Anthony Stevens-Acevedo, *The Santo Domingo Slave Revolt of 1521 and the Slave Laws of 1522* (2019), 66n27. As to scholarship published

in English, it was practically only after the pioneering 1998 doctoral dissertation by Lynne Guitar about Indians, Africans, and Spaniards in La Española during the first half of the 1500s, that scholars, mostly US-based, have begun to mention or comment on slavery, or some aspects of it, in La Española during the early colonial period in general (Richard Turits, 2003; Laurent Dubois and Richard Turits, 2019; and to a lesser degree Ida Altman and Thiago Krause, 2020 as well as Alex Borucki, David Eltis, and David Wheat, 2020), and more particularly on sixteenth-century slavery in that colony (Ida Altman, 2007, 2012, 2017, 2018, and especially 2013; Alejandro de la Fuente García, 2008; Erin Stone, 2013 and 2017; Lissette Acosta-Corniel, 2015 and 2016; David Wheat, 2016; Ana Ozuna, 2018; Robert Schwaller, 2018; Gabriel Avilez Rocha, 2018; Ida Altman and David Wheat, 2019; Marc Eagle, 2019; Richard Turits, 2019; and Marc Eagle and David Wheat, 2020. Of these works, it is probably Wheat's 2016 regional monograph highlighting the role of the Black population as surrogate colonizers of the Spanish Empire in the Caribbean the one that contributes the widest analytical considerations for La Española's case. Yet it is probably the online platform *First Blacks in the Americas* (2016) that offers the most diverse set of new data about the lives of Black folk in La Española at the time, both through all the archival sources included in the platform as well as the thematic summaries and contextual commentary that accompany them.

    8. This chapter is part of a larger, long-term research project about the overall social world of sixteenth-century La Española and, more specifically, the social world of the early-colonial sugar plantation economy of Santo Domingo.

    9. Dates are firmly indicated for the ordinances of 1528 and 1544. In the case of the laws reportedly issued in the years of 1535, 1542, and 1545 (with dates only indicated in a general heading, but not in the body of each ordinance or fragment of ordinance), we will assume that the textual sequencing in the manuscripts corresponds at least to the chronological order mentioned.

    10. There is a potent deposition on regular slave flight from La Española's plantations, for instance, in a declaration by the royal accountant of Santo Domingo's colonial treasury office Pedro Serrano in the 1570s. See "Pleito Fuenmayor-Torres," ca. 1570, AGI, Justicia 24-A, f. 799v–f. 800v. As to black slaves in that colony claiming freedom as a supposed by-product of entering Christian marriage as promoted by their masters, see a royal order from King Charles V of June 28, 1527, Archivo General de Indias, Indiferente, 421, L.12, f. 151r–152r.

    In relation to the use by enslaved blacks of appeals to delay probable lethal sentencing, there is a 1537 decree from Emperor Charles V where the king ordered the Santo Domingo *Audiencia* to assume the role of appeals court in these cases. By taking charge of the review of the appeals of its own sentences done as a court of first instance, the *Audiencia* would impede the use of the appeals as a delay tactic by slave defendants. See Archivo General de Indias, Santo Domingo, 868,

L.1, f. 14v–15r. See also, *First Blacks in the Americas*'s document no. 029 (http://firstblacks.org/en/manuscripts/fb-primary-029-manuscript/translation/).

11. De la Fuente García, Alejandro, *Havana and the Atlantic in the Sixteenth Century*, 280–85. I appreciate the recommendation by a blind reviewer of this essay to check sources like *Actas Capitulares del Ayuntamiento de La Habana*, edited in four volumes by Emilio Roig between 1937 and 1946, as well as *Historia documental de Puerto Rico, Vol. 1, El concejo o cabildo de la ciudad de San Juan de Puerto Rico (1527–1550)*, compiled by Vicente Murga (1956), and possible similar compilations about Cartagena de Indias, Caracas or other early colonial towns in the Spanish-dominated Caribbean territories. Yet aside from the fact that such a scope of coverage was not part of the original plan for this essay, the suggestion arrived at a time when the COVID-19 pandemic had restricted the capacities of this author considerably. As a result, we were only able to consult the volumes published by Roig. They clearly show that there were orders issued by Havana municipal colonial authorities about the enslaved Black population of the town as part of their ordinary regulatory practices, but no evidence is shown in this source as to the issuing of any set or body of ordinances resembling a code and focusing on that population. The closest thing to a Cuban Black code that we know of for the 1500s is of a later date; the series of orders included in the "Ordenanzas Municipales de la Habana" of 1574, written in Cuba by La Española's Audiencia oidor Alonso de Cáceres (Altamira et al. 1951), a set of regulatory provisions that almost inevitably reminds us of the Santo Domingo codes issued throughout the first half of the century, especially when we consider that their author had been exposed to La Española's social setting that produced those codes to begin with. Coincidentally, well after this essay has entered the final editorial revisions phase, a new interesting publication appeared, *La vida cotidiana de los esclavos en la Castilla del Renacimiento* by Raúl González Arévalo (2022), that uses Medieval and Early Modern Spanish legislation as a source to study the lives of the enslaved Black population in Iberia during those periods. It includes a few pages on the early colonial Spanish ordinances issued in the Americas, apparently almost totally based on previously published comments by Manuel Lucena Salmoral (1996).

12. The laws of 1522, promulgated after the 1521 slave rebellion, were inclusive of the white enslaved population that may have existed in the island.

13. The *Código Negro Carolino* draft text contains a rather extensive and organized code proposed to regulate the Blacks of La Española of the 1780s, and it constitutes a great source for the study of the status of the Black population in the late Dominican eighteenth century, but in this essay we are focusing only on the part of the materials pertaining to the 1500s that appear attached to the *Código*. In Dominican historiography, the most commonly known edition of this code is probably that of Javier Malagón Barceló, ed., *Código Negro Carolino o Código Negro Español* (Santo Domingo, 1784).

African Slavery and Laws in La Española | 131

14. The laws of 1522 were first published by Carlos Esteban Deive in 1989, as an appendix to his book *Tangomangos: Contrabando y piratería en Santo Domingo, 1522-1606*. Subsequently, historian Manuel Lucena Salmoral also published a transcription of these laws in his 1996 volume *Los códigos negros de la América Española*, but with some important transcription flaws. The source for the archival manuscript is Archivo General de Indias (AGI), Patronato 295, no. 104, fos. 1r-8v. For a line-by-line paleographic transcription of these ordinances, see Anthony Stevens-Acevedo *The Santo Domingo Slave Revolt of 1521 and the Slave Laws of 1522*.

15. First published by Cipriano de Utrera in his *Historia Militar de Santo Domingo*, vol. 1, 1947, 202-10. The archival source used by Utrera was AGI, Santo Domingo, 1034. In 1951, historian Vetilio Alfau Durán, under the title "Ordenanzas para el gobierno de los negros de la Isla Española," published an additional version of these ordinances held at Biblioteca Nacional de Madrid, Mss. no. 8,734.

16. "Ordenanzas: buen tratamiento de negros para su conservación," AGI, Patronato, 171, N. 2, R.10. First published in *Colección de documentos inéditos*, Tomo XI, 82-90. However, the publication only included a general source reference to AGI, with no indication of *legajo* or bundle number.

17. For some reason that we do not know yet, there is no evidence that the draft was ever promulgated in La Española, or of why that was the case, though the existence of a partial copy at AGI is a likely proof that at least it arrived at the metropolitan court's circuits.

18. Cipriano de Utrera was as well the first scholar to publish these 1530s and 1540s ordinances on Blacks of La Española, inserted in his 1947 *Historia Militar de Santo Domingo*, vol. I, 211-20.

19. A compilation of old ordinances and segments of ordinances on Blacks from La Española in the 1500s was done by Audiencia officials of the colony in the 1760s, and they all seem to have survived as part of a new draft of a Black code prepared by these authorities under the title of *Código Negro Carolino*. Four different manuscript versions, some more succinct than others, have made it into our time, three at Archivo General de Indias (Santo Domingo, 1034; Santo Domingo, 49; Estado, 7, N. 3), one at Biblioteca Nacional de España (Manuscrito 8734-2) and another at Archivo Nacional de Cuba (Documento Secreto 243). For a complete bibliographic reference to these archival sources, see the "Works Cited" section of this essay.

20. To simplify the referencing throughout this chapter to this entire set of ordinances on Black slaves produced from 1522 to 1545, and to avoid the repetition of their lengthy titles, hereafter in these endnotes they will be identified as "1522 Laws," "1528 Laws," "1535, 1542, 1545 Laws," "April 1544 Laws," and "May 1544 Laws." The draft ordinances prepared by Bishop-Governor Ramírez de Fuenleal will be identified as "1530 Laws." Except for the 1522 ordinances issued by Diego Colón and the draft ordinances prepared by Governor Ramírez

de Fuenleal around 1530, which are referenced to their first published editions by Deive (1989) and Torres de Mendoza (1869), respectively, the citation of all the others will be based on their earliest edition and publication by Cipriano de Utrera, in his *Historia Militar de Santo Domingo* of 1947. Utrera's edition poses a number of problems, like the fact that the texts of the different ordinances are interspersed with texts of other documents thematically related to La Española's enslaved Blacks of the first part of the sixteenth century. Yet at the same time, the ordinances transcribed and published by Utrera in 1947 are the only ones for which there is a readily accessible original archival manuscript, preserved at Archivo General de Indias under the archival call number "Santo Domingo, 1034."

21. The text of the 1528 laws seems ambiguous on the matter, indicating first that slaves are given fifteen days to return without punishment—in case they did not commit any other crime while away—but then warning that "for the second time that they are absent for twenty days," once captured, they will get a foot cut off. Utrera 1947, 202.

22. This provision seems to imply that the authorities issuing this set of laws contemplated the possibility of a slave who had suffered the amputation of a foot still being capable of running away again even with such a condition or handicap.

23. 1522 Laws, ordinance 1, fo. 2v. Stevens-Acevedo 2019, 37.

24. 1522 Laws, ordinance 1, fo. 1r-1v. Stevens-Acevedo 2019, 31, 33; 1528 Laws, §1. Utrera 1947, 202.

25. For the differences between *ladinos* and *bozales*, see an essay on the topic in *First Blacks in the Americas*, http://firstblacks.org/en/summaries/arrival-02-ladinos-and-bozales/.

26. 1528 Laws, §4. Utrera 1947, 203.

27. 1535-1542 and 1545 Laws. ordinance 5. Utrera 1947, 211-12.

28. 1528 Laws, ordinance 2. Utrera 1947 2023.

29. 1522 Laws, ordinance 2, fo. 2v. Stevens-Acevedo 2019, 37; 1528 Laws, §7. Utrera 1947: 203-4.

30. 1522 Laws, ordinance 2, fo. 2v, and Ordinance 9, fo. 4r. Stevens-Acevedo 2019, 37.

31. 1535-1542 and 1545 Laws, ordinances 2 and 3, Torres de Mendoza 1869, 83-84.

32. 1522 Laws, fo. 3r. Stevens-Acevedo 2019, 39.

33. 1522 Laws, fo. 3r. Stevens-Acevedo 2019, 39.

34. 1522 Laws, fo. 3v. Stevens-Acevedo 2019, 41.

35. 1528 Laws, ordinance 8. Utrera 1947, 204.

36. 1535, 42 and 45 Laws. Utrera 1947, 263.

37. 1522 Laws, fo. 2v. Stevens-Acevedo 2019, 37.

38. 1535-1542 and 1545 Laws, ordinance 9. Utrera 1947, 212.

39. 1535-1542 and 1545 Laws. Utrera 1947, 216.

40. This perception coincides with David Wheat's relatively recent call of attention to, and reassessment of the dimension and role of the social presence of Blacks in the early colonial Spanish Caribbean (Wheat 2016, 14, 18).

41. -1542 and 1545 Laws, ordinance 8. Utrera 1947, 216.

42. Laws, ordinance 9, fo. 4r. Stevens-Acevedo 2019, 43. This collection of a daily fee by the slave owners is described in the ordinance as something of "great damage" ("mucho perjuizio"), but no explanation is given as to how that was the case. We do not know whether it was perceived as an undesirable practice because too many *vecinos* were doing it and in the process allowing too many slaves to wander around with some degree of freedom that the authorities saw as inconvenient, or whether there was any other reason for the concern on the part of government officials.

43. 1528 ordinances, ordinance 12. Utrera 1947, 205. The ordinance talks about "*jornales y alquileres*" (daily pay and rent) as the forms of compensation that was used to pay these rented-out slaves. As to why the daily pay mechanism would implicitly be allowed to a nonskilled enslaved worker, at this point we do not have an explanation for, lest we are not grasping correctly the grammar of the manuscript.

44. Stevens-Acevedo 2019, 12.

45. 1535–1543 and 1545 Laws, ordinance 3. Utrera 1947, 215–16.

46. May 20, 1544 Laws, ordinance 3. Utrera 1947, 219.

47. 1535, 1542 and 1545 Laws, ordinance 21. Utrera 1947, 213.

48. April 9, 1544 Laws, ordinance 1. Utrera 1947, 217.

49. 1535–1543 and 1545 Laws, ordinance 4. Utrera 1947: 216.

50. 1535–1543 and 1545 Laws, ordinance 5. Utrera 1947: 216.

51. 1535, 1542 and 1545 Laws, ordinance 2. Utrera 1947, 215.

52. April 9, 1544 Laws, ordinance 5. Utrera 1947, 218.

53. May 20, 1544 Laws. Utrera 1947, 219.

54. April 9, 1544 Laws, ordinance 1. Utrera 1947, 217.

55. 1535, 1542 and 1545 Laws, ordinance 11. Utrera 1947, 216.

56. May 20, 1544 Laws, ordinance 1. Utrera 1947, 219.

57. 1528 Laws, ordinance 22. Utrera 1947, 207.

58. 1528 Laws, ordinance 23. Utrera 1947, 208.

59. 1535–1542 and 1545 Laws. Utrera 1947, 215.

60. May 20, 1544 Laws. Utrera 1947, 219.

61. Richard L. Turits, *Foundations of Despotism*, 32–34 and 47–48.

62. Richard L. Turits, Review of *Havana and the Atlantic in the Sixteenth Century*, 684–85.

63. De la Fuente García, Alejandro. *Havana and the Atlantic in the Sixteenth Century*, 180.

64. Richard L. Turits, Review of *Havana and the Atlantic in the Sixteenth Century*, 685. In a new publication of 2019 by Turits and Laurent Dubois, *Freedom*

Roots: Histories from the Caribbean, 53–54, Turits's observation on the colonial beginnings of the racialization of slavery in Santo Domingo has been expanded to the entire Caribbean region as the locale of its origin.

65. De la Fuente García, Alejandro. *Havana and the Atlantic in the Sixteenth Century*, 180.

66. "Traslado de las ordenansas de los Negros," Archivo General de Indias, Patronato, 295, Número 104, fo. 1r.

67. For an English translation of the 1522 laws, see Stevens-Acevedo 2019, 23–29.

68. "Copy of the ordinances on Blacks," fo. 3r. Stevens-Acevedo 2019, 25.

69. "Ordenanzas: buen tratamiento," 82–83, 83–86.

70. Utrera 1947, 212–14.

71. Utrera 1947, 215–17.

72. May 22, 1544 Laws, fo. 1v. Utrera 1947, 217–18.

73. May 20, 1544 Laws. Utrera 1947, 219.

74. 1522 Laws, fo. 1v. Stevens-Acevedo 2019: 33.

75. 1528 Laws.

76. 1535–1542 and 1545, ordinance 34. Utrera 1947, 215.

77. 1535–1542 and 1545 Laws, ordinance 8. Utrera 1947, 216. April 9, 1544 Laws. Utrera 1947: 217.

78. 1522 Laws, ordinance XIV, fo. 5v. Stevens-Acevedo 2019, 49.

79. 1528 Laws.

Bibliography

Archival Sources

Archivo General de Indias, Justicia, 24-A.

Archivo General de Indias, Indiferente, 421, L.12.

Archivo General de Indias, Patronato 171, Número 2, Ramo 10. PARES, Portal de Archivos Españoles S.41091.AGI/29.7.10.2//PATRONATO,171, N. 2, R.10, n.d.

Archivo General de Indias, Santo Domingo, 868, L.1.

"Extractos de Ordenanzas formadas para sosiego y seguridad de los esclavos negros de la Isla Española, aprovadas en 12 de Octubre de 1528, 1535, 42 y 45, (Estas tres épocas solo constan por enunciativa del Fiscal, fol. 73 del Testimonio en que se hallan) 29 de Abril de 1544, 22 de Mayo del mismo año, Confirmadas por el Consejo de Yndias en 22 de Septiembre de 1547, y de otras formadas por el Cabildo Secular de aquella Ysla, y pressentadas a la Audiencia en 27 de abril de 1768." In *Papeles referentes a los esclavos negros en América*, Biblioteca Nacional de España, Manuscrito 8734, Biblioteca Digital Hispánica.

"Extracto de Ordenanzas formadas para el sosiego y seguridad de los Esclabos Negros de la Ysla Española, aprobadas en 12 de Octubre de 1528, 1535, 42 y 45, (Estas tres Épocas solo constan por enunciativa del Fiscal, fol. 73 del Testimonio en que se hallan) 29 de Abril de 1544, y 22 de Mayo del mismo año, confirmadas por el Consejo de Yndias en 22 de Septiembre de 1547; y de otras formadas por el Cabildo Secular de aquella Ysla y presentadas a la Audiencia en 27 de Abril de 1768." Archivo General de Indias—Estado, 7, N.3. PARES—Portal de Archivos Españoles, ES.41091. AGI/21/ESTADO, 7, N.3.

"Ordenanzas Municipales de la Habana y de los demás pueblos de la Isla de Cuba por el oidor D. Alonso de Cáceres," Archivo General de Indias, Santo domingo, 117. In Rafael Altamira y Crevea, Manuel Carrera Stampa, Francisco Dominguez y Compañy, Agustín Millares Carlo, and Erwin Walter Palm, *Contribuciones a la Historia Municipal de América*, 76–107.

"Testimonio de las ordenanças antiguas de la Ciudad de Santo Domingo de la Ysla Española." Archivo General de Indias, Santo Domingo 1034, fos. 25v–47r.

Torres de Mendoza, Luis (ed.). "Ordenanzas: buen tratamiento de negros para su conservación." *Colección de documentos inéditos, relativos al descubrimiento, conquista y organización de las antiguas posesiones españolas sacados de los archivos del reino, y muy especialmente del de Indias*, Tomo XI. Madrid, Spain: Imprenta de J. M. Pérez, 1869, 82–90.

"Virrey de Indias: ordenanzas sobre los negros y sus amos" [1522]. Archivo General de Indias, Patronato 295, Número 104—PARES, Portal de Archivos Españoles ES.41091.AGI/29.4.2//PATRONATO, 295, N.104.

GENERAL SOURCES

Alfau Durán, Vetilio. "Ordenanzas para el gobierno de los negros de la Isla Española." *Anales de la Universidad de Santo Domingo* 16, no. 57–60 (1951).

Deive, Carlos Esteban. *Tangomangos: contrabando y piratería en Santo Domingo, 1522–1606*. Santo Domingo, Dominican Republic: Fundación Cultural Dominicana, 1996.

De la Fuente, Alejandro, with the collaboration of César García del Pino and Bernardo Iglesias Delgado. *Havana and the Atlantic in the Sixteenth Century*. Chapel Hill: University of North Carolina Press, 2008.

Lucena Salmoral, Manuel. *Los códigos negros de la América Española*. Madrid, Spain: Ediciones UNESCO and Universidad de Alcalá, 1996.

Malagón Barceló, Javier. *Código Negro Carolino o Código Negro Español* (Santo Domingo, 1784). Santo Domingo, Dominican Republic: Ediciones de Taller, 1974.

Stevens-Acevedo, Anthony. *The Santo Domingo Slave Revolt of 1521 and the Slave Laws of 1522: Black Slavery and Black Resistance in the Early Colonial Americas*. New York: CUNY Dominican Studies Institute, 2019.

Torres-Saillant, Silvio. *Introduction to Dominican Blackness*. 2nd ed. New York: CUNY Dominican Studies Institute, (1994) 2010.

Torres de Mendoza, Luis (ed.). "Ordenanzas sobre el buen tratamiento que se debe dar a los negros para su conservación." *Colección de documentos inéditos relativos al descubrimiento, conquista y organización de las antiguas posesiones españolas.* Tomo XI. Madrid, Spain: Imprenta J. M. Pérez, 1869.

Turits, Richard Lee. "Freedom in *el Monte*. From Slaves to Independent Peasants in Colonial Santo Domingo." *Foundations of Despotism. Peasants, the Trujillo Regime, and Modernity in Dominican History.* Stanford, CA: Stanford University Press, 2003.

Turits, Richard Lee. "Havana and the Atlantic in the Sixteenth Century," review of *Havana and the Atlantic in the Sixteenth Century* by Alejandro de la Fuente, César García del Pino and Bernardo Iglesias Delgado. *Hispanic American Historical Review* 89, no. 4 (2009): 683–85.

Turits, Richard Lee, and Laurent Dubois, *Freedom Roots. Histories from the Caribbean.* Chapel Hill: University of North Carolina Press, 2019.

Utrera, Cipriano de Utrera. *Historia Militar de Santo Domingo*, vol. 1, 1947. 2nd ed. Santo Domingo, Dominican Republic: Banco de Reservas de la República Dominicana, 2014.

Chapter 5

Black Women in Sixteenth-Century Santo Domingo

Free, Enslaved, Founders, and Explorers

Lissette Acosta Corniel

Black women in sixteenth-century La Española[1]—their experiences, contributions, and history—have yet to make it into many book chapters, journal articles—or most importantly, a book. This has unequivocally omitted Black women from the many disciplines that investigate the colonizing of the New World.[2] This chapter aims to serve as a stepping stone into a field that deserves more attention within the topic of Atlantic slavery by sharing microstories about free and enslaved women in early colonial Santo Domingo. With the production of more works of this kind, we hope to write a more comprehensive history about the free and enslaved Black women in the early years of the Transatlantic Slave Trade.

For instance, one can aim to question whether there were enslaved Black women among the 2,500 passengers said to have accompanied Nicolás de Ovando in his founding trip of 1502. To this point, historians have not been able to reach a conclusion as to the list of passengers, due to the delicate condition of the original documents and because those documents are out of order. About this problem, historian Ursula Lamb explained that "the abundant and complete bundle of the *Contratación* of the archives in Seville related to Ovando's fleet, is known to exist, but is not in order. It is, therefore, impossible to attempt a detailed description of the organization of the fleet's crew."[3] This may allow the suggestion of a reappraisal of passenger lists of all the expeditions recorded to have sailed to Hispaniola between 1492 and 1502. In addition to the voyages of Christopher Columbus and before Nicolás de Ovando's voyage, approximately eight expeditions are registered to have docked in Hispaniola between 1492 and 1502.[4]

Black Women in Early Hispaniola

The importance of Black women as part of the foundation of American society began to be noticed by the local authorities during the first decades after the foundation of the colony of Hispaniola. In 1518, Governor Alonso Zuazo wrote to the Spanish Crown, asking that they send young Black *bozales*,[5] and also send Black women so that Black men and women could marry and be part, specifically, of the foundation of cities or—more generally—the expansion of the colonized population. This is a clear example of how Black women were used as bait to preserve enslaved communities. In this statement, the governor urges that the Crown, "bring all the black men and women and they could be eighteen- and twenty-year-old *bozales* who will live on this island and learn our customs and they can be taken to towns where they will be married with their wives."[6]

In the same document, Governor Zuazo insists, with more detail, on the importance of sending enslaved Black women to Hispaniola. The document mentions the significance of marriage as the axis of settlement and suggests that Blacks should be married. The statement also sounds like a pitch to lure people into visiting or moving to such a wonderful place, a place so full of grace that this is where you would want to spend the last days of your life. The governor's words implied that Hispaniola was a paradise for everyone when he said, "This land is the best in the world for blacks, for women, for old men, and for the wonders that you are allowed to see when in this land you die. The groups of blacks do not have to be permanent, but temporary, chosen every year and that the selected one be married so that he may have love for the land."[7] Nine years later in 1527, and with different objectives than those of populating the island, the Spanish Crown ordered that Blacks be encouraged to marry.

> Don Carlos Etcetera for we are informed that as a result of too many blacks having gone to the island of La Española and

there being a few Spanish Christians, it could be the reason of possible unrest or rebellion by said blacks. . . . It seems that it would be a great remedy to marry the blacks who are taken to the island from this point forward and the ones living there now and that they each may have a wife because that and the love they may have for their wives and children and the institution of marriage, would be cause of much pacification for them . . . and to marry them by law and blessings . . . they would be forced to marry within fifteen months after the promulgation of this letter being it the wish of said black men and women. Because marriage should be voluntary and not obliged . . . by this letter we declare that to marry and having the permission from their masters would not constitute freedom, but slaves as if the said marriage did not take place.[8]

The intention of marrying Blacks was a strategy to control enslaved men who escaped. With what is proposed, the Spanish Crown executed two objectives. First, control Blacks, and second, institute the law of Catholic marriage among the enslaved. The reason for using marriage as a means of control for Blacks must have developed in an effort to try to prevent another slave revolt like the rebellion of 1521, generally known—until now—as the first big revolt by enslaved Blacks in the Americas.[9] Little is known of the participation of Black enslaved women in uprisings in Hispaniola, except the mention in the ordinances of the Black code (1768) about the punishment enslaved Black women would receive if they were participants or accomplices when the enslaved escaped.[10] This reprehensive statement seems to indicate that there were indeed cases of female complicity that needed to be repressed or were of concern for the colonial authorities, and such collaboration needed to be prevented. Most important is the fact that these collaborations might have existed all the way to 1784, when laws highlighting the need to control these activities continued to be created.

Complicity and collaborations to protect—to an extent—the enslaved included others colonists. We do not know the name of the enslaved Black woman, we do know that her case became very popular when the church tried to save her from her death sentence. We know that she was burned after being accused of poisoning her mistress with mercury.[11] This case is documented by Governor Alonso Zuazo, who writes to the Spanish Crown describing the details of how a clergyman opposed the punishment that the enslaved Black woman had been sentenced to. Zuazo took this opportunity to complain to the Spanish Crown that the clergy had more enslaved people than the laity, and that to reject the punishment of Blacks by the secular authorities threatened the peace of the colony.[12]

Despite the instability of the state in Hispaniola, partly because of the resistance exerted by the enslaved Blacks and the dwindling aboriginal population, there were those who advised continuing to bring Blacks into the island. In Roberto Marte's publication of the Juan Bautista Muñoz collection of colonial documents, there is a letter written by "some of the most important residents" of the island, dated 1528–1529, in which the residents proposed the importation of fifty neighbors from Spain to establish a town. Twenty-five of these neighbors would be from Castile and the other twenty-five would be "blacks or mestizos all with their wives."[13] It is important to note this proposal by some of the leading citizens in Hispaniola, of recommending that twenty-five Blacks or mestizos with their women go to Hispaniola and be part of the citizens who would establish and settle in a city.

This proposal could be seen, at first, as politically ambiguous, because it seems to be portraying the acceptance of the inclusion of Blacks as residents and founders of one of the first American cities. However, in another paragraph, the residents also ask the Spanish Crown to allow the 25 incoming Castilian residents to each bring 100 Black males and 100 Black females. It is assumed that the Blacks being brought by each of the 25 incoming residents would be enslaved. On the other hand, there remains the question of what would be the status and civil rights of the 25 Blacks or mestizos who would travel as residents and with their wives. While this may be a vague interpretation of the events, it becomes part of a series of small details that allow us to compose part of the untold history of the Black people in sixteenth-century Hispaniola.

In addition, as vague as they may be, these details allow us to at least imagine Black women being present at the same time that Black men were. It is likely that the first Black women arrived in the Americas as domestic slaves accompanying the first families that arrived with Nicolás de Ovando to colonize the island. In the ensuing years, sugar was the largest production and trade activity in the colony and the presence of Black women in this process was recorded at least from the 1540s onward, although for prior periods we may infer their presence even when in many cases we do not have their names. This is the case of the Black women who were probably among 2,510 Blacks who worked in the 13 mills that existed in Hispaniola in 1533. I have arrived at this conclusion given the earlier eagerness of some of the colonial authorities to have Black females brought to the island, on the one hand, and because there is no reason to believe that the earliest sugar plantations did not see a benefit in including female enslaved labor as they did in plantations in subsequent decades and in other colonies, on the other hand. In a way, the absence of enslaved Black women in colonial documents about Santo Domingo may be compared to the hundreds of Spanish women who traveled to Santo Domingo between 1492 and 1530, and appear listed nameless and/or only as attachés of their husbands, fathers, and brothers—as if they were pieces of luggage. For example, many women are listed as "traveled with his wife" or "with his mother, sister Catalina and two or three more sisters."[14] Aida Altman explains that by 1514 Spanish women lived all throughout Hispaniola except for Salvatierra de la Sabana, and that most of the Spanish women lived in the city of Santo Domingo.[15] At least these Spanish women can be traced to their male relatives. Black women, on the other hand, can be found quantified in phrases like "100 black males and 100 black females." Altman adds that "Not only are the lives of non-European women largely inaccessible to us but also the nature of relationships across ethnicities can be difficult to discern."[16] Historian José Luis Sáez studied the population in the thirteen mills in Hispaniola in 1533, and explains that the number of enslaved Blacks is available, but there is no specific information about their gender except "100 blacks reside in this mill."[17] However, in his study of the mills in 1547, Sáez explains that there were thirty-two enslaved Black females of six different ages at the Ingenio Santiago de la Paz in the city of Azua, owned by Hernando Gorjón. One of the women is registered as deceased, having perished while giving birth.[18] The varying ages of the enslaved women lead to several questions. Unfortunately, we do not know the arrival and purchase date of any of the women. We also do not know if they were creole or *bozales* and/or if they were kin to one another. The following table provides the breakdown of the ages of the women at the mill. Fourteen of the women were between the ages of fifty and seventy, which can suggest that they had been at the mill since an early age and aged there. Given the structure of slavery, the future of the remaining 18 women would be the same unless they escaped, bought their freedom, or died, whether by natural cause or suicide. Many enslaved saw death as a form of freedom.

Three decades later, in 1577, we can see even greater numbers of Black women in the sugar mill inventories. For example, mill Boca de Nigua in the Province of San Cristóbal reported thirty-eight, and mill

Table 5.1. Division of Enslaved Black Females by Age at the Mill Owned by Hernando Gorjón.[19]

Age	Enslaved Black Females
3–15	6
17	1
20	1
25	2
30	3
40	3
50	8
70	6
80	1

Source: S. J. José Luis Sáez. *La iglesia y el negro esclavo en Santo Domingo: una historia de tres siglos*, Santo Domingo, Dominican Republic: Patronato de la Ciudad Colonial de Santo Domingo, 1994, 267.

La Concepción de Nuestra Señora owned by Álvaro Caballero reported 51 enslaved Black women.[20] Genaro Rodríguez Morel explains that four of the 51 women at the mill La Concepción de Nuestra Señora appeared as married and that their known ages varied between newborn and 60 years old. The age of 32 of the women is unknown.

This information shows how Black women left their presence and role recorded in Hispaniola's enslaved African society. And, although their representation is more related to the slave trade and sugar production, there were times when restricted spaces offered some Black women an opportunity to resist and to leave traces of their agency. That is the case, for instance, for free Black women who traveled to explore the newly conquered territories in the Americas.

Free Black Women Who Crossed the Ocean

There are documented cases of Black women *horras*,[21] who requested licenses to travel to Hispaniola, accompanied by their sons or daughters as early as the second decade after the founding of the colony. Such is the case of a Black woman named Catalina and her son Diego who were granted a license to travel to the Indies in 1513, after presenting a letter of *ahorría* or manumission.²² Similarly, in 1527, Inés, "of black color," requested to go to Santo Domingo with her daughter Beatríz.²³ In 1536, Catalina Hernández, "of black color" and a resident of Seville, also asked for permission to go to Santo Domingo with her daughter Francisca de Castilla, after submitting letters of *ahorría* for both of them. Catalina and Francisca entered Hispaniola in 1539.²⁴

What compelled these Black women to migrate, apparently voluntarily, to Hispaniola? We do not know, but as Ida Altman points out, a transatlantic and intracolonial migration developed during the first two or three decades of the arrival of Christopher Columbus and this subject remains to be explored.²⁵ Equally interesting is the migration of enslaved Blacks from Hispaniola to Seville as companions of their masters in Seville, who obtained their freedom while there. It seems that some of these newly freed Blacks also petitioned to return from the capital of the empire's economy back to Hispaniola. Although a case of a Black male, it is worth mentioning Miguel de Torquemada, an eighteen-year-old free Black male who in 1553 asserted that he would like to return from Seville to Santo Domingo, because he would like to go back to his mother and to his estate.²⁶ Miguel de Torquemada is described as a short young man with a scar on his forehead. There are no more details of his mother and his alleged farm in Santo Domingo. However, Miguel's case is evidence that toward the middle of the sixteenth century, it was a reality that a Black woman and her son owned a farm and that Black women in Hispaniola were active agents in that society.

Black women were also property owners in other Spanish colonies such as Cartagena de Indias, Mexico, and Havana, and their ventures varied, adding to their diversified contributions throughout the Americas. David Wheat explains that in 1620 Gethsemaní, fourteen Black women listed as *morenas* and mulattas owned property that they used as their residence and also rented them. Some women, Wheat continues, hired property managers such Luis de Soto, who appeared as the property manager for "an unnamed mulata."²⁷ In late sixteenth-century Havana, the roles of Black women can be found documented as a result of the skills and services they offered. For example, many Black women cooked and washed clothes for soldiers who often took months and years to pay. In some instances, the women used the credit or debt owed to pay for their own debts.²⁸ Daniel Terrazas-Williams discusses the life of free Black women's economic agency in colonial Mexico where they accrued wealth owning slaves either through purchase or inheritance.²⁹

These cases show that a thorough study of Black women in the early Americas would yield more information about their lives and journey. For instance, Nicole von Germeten wrote about Paula de Eguiluz, who was born in Santo Domingo into slavery in 1592. According to von Germeten, Paula was the daughter of an enslaved mother and a free father. The mother is said to have been of Cazanga ethnicity and the father Bañon.[30] Paula was accused of witchcraft in Cuba, and tried by the Spanish Inquisition in Cartagena in 1624. She served a two-year sentence and was tried again at forty years old after rumors arose that she was practicing again in 1632.[31] Ana María Silva Campo also wrote about Paula de Eguiluz's trials in Los Jagüeyes, New Granada, and like von Germeten, Silva Campo discusses other women mentioned in Paula de Eguiluz's trials.[32] One of the women questioned as a result of Paula de Eguiluz's testimony was Luisa Domínguez, a free Black who was said to be twenty-six or twenty-seven years old, born in Santo Domingo and enslaved by Diego López. According to Silva Campo, Luisa Domínguez lived free in Los Jagüeyes, and made "a living by washing and starching clothes, and by making filled buns (bollo) and empanadas."[33]

Another case worthy of discussion is that of María de Cota, an *horra* residing in Seville in 1575. María was granted her freedom by her owner, Alonso de Avellaneda Farfan, following his wife's request in her will. The letter of *ahorría* was given to María in 1568, and on November 6, 1575, María requested a license to travel to Peru. The license was granted on December 13, 1575. In her will, Mrs. Barbola left 20 ducats to be given to María and also expressed that she would like María to be priced at the same value that she purchased her, and that María no longer appear as one of her possessions. It seems that Mrs. Barbola wanted to make sure that María was not included as one of her possessions after her death, in order to grant María her freedom. In addition, by asking that María be priced at the same value of the 100 ducats that she paid for her, Mrs. Barbola is gifting María a total amount of 120 ducats, given that María will not have to pay the 100 ducats that she is worth to buy her own freedom and she is also receiving 20 ducats. The stipulations on the will also forbid María's temporary owner from raising her price, something that perhaps would have made it more difficult for María to obtain her freedom and plans for travel.

As indicated above, María requested a travel license to go to Peru, but the veracity of her freedom status was questioned and her case went to trial. In her testimony of 1575, María de Cota explained that she was born in Santo Domingo, and that she arrived in Seville approximately eighteen years ago, possibly making the arrival year to be 1557. According to Joana Martínez, one of the witnesses, when María de Cota requested her license to travel to Peru, María was twenty-six years old. If Joana Martínez is correct in her estimate of María's age, María was born in 1549 in Santo Domingo, and was eight years old when she arrived in Seville in 1557, along with Joana Martínez and their mistress Mrs. Barbola de Arana. This chronology makes Joana four years older than María and places Joana as being born in Santo Domingo in 1545. It is important to note that Joana Martínez was also an enslaved woman owned by Mrs. Barbola, also manumitted in her testament, and gifted 20 ducats. In her request of 1575, María presented two female witnesses said to have grown up with her in the same house in Santo Domingo, who traveled to Seville on the same ship. Judging by witness Joana Martínez and Mrs. Barbola's will, it is highly probable that one of those women was Joana Martínez.

While one document places María on her way to Peru in the ship of Lazaro Gutiérrez on December 13, 1575, a document in 1580 shows that María was requesting once again, or still, a license to travel to Peru from Seville. In the 1580 document, María reiterated that she was born in Santo Domingo, and added that she had a three-year-old daughter named Magdalena who was also born in Santo Domingo. During her travel license request in 1580, María presented three male witnesses, one of which was Mrs. Barbola's widower Alonso de Avellaneda Farfan, who vouched for María and assured that she had a three-year-old daughter named Magdalena.

María's license request, on separate occasions, is evidence of inter-colonial migration by Blacks, especially women. It is worth noting that in 1575, María was a resident of Seville asking to go to Peru. In 1580, she is also a resident of Seville asking to go to Peru with her three-year-old daughter, who according to María and three witnesses, was born in Santo Domingo. The time line and testimony of the witnesses suggests that María began her journey to Peru between 1575 and 1577, and Lazaro Gutierrez's ship probably anchored in Santo Domingo where María remained for some time until she returned to Seville with her newborn, Magdalena, who was three years old at the time of her 1580 license request to go to Peru.[34] María's case is not only important because of the details about her mobility, but also because in her second travel license request María explained that she wished to go back to Santo Domingo because she owned a large farm there and would be more comfortable there. She also stated that she was not married, a declaration that perhaps was important because as a single woman she had nothing tying her to Seville. We can also suggest that María had no special reason to go to Peru, other than to explore and try new ventures and that this plan changed when she visited Santo Domingo between 1575 and 1580. It is also possible that María was pregnant when she sailed to Peru, stopped in Santo Domingo, and gave birth there, and then returned to Spain to tend to personal business. While no further details are available, María de Cota's brief account illustrates what life was like for some of the free Black women in sixteenth-century Santo Domingo.

Certainly, there are several examples that show Black women in the early Americas were as enterprising as Spanish women, risking their way in a place that constantly denigrated their position in society for being Black and for being female. We do not know the full details right now as to why María de Cota wanted to immigrate to Peru, especially if in 1580 we learn that she wanted to return to Santo Domingo in Hispaniola, where she had "a farm and more comfort."[35] At first glance, Peru being a thriving mining center, it is understood that Peru would prove a more attractive destination than Hispaniola, but in her second travel request of 1580, María de Cota explained that she would be better off in Santo Domingo than in Seville. To some extent, the reasons for María de Cota to want to travel to Santo Domingo or Peru can relate to those of Catalina Hernández, and to Catalina and Inés discussed earlier in the chapter, wanting to emigrate to Hispaniola in 1513 and 1527, respectively. Simply put, they wanted to go where they could and where things seemed to be better. These cases call for new studies that focus on the economic status of Blacks in Seville requesting licenses to travel to the Indies in the sixteenth century, especially to Santo Domingo and during the Transatlantic Slave Trade. These new studies would open doors for interactive conversations about and between what was happening in Spain and what was happening in the colonies. In chapter 2 of this volume, Rocio Periañez Gómez discusses laws, resistance, and the consequences that came with being Black and/or helping a Black person in Extremadura, Spain. It seems that María de Cota, Catalina and Inés, and Catalina Hernández decided to try their luck in a new place in hopes of a better life for themselves, Blacks, and for women.

Perhaps the Ginés sisters thought the same when they left Santo Domingo. These two Black *horras* migrated during the 1580s from Santiago de los Caballeros, in Hispaniola, to Cuba where they became popular and are remembered to this day. We are referring to the sisters Micaela and Teodora Ginés, recognized as the pioneers of the Cuban rhythm best known as *son*. Alejo Carpentier places the Ginés sisters living in Santiago de Cuba and as members of a band where the sisters became well-known for playing the *bándola*.[36] Micaela moved to Havana while Teodora remained in Santiago de Cuba where she made famous a song titled "Son de Ma' Teodora." It is not exactly clear if they were born in Hispaniola. What is certain is that they lived there and are credited with being the pioneers of Cuban *son*, or at least one of the first to introduce this music genre in the island of Cuba. We must also assume that if they arrived in Cuba as musicians, they must have also played in Santo Domingo, but there are no records of their mention as musicians in Santo Domingo. Nonetheless, with a rhythmic and lyrical combination of Spaniard and African heritage, the Ginés sisters left an imprint in the history of music in Latin America.

> ¿Dónde está la Má Teodora?
> Rajando la leña está.
> ¿Con su palo y su bandola?
> Rajando la leña está.
> ¿Dónde está que no la veo?
> Rajando la leña está.
> Rajando la leña está.
> Rajando la leña está.[37]

According to Carpentier, the call and response style of the song is inherited from African games brought to the colonies. The song asks, "Where is Ma' Teodora?" with the response, "chopping the wood," an expression used to mean that the person was working. The second question, "With her stick and *bandola*?" alludes to Ma' Teodora working either as the person who directs the band or the person who directs people to dance at the same time that she also plays the *bandola*.[38]

The First Black Woman of the Americas in Colonial Documents

The first mention of the presence of a Black woman in the Americas refers to a Black *horra*, who is said to have founded the first hospital in the Americas before 1502. Yet the founding of the hospital has been documented as being done by Governor Nicolás de Ovando, after his arrival to Hispaniola in 1502. Documents that provide specific details about the life of "the black woman from the hospital," have yet to be found. However, there exist two letters written in Santo Domingo, one on December 2, 1695, and another on August 24, 1783, respectively, which mention the Black woman. The first letter was written in response to King Carlos II who writes nearly 200 years after the colonization of the island to ask about the veracity that the hospital of Saint Nicholas was founded by a Black woman. What follows is part of the response to the King from Archbishop Carvajal y Ribera of Santo Domingo in 1695:

> For the Real decree on October 6, 1693, your Majesty requests to be informed of how the hospital of Saint Nicholas was erected and the daily and yearly administration by six deputy officers and their manager. . . . To which I respond. The beginning of the foundation of the hospital was a hut next to where today is the Chapel of the virgin of Altagracia, belonged to a pious black woman who took in the poor people she could and healed them as she could as there was no hospital in the city.[39]

One of the most important details in this letter is the fact that according to Archbishop Carvajal y Ribera, the Black woman increased the services she provided as a result of receiving donations from some of the town's residents. A major significance of this document lies in the detail that *vecinos* or residents contributed with donations, and *vecinos* was a term used to describe only colonists, and not Blacks, whether free or enslaved.[40] Also, the donors not only trusted the Black woman with administering the medical-like facility but also trusted her with their health.

The prelate continued, adding that on his arrival, Governor Nicolás de Ovando "took over this holy work and raised the building where the hospital is found today. . . . And in gratitude to this noble man and protector of the hospital, the people dedicated it to God and gave it the name of Saint Nicholas Hospital."[41] The archbishop added, "that all these authentic instruments burned when Privateer Francis Draque invaded the city."[42] Everything seems to indicate that the humanitarian acts made by the Black woman remain in oblivion, buried under the empire of colonization, and burned in the fires caused by the ambition of the pirates.[43] However, and still without conclusive evidence except for the conviction of oral history maintained apparently by people who remembered the Black woman, and/or the existence of Archbishop Carvajal y Ribera's letter written in 1695, Archbishop Rodríguez Lorenzo wrote to King Carlos III in 1783, again, reiterating the information we have shared about the "black woman from the hospital."⁴⁴ King Carlos III wrote his inquiry about "the black woman from the hospital" 88 years after King Carlos II wrote his in 1693. These royal inquiries reveal that whether the story of the "black woman from the hospital" was invented or real, the legacy of the "black woman from the hospital" had prevailed in the historical memory of some citizens of the island for approximately 281 years. For this reason, in one of the most complete interpretations of the actions of the "black woman from the hospital," Fray Cipriano de Utrera explains that the condition of anonymity of the Black woman is the result of the obvious circumstances surrounding society at the time, a period when there seemed to be no space to acknowledge the contributions of Blacks.⁴⁵ Today, the ruins of the hospital located on Calle Hostos in the Colonial Zone of the city of Santo Domingo in the Dominican Republic, showcases a descriptive plaque crediting the foundation of the hospital to Governor Nicolás de Ovando, and makes no mention of the origins of the hospital and the contributions of the Black woman. Governor Nicolás de Ovando was the highest authority in the island and his action and responsibility as governor to provide a better place for the hospital could not have been overshadowed by the work, however pious, of a Black woman. Nonetheless, even if the actions of the "black woman from the hospital" were overshadowed by the norms of a racialized-classist-patriarchal system, her entrepreneurship and generosity still lives on in official colonial documents.

Black Women of the Sixteenth Century in Judicial Documents

While Black women in sixteenth-century Hispaniola have been outshone in history, being mentioned mostly as Black or enslaved or in a travel license to the Indies accompanying their mistresses and masters, it is time to begin writing about Black women, utilizing as source the various colonial documents that can help us reconstruct their stories and add to the history of slavery. Among these sources are judicial documents where Black women are the protagonists either as witnesses or complainants. As an example, this work presents five Black enslaved women who participated as witnesses in 1549–1554 Hispaniola, in the femicide case of Catalina de Tinoco who was allegedly having an affair and allegedly murdered by her husband, Francisco Bravo. It is because these women were called to

Table 5.2. Black Female Slaves in the *Judicial Case of Catalina de Tinoco v. Francisco Bravo Hispaniola*, 1549–1554.[46]

Name	Description
Ana Jelofa [sic]	Ladina
Catalina Bran	Little Black slave who spoke clear
Catalina Rodríguez	Mulata
Juana Gelofa Pelona	17- or 19-year-old
Luisica	12-year-old ladina

Source: AGI, Justicia 103B, 104A.

testify that we have the opportunity to learn a few details about Catalina Bran, Juana Gelofa Pelona, Ana Ladina, Ana Jelofa, and Luisica.

When they were called to testify, the women stated what they knew about the alleged illicit relationship between Catalina de Tinoco and her alleged lover López de Salazar. However, it seems that some of the women spoke more than others, being that when other slaves were called to testify, they stated that what they knew they had heard from a specific slave they referred to as "*negrita* or *negrilla*."[47] Similarly, some of the witnesses indicated the name of the slave from whom they heard the rumors about Catalina de Tinoco. Although the enslaved woman who is referenced the most by the witnesses is Catalina Bran, the actions of Juana Gelofa Pelona and her rebellious nature might suggest that Juana was one of the slaves they referred to as "the little black slave," from whom they received most of the gossip. Juana challenged her master, who threatened to whip her and burn her with hot wax if she testified against her former mistress Catalina de Tinoco. Juana, not fearing her master's threats, lambasted against her former mistress Catalina, and declared everything she allegedly knew.[48] As we have come to realize and as mentioned before, Black women were part of everyday society in sixteenth-century Hispaniola, applying their abilities to what was happening in the colony. Clearly, judicial cases can be an important source of information on topics about sixteenth-century Hispaniola and particularly for the Black population. Such documents provide important details that would help bring to light the history of these women who deserve to be included in the history of Atlantic slavery.

Black Women in the Economy during the First Century of the Conquest

Uncovering the participation of Black women in the development of the economy in the Americas has been reduced to documenting their condition as slaves to be used as producers of wealth for their owners through hard labor or through breeding. But there is evidence of the participation of Black women in the economy during the first decades of colonization of Hispaniola. First, a Black *horra* assisted sick people from her hut. We can argue that her economic contribution was to assist people who could then integrate back to their daily working life. Then, it is presumed that several Black women accompanied their owners traveling as domestic slaves from Spain to Hispaniola and vice versa. Also, the arrival of imported indispensable Black women was part of a strategy to control Black males on the island and those Black slaves who were yet to arrive. This maneuver allowed colonizers to have Black slaves feel more settled with their wives, and as such have a secured labor force in the mines, sugar plantations, farms, and construction projects. Another key contribution was the case of Black women who played various roles in the sugar mills. The participation of Black women working in the plantations is evidenced in the case of a Black woman who appears to have worked as an *hornera* in the mill La Concepción de Nuestra Señora in 1577.[49]

Similarly, Black women were essential for the livelihood of colonizers who depended on the daily work of the enslaved, either by renting them or sending them to the streets as vendors. The women vendors were known as *ganadoras*.[50] The ordinances of 1544, preserved in the Spanish Black Code, stipulated the public spaces and the times that enslaved Black women could sell products, exclusively during morning and afternoon. The ordinances indicated that the punishment of a hundred lashes be given to the women who violated these laws.[51] However, the ordinances clearly explained the importance of *ganadoras* to assist in the support of widows who lived in poverty and others who were in the same penurious state as the widows. We must assume that, although not specified, the reference to others who also lived in poverty should include men whose survival depended on the labor and earnings of the *ganadoras*. It is important to highlight that if the work of the *ganadoras* was convenient for their owners, it was convenient for the *ganadoras* too because they enjoyed privileges of spatial mobility, unlike some of the other enslaved. Another advantage for the *ganadoras* was that through their work, it was easier for them to save money to buy their freedom. This fact was also highlighted in the ordinances of the Spanish Black Code.

> Because too many black men and women walk about in the city earning in various trades, agreements and contracts and arrangements with their masters and also arrange to give their masters a certain amount per month or per week or per day and this causes too many inconveniences, specially that many do not acknowledge their masters because the slaves are gone for so long, nor do they come into their homes but only when they are due to pay their wages and slowly begin to obtain their way to freedom.[52]

As a result of the above, the law established that slave owners brought the slaves to a specific location for the day where the enslaved would be available for hire and return at a specific time when they would be picked up by their masters and then brought home. Owners could also rent out slaves for more than one day, but the renter would be responsible for following the same rules of making sure that the enslaved returned to their original home. It could have been the cunning character of some of the Black women *ganadoras*, or the inheritances received from their owners—as was the case of María de Cota who inherited 20 ducats—that helped many enslaved Black women with buying their freedom and owning a house, shops, and/or farms. This may explain why we found forty-five Black women in the 1606 census conducted by Governor Antonio de Osorio, after the removal of the residents of La Española in the west and northwest regions of the colony in the operation known as "*Devastaciones*." These forty-five women are registered under the categories of "free black," "free mulata," "*horra*," and with specifications such as "own a shop" to refer to women who owned property. The census does not provide the names of the 9,648 enslaved people said to be in the island. However, it does provide details on the free Black women and men. And these details, however small, contribute to the process of building the history of society at the time, especially in relation to Black women.

The list of Black women includes other women who appear as wives of Black men, as in the case of Andrés Hernández who is described as a mulatto and is registered as having a wife and family. Because we cannot determine whether Andrés Hernández's wife was also a mulatta and/or

Table 5.3. Black Women in the Census of Santo Domingo, 1606.[53]

Name	Census Description	Residence	Property	Family
Maria Hernandez	Mulata	Santo Domingo	Slaves	With family
Mariana Suazo	Mulata	Santo Domingo	Slaves	With family
Ines de Carmona	Morena libre	Santo Domingo		With family
Pascuala de Carvajal	Morena horra	Santo Domingo		With kids and family
Lucia	Mulata	Santo Domingo	Store	
Marcela de Sant Estevan	Morena horra, widow	Santo Domingo		With family
Isabel de Morales	Morena horra	Santo Domingo		With family
Ines de Aguilar	Mulata libre	Santo Domingo		With family
Maria Magdalena	Mulata	Santo Domingo		With family
Ana de Benavides	Mulata	Santo Domingo		With family
Brigida Diaz	Mulata libre	Santo Domingo		With family
Mari Diaz	Negra libre	Santo Domingo		With family
Ana de Guzman	Mulata libre	Santo Domingo		With family
Dominga	Morena horra	Santo Domingo		
Luisa Gobea	Morena libre	Santo Domingo		With family
Paula de Almansa	Morena libre	Santo Domingo	House	
Olaya Dabila	Mulata libre	Santo Domingo	House	
Luisa Rodriguez	Morena libre	Santo Domingo		Kids and family
Maria Nunez	Mulata libre	Santo Domingo		Kids and family
Bernardina Solano	Morena libre	Santo Domingo		kids and family
Marcela Suazo	Mulata libre	Santo Domingo		With family
Maria de la Requena	Mulata libre	Santo Domingo		With family

continued on next page

Table 5.3. Continued.

Andrea de la Roca	Mulata libre	Santo Domingo		With family
Costança Perez	Mulata libre	Santo Domingo		With family
Francisca Minaya	Mulata libre	Santo Domingo		With family
Juana de Esquibel	Horra	Santo Domingo		With family
Felipa de Tapia	Mulata libre	Santo Domingo		With family
Elena Carrasco	Morena horra	Santiago de los Caballeros		
Marta Ximenez	Mulata libre	La Vega		
Leonor	Negra libre	La Vega	Cassava, corn, vegetables	
Ana Alarcon	Negra libre	La Vega	Cassava, corn, vegetables	
Beatriz Hernandez	Morena libre	Cotui		
Joana de la Puebla	Negra libre	Savana de la Venta y la Esperilla y Saona	Cattle ranch	
Cathalina Bran		Isabela	Cassava, corn, vegetables	
Alvira	Negra horra	Nigua	Cassava, corn, vegetables	
Marta	Negra libre	Azua	Cassava and other vegetables	

Source: AGI, Santo Domingo 83.

free Black or any other phenotypic description used in the census, we chose to include her and assume that all the wives of Black men were Black and not white. The total number of men described as Black *horro*, tan color, *horro*, and mulatto with wife and family is nine, raising the number of Black women to forty-five. The final figure in table 4 exceeds the number of women because some of these women meet more than one category. This number represents the documented free women in the entire island with the majority, twenty-seven women, residing in the city of Santo Domingo, along with those who owned farms near the capital of Santo Domingo, and the nine who are listed as wives of the free Black men who also lived in the city of Santo Domingo.[54] For comparison purposes, while six of the forty-five Black women are listed as farm owners, Black men led in this area with eleven free Black men listed as farm owners. On the other hand, in terms of free people of color, mulattas took the lead with sixteen mulattas of the thirty-six Black women compared to five mulatos of the thirty-one free Black men. This may support the theory of social mobility of light-skinned women in the colonial period, especially during the early developments of slave society in the Americas. On other hand, *negras*/Blacks led in property ownership with five *negras* listed as owning a farm. The above numbers correspond to the census of 1606, but as David Wheat points out, in 1604, Governor Antonio Osorio traveled around the island in preparation to relocate the residents in less populated towns. And during his tour, the governor took care of other businesses that were important under colonial standards. The governor fined men and women whom he found living in concubinage, whether in adultery or simply not married by the church. Some of the women found violating both included free Black women in several of the towns, including Azua and Santo Domingo. However, it is not clear if these women were included in the 1606 census.[55]

The question remains: what implications does this information about free Black women and men in 1606 Hispaniola have on the total number of 9,648 enslaved and the 5,545 whites listed in the census? Perhaps 45 free Black women and 31 free Black men may seem like low numbers compared to the enslaved population and whites. The numbers were not much higher over a century later in the neighboring colony of Saint Domingue. According to John D. Garrigus, in 1789 Saint Domingue, only 100 to 200 free people of color were planters and merchants out of approximately 25,000 free people of color.[56]

Possibly, the explanation for this phenomenon may be provided in the footnotes by Fray Cipriano de Utrera in Emilio Rodríguez Demorizi's *Relaciones históricas de Santo Domingo*. The friar explained that only heads of household were included in the census and that several married women were incorporated into the category of widow because they didn't have economic autonomy.[57] Although only one free Black woman is listed as a widow and the strategy explained above may not help our numbers, there are no additional details and social status of the people listed as "relatives" for twenty-three of the free Black women and seven of the free Black men. This may indicate that there could have been more free women of African descent who were not included in the census for not meeting the required economic status. Nonetheless, however small, the number of Black women in the census is a marker of the presence and participation of Black women in the economy of Hispaniola, at a time when the colony was undergoing a catastrophic economic crisis that led authorities to the process of depopulation in certain areas of the country.

Among the women described as "black," we observed that of the seven in total, five were farm owners. Out of those referred to as "mulata," only two of sixteen appear as slave owners. It should be noted that owning slaves at the time was another indication of status in the colonies. Two mulattas appear as house owners. We do not know if the "blacks" classified as "farm owners" also owned their homes or only owned the farms and did not own their homes, or if the homes were in different locations than the farms.

Whether the number of women who owned farms and other property was zero or 100, Black women—in my opinion—had the biggest role in the slave trade financial enterprise. Black women were responsible for the production of the most important product in the sugar economy. They birthed the enslaved children. The significance of this reality is highlighted by Jennifer Morgan as she explains the case of Richard Harris, a slave owner in 1711 Carolina, who made sure to include in the will to his children a male and female slave and "the increase" of the female slave. A Black woman's body had so much value that her unborn or yet final product was considered an asset.[58] The value of Blacks—especially Black women as "human property"—was so critical for the continuity of a thriving society that slave owners predicted the possible increase of share or stock through the ownership of a Black female slave. Enslaved Black women constituted the raw material of mass production and reproduction.[59] How enslaving societies created and recreated unrestricted access to enslaved people as can be found in the archives. In 1699 Santo Domingo, Juan Gil sold one-fourth of Manuela, the enslaved woman that they had inherited from their mother, to his brother Domingo Dias. How they were administering and distributing Manuela is not explained in the bill of sale. What is clearly stated is that Gil sold his share of Manuela (the property) to Días, who can now have access to one fourth of Manuela and "sell, trade, exchange, annex, and have access to it as he wished."[60] As illustrated in Manuela's case, enslaved people could be sold in fractions, although in the case of Black enslaved women, their most important fractions were their children, which were taken from them. But this is not something that was happening only during the thriving years of the Transatlantic Slave Trade, which takes us back to the main argument of this chapter, that Black women were present and important in the Americas since the beginning of the conquest. In 1555 Santo Domingo, Diego López, who purchased an enslaved Black woman, demanded the reimbursement for what he paid, alleging that the woman was severely sick. López requested that a doctor and midwives inspect his property, given that he believed that she suffered from having a fallen womb. His diagnostic was corroborated by both the doctor and the midwives and as a result, the enslaved Black woman was returned as damaged merchandise.[61] This document could not be more relevant to the experience of Black women and their contributions to the "wealth of nations."

In short, we have seen how Black women were present in the Americas since its inception. And most importantly, Black women were part of the foundation of society from the beginning as we have seen in the example of the "black woman from the hospital." We also know now that Black women were not afraid to venture out on their own, as they requested licenses to cross the ocean to travel to foreign lands, also taking their children. More important, it has been proven that Black women showed resistance from the first years of being subjected to slavery in Hispaniola.

In that sense, we have demonstrated that Black women in Hispaniola in the sixteenth century are buried in archives waiting to be brought back from anonymity, from those "graves," as historian Alice Gould called the repository of files that she wanted to investigate in search of the passenger list of the first voyage of Christopher Columbus.[62] To that end, historians must continue to dig in the archival mass graves where too many Black women lay buried.

Notes

This chapter is a translation and revised version of "Negras, mulatas y morenas en La Española del siglo XVI (1502–1606)," in Esclavitud, *mestizaje y abolicionismo en los mundos hispánicos*, ed. Aurelia Martín Casares (Granada, Spain: Universidad de Granada, 2015), 201–18.

1. In this work, we use Santo Domingo, the main city, which was used interchangeably to refer to the whole island.

2. Carlos Esteban Deive's *La mala vida: delincuencia y picaresca en la colonia española de Santo Domingo* (Santo Domingo, Dominican Republic: Taller, 1997), is one of the most complete works about sixteenth-century La Española and part of the seventeenth century that includes several mentions of free and enslaved Afro-descendant women. This text is a must-read for the study of everyday life during the first decades of the foundation of the Americas, and most importantly, for the study of Black women in the early years of the conquest. The only exhaustive work that we know of so far about Black women in La Española is the work of Celsa Albert Batista. *Mujer y esclavitud en Santo Domingo* (Santo Domingo, Dominican Republic: Búho, 1993). It contains an ample bibliography about the topic of African slavery in the Indies where Black women are mentioned. Another text with information about Black women in colonial Santo Domingo is the work of Alejandra Liriano. *El papel de la mujer de origen africano en el Santo Domingo colonial (siglos XVI–XVII)* (Santo Domingo, Dominican Republic: Centro de Investigación para la Acción Femenina, 1992).

3. Ursula Lamb, *Frey Nicolás de Ovando: Gobernador de las Indias, 1501–1509* (Madrid, Spain: Consejo Superior de Investigaciones Científicas, Instituto Gonzalo Fernández de Oviedo, 1956), 104. For more information about the condition of the archives with information on Nicolás de Ovando, see also: Gil, Juan. "La Gente de Ovando en los protocolos hispalenses," *Anuario de Estudios Americanos*, Sevilla, 63, no. 1 (January–June 2006): 255.

4. For more information about voyages to La Española see, Henry Harrisse, *The Discovery of North America; a Critical, Documentary, and Historic Investigation* (Amsterdam: N. Israel, 1961), 663. Another text with ample information about the voyages to the Indies is Demetrio P. Ramos, *Audacia, negocios y política en los viajes españoles de descubrimiento y rescate* (Valladolid, Spain: Casa-Museo de Colón, Seminario Americanista de la Universidad, 1981).

5. *Bozales* was the term used to refer to enslaved Africans who did not speak Spanish and had not been Christianized.

6. AGI, Patronato, 174, R. 8. F. 47r. FB, document no. 56.

7. AGI, Patronato, 174.

8. AGI, Indiferente, 421, L.12, F.151R–52R, fo. 508r-v.

9. AGI, Patronato, 295, N. 104. See Anthony Stevens Acevedo, *The Santo Domingo Slave Revolt of 1521 and the Slave Laws of 1522: Black Slavery and Black Resistance in the Early Colonial Americas* (New York: Dominican Studies Institute, 2019). Stevens-Acevedo's comprehensive account of the laws of 1522 provides important details that allow us to have a glimpse of what the enslaved Black people experienced. See also Carlos Esteban Deive, *Los guerrilleros negros:*

esclavos fugitivos y cimarrones en Santo Doming (Santo Domingo, Dominican Republic: Fundación Cultural Dominicana, 1989), 33. Sued Badillo argues that the first of several Black uprisings took place in 1514 Puerto Rico. See his work, "From Tainos to Africans in the Caribbean Labor Migration and Resistance," in *The Caribbean: A History of the Region and its People* (Chicago, IL, and London: University of Chicago Press, 2011), 127–28.

10. Javier Barceló Malagón, *Código negro carolino* (Santo Domingo, Dominican Republic: Taller, 1974), 122, Art. 31; 123, Art. 34.

11. The document explains that the enslaved woman used *soliman*, which was popular in the colonial period as a cosmetic and as poison.

12. AGI, Santo Domingo, 49, R. 1, N. 2, fo. 2R.

13. Roberto Marte, Santo *Domingo en los manuscritos de Juan Bautista Muñoz* (Santo Domingo, Dominican Republic: Fundación García-Arévalo, 1981), 292.

14. In her seminal work, *Pasajeros a La Española: 1492–1530*, Vilma Benzo de Ferrer offers a list of passengers to La Española, which includes hundreds of women and many of them registered unnamed.

15. Ida Altman, *Life and Society in the Early Spanish Caribbean: The Greater Antilles (1493–1550)*. Baton Rouge: Louisiana State University Press, 2021, 162.

16. Altman, *Life and Society*, 189.

17. S. J. José Luis Sáez documents the presence of enslaved Blacks in Santo Domingo and their role in the production of sugar in *La iglesia y el negro esclavo en Santo Domingo: una historia de tres siglos* (Santo Domingo, Dominican Republic: Patronato de la Ciudad Colonial de Santo Domingo, 1994), 267.

18. Sáez, *Iglesia y el negro esclavo*, 267.

19. Sáez, *Iglesia y el negro esclavo*, 278.

20. Genaro Rodríguez Morel, *Orígenes de la economía de la plantación de La Española* (Santo Domingo, Dominican Republic: Editora Nacional, 2012), 151 and "El sector azucarero" in *Historia General del pueblo dominicano*, Tomo I. Roberto Cassá y Genaro Rodríguez Morel, ed. (Santo Domingo: Academia Dominicana de la Historia, 2013), 399, 405.

21. *Horro* was the term used to refer to an enslaved person who had obtained his or her freedom through savings. *Ahorrar* in Spanish means to save. The term was also written as *jorro*.

22. AGI, Contratación, 5536, L. 1, F. 225 (4).

23. Benzo de Ferrer, *Pasajeros a La Española*, 195.

24. AGI, Contratación, 5536, L.5, F. 197 R (5).

25. Ida Altman, "Marriage, Family, and Ethnicity in the Early Spanish Caribbean," *William and Mary Quarterly* 70, 2, Centering Families in Atlantic Histories (April 2013): 225.

26. AGI, Contratación, 5217B, N.9, R.15.

27. In "Nharas and Morenas Horras" of his groundbreaking work, *Atlantic Africa and the Spanish Caribbean (1570–1630)* (Chapel Hill, University of North

Carolina Press, 2015), Wheat discusses the impact, agency, and contributions of Black women in the Americas. Discussed here, 146, 148–49.

28. Wheat, *Atlantic Africa and the Spanish Caribbean*, 149.

29. Danielle Terrazas Williams, *The Capital of Free Women: Race, Legitimacy, and Liberty in Colonial Mexico* (New Haven, CT, and London, Yale University Press, 2022), 87.

30. Wheat, 62. According to Wheat, these two ethnonyms were of African groups in Upper Guinea.

31. Nicole von Germeter, "Paula de Eguiluz, Seventeenth-Century Puerto Rico, Cuba and New Granada (Colombia)," in *As if She Were Free: A Collective Biography of Women and Emancipation in the Americas*, ed., Erica L. Ball, Tatianna Seijas, and Terri L. Snyder (New York: Cambridge University Press, 2020), 43, 47.

32. For the story on Paula de Eguiluz and other free Black women, see Ana María Silva, "Fragile Fortunes: Afrodescendant Women, Witchcraft, and the Remaking of Urban Cartagena" *Colonial Latin American Review* 30, no. 2 (2021): 197–213, 198–99, and 204.

33. Silva, "Fragile Fortunes: Afrodescendant Women," 204.

34. PARES, Portal de Archivos Españoles, AGI, Indiferente 2060, N. 10, obtained through the *First Blacks in the Americas* database, www.firstblacks.org.

35. PARES, *First Blacks in the Americas*.

36. A *bandola* is a small stringed instrument in the guitar family.

37. Alejo Carpentier, *Music in Cuba* (La música en Cuba), 1946, trans. Alán West-Durán (Minneapolis: University of Minnesota Press, 2001), 40–43.

38. Alejo Carpentier, *Music in Cuba* (La música en Cuba), 1946, trans. Alán West-Durán (Minneapolis: University of Minnesota Press, 2001), 40–43. See also, Lissette Acosta Corniel, Micaela Ginés, Teodora Ginés, and Juana Gelofa Pelona, in, *Dictionary of Caribbean and Afro-Latin American Biography*, edited by Henry Louis Gates Jr. and Franklin Knight; subject editor, Silvio Torres-Saillant, New York: Oxford University Press, 2016.

39. AGI, Santo Domingo 93, R.6. There is a second document that exists with the same date and around the same topic, which demonstrates the topic was being discussed from various angles by the Crown. AGI, Santo Domingo 876, L. 27.

40. Earlier in the chapter we learned of colonial officials referring to Blacks as residents in 1528–1529. However, this author does not have documentation yet, to be convinced this was the case in the earlier years.

41. AGI, Santo Domingo 93, R.6.

42. AGI, Santo Domingo 93, R.6.

43. La Española was invaded by corsair Francis Drake in 1586, suffering great loss as a result of the fires he caused.

44. De Utrera, *Dilucidaciones históricas*, 290. The old AGI citation is June 13, 1978. The new citation to locate this document is AGI, Santo Domingo, 93, R. 6.

45. De Utrera, *Dilucidaciones históricas*.

46. AGI, Justicia, 103-B, fo. 4116r, 4128v, 4161v, 4162r, 4164r–65r, 4240r–46r.
47. *Negrita* or *negrilla* is the diminutive adjective for *negra*. The diminutive was used to refer to children.
48. For more on Juana and her participation in the trial read Lissette Acosta Corniel, "Juana Gelofa Pelona: An Enslaved but Insubordinate Witness in Santo Domingo (1549-1555)," *PerspectivasAfro* 1/2 (January–June 2022): 77–90.
49. Rodríguez Morel, *Orígenes de la economía*, 170.
50. Marte, *Santo Domingo en los manuscritos*, 397. The English translation for *ganadoras* is *earner*.
51. Malagón Barceló, *Código negro*, 147.
52. Malagón Barceló, *Código negro*, 142.
53. AGI, Santo Domingo, 83. This census was also published by Emilio Rodríguez in *Relaciones históricas de Santo Domingo* (Santo Domingo, Dominican Republic: Sociedad Dominicana de Bibliófilos, 2008), 375. This current work utilizes the version transcribed by Laura Gutiérrez Arbulu, and revised by Anthony Stevens Acevedo for CUNY DSI.
54. There are thirty-five women listed on the census identified as Black, six of whom are listed as farm owners. However, I am also including Catalina Bran, who is listed as having a cassava, corn, and other legumes farm in Nigua. This raises the number of women to thirty-six. Bran was one of the ethnic groups that many of the enslaved people belonged to. Similarly, the number of free men of color is thirty, but I am also including a Black man, Juan Romero Prieto, because of his last name. Like Bran, Prieto was generally a name given to Blacks. This brings the number of free Black men in La Española to 31. For reference on Catalina Bran, see entry #103 in the census under *"Estancias de Nigua, de Yuca y maíz y otras legumbres*. For reference on Juan Romero Prieto, see entry #62 in the census under *"Vezinos de la ciudad de Sant Antonio de Monte de Plata."* Also, Bartolomé Rodríguez, entry #616 is listed as a maroon, *"simarron"* and as having a wife and relatives.
55. Wheat, 166.
56. John D. Garrigus, "Vincent Ogé "jeune" (1757–1791): Social Class and Free Colored Mobilization on the Eve of the Haitian Revolution," *The Americas* 68, no. 1 (July 2011): 33.
57. Emilio R. Demorizi, *Relaciones históricas*, 377. Footnote by Fray Cipriano de Utrera. The Spanish version of this chapter published by this author in 2015, listed only forty-two Black women, focusing on the women listed in the city of Santo Domingo, and did not include the additional three women residing in Santiago de los Caballeros, San Juan Baptista de Bayaguana, and Cotuí.
58. Jennifer L. Morgan, *Laboring Women*, 91.
59. Morgan, *Laboring Women*, 92.
60. AGN, Rep. Dom., Archivo de Bayaguana, fo. 1v. This case was first cited by Alejandrina Liriano in Alejandra Liriano: *El papel de la mujer de origen afri-*

cano en el Santo Domingo colonial, siglos XVI–XVII. Santo Domingo, Dominican Republic: Centro de Investigacion para la Accion Femenina, 1992.

    61. AGI, Justicia 103-A, F. 3608R–3608V, CUNY DSI Dominican Colonial Documents Collection.

    62. Alice B. Gould, *Nueva lista documentada de los tripulantes de Colón en 1492* (Madrid, Spain: Real Academia de la Historia, 1984), 2.

Archives

Archivo General de Indias, Seville Spain (AGI).
Archivo General de Puerto Rico (San Juan) (AGPR).
Archivo General de la Nación, Dominican Republic (AGN-DR).
Collection of Colonial Documents, CUNY Dominican Studies Institute.

Bibliography

Acosta Corniel, Lissette. "Juana Gelofa Pelona: An Enslaved but Insubordinate Witness in Santo Domingo (1549–1555)." *PerspectivasAfro* 1/2 (January–June 2022): 77–90.

Albert Batista, Celsa. *Mujer y esclavitud en Santo Domingo*. Santo Domingo, Dominican Republic: Instituto Dominicano de Estudios Africanos y Asiáticos, 2013.

Altman, Ida. *Life and Society in the Early Spanish Caribbean: The Greater Antilles (1493–1550)*. Baton Rouge: Louisiana State University Press, 2021.

Altman, Ida. "Marriage, Family, and Ethnicity in the Early Spanish Caribbean." *William & Mary Quarterly* 70, no. 2 (2013): 225–50.

Benzo de Ferrer, Vilma. *Pasajeros a La Española, 1492–1530*. Santo Domingo, Dominican Republic: n.p., 2000.

Carpentier, Alejo. *Music in Cuba*. Minneapolis: University of Minnesota Press, 2001.

Cipriano de Utrera. *Santo Domingo: dilucidaciones históricas*. Santo Domingo, Dominican Republic: Secretaría de Estado de Educación, Bellas Artes y Cultos, 1995.

Deive, Carlos. *Carlos Esteban Deive's La Mala Vida: Delincuencia y Picaresca En La Colonia Española de Santo Domingo*. Santo Domingo, Dominican Republic: Taller, 1997.

Esteban Deive, Carlos, and Fundación Cultural Dominicana. *Los guerrilleros negros: esclavos fugitivos y cimarrones en Santo Domingo*. Santo Domingo, Dominican Republic: Fundación Cultural Dominicana, 1989.

Garrigus, J. D. "Vincent Ogé Jeune (1757–91): Social Class and Free Colored Mobilization on the Eve of the Haitian Revolution." *Americas Americas* 68, no. 1 (2011): 33–62.

Gil, Juan. "La gente de Ovando en los protocolos hispalenses." *Anuario de Estudios Americanos* 63, no. 1 (2006): 255–87.
Gould, Alicia B. *Nueva lista documentada de los tripulantes de Colón en 1492*. Madrid, Spain: Real Academia de la Historia, 1985.
Harrisse, Henry. *The Discovery of North America: A Critical, Documentary, and Historic Investigation*. Amsterdam: N. Israel, 1961.
Lamb, Ursula, and Miguel Muñoz de San Pedro. *Frey Nicolás de Ovando gobernador de las Indias (1501–1509)*. Madrid, Spain: CSIC Instituto Gonzalo Fernández de Oviedo, 1956.
Liriano, Alejandra. *El papel de la mujer de origen africano en el Santo Domingo colonial, siglos XVI–XVII*. Santo Domingo, Dominican Republic: Centro de Investigación para la Acción Femenina, CIPAF, 1992.
Malagón Barceló, Javier. *Código negro carolino o Código negro español*. Santo Domingo, Dominican Republic: Ediciones de Taller, 1974.
Morgan, Jennifer L. *Laboring Women: Reproduction and Gender in New World Slavery*. Philadelphia: University of Pennsylvania Press, 2004.
Muñóz, Juan Bautista, Roberto Marte, Manuel Antonio García Arévalo, and Fundación García-Arévalo. *Santo Domingo en los Manuscritos de Juan Bautista Muñoz*. Santo Domingo, Dominican Republic: Fundación García Arévalo, 1981.
O'Sullivan-Beare, Nancy. *Las mujeres de los conquistadores; la mujer española en los comienzos de la colonización americana*. Madrid, Spain: Compañía bibliográfica española, 1957.
Palmié, Stephan, and Francisco A. Scarano. *The Caribbean: A History of the Region and Its Peoples*. Chicago, IL: University of Chicago Press 2011.
Ramos, Demetrio, Universidad de Valladolid, and Seminario Americanista. *Audacia, negocios y política en los viajes españoles de "descubrimiento y rescate."* Valladolid, Spain: Universidad. Seminario Americanista, 1981.
Rodríguez Morel, Genaro. *Orígenes de la economía de plantación de La Española*. Santo Domingo, Dominican Republic: Editora Nacional, 2012.
Sáez, José Luis. *La Iglesia y el negro esclavo en Santo Domingo: una historia de tres siglos*. Santo Domingo, Dominican Republic: Patronato de la ciudad colonial de Santo Domingo, 1994.
Silva Campo, Ana María. "Fragile Fortunes: Afrodescendant Women, Witchcraft, and the Remaking of Urban Cartagena." *Colonial Latin American Review* 30, no. 2 (2021): 197–213.
Terrazas Williams, Danielle. *The Capital of Free Women: Race, Legitimacy, and Liberty in Colonial Mexico*. New Haven, CT, and London, Yale University Press, 2022.
von Germeter, Nicole. "Paula de Eguiluz, Seventeenth-Century Puerto Rico, Cuba and New Granada (Colombia)." In *As if She Were Free: A Collective Biography of Women and Emancipation in the Americas*, edited by Erica

L. Ball, Tatianna Seijas, and Terri L. Snyder, 43–57. New York: Cambridge University Press, 2020.

Wheat, David. *Atlantic Africa and the Spanish Caribbean, 1570–1640.* Chapel Hill: University of North Carolina Press and the Omohundro Institute of Early American History & Culture, 2018.

Chapter 6

Transgressing Social, Gender, and Sexual Norms in Colonial Santo Domingo (1716–1719)

JACQUELINE JIMÉNEZ POLANCO

Circumventing or transgressing the customs and norms of capitalist societies is not a new experience for Dominican women, neither it is something exclusively derived from their fruitful migratory journey. It is rooted in a rich cultural heritage that has transcended time, space, and political systems. Historical documents of the colonial era show, for instance, that despite the rigid rules of the Spanish government, Dominican women were either bypassing the norms to play key roles in social, political, and economic realms of early Dominican society, or breaking the prevailing public regulations as a form of resistance against rigid and oppressive patriarchal institutions.

In this chapter, I explore the transgressing journeys of María de las Nieves, Isabel Lorenzo, María Magdalena, and Andrea Díaz: four urban Dominican women in eighteenth-century Santo Domingo, who did not conform to the strict marital, monogamous, modest, and secluded sexual and social status imposed on women by the confessional Catholic state of the Spanish Empire. They challenged the colonial dominant culture by being single and mothers of illegitimate children, nurturing passionate sexual relationships, and living in women-only households.

Three of the women, María de las Nieves, María Magdalena, and Andrea Díaz, were mulattos born in La Española. The fourth woman, Isabel Lorenzo, was born in the Canary Islands. As free mulatto women, María de las Nieves, María Magdalena, and Andrea Díaz had more upward social mobility than Black women, but their access to wealth was limited by their lack of "clean blood." As pointed out by Asunción Lavrin, mulatto women in the Spanish colonies were an important component of the labor market in the cities and in rural areas. Some of them were sellers or owners of small shops, houses, and plots. They had the same interests in material possessions that white Hispanic people did. When it came to marriage, mulatto women nurtured relationships with men from different ethnic groups but they mainly ended up marrying men from their own groups.[1] The mulatto women discussed in this chapter were poor, had little or no valuable properties, and were single.

The acts of deviance committed by these women against the cultural norms of sexual behavior that sustained the official matrimonial structure were severely punished during this colonial period, as they followed the laws of Las Siete Partidas. The laws of Las Siete Partidas of Alfonso X in Castille severely punished acts of sexual misconduct committed by women. For example, for adultery, the husband was allowed to kill the wife if she cheated and was caught. Also, women who were considered prostitutes were expelled from their hometowns.[2] In essence, the laws of Las Siete Partidas changed the notion of partnership and marriage prevailing until the Council of Trent, during which, as stated by Sperling, "informal domestic partnerships were a very common form of marriage in most Catholic countries, especially in the Iberian Peninsula."[3]

The social, economic, political, and cultural order imposed by Las Siete Partidas created strict governmental and religious mechanisms targetted at cutting down the popular perceptions of sexuality as the symbolic expression of passionate love and imposing the traditional Catholic sexuality based on the economic and social basis of the marital union.

Historiographical studies observe differences in the emergence of the symbolic expression of love and sexuality in Europe and the North American colonies. According to Stone, the eighteenth century marked the origin in England of the first expressions of romantic love and its association with marriage. He states that romantic love became a respectable motive for marriage among the propertied classes in 1780, and it became fashionable and more common in the mid- and late eighteenth centuries.[4] LaFleur observes that in the North American colonies there was also an increasing visibility of sexual behavior in the eighteenth century, in which "the environmental logic fundamentally shaped the way sex was understood."[5] Hardwick, on the other hand, states that expressions of romantic love and its association with marriage existed earlier in France, at least throughout the sixteenth and eighteenth centuries. She argues that an elite interest in sexual pleasure was evident from the sixteenth century, and passionate love was commonly practiced among ordinary people, including single individuals who engaged in intercourse before marriage.[6]

Analysis of sexuality in the Spanish colonies observes that the subliminal element of romantic love that fused affectionate and spiritual connotations with sexual attraction in the empire, and whose practice endured at least until the Council of Trent (1545–1563), was not exported to the colonies in the Americas. Here the economic and social nature of the sexual matrimonial link always prevailed, either to increase the indigenous and Black labor force or to guarantee the heredity rights of colonizers and their descendants; and, ultimately, to guarantee the benefits that the metropolis derived from in both cases. As examined by Samudio in Venezuela, the preservation of the socioeconomic status as a precondition for marriage was still in force even during the demise of the colonial era in the nineteenth century, which in any event propelled clandestine marriages that were forbidden and severely punished by royal decrees (*reales cédulas*).[7]

In colonial Santo Domingo, the control of people's intimacy and sexuality was so profuse that, as stated by Moya Pons, the governor, who was also the captain general and president of the colony, spent long nights walking in the dark through the paved dirty streets of the city followed by notaries and bailiffs, to respond to complaints about "communications and awkward and ilicit treatments" (*"comunicaciones y tratos torpes e ilícitos"*). Those who were punished for "public sins" were Blacks, brown, free mulattos, simple shoemakers, slaves, or *grifos* of "bad living" (*"de mal vivir"*).[8]

María de las Nieves, Isabel Lorenzo, María Magdalena, and Andrea Díaz were conscientious objectors who lived out of the ordinary. Not only did these women violate the institutional norms and customs that established the matrimonial link as the only legitimate mechanism for sexual relationships, parenthood, and socialization; but they took responsibility for their "illegal" and "immoral" behavior (*pecados públicos*) and the recurring punishments imposed by the colonial judicial system. These women's violation of the prevailing marital social and sexual order could be analyzed as a form of resistance of the common people against the dominant colonial norms. And it could be so by the sole fact of disrupting the strict rules, even though in some cases they admitted it, and, in other cases, they denied it. Popularly known as *golfas* and *rubizas*, or *mujeres de amor* (i.e., women of love) for being single and self-reliant,[9] these women lived a passionate sexuality that went beyond the institutional and social requirements that imposed heterosexual marriage as the only legitimate form of social and family relationships.

Trial against María de las Nieves, Isabel Lorenzo, and María Magdalena

In the city of Santo Domingo the fifteen of March of seventeen nineteen, Your Honor Sir Don Fernando Constanzo y Ramires Cauallero of the Order of Santiago, Brigadier and Major General of the Royal Armies of his Majesty, President of the Royal Audience and Governor and Captain General of this Island Española said that he received the news that three women with bad reputation, María de las Nieves, Isabel Lorenzo, and María Magdalena, live in the site of Santa Ana and their scandalous behavior disturbs the vicinity and generates discord among the neighbors, with grave harm for the service of his Majesties, especially now during the Holly Lent.[10]

The rigorous trial involved the accusation, imprisonment, confiscation of the possessions the women had in their rented thatch-roofed houses (*bojíos*), and conviction. The judge ordered that the three women were secluded in separated rooms in jail, so that they could not communicate among themselves. The imprisonment and confiscation of properties of María de las Nieves, Isabel Lorenzo, and María Magdalena preceded the hearing of nine witnesses (four female and five male neighbors), the confessions of the four women, and that of Sebastián López, a canoe builder. As pointed out by Ana María Silva Campos, confiscation of property during a trial was a colonial practice intended to dispossess Afro-descendant women and disrupt their tight-knit communities in desirable areas of the city.[11]

DEPOSITIONS OF THE WITNESSES

The witnesses Ana Rodríguez, María Escaño, Fabiana Rodríguez, María de la O y de Moya, Pedro Padilla, Juan Valera, Christoval Padilla, Juan

Ximenez, and Manuel Marques stated under oath and after gesturing the cross signal, that they knew those women and described them as scandalous prostitutes (*rameras*) and single or unmarried women who quarreled often.[12]

Fabiana Rodríguez stated that María de las Nieves lived alone in a house in the site of Santa Ana, and was sexually involved with the canoe builder Sebastián López, who was the only man who visited and sustained her and with whom she had a daughter who had died. She added that on the holiday of Three Kings Day (*el día de los Santos Reyes*) María de las Nieves came into the witness's house, running away from Sebastián López because he wanted to beat her. She also stated that the other two women, Isabel Lorenzo and María Magdalena, were living together in a rented house in the same area of the city and allowed anyone who brought them money to come into their house, and they often yelled to one another when they were quarreling, which bothered and scandalized the neighborhood. Fabiana Rodríguez also said that sometimes she had lodged complaints to these women for their scandals and quarrels and they had responded with expletives. She also said that she wanted no scandal with anyone, because she was married to a boat maker and did not want her husband to lose control by confronting these women, who were uncontrollable.

María de la O y de Moya declared that these single women were often quarreling, using as a pretext a chicken or a hen and publicizing the bad life they had, yelling at each other whether they got pregnant, delivered babies out of wedlock, or other "dishonest" things that she omitted to say for the sake of modesty and respect to justice. When asked whether she knew who came into these women's houses, whether they had children, and what they did for a living, she said that Isabel Lorenzo had three children with an unknown man and that she'd seen her sometimes hanging washed clothes, knitting, and sewing; but she didn't know if anyone entered Isabel's house because the only thing she could see from her house was the patio's door.

In their separate depositions Pedro Padilla, Juan Valera, Christoval Padilla, Juan Ximenez, and Manuel Marques affirmed that the three women were not married or single and were public prostitutes (*rameras*), and they knew that because they had heard them squabbling and yelling dishonest words. Juan Ximenez Christoval Padilla and Manuel Marques indicated that although they knew these women were prostitutes, they did not know whether they had illicit friendships with some men; except for María de las Nieves's illicit friendship with Sebastián López, whose clothes she washed and for whom she cooked breakfast, lunch, and dinner when he came to stay in her house, and with whom she had a daughter who had died. The witnesses added that both María de las Nieves and Sebastián López had been incarcerated twice in the Royal Prison (*Cárcel Real*) for their illicit friendship.

Juan Valera stated that Isabel Lorenzo was the mother of three children; two of them she procreated with Juan de Pineda, but he did not know who the father of the other child was. The last male witness, Manuel Marquez, said that María de las Nieves had one child and María Magdalena had a child who died, but he had not heard who the fathers of those children were.

Confession of Sebastián López

In his confession, Sebastián López said that he knew María de las Nieves (or María Paula) and that he used to visit her house because she cooked and washed the clothes for him, and he paid her for doing that work. He added that he visited María Paula because he was a foreigner and didn't know another person who could cook or wash for him. He also explained that he came into María Paula's home at a proper time and that he lived in a separate room he had rented to stay over when he came to the city for eight or ten days, because the rest of the time he was working in the countryside.

Confession of María de las Nieves

In her confession, she said her name was María de las Nieves (alias María Paula), born and raised in the city of Santo Domingo, did not know her age, and was a single woman who had never been married. The governor indicated that she seemed to be between thirty-two and thirty-three years old. She admitted that she had been in prison twice in the last two and a half years for an illicit friendship with Sebastián López, an official canoe builder (*Official de Canoero*). The last imprisonment was one month and a half ago and only lasted two days. She was released for lack of evidence against her.

María de las Nieves affirmed that she'd returned to the illicit friendship with Sebastián López because one year ago he'd told her that he'd received news that his wife had died in Campeche (Yucatan Peninsula, Mexico), and that he was determined to marry her because of the love he felt for her (*por el cariño que le tenía*).¹³ She also said that she didn't want him to convince her, and she told him that she wouldn't give him a response because she didn't want him to come and deceive her, getting her in trouble with the law. He told her that he was not deceiving her and gave the name of a coworker who could confirm he was telling the truth. María de las Nieves declared that she had decided to reestablish communication with Sebastián approximately a month before the last storm seven months ago. She stated that she did so supposing that he would eventually become her husband.

At the end of the hearing, María de las Nieves was asked if she had any doubt that what was the cause of arrest, as she had confessed, was that she had relapsed in her illicit friendship with Sebastián López, which had caused the noise and scandalous behavior described in the summary. She replied that she knew that the cause of her arrest was that illicit friendship although she originally thought it was for a dispute (*pendencia*) she had with another woman (Fabiana, the wife of Manuel Marquez), whose last name she did not know. Then, María was asked how was it that she had relapsed in her illicit friendship with Sebastián, after being warned the first time she was in jail to abstain from committing the crime of illicit friendship and to live in modest seclusion, because otherwise she would be judged with all the rigor of the law and would be indicted with the punishments established in the code.

María was also asked how was it that she had dared to continue to live in concubinage with such little fear of the divine and human laws, disrespecting and disobeying justice. She responded that, "failing as a poor and ignorant woman she let the so-called Sebastián López deceive her under the assumption that he would be her husband and that she had nothing more to say (*herrando como una pobre mujer ignorante se dejo engañar del dicho Sebastian Lopez en el supuesto de que avía de ser su marido y que no tiene que decir otra cosa*)."¹⁴ María's experience replicated the common practice in colonial Santo Domingo of men not fulfilling promises of marriage in order to obtain sexual favors that, as stated by Deive, often resulted in women's rape, undesired pregnancy, and the trickster's runaway.¹⁵

CONFESSION OF ISABEL LORENZO

In her confession, she said her name was Isabel Lorenza, originally from the Canary Islands, that she was thirty years of age, more or less, and was not a married or a widow, but a "single woman." Throughout the hearing, Isabel denied all the accusations. She was asked how it was that she did not know why she was imprisoned when the summary indicated that she had led a scandalous life and had been publicly receiving different men in her house, and causing many disputes with other neighbors. She said that although the witnesses had said in the summary that her life was scandalous, it was not true. She said that she sustained her three children (two little baby boys and one nine-year-old girl) with the money she earned sewing other people's clothes and knitting, and that she spent most of the day "washing clothes in a tray to avoid doing illicit things (*estando lo mas del dia lavando en una vatea por no hazer cosa ilicita*)."[16]

Isabel was then asked how was it that she said she did not have a scandalous life and was not a *mujer de mala vida* (a prostitute) because she was not married and had not been married when she gave birth to her three children. She replied that she did not deny she had three children, but she procreated them with a man who left the city six years ago, and she made that mistake under the assumption that he would be her husband; but he had died leaving her with that load and without a remedy. Isabel was then asked how was it that she said she did not commit that sin again, when the witnesses declared in the summary that she was a prostitute who allowed anyone who brought her money to come into her house, which resulted in her scandalous and bad life; and that when she and the other women quarreled, they yelled at each other that they were involved in those crimes. She replied that she could not shut off the world's mouth, but it was false that she or any of the other women were having illicit friendships, were saying indecent words, or making noise. She also denied what the witnesses had said of having heard her saying that she procreated her children with Juan Pineda. She did not sign her confession because she said she did not know how, and the judge signed for her.

Confession of María Magdalena

In her confession, María Magdalena said that she was born in Maniel, Azua, was twenty-two years old, was single, and had never been married. Since she was more than twenty-two years of age and less than twenty-five, she was told that she needed a curator, and the judge ordered her to suspend her confession until she had named a curator *ad litem* who defended her, unless she wanted a legal aid. She named the attorney general to the Royal

Court as her curator *ad litem*, who accepted, took the oath and signed his nomination, and then named as guarantor the porter of the Royal Court. María Magdalena could not sign the nomination because she said she did not know how. She was asked whether she knew why she was imprisoned, and she replied she guessed it was because Fabiana (Manuel Marquez's woman) lodged a complaint against her, María (de las Nieves) de Paula, and Isabel (Lorenzo) Lorenza. She was asked the reason and she said that she presumed it was due to a noise in María (de las Nieves) de Paula's house on Tuesday night, because Sebastián López wanted to kill another man for a bottle of rum that was missing.

Then María Magdalena was asked how was it that she denied the cause of her imprisonment, responding to the question about another cause; she replied that if that was not the cause for the complaint against her, she did not know another cause. She was asked how she could have denied not knowing another cause if the information in the summary indicated that she was a public prostitute who scandalized her vicinity.

María Magdalena replied that she denied having caused a scandal in her vicinity and that none of her neighbors could have witnessed that because, although as a girl she had fallen into some feebleness, she had left all that well before the last storm, following the advice of her father who had arranged for her to marry a Black man from Azua, who seemed to be a slave of the Ramirez, and would be waiting for her on Easter or soon afterward.

María Magdalena said that she denied the accusations of being continuously quarreling with María (de las Nieves) de Paula and Isabel (Lorenzo) Lorenza and yelling dishonest words that had disturbed people in the vicinity, because she had spent most of the time in the countryside, and although she lived with Isabel, she had never had any fights with her. She had had some fights with María (de las Nieves) de Paula, but only over some baby chicken that she was raising because when they went into María's house they damaged her house and she killed them. But they did not say dishonest words to each other.

María Magdalena was asked how was it that she said she was not a prostitute, meaning that she was living with Isabel Lorenza, who had three children without being or having been married—meaning that there were witnesses who said that she and Isabel allowed anyone who brought them money to come into their house. She said it was false that she persisted in hanging out with men, because she had stopped doing that many days ago; and she was intended for marriage and could lose this convenient agreement. She did not sign her confession because she said she did not know how, and the judge signed for her.

Confiscation of Properties

In the requisition of the rented houses of the three women, the authorities did not find properties that could be confiscated in María de las Nieves's home, but only useless pieces of furniture that had no value. In Isabel Lorenza and María Magdalena's house the colonial authorities found some valuable pieces that were confiscated, such as a bed with an old mattress of Ceyba wool, two benches, an old spitting bowl, and a lamp bowl. Recent studies on women's trials in Spanish colonies inform that seizure of their properties through confiscation involved a final sale at auctions in which men (in some cases members of the elite) were the ones who purchased the accused women's properties, which allowed them to expand their property holdings. Therefore, as Silva Campo states, removing a woman for trial "meant not only apprehending her body but also upending and refashioning her connections to the social and material worlds that she inhabited."[17]

The Verdict

The judge declared the three women guilty, especially María de las Nieves (alias de Paula) for her illicit friendship with Sebastián López, a married man who lived with her in the same house and for whom she was there for whatever he needed—scandalizing people in her vicinity with her behavior as it was explained in the witnesses' summary. The judge also found María de las Nieves guilty of relapsing in the same crime for which she was previously found guilty in 1716, although she was pardoned on the day of Sir Saint Louis, after spending some time in prison, with the obligation to live in modest seclusion. She was then warned that if she did otherwise, the corresponding punishments would be rigorously applied, particularly if she had allowed Sebastián López to come into her house, which she admitted she did in violation of the law and with little fear of God and her conscience.

María de las Nieves's pardon followed her first imprisonment three years before, after the trial against her and Sebastián. The judge's pardon to María de las Nieves was preceded by a letter she sent to the judge, in which she asked to be released from jail. In the letter she said that she had sent it with her little daughter, because she did not have another person whom she could rely on. She also said that she was experiencing many difficulties in jail; there were days when by 4:00 p.m. she had not eaten breakfast yet; she was afflicted for the calamities of her daughter, and she had neither money nor a guarantor since she was alone in Santo Domingo City. In that trial she denied having an illicit friendship with Sebastián, although she admitted she cooked for him and washed his clothes to sustain herself and her children, as the "extremely poor woman she was (*pobre de solemnidad*)."[18] Sebastián also denied the accusation and affirmed he was originally from Alicante and was married to a woman in Spain. In his verdict, the judge stated that the fact that María de las Nieves had children without having been married was considered scandalizing, although she did not have those children with Sebastián. It was also considered illicit that Sebastián was living in the island for over six years without his wife. The judge ordered that María de las Nieves be remitted to the Ville of Guava, where the female shortage had allowed other women like her to find men who married them, which avoided scandalous behaviors. The judge released Sebastián under parole following his petition of paying a fine after finishing the construction of some canoes in Najayo Beach. He was warned of not relapsing in the illicit friendship and communication with María (de Paula) de las Nieves. The judge also found Sebastián López guilty and ordered his imprisonment and the confiscation of his properties.[19]

When María de las Nieves was notified of the provisional sentence in the Royal Prison, she told the scribe that she did not have any defense and consented that the judge dictate a definitive verdict in her case. The judge emitted a decree in which María de las Nieves was notified that she needed to discharge and defend herself in the term of three days, and that after the expiration of that term there would be another five-day term for the final verdict, and then she could allege and justify what she considered convenient for her. In the final verdict against Isabel Lorenza and María Magdalena, the judge stated that, since they had not been previously admonished for these excesses, he would order that they be released from prison. He warned them to live an honest and secluded life from now on, with no scandalous behavior, "without causing trouble (*sin dar nota*)"[20] or quarreling with any person, and using modesty in their words; otherwise, they would be punished by the law.

The judge ordered that Isabel Lorenza move away from María Magdalena's thatch-roofed house (*bojío*) and from that neighborhood, since it was considered inauspicious that she lived there and in the company of María Magdalena. It was also ordered that María Magdalena's father be notified to pick her up and arrange her marriage with a Black (*un moreno*)[21] man from the Ville of Azua, in compliance with what she had expressed in her confession.[22]

Trial against Andrea Díaz

The governor said he received information about a woman with bad reputation,[23] Andrea, who lived in Convento de San Francisco Street and whose scandalous behavior disturbed the vicinity, with great harm for the religious service of his Majesty, especially during Lent (*Quaresma*). The trial included the accusation, imprisonment, confiscation of properties, the hearing of five male witnesses (three soldiers, the reformer of the neighborhood precinct, and a neighbor), Andrea's confession, and her conviction.

Deposition of the Witnesses

The witnesses Alferez Joseph Luis, Francisco de Fonseca, Nicolás de la Concepción, Domingo Moreno, and Phelipe Lozano affirmed under oath, and gesturing the cross signal, that they knew Andrea, who lived as a single woman and prostitute and who was *dando la nota* (scandalizing) the vicinity with the frequent visit to her house of a friar (*un fraile lego*) from one of the convents of the city. The witnesses declared that Andrea was the mother of several children (aged three, four, or five) and a baby that she was breastfeeding, and that they did not know who the father of her older children and baby was. Nicolás de la Concepción stated that the friar had been visiting Andrea during naptime (*siesta*) for the last seven years, and that these visits had taken place during daytime. During their depositions, the witnesses indicated the name and convent of the friar, but this information was not included in the description of the case.

Confession of Andrea Díaz

In her confession, Andrea said that she was born in the city of Santo Domingo and was more or less thirty-five years old. She also said that she was single, for she had never been married. When she was asked whether she knew the reasons why she had been imprisoned, she responded that she did not know. The judge asked her how she could say that she did not know the reasons for being imprisoned, meaning that she was breastfeeding a baby girl and raising other older children, which caused a grave scandal, considering that she confessed she was not married and had never been married.

Andrea admitted that she had never been married, was breastfeeding a baby girl and raising two more girls—one was twelve years old and the other was fourteen years old—plus a boy who was seventeen years old. She alleged that no one had come to live in her house (*no ha entrado nadie de asiento*) and that she had gotten pregnant four months ago by chance or disgrace, since she fell "as a fragile woman (*fue por una casualidad o desgracia suya, en que cayó como mujer frágil*)."[24] The judge asked Andrea which people visited her house as friends, neighbors, or as her clients for cooking and other services. She said that some countryside people stopped by to sell or buy products, and that the only person who visited her house on a regular basis was a friar, whose name and religion she did not mention out of respect to his habits. She informed the judge that the friar visited her house to give her good advice since she had been washing his clothes for the last eight years.

Andrea was asked how she could say that the religious man entered her house to give her good advice if the summary indicated that she had maintained a long-term illicit friendship with him, causing a grave and notorious scandal to all the vicinity. She replied that it wasn't true that she maintained an illicit friendship with the friar, whom she took for a saint, and that she didn't cause any scandal in the vicinity. The judge stated that he had heard that the baby Andrea was breastfeeding was the friar's child. Andrea attested, reaffirming what she had said. She added that the friar used to go to her house, sometimes during naptime and after praying, to look for oil (*manteca*) to fuel the *Santisimo*'s lamp that she kept in her house, as the prelate knew.

Andrea was asked how she claimed that she did not have an illicit friendship with the friar when the summary stated that she was cohabiting with him, took care of him when he was sick, cooked for him, and washed his clothes. She responded that, indeed, she took care of his clothes and meals and made some remedies for him when he was sick, but that she did not do that "with bad intentions but for good friendship (*nada de esto era por mal fin sino con buena amistad*)."[25] She did not sign her confession because she said she did not know how, and the judge signed for her.

CONFISCATION OF PROPERTIES

The authorities confiscated Andrea's thatch and palm leaf house, two cedarwood boxes with Andrea and her daughters' clothes and tiny gold pieces, a copper mortar, a copper cauldron, a copper weight with iron weighs, two old mahogany tables, three stools, and a small white mud pitcher.

THE VERDICT

The judge found Andrea, who had been imprisoned and whose properties had been confiscated, guilty. In his final verdict, the judge ordered Andrea to move from her neighborhood so that she could live far away from the friar to avoid any sort of communication with him, and to live honestly. The judge also stated that he would consult the superior prelate so the court ordered the appropriate punishment for the excess and scandal caused by the visit of the friar to Andrea's house.

Institutional Mechanisms to Control Social and Sexual Behavior in the Spanish-American Colonies

As we saw in the narrative of the legal trial of María (de Paula) de las Nieves, Isabel (Lorenzo) Lorenza, María Magdalena, and Andrea Díaz, the main concerns of the judge were that these women were living scandalous lives as single, never married, nonwidowed women, and in three cases they were the mothers of children they procreated with nonlegitimate fathers. These women's civil status as single (never married or widowed) and the mulatto racial component of María (de Paula) de las Nieves, María Magdalena, and Andrea Díaz was basic to their lower socioeconomic conditions and class status. The Royal Archives of Higüey show that between the seventeenth and twentieth centuries, the participation of women in commercial activities was common, and that divorced and widowed women fostered commercial relations. This was salient in the eighteenth century, the time of this trial, when contraband, cattle, estate, and slave business prevailed, and women purchased and sold slaves in the domestic sphere of the family. And yet, widowed and divorced entrepreneurial women reacted against the establishment, for instance, for the prohibition of getting involved in the illicit activity of mercery, but they did so in the specific margins allowed by the Catholic Church and the dominant society.[26]

The four women discussed in this chapter were single and had never been married or widowed. They were poor and illiterate,[27] had no properties, and were imprisoned, dispossessed of their little possessions, and judged, although only in one case (María de las Nieves's), could the court attest that the neighbors had actually seen them hanging out with men or nurturing illicit friendships with men. Consequently, from a legal/religious standpoint, María de las Nieves was depicted as an unredeemed deviant, a criminal, and ultimately as an outcast whose only place was prison. First, she violated the verdict of the first trial that ordered her to move to Ville of Guava and marry a man there after she had denied her illicit friendship with Sebastián *el canoero*, and four years later she admitted her illicit friendship with the same man in a second trial.

In contrast, the possibility of marriage for María Magdalena, even when the future groom was a Black slave, would change her fate, eventually placing her in a less marginal social stratum that would redeem her from her past crimes and sins. That is why the judge ordered Isabel Lorenzo to move out of the home she shared with María Magdalena, so as to avoid María Magdalena continuing to contaminate the future bride and now innocent girl with her hideous and illicit behavior. The eventual marriage between María Magdalena and the *moreno* from Azua would be possible because of the medieval laws of *Siete Partidas*, which regulated that the slavery system in the Spanish-American colonies follow the Roman legislation, in which *the slave was legally considered a thing, with growing probabilities of assimilating the concept of person*. The application to the slaves of the "concept of person" implied that they could get married following the Christian ritual, whether or not their masters consented to their marriage. And although the matrimonial unit did not emancipate them, slaves were allowed, however, to marry other slaves or free persons. To avoid the dissolution of the marital unit, *the Partidas* established that the enslaved couple could not be sold separately. This meant that once the slave had married a free or enslaved person, he or she could not be separated from his wife or her husband. That matrimonial condition was addressed at perpetuating the slavery system through the grounded and sacred structure of the family.[28]

Also, since María Magdalena was underage, she needed the consent of her father. Since the application in Spain of the Toro Laws in 1505, and their interpretations in the colonies, the male parent could disinherit an underage offspring (male or female) who married clandestinely and without his consent. However, until 1776, the control of marriage depended almost exclusively on the archbishop's jurisdiction and the ecclesiastic courts that generally rejected the male parent's objection to consent to the marriage based on ethnic and economic reasons. This contributed to an increase of interracial/interethnic and interclass marriages that lasted until after the application of the Pragmatic Sanction of the Bourbon King Carlos III. The Pragmatic Sanction was intended to control the marriage between "unequals," and at limiting the jurisdiction of the Church in the family issues by transferring them to the courts (*Audiencias*). It reestablished the parental control over marriage and included the disinheritance and later the inability to occupy public positions (1790) as contraventions to clandestine marriages. This legislation applied to everybody: whites, Blacks, and indigenous people. Some authors maintain that this law marked the origin of the patriarchal authority in the Americas.[29] As stated by Verena Martinez-Alier, "by severely restricting freedom of marriage, the Royal Pragmatic lent legal support to the aspiration of social exclusiveness."[30]

In the colonial era the family (heterosexual family) was, therefore, perceived as a main social place where the behavioral norms were established. It constituted the social basis for the preservation of customs, order, and certain traditions that were considered as normal behavior. And until the second half of the eighteenth century, the flexibility of the ecclesiastic courts toward interethnic/interracial and interclass marriages was aimed at promoting marriages as a means of social control and increasing the population. This may explain why during the trial, nothing was said about the possibility of María de las Nieves, Isabel Lorenzo, and María Magdalena being involved in a "no-natural" woman-to-woman or lesbian relationship, not even in the case of Isabel Lorenza and María Magdalena, who lived in the same *bojío* and who, based on their own confessions, admitted to having a good friendship.

In the case of Andrea Díaz, the judge punished her with prison and ostracism for her illicit friendship with a friar who was excluded from any punishment. The narrative of the trial indicates the clear intention of the judge to protect the good name of the religious figure who, as stated by González Marmolejo, was imbued with a kind image promoted to help and convey peace,[31] while Andrea persisted in her having a good friendship with the friar as her adviser. González Marmolejo points out that the exchange of sexual favors for the absolution of sins was a common practice in the Spanish colonies during the eighteenth and nineteenth centuries. In Spain, Mexico, and other Spanish colonies (Filipinas, Nicaragua, Honduras, and Guatemala), the Inquisition called it crime of solicitation (*delito de solicitación*), interpreted as any form of sexual initiation that a cleric imposed on her spiritual daughter. It was considered a transgression to ecclesiastical celibacy and, conjointly with forbidden literature and bigamy, was highly persecuted and punished with the clerics' imprisonment and confiscation of properties. Also, other punishments were the exile of the clerics and the perpetual prohibition to receive the confession of women.[32] In the analysis of 800 denunciations in the Archbishop of Mexico, González Marmolejo found a wide range of testimonies detailing the relationships between the clerics and their female congregation. Most of the clerics' illicit relationships involved single young women.[33] The clerics used a wide variety of methods to seduce their spiritual daughters, including aggression and violence. In all the cases studied by Marmolejo, the clerics accused were punished. The punishment, however, did not stop the crime of solicitation, which in many cases was committed with the complicity and simulation of society. In addition, as pointed out by Lavrin, clerics were rarely expelled from the church for seducing a woman.[34]

As observed in Andrea Díaz's case, unlike other Spanish colonies where the clerics were persecuted and punished for the crime of solicitation, in Santo Domingo sexual relationships between clerics and female congregations implied the punishment of the women and the dismissal of the religious men, for whom the sexual misconduct was seen as a scandalous anecdote.

Conclusion

María (de Paula) de las Nieves, Isabel (Lorenzo) Lorenza, María Magdalena, and Andrea Díaz transgressed the social, gender, and sexual norms in colonial Santo Domingo, during a historical period when the strict laws ruling sexuality, marriage, and family were controlled by both the state and the church. The state was interested in conferring a legal character to the marital union that guaranteed the inheritance and division of goods between the couple and the offspring. The church had established its sacramental cohesion to maintain a link between the material and the spiritual.

In essence, the state framed sexual behavior on the basis of a socioeconomic and political goal, and the protection of capitalist interests of the metropolis, the colonizers, and their heirs. The church constricted all expressions of sexuality to the achievement of a theological goal: the salvation of the soul.[35] Ultimately, the nonconformist behavior of these common women, alongside others from different socioeconomic strata and historical eras, planted the seeds of a cultural heritage that has nurtured the Dominican people for centuries and persists in today's postmodern era as women of color continue to circumvent or transgress the unequal gender rules of the patriarchal capitalist system.

Notes

1. Asunción Lavrin, "La mujer en la sociedad colonial hispanoamericana," in *Historia de América Latina*, ed. Leslie Bethel (Barcelona, Spain: Editorial Crítica, 1990), 23–24.

2. *Las Siete Partidas del Rey Don Alfonso el Sabio* (Madrid, Spain: Ediciones Atlas, 1972), Título 17, Ley 13; Título 22, Ley 2.

3. Jutta Sperling, "Marriage at the Time of the Council of Trent (1560–70): Clandestine Marriages, Kinship Prohibitions, and Dowry Exchange in European Comparison," *Journal of Early Modern History* 8, no. 1–2 (2004): 69.

4. Lawrence Stone, *The Family, Sex and Marriage in England, 1500–1800* (London: Penguin Books, 1990), 184–85.

5. As stated by LaFleur, during the eighteenth century, natural historians agreed that "human variety was due at least in part to one's environmental circumstances, including exposure (or lack thereof) to the sun's rays, the relative warmth of the climate, the food and drink one consumed, and even the social and political organization of one's society." Greta LaFleur, *The Natural History of Sexuality in Early America* (Baltimore, MD: Johns Hopkins University Press, 2018), 6, 7.

6. Julie Hardwick, "A Sexual Revolution in the Eighteenth Century?" *Age of Revolutions*, 2021, https://ageofrevolutions.com/2021/03/15/a-sexual-revolution-in-the-eighteenth-century/.

7. Edda O. Samudio A., "Un matrimonio en Mérida en el ocaso del período colonial," *Procesos Históricos: Revista de Historia y Ciencias Sociales* 4 (July–December 2003): 2–10.

8. Frank Moya Pons, *La vida escandalosa en Santo Domingo en los siglos XVII y XVIII*. Colección Inchaustegui (Santiago, Dominican Republic: Universidad Católica Madre y Maestra, 1976), 8.

9. Carlos Esteban Deive, *La mala vida: Delincuencia y picaresca en la colonia española de Santo Domingo* (Santo Domingo, Dominican Republic: Fundación Cultural Dominicana, 1988), 123.

10. Archivo General de Indias, Legajo No. 256 (February 22, 1722), 13.

> En la ciudad de Santo Domingo en quinze días del mes de marzo de mil setecientos y diez y nueve años Su Señoria el Sr. Dn Fernando Constanzo y Ramires Cauallero del Orden de Santiago Brigadier y

Magor Gral. De los Reales Exercitos de su Magd. Presidente de la Real Audiencia y Governador y Capitán Gral. De esta Isla española dijo que por quanto se le ha dado noticia a Su Señoria de que en el solar que llaman de Santa Ana viven tres mujeres de mala vida nombradas Maria de las Nieves, Isabel Lorenzo y Maria Magdalena y que con sus escándalos tienen alborata y en continua discordia aquella vecindad con grave perjuicio del Servicio de ambas Magestades mayormente en el Santo y presente tiempo de Quaresma.

11. Ana María Silva Campo, "Fragile Fortunes: Afrodescendant Women, Witchcraft and the Remaking of Urban Cartagena," *Colonial Latin American Review* 30, no. 2 (2021): 198.

12. According to Lavrin, there is little reference to prostitution in the colonial era, and there is doubt about its flourishing in the Americas as it did in Spain and the rest of Europe. This lack of information persists even though the Crown conferred a license to open a prostitution house in La Española in 1526. The professional practice of prostitution could prosper only in some large cities, because it was highly controlled by the church in small towns. Lavrin, "La mujer," 12–13.

13. Archivo, 21.

14. Archivo, 22.

15. Carlos Esteban Deive, *La mala vida*, 104.

16. Archivo, 23.

17. Ana María Silva Campo, "Fragile Fortunes," 198.

18. Archivo, 5.

19. Bigamy constituted a crime whose transgression had been tried by the Inquisition Court since the early sixteenth century until 1788, when bigamy was passed to the civil jurisdiction, as well as other regulations of marriage. Diana Marre, "La aplicación de la Pragmática de Carlos III en América Latina: Una Revisión," *Quaderns de l'Institut Catalá d'Antropologia* 10 (Winter 1997).

20. Archivo, 29vo.

21. Archivo, 30.

22. The fact that María Magdalena was twenty-two years old (or younger than twenty-five), was assigned a curator, and her father was ordered to organize her future marriage implies that she was a minor and, therefore, the judge was fulfilling the requirements of the Carlos III Royal Pragmatic of 1776 regarding the marriage of family's children, according to which minors could not marry without the authorization of their fathers. Rodrigo Andreucci Aguilera, "La pragmática de Carlos III sobre el matrimonio de los hijos de familia y su pervivencia en el derecho chileno," *Revista de Estudios Histórico-Jurídicos* 22 (2000).

23. *"El gobernador dice haber recibido noticia de que en la Calle del Convento de San Francisco vive una mujer de mala vida."* Archivo, 1.

24. Archivo, 8vo.

25. Archivo, 9no.

26. Dora Dávila-Mendoza, "Un concierto de voces: Mujer, familia y sociedad en Santo Domingo colonial," Dominican Studies Institute Working Paper 3 (1999).

27. Illiteracy was something common among lower-class women in the colonial era, when the lack of formal education wasn't seen as an obstacle to carry out activities outside the sphere of the house. Illiteracy was not an obstacle for legal transactions that were notarized in the presence of witnesses. Illiterate women could work in small shops and bakeries. Lavrin, "La mujer," 16–17.

28. Manuel Lucena Salmoral, *Leyes para esclavos y el ordenamiento jurídico sobre la condición, tratamiento, defensa y represión de los esclavos en las colonias de la América española*, vol. 1 (Madrid, Spain: Fundación Histórica Tavera, 2000), 8, 9, 25.

29. Diana Marre, "La aplicación de la Pragmática de Carlos III en América Latina: Una

Revisión," *Quaderns de l'Institut Catalá d'Antropologi*. 10 (Winter 1997): 217–49. Asunción Lavin, *Sexualidad y matrimonio en la América hispánica, Siglos XVI–XVIII* (Mexico City, Mexico: Consejo Nacional para la Cultura y las Artes, Editorial Grijalbo, 1991), 15–16.

30. Verena Martinez-Alier, *Marriage, Class, and Colour in Nineteenth-Century Cuba* (Cambridge, UK: Cambridge University Press, 1989), 1.

31. Jorge René González Marmolejo, *Sexo y confesión: La Iglesia y la penitencia en los siglos XVIII y XIX en la Nueva España* (Mexico City, Mexico: Instituto Nacional de Antropología e Histora, Plaza y Valdés Editores, 2002), 16.

32. Lavrin, "La mujer," 12.

33. González Marmolejos, *Sexo*, 214.

34. Lavrin, "La mujer," 12.

35. Lavrin, *Sexualidad*, 15–16.

Bibliography

Aguilera, Rodrigo Andreucci. "La pragmática de Carlos III sobre el matrimonio de los hijos de familia y su pervivencia en el derecho chileno." *Revista de Estudios Histórico-Jurídicos* 22 (2000), http://www.scielo.cl/scielo.php?script=sci_arttex&pid=S0716-54552000002200010.

Archivo General de Indias, *Legajo No. 256, 22 de febrero de 1722*, 1–30, 1–11.

Archivo Histórico Documental Incháustegui Cabral, Pontificia Universidad Católica Madre y Maestra. Santiago, Dominican Republic.

Dávila-Mendoza, Dora. "Un concierto de voces: Mujer, familia y sociedad en Santo Domingo colonial." Dominican Studies Institute Working Paper 3 (1999).

Deive, Carlos Esteban. *La mala vida: Delincuencia y picaresca en la colonia española de Santo Domingo.* Santo Domingo, Dominican Republic: Fundación Cultural Dominicana, 1988.

González Marmolejo, Jorge René. *Sexo y confesión: La Iglesia y la penitencia en los siglos XVIII y XIX en la Nueva España.* Mexico City, Mexico: Instituto Nacional de Antropología e Historia, Plaza y Valdés Editores, 2002.

Hardwick, Julie. "A Sexual Revolution in the Eighteenth Century?" *Age of Revolutions*, 2021, https://ageofrevolutions.com/2021/03/15/a-sexual-revolution-in-the-eighteenth-century/

LaFleur, Greta. *The Natural History of Sexuality in Early America.* Baltimore, MD: Johns Hopkins University Press, 2018.

Las Siete Partidas del Rey Don Alfonso el Sabio. Madrid, Spain: Ediciones Atlas, 1972.

Lavrin, Asunción. "La mujer en la sociedad colonial hispanoamericana." In *Historia de América Latina*, edited by Leslie Bethell. Barcelona, Spain: Editorial Crítica, 1990.

Lavrin, Asunción. *Sexualidad y matrimonio en la América hispánica. Siglos XVI–XVIII.* Mexico City, Mexico: Consejo Nacional para la Cultura y las Artes, Editorial Grijalbo, 1991.

Lucena Salmoral, Manuel. *Leyes para esclavos y el ordenamiento jurídico sobre la condición, tratamiento, defensa y represión de los esclavos en las colonias de la América española.* Madrid, Spain: Fundación Histórica Tavera, 2000.

Marre, Diana. "La aplicación de la Pragmática de Carlos III en América Latina: Una Revisión." *Quaderns de l'Institut Catalá d'Antropologia* 10 (Winter 1997): 217–49, http://www.ub.es/geocrit/sv-22.htm.

Martinez-Alier, Verena. *Marriage, Class, and Colour in Nineteenth-Century Cuba.* Cambridge, UK: Cambridge University Press, 1989.

Moya Pons, Frank. *La vida escandalosa en Santo Domingo en los siglos XVII y XVIII.* Santiago, Dominican Republic: Universidad Católica Madre y Maestra, 1976.

Samudio A., Edda O. "Un matrimonio clandestino en Mérida en el ocaso del período Colonial." *Procesos Históricos: Revista de Historia y Ciencias Sociales* 4 (July–December, 2003): 2–10, https://dialnet.unirioja.es/servlet/articulo?codigo=1251449&orden=185531&info=link.

Silva Campo, Ana María. "Fragile Fortunes: Afrodescendant Women, Witchcraft and the Remaking of Urban Cartagena." *Colonial Latin American Review* 30, no. 2 (2021): 197–213.

Sperling, Jutta. "Marriage at the Time of the Council of Trent (1560–70): Clandestine Marriages, Kinship Prohibitions, and Dowry Exchange in European Comparison." *Journal of Early Modern History* 8, no. 1–2 (2004): 67–108.

Stone, Lawrence. *The Family, Sex and Marriage in England, 1500–1800.* London: Penguin Books, 1990.

Chapter 7

Fostering a Sense of Community in Seventeenth-Century Puerto Rico

The Godparenthood of Enslaved Infants, Children, and Adults in San Juan, 1672–1706

DAVID M. STARK

On January 7, 1687, an infant named Juan José was baptized in the cathedral in San Juan, Puerto Rico. Juan José was the oldest child born to Graciana, an unmarried slave who belonged to Captain Fernando Castilla. A soldier, Francisco Alonso, and his wife, Francisca Serafina (de Rivera), stood as the infant's godparents.[1] Graciana gave birth to three more children over the next seven years and chose a different soldier for each child as the sole godparent. Choosing a godparent for an infant required careful consideration. In the event of an accident or the illness or death of the parent, the godparents and/or the slave owner would become responsible for the spiritual guidance and material well-being of the child. Among the many infants born to slave parent(s) baptized in San Juan were Jacinto de la Rosa, Juana María, and Francisco Xavier, on September 3, 1699, October 29, 1701, and December 30, 1703, respectively. Their mother was Francisca, an unmarried slave who belonged to Catalina Traspuesto. A *pardo*, or nonwhite male, named Silverio de Moya was the godfather for all three.[2] Francisca did not select godmothers for these children. Other examples of baptismal sponsorship include Alejandro, who was baptized on May 23,

1702, and Patricio, who was baptized on April 4, 1704.³ Both were born to Maria, an unmarried slave mother who belonged to Francisco de Muñoz.⁴ The godfather, Juan Alonso Gonzalez, had received minor orders—he was authorized to perform the functions of porter, lector, exorcist, and acolyte—while studying for the priesthood.⁵ Maria did not select godmothers for her two sons. Enslaved African children and adults were also baptized. One adult, named José, who was baptized on November 9, 1700, belonged to Francisco Calderon de la Barca. One of de la Barca's slaves, Antonio, served as the sole godparent for José.⁶ Baptizing enslaved infants and adults was not uncommon in San Juan, but the range of identities of people selected as godparents—some were Black, some were white, some were free, and some were enslaved—merits closer attention.

Until recently, our study of godparenthood among enslaved populations was focused on the kinds of people selected and how often they were chosen as godparents, who were also known as baptismal sponsors.⁷ Much like their free counterparts, slaves established fictive kinship networks and cultivated social relationships through baptism and godparenthood. However, as Herman Bennett has noted, we know little about the relationships slaves created or could forge.⁸ While some studies have looked at that issue among free people in Latin America, few have examined how enslaved people created, expanded, or strengthened social ties in the Spanish Caribbean.⁹ We also know little about why free people, especially soldiers and priests, were willing to take on the responsibility of godparenthood.

Slaves likely preferred free godparents because they might be able to act as an advocate or intercessor between an owner and their enslaved godchild in times of conflict between the two. However, owners seldom sponsored infants born to slaves they owned. Neither did relatives of the slave owner.¹⁰ Ana María Lugâo Rios argues that another reason why slaves may have chosen free godparents was that they "could not represent themselves legally nor conduct commercial transactions."¹¹ Slaves may have considered it advantageous to have someone who could represent them in the world of free persons, and given the close ties sponsorship created between godparent(s) and parent(s), it made sense to ask a free person to be a godparent.¹² What about African slaves brought to the Americas? David Wheat found that in the late 1500s, Biafadas (Upper Guineans) in Havana demonstrated a strong preference for establishing social ties with one another and with traditional trade partners but avoided people to whom they had been militarily or politically subjugated.¹³ While the historiography affords an invaluable glimpse into who was selected, it does little to address how godparenthood impacted the communities enslaved people lived in. One way to learn about their lived experience is to pay more attention to social interactions and understand what they meant and how they benefited enslaved infants and adults and their godparent(s).

Baptismal records offer a wealth of biographical and demographic data. Baptismal registers tell us the age of the infant, child, or adult; the name(s) of the child's parent(s); the ethnic and racial designations of the infant and its parent(s), child, or adult initiate, previous or *in articulo mortis* (in danger of death) baptism; the names of the godparents; and the names of the witnesses. However, not all this information was always listed; priests (or scribes) sometimes forgot to include some details. The baptismal records in San Juan for the period 1672 to 1706 are particularly useful because they provide most of this information, though they occasionally omit racial status. From them, we can learn the identity of many godparents from this period. This data shows that a cross-section of San Juan's inhabitants, including free and unfree individuals, were selected as godparents. This prompts two questions: Why would slaves such as Graciana, Francisca, María, and José select individuals such as the soldier Francisco Alonso, the pardo Silverio de Moya, the future priest Juan Alonso Gonzalez, and the slave José—people with whom they had no biological relationship—to take on the spiritual and potential economic obligations associated with godparenthood? And how might individuals benefit by serving as baptismal sponsors?

The answers to these questions are hard to come by. Baptismal registers did not record the thoughts and motivations of those who participated in the ceremony. Research on individuals who served as godparents for infants born to a slave parent has long centered on why they were selected. Young godparents were probably chosen with an eye toward the future in the event that they might have to care for an infant's well-being or to provide aid to the parent(s) or the infant.[14] As Katherine Gerbner has noted, selecting free or freed godparents enabled slaves to develop social networks that extended beyond the boundaries of the slave owner's property and to establish links of association or ties of kinship outside the bonds of slavery.[15] Selecting enslaved godparents enabled slaves to reinforce and strengthen family and social ties. Looking closely at who was selected as a godparent can tell us about the creation and consolidation of the tightly knit communities that both unfree and free populations formed.

This study examines godparent selection for 795 infant slaves and 182 enslaved adults baptized in San Juan from 1672 to 1706.[16] It broadens our understanding of baptismal sponsorship by looking at how communities formed and how people cultivated and strengthened social networks. My findings reveal that the number of children who had godfathers was greater than the number who had godmothers. Although men served as godparents multiple times more frequently than women, they generally sponsored only one child of a slave parent or parents. They may also have served as baptismal sponsors for infants born to free parents; if that was the case, they were likely reluctant to take on responsibilities associated with spiritual kinship for the child of a slave, who would have fewer resources when a parent died. A godparent's responsibility for an enslaved child was greater than it probably would have been for the child of a free parent.

Social networks among enslaved subjects connected people across lines of legal and racial status, fostering a sense of community. While most godparents were free, their race varied: parish records show that they were white, Black, and brown (mixed race). Slaves undoubtedly sought to avail themselves of the influence, wealth, or status of the godparents they chose. It was neither uncommon nor socially unacceptable for free (white) members of the community to serve as godparents for children born to slaves or former slaves. They often did so as a way of enhancing their prominence or asserting their honor in the community. That so many godfathers were free is not surprising, because white men made up a majority of San Juan's male population, according to the 1673 census.[17] However, many godfathers were immigrants who had been born in Europe, including numerous soldiers like Francisco Alonso. Because the economy of Puerto Rico was chronically short of coinage, individuals, particularly soldiers, were heavily dependent on credit. As Scott Taylor has noted, in situations where individuals were forced to make do with informal credit for everyday transactions, it was important that they demonstrate how well they were integrated into the community.[18] One way to do this was by taking on the role of a godparent, because it allowed them a certain level of respect. Generally, godparents were carefully selected because they were perceived as reliable people. This was also important for free men of color such as Silverio de Moya, who likely sought to elevate their social standing to acquire honor and reputation—or to enhance those assets.

I selected San Juan because it has the oldest series of parish registers on the island for a period that is one of the least studied in the Spanish Caribbean.[19] One has to wonder how generalizable the practices surrounding godparenthood I have observed in San Juan are to other parts of Latin America (or the world). The Catholic Church had (and still has) specific guidelines for the administration of baptism that all Catholics followed. For example, the wording of the ritual and the regulations about the administration of the sacrament were the same everywhere.[20] There were also universal guidelines about the minimum age requirements for godparents and who could serve as a godparent. A godparent also had to be in good standing with the Church, which meant that he or she had received the sacraments of penance and communion during the preceding year. In this regard, the practices associated with baptism were similar in all locations in the seventeenth and eighteenth centuries. Where they differed was in who was selected as godparents. Regional variations in who was chosen certainly existed in the late seventeenth and early eighteenth centuries. However, across Puerto Rico and the Spanish Caribbean, slave parents used godparenthood to formalize social networks and strengthen bonds of racial community.

Society in Seventeenth-Century San Juan

Microanalysis of communities such as San Juan provides a deeper understanding of how people lived in the past. San Juan, the second oldest city on the island, was settled in 1521.[21] It was situated on the small islet of San Juan Bautista and was connected to the island's northeastern mainland by a bridge. Living space was at a premium and the population spilled over into adjacent areas. Information from a census taken in 1673—the only one taken in the seventeenth century for the city and the island—enumerated 1,794 individuals aged ten or older. Of these, 820 (46 percent) were white, 662 (37 percent) were enslaved, and 312 (17 percent) were free Black people or persons of mixed race.[22] There was no indigenous population in the city. San Juan was the seat of civil, military, and religious authority. It was home to colonial officials and their families and/or households. This, along with the presence of a military garrison, created an ongoing demand for goods and services, and a service economy developed in San Juan that was not present in other island communities. Sugar was grown, albeit in small quantities, in outlying areas of San Juan. Owners of sugar *ingenios* (mills), such as Juan de Amezquita, María de los Rios, and Constanza de Torres, figured prominently among the city's elite and were some of its largest slaveholders.[23] Like other islands throughout the Caribbean, enslaved and free nonwhites outnumbered whites in Puerto Rico. However, the proportion of whites in San Juan's (and probably the island's) population, at that time, was greater than that in the British, Dutch, and French sugar-producing islands.

Legal trade between Spain and the Spanish Caribbean was practically nonexistent for the second half of the seventeenth century. If we are to believe contemporary accounts, from 1651 to 1675, only eight ships departed from Seville for San Juan.[24] Perhaps because of this, an illegal trade with the British, Danish, and Dutch thrived. As Joseph Dorsey notes, "From approximately 1670 to 1765, Puerto Rico was the center of international contraband trade in the Caribbean."[25] The hub of the contraband trade in this period was San Juan, where Francisco Calderón de la Barca and his brother-in-law Antonio de Robles and his father-in-law Juan de Amezquita were among the principal protagonists. They exported hides, dried meat, horses, mules, dairy cows, and possibly sugar to the Danish Virgin Islands (St. Thomas) with relative ease.[26] Although little, if any cash, exchanged hands, goods were readily bartered. Contraband trade integrated European colonies throughout the Caribbean because ideas as well as goods were exchanged through informal communication networks.[27] In this way, the Spanish Caribbean, especially Puerto Rico, was not nearly so marginal in the Atlantic world as was once thought.

Information from the 1673 census demonstrates that slaveholding was widespread in San Juan: 142 of the city's 259 households, or 55 percent, contained at least one enslaved person. The average number of slaves per household was nearly five. However, two-thirds of all owners had fewer than five enslaved persons, and they collectively controlled only one-third of the enslaved labor force. Most owners (56 percent) had between one and three enslaved persons. Masters with six to ten charges constituted one-fourth of the slave-owning population, but they controlled the bulk—41 percent—of San Juan's enslaved persons. Eight owners—6 percent of the total number of people who had eleven to fifteen slaves—controlled 15 percent of San Juan's servile labor.[28]

Because San Juan was the island's capital and the only true city, many of its enslaved persons were employed as household domestics. Moreover, as a port city there was a demand for certain services (from vendors, washerwomen, seamstresses, and sex workers) in San Juan that did not exist on a similar scale elsewhere on the island. Enslaved females actively participated in the urban economy, serving the needs of the city's elite and providing food and lodging to soldiers who lived in the military garrison. In doing so, they may have exercised a degree of independence in their activities that was not available to their counterparts in other colonial Caribbean cities at that time. Alejandro de la Fuente and César García del Pino noticed a similar pattern among the enslaved women of Havana in the late sixteenth century.[29] Not all slaves were domestics or provided food, entertainment, or other services needed by the city's inhabitants, especially males. The Crown employed enslaved persons in the construction and upkeep of military fortifications and the city walls. Seventeenth-century *Contaduría*, or auditing records, from San Juan denote payments made to masters who hired out their male slaves for work in the *reales fábricas*, or royal works.[30] This evidence shows that enslaved women and men interacted frequently with members of the free population, some of whom may have been free Black people or people of mixed race. Close proximity tended to blur social distinctions between white, Black, and brown people, who mixed and mingled freely.

The experience of enslaved populations in San Juan was different from those of their counterparts in the sugar-producing areas of the Caribbean. Although some sugar was grown in outlying areas of San Juan, the number of slaves who worked on these ingenios was probably much smaller than on sugar plantations in English colonies such as Barbados. Like their counterparts in the non-Hispanic Caribbean, ingenio owners such as Juan de Amezquita, María de los Rios, and Constanza de Torres probably owned a larger number of male than female slaves because they needed them to do demanding agricultural work. However, in the city the situation was different. Females outnumbered males by more than two to one in San Juan. The proportion of women to men in this category was fairly uniform across the distribution: 74 to 26 among holdings with fewer than five slaves, 62 to 38 among holdings with six to ten slaves, and 67 to 33 among holdings with eleven or more slaves.[31] The presence of so many women among the enslaved population might reflect a preference among owners for females. According to Pedro Welch, "Females tended to be cheaper, they offered prospects of increasing the initial investment through childbirth, their domestic service conferred an enhanced social status on the owner and they provided the 'start up' capital which could be bequeathed to children, particularly daughters."[32] These were all likely important reasons for the predominance of females among San Juan's enslaved population.

Women outnumbered men in San Juan by a ratio of more than two to one among white people, free Black people, and persons of mixed race. Of the 820 individuals census takers identified as white in the 1673 census, 551 (67.2 percent) were women, and 269 (32.8 percent) were men. Among the 312 people identified as free Black or of mixed race, the proportion is strikingly similar; 214 (67.4 percent) were women and

98 (32.6 percent) were men. A similar shortage of men did not exist in other Caribbean cities. We know, for example, that there were more men than women in Bridgetown, Barbados, in 1680; and Arlette Gautier describes seventeenth-century French Antilles as a "masculine" society.[33] In this regard, San Juan was very different from both its English and French counterparts.

The scarcity of enslaved men meant that women's opportunities for marriage were limited. We see this reflected in the proportion of births that occurred outside the context of marriage. From 1672 to 1706, 795 infants were baptized in San Juan; the annual average was 23 births. Of these, 163 infants, or 20.5 percent, were born to married couples, and 632, or 79.5 percent, were born to unmarried mothers.[34] Very little research has been done on the proportion of legitimate births among enslaved populations elsewhere in the Americas in this time period, but my findings are much higher than those in the city of Santo Domingo on the nearby island of Hispaniola. From 1636 to 1670, 435 infants were baptized in Santo Domingo; the annual average was 13 births. Of these, only 12 infants, or 2.8 percent, were born to married couples, and 423, or 97.2 percent, were born to unmarried mothers.[35] Perhaps the shortage of males in Santo Domingo was more pronounced than it was in San Juan. The difference between the two cities is striking. Slaves likely had greater opportunities to marry and/or establish family lives of their own in port cities like San Juan, where the decline in sugar production in outlying areas in the mid-seventeenth century and the presence of the military garrison created ongoing demands for the provision of goods and services associated with a service economy as well as opportunities for masters to hire out slaves to the Crown.

Little is known about how many slaves were imported to Puerto Rico in the seventeenth century. Following the cancelation of the *asiento* with Portugal in 1640, few, if any, African slaves were legally brought to the island.[36] These numbers are particularly difficult to gauge because few official records or estimates of the slave trade have survived. We do know it is likely that no adult slaves were baptized in San Juan from June 1638 to March 1657.[37] However, information in San Juan's baptismal register can be used to locate and identify Africans for the period 1672 to 1706, much as Mary Karasch did in her study of Central Africans in Goiás, Brazil, in the late colonial period and Matthew Restall did in his work on Afro-Yucatecans in eighteenth-century Mérida, Yucatan.[38] Because *Voyages: The Trans-Atlantic Slave Trade Database* does not include information about the number of African arrivals to Puerto Rico from 1675 to 1726, information gleaned from San Juan's baptismal register fills a gap in our knowledge of the slave trade.[39]

The small number of adult slaves—both those of African origin and those who had been born elsewhere—who were baptized in San Juan during these years corroborates documentary evidence that suggests that levels of legal slave importation were low in this period. A total of 182 children and adult slaves from abroad were baptized in San Juan from 1672 to 1706, an annual average of just over 5 slaves. These account for 18.6 percent of the 977 total slaves who were baptized in San Juan in this time period. Eighty-one percent of the slaves who were baptized in this period were native-born infants, strong evidence that the Puerto Rican slave population was reproducing itself. By way of comparison, in the city of Santo Domingo, 324 children and adult slaves were baptized from 1636 to 1670, an annual average of nearly 10 Africans.[40] The number of children and adult slaves baptized in Santo Domingo increased to 1,259 from 1673 to 1707, an average of 37 individuals baptized annually. These account for 72 percent of the 1,755 slaves who were baptized in this period; only 28 percent of the baptized slaves were infants.[41] The contrast in the level of slave imports and the demographic behavior of the enslaved populations in San Juan and Santo Domingo is striking. Of the two, San Juan was more peripheral in the extent of legal and illegal commercial traffic, as reflected in the lower volume of slave imports. San Juan's enslaved population was dependent on natural increase to sustain itself in these years, whereas Santo Domingo's slave population was unable to do so, and owners had to replenish the labor force from outside sources.

The only recourse for planters in San Juan who wanted to purchase slaves was to rely on contraband trade. However, after 1663, when direct trade ended, enslaved individuals did not arrive straight from Africa.[42] African transports were received in several ports throughout the non-Hispanic Caribbean, such as Curaçâo, St. Eustatius, and St. Thomas, from which they were reexported to Spanish ports. The Africans who were brought to San Juan, for whom geographic origin was identified (35 of 182, or 19 percent) came from various Caribbean entrepôts, including Curaçâo and St. Thomas. The geographic proximity of St. Thomas meant that it was ideally positioned to supply Puerto Rico with contraband slaves. Many of the slaves purchased by the largest slaveholder(s) in San Juan at that time, Francisco Calderón de la Barca and members of his immediate family, undoubtedly came from this nearby Danish island, where the Calderón de la Barca's had extensive business dealings.

Children and adult slaves baptized in San Juan for whom geographic origin was identified were brought from West Africa, primarily from Tari (a small state located between Whydah and Allada in modern-day Benin) and from West Central Africa, primarily from Angola, Congo, and Loango.[43] Among the 182 Africans brought to San Juan, most—129, or nearly 71 percent—were males. One of the notable characteristics of the period 1672–1706 was the substantial number of children introduced. Children under the age of fifteen constituted 41 of 65 (63 percent) of human cargo that arrived from Africa or from the Caribbean islands. Because San Juan's enslaved population was mostly native born, newly arrived Africans would have found it difficult to create a community of their own, in which they could continue to engage in their own spiritual practices or religious beliefs. This would have been especially difficult for young Africans. Creolization rather than African retention was the likely outcome.

Catholicism was the official religion of Puerto Rico. Many of San Juan's residents likely attended mass regularly at the cathedral, which was the only church in the city. Parishioners learned their prayers and the rudiments of the faith at a young age, and the sermons they heard at mass on Sundays and on holy days reinforced the tenets of faith and precepts of the Church. Reception of the sacraments also figured prominently in religious practice and was the norm in late-seventeenth- and early-eighteenth-century Puerto Rico. Of course, some island inhabitants did not actively participate in liturgical events or partake in the sacraments because of cost, the distance, and time involved, or indifference, but the archival record indicates that even among the enslaved population, reception of the sacraments—especially baptism—was widespread. Because there was no religious tolerance in Spanish colonies, infants and adults were baptized. One must wonder whether slaves were baptized voluntarily. Slaves likely embraced the sacrament of a Christian baptism because, as Herman Bennett noted in his study of Black people in colonial Mexico, "even individuals who refused to abide by Christian values in other aspects of their lives ascribed symbolic importance to baptism."[44] Slaves may also have viewed baptism as a way to gain access to rights, including the right to marry.[45]

The Catholic Church also took baptism seriously. Infants who were baptized at home in danger of dying—such as Clemencia, the daughter of Graciana, a slave who belonged to Gerónimo de Aguero, or María, the daughter of Francisco and Isabel, slaves who belonged to Ana de Carrasquillo—were baptized again at the cathedral when they had recovered from illness.[46] Masters had their own reasons for ensuring that Africans newly purchased from slave traders and newborn slaves were baptized promptly: baptisms were recorded in the parish register and such records served as proof of ownership, because the legal status of the person who was baptized was noted.[47] Both free and unfree inhabitants likely took advantage of opportunities to participate, redefine, and utilize the institutions and rituals of the Church on their own terms.

Baptismal Sponsorship

Baptism fulfilled a wide variety of spiritual and social functions. For Catholics, baptism cleanses the individual of original sin. They believe that if a child who has been baptized dies before the age of moral responsibility, usually at six or seven, its soul goes straight to Heaven. Should the child die unbaptized, the child will go to Limbo, if not to Hell.[48] Additionally, baptism symbolizes an individual's spiritual birth into the Christian community. For this reason, the Catholic Church places great emphasis on the selection of godparents to ensure that a child will receive religious education and guidance, especially if the child loses one or both parents.[49] Because of its importance, baptism could only be conferred at the parish church.[50]

The baptismal ceremony also served as a rite of initiation into the biological family (for newborns) and the local community (for older children and adults).[51] At the time of baptism, the child (or the adult) publicly assumed his or her own individual social identity through the ritual acquisition of a Christian name.[52] This name was usually that of a saint, under whose patronage the child (or adult) made its entry into the Christian community.[53] At first glance, a slave's willing and outward embrace of Christianity possibly signaled acquiescence to their enslavement, to their owner, and submission to the parish priest. However, according to Kathleen Higgins, slaves and owners "interpreted the worldly outcomes of baptisms differently and attempted to manipulate their interests in these outcomes accordingly."[54] Some slaves may have transformed the Catholic sacrament of baptism into a strategy of belonging by forging community ties with other Afro-descended peoples. This may have been the case when Catalina, an eighteen-year-old slave who belonged to Sergeant Major Antonio de Robles, was baptized on February 2, 1700. Her godfather was Francisco Alvarez, a soldier of a lower rank (*cabo de escuadra*, or squadron commander).[55] No information is known about Francisco Alvarez. He was not married in San Juan, and only served once as a godparent for an infant born to slaves. It may be the case that de Robles selected this godfather because Catalina was so young and because she had recently arrived from Africa. Later, Catalina had a daughter, Maria Germana, who was baptized on June 28, 1701. The godfather was Adriano González, a mixed-race soldier of lower rank (*alférez*, or second lieutenant) who served in a company of nonwhite (*pardo*) soldiers.[56] Although it is not clear why Catalina selected Adriano González as a godparent for her daughter, perhaps she found it advantageous for her integration into kinship networks in the city.

Although the Church allowed only one godfather and one godmother for each child, there were no restrictions on the legal, racial, or social status of godparents. We do not know what proportion of the population served as a godparent, but the practice appears to have been widespread among males in San Juan.[57] Although the minimum age for serving as a godparent in the diocese of Puerto Rico was fifteen, younger individuals sometimes served.[58] Whether this was the case with slaves who served as godparents is not known. The godparents usually assumed the expenses associated with the celebration of this sacrament.[59] Godparents were also responsible for bringing the newborn infant to the cathedral for baptism. It is not known at what age infants were baptized in the late seventeenth century, but infants in eighteenth-century Puerto Rico were typically baptized when they were ten to twenty days old.[60] Some baptisms happened earlier or later than that because of problems with the infant's health and/or difficulties related to traveling to the parish church.

According to Frank Proctor, when parents selected relatives of the owner as godparents, they probably did so because they had forged intimate ties with them in the domestic sphere—for example, when the slave's mother and the owner's daughter had grown up together.[61] From a slave's standpoint, selecting a member of the owner's family afforded greater opportunity to know them on a more personal level, something that might lead to greater possibilities for manumission. That such possibilities existed is suggested by the greater incidence of manumission in the waning years of the eighteenth century, when one of every eight slaves were manumitted in San Juan, as Adám Szasdi has noted.[62] While the extent of manumission is not known in the late seventeenth century, it was not uncommon for slaves to select the sons and daughters of the wealthiest, most prominent, and most powerful members of the city to serve as godparents.

The role of godparents in the lives of infants after baptism is difficult to determine. Godparents occasionally gave their name to the infant and/

or may have given them gifts at birth. They may even have remembered them in their wills, but a more active role beyond that cannot be established. The spiritual kinship that godparenthood created was probably a parent's way of assuring that their child would have help or assistance in times of need.[63] This was true among the free population and may have also been the case among slaves. Godparents' responsibilities toward their godchildren and vice versa were defined by custom, not law.[64] Although a godparent's obligations largely depended on their personal wishes, they were probably enforced through gossip, community pressure, and the threat of ostracism.

The fundamental problem in the study of godparenthood among enslaved populations is the issue of choice. How much control and/or influence did owners, slaves, or parish priests exercise over the selection of baptismal sponsors? When free godparents were selected, was it because owners used their authority to create or reinforce patron-client relationships? When an unfree godparent was selected for the child of a slave parent, is that evidence that slave parents expressed agency by establishing or strengthening kinship ties in the ranks of the enslaved?[65] Although the process by which godparents were chosen is not known, variations in who was selected to sponsor baptism suggest that while the initiative came from the parents most often, on some occasions it came from owners, especially in the case of African children and adults. Regardless of who selected the godparents for enslaved infants and adults or how they were selected, baptismal sponsorship could be used in a variety of ways that included cultivating social ties with people of diverse legal and racial status and strengthening family and social ties among enslaved people.

Selection of Godparents

In San Juan, from 1672 to 1706, there were 790 baptisms of infants born locally with a slave parent(s), of which 368 were boys and 422 were girls.[66] Every infant had at least one godparent, but most (745) had only one.[67] Of these infants, 744 had a godfather. Only Clemencia, whose mother Graciana was a slave who belonged to Gerónimo de Agüero, had a sole godparent who was female. When Clemencia was baptized on April 25, 1699, Ana Mujica sponsored the sacrament.[68] José Luis Sáez observed a similar pattern in his study of baptisms in Santo Domingo in the period 1636–1670, when all but two infants had one godparent and that godparent was male.⁶⁹ This custom continued in San Juan well into the eighteenth century; godmothers were seldom selected.⁷⁰ Such findings demonstrate the social importance of the godfather. For a child to have an adult male as a godparent was more important, possibly to serve as a benefactor or patron who could intercede on their behalf, than it was to have an adult female. No infants were baptized in San Juan, or other communities examined in Puerto Rico, with saints as godparents, as had been the case in some Brazilian communities.⁷¹ In Brazil, for example, infants were baptized with female Catholic saints as godmothers. This was not the case in Puerto Rico. That Catholic saints were not chosen as godparents in Puerto Rico could explain why many enslaved infants lacked a godmother in San Juan. While it was common for godfathers to serve as the sole godparent in San Juan, a total of 50 infants (5.1 percent) baptized in San Juan in the years covered by this study had both a godfather and a godmother.⁷²

The selection of a godmother was common among free and unfree infants baptized in other communities on the island. In Arecibo, located along the northern coast of the island, from April 1708 to November 1732, it was uncommon for godfathers to serve as the sole godparent. However, from that later date until March 1737, only seven godmothers were chosen (of 677 baptisms). In the years that followed, godmothers were increasingly selected. For example, only 14 percent of infants baptized in the years 1764–1772 had a sole godparent who was male. This may indicate a growing concern with the well-being of the child should something happen to their mother. A similar practice likely prevailed in Caguas, where godmothers were infrequently selected for free and unfree infants who were baptized from 1730 to 1741. After the arrival of a new pastor in August 1741, the presence of a godmother at baptism became more common. Perhaps the new pastor Pedro Alcantara Serrano initiated this change. He was a native of Arecibo, where it was a common practice to select women as godparents at the beginning of the eighteenth century. The only other community on the island with baptismal records in the early eighteenth century is Coamo, located along the island's southern coast, where 141 of 163 infants, or 86.5 percent, with a slave parent had two godparents during the years 1700–1722. No other baptismal records exist for the early years in the eighteenth century, and it is not known why having two godparents was more common in Coamo than elsewhere on the island.

Altogether, 1,027 baptismal sponsors were selected in San Juan from 1672 to 1706. Of these, 958 were male and 51 were female. Eighteen infants had no godparents.⁷³ When the number of repeat selections is disregarded, this reveals a total of 599 individuals—549 men (510 free and 39 unfree) and 50 women (45 free and 5 unfree)—who were godparents. Most godparents for infants (69 percent) served only once. Among the males who were selected once, 335 (66 percent) were free and 31 (79 percent) were unfree, whereas among females 40 (89 percent) were free and five (100 percent) were unfree. The reason for this may be that free men and women also served as baptismal sponsors for infants born to free parents. Having already served as godparents multiple times, they were probably disinclined to sponsor infants born to slave parents. Another interpretation might be that given the greater likelihood that a slave parent would die young, males were more likely than females to have the economic resources to support an orphaned child.

The most frequently selected godfathers in this study were Sebastián Cortijo (who served 12 times), Juan Alonso González (10 times), and Juan de San Juan (10 times). No information is known about Sebastián other than that he was a Spanish soldier. Sebastián served as godparent with a female counterpart twice: the first time he was selected, in 1687, when he was paired with Francisca del Rosario in 1687, and again in 1690, when he was paired with Andrea Mexia.[74] After that, he was a sole godparent. Juan Alonso González was the son of Cristóbal González and Catalina Ximénes de Hermosilla, who were married on July 16, 1663, in San Juan. Juan's father, who was from the city of Zafra in the Spanish province of Badajoz, was a soldier in the company of Captain Pedro de Aranguren.[75] His mother, Catalina, was a native of San Juan. Juan Alonso's age is unknown because many of the baptismal records for whites do not exist for the late seventeenth century. When Juan was first selected as a godparent, in 1699, he was preparing for a career in the priesthood and had been tonsured (i.e., some or all the hair on his scalp had been shaved).[76] When he served as a godparent the second time, in 1704, he had advanced to the minor clergy. By 1708 he was *cura capellan*, or chaplain, in Ponce, which suggests that he had been ordained as a priest in the year or two after 1704.[77] Sebastián Cortijo may have been selected because he was a soldier and, as an outsider, likely welcomed the opportunity to enhance his honor and prestige in the community (but more on this later). On the other hand, Juan Alonso was native born, and his family had lived in San Juan for thirty years or more, which indicates he and his family were well known in the city.

Juan de San Juan was first selected in 1676, when he was an unmarried slave who belonged to Catalina Malave.[78] He married Ana de Espinosa on May 22, 1678, in San Juan. According to the marriage record, Juan was born in San Juan. Although the name(s) of his parent(s) were not recorded, this was the common practice among slaves and former slaves in that period.[79] When he was selected again as a godfather in 1692, he was a free man who had several children of his own, including Felipe de San Juan, who later served seven times as a godparent.[80] Married men, especially if they were enslaved, probably wished to avoid taking on the additional responsibilities that came with godparenthood and instead chose to devote themselves to caring for their own families. Perhaps Juan served as a godparent after he had attained his freedom and availed himself of the opportunity to affirm his new identity and social standing as a freed man in San Juan.

The most frequently selected godfathers among enslaved men were Bernabe, who belonged to Victoria Pantoja, and Melchor, who belonged to Miguel Enríquez. Bernabe was selected twice in 1700, first on February 26 for an infant born to Catalina, a slave who belonged to Francisco Calderón de la Barca, and again on October 8 for an adult African named Francisca who belonged to Ana de Carrasquillo.[81] Melchor's identity is complicated. He was a godfather in 1691 for Jacinto, the son of Francisca, who belonged to María Falcon. However, the baptismal register does not identify Melchor as a slave; instead he is listed as Melchor, a *moreno* (a Black person).[82] In 1696, Melchor served as a godfather twice. The first time was on January 19 for an infant born to Josefa, a slave who belonged to Francisco Calderón de la Barca, and the second time was on March 6 for an infant born to Ana María, a slave who belonged to Jacinto Felipe. Again, Melchor was not identified as a slave and instead appears as Melchor Enríquez, a *moreno*.[83] In 1699, when Melchor was a godfather again, he was identified as a slave who belonged to Miguel Enríquez.[84] Because the original baptismal record book was badly deteriorated and was recopied at the end of the eighteenth century, the transcriber may have been confused about Melchor's legal status (and that of others).

No information is known about the woman selected most often as godmother, María de Chávez Mujica, who served three times, once in 1691 and twice in 1701.[85] Similarly, little is known about godmothers who were selected two times. Francisca Serafina (de Rivera) was a native of San Juan and a widow when she married the Spanish soldier Francisco Alonso on December 28, 1669.[86] Eighteen years passed before she served as a godmother, which she did twice in 1687.[87] Luisa Valdés was a native of San Juan who married Antonio de Gorgoran Castilla on September 28, 1676.[88] Seventeen years passed before she served as a godmother, which she did in 1693 for adult slaves who were baptized on the same day.[89] Nothing is known about Sebastiana de Ayala, who was a godmother in 1685 and 1692, and María de Viveros, who was selected twice in 1687.[90] Francisca and Luisa may have been reluctant to serve as godmothers while their children were young. This might explain why they waited so long to sponsor slave infants and adults. All five of the unfree women who served as godmothers were selected only once. No information is known about them.

What did it mean for slaves to select a soldier like Sebastián Cortijo, someone preparing for a career in the priesthood like Juan Alonso González, or a free person who had once been enslaved like Juan de San Juan? These are difficult questions to answer; we can only speculate about why godparents were selected. However, San Juan's defense system likely was a factor in this process.

From its inception, San Juan had to protect itself against foreign incursions. The threat of French corsairs, which began in the 1530s and continued through the 1550s, prompted the first efforts to fortify the city. Initially local militia protected the city, but as the Crown became increasingly concerned about foreign interlopers, it assigned a garrison of professional soldiers to defend it in 1582. The Crown also allocated funds called the *situado* for the upkeep of the garrison, as was the common practice in other fortified cities throughout the Caribbean.[91] The British were also a threat. In November 1585, Sir Francis Drake attacked San Juan, and three years later, in the summer of 1598, George Clifford, the third earl of Cumberland, attacked the city again. In response, the Crown authorized further improvements in the city's fortifications and increased the size of its garrison.[92] These events hastened San Juan's transformation into a military presidio. As this process unfolded, the prominence of the military in local society increased at the expense of other segments of the population. Nearly all military and civil authorities in the first half of the seventeenth century came from Spain. Many of these men married the daughters of prominent local families, forming the nucleus of a stratified, hierarchical society.

We do not know how many soldiers were living in San Juan, because the 1673 census did not enumerate them. Three companies of soldiers were assigned to San Juan at the end of the seventeenth century: two infantry and one artillery. Each infantry company should have been comprised of 150 troops, while the artillery company should have been comprised of 100 troops, making for a total troop strength of 400 soldiers.[93] This is similar to the troop strength in Havana at the beginning of the seventeenth century, which amounted to 450 soldiers.[94] However, as table 1 demonstrates, total troop strength in San Juan was well below what it should have been.

In the eighteen years for which data on troop strength is available, the size of the garrison in San Juan averaged 170 soldiers, or only 42.5

Table 7.1. Troop Strength in San Juan for Selected Years, 1648–1700

Year	Infantry 1st Company	Infantry 2nd Company	Artillery	Total	Notes
1648	84	68	29	181	
1650	55	47	12	114	
1651	29	32	6	67	Only reinforcements
1652	124	—	45	169	Data for 2nd Company missing
1655	109	95	—	204	Data for Artillery Company missing
1656	51	35	16	102	
1657	87	73	37	197	
1659	122	104	45	271	
1660	38	63	35	136	
1661	71	61	10	142	
1662	23	20	9	52	Only reinforcements?
1663	88	139	26	253	
1688	45	47	23	115	
1691	93	88	46	227	Excluding 62 prisoners forced to serve as soldiers
1697	93	98	37	228	
1698	92	93	—	185	Data for Artillery Company missing
1699	83	87	40	210	
1700	85	92	33	210	

Source: Archivo General de Indias (hereafter AGI), Contaduria 1078, 1079, 1080; AGI, Santo Domingo 167 and 173.

percent of anticipated troop strength.[95] Of course, some of these soldiers may have been old and infirm, as was frequently the case with those assigned to Havana's military garrison.[96] Troop strength fluctuated from year to year, sometimes because of natural disasters such as the plague that struck the island in 1647, and sometimes because of troop movements.[97] By all accounts, the early 1660s were years when troop strength at the San Juan garrison reached its nadir, though it seems to have increased from 1663. Nevertheless, a letter from members of the *cabildo eclesiástico*, or cathedral chapter, written in 1669, to the queen (Mariana of Austria, who acted as Regent for much of Charles II's reign), states that troop strength was less than half of what it should have been.[98] Many soldiers remained in the city when they retired, as was the case with Captain Pedro González Manos de Oro, a native of Granada who married Inés de Sanmillán, a native of San Juan, on March 1, 1654.[99] When the census was conducted nineteen years later, Pedro González Manos de Oro was living in the city with his three children, Gabriela, Pedro, and Manuel.[100] No mention is made of his wife, so she might have died by then.

The island's (and the city's) dependence on the *situado*, which provided the largest supply of specie for the island, also made matters worse. No situado arrived from Mexico in seventeen of the years in the period 1650–1700, and only 53 percent of the total that should have arrived reached Puerto Rico in these years.[101] Such shortfalls meant that months or years might pass when no official salaries were paid. This forced residents to rely on credit or loans from local merchants and resulted in periodic economic downturns. In the years when the situado arrived, it provided a much-needed infusion of capital that helped fund the local market and generated a greater demand for goods and services. Historian Ángel López Cantos describes the period from 1650 to 1700 "as the period of lowest economic activity in Puerto Rico."[102]

Dire economic conditions in port cities such as San Juan meant that soldiers had to depend on credit or loans. For Spanish soldiers with few, if any, social ties to the community, it was imperative that they start building an honorable reputation and expanding their social network in the city so they could gain access to these resources. Honor was an important element in the decisions potential creditors made about people who sought financial assistance. Although it was an ephemeral quality that could not be measured, it was manifested through a person's actions.[103] Failing to establish an honorable reputation probably meant economic hardship, because it is probable that most Spanish soldiers came from very poor families. As Peter Guardino has speculated, impoverished soldiers likely sought to acquire a measure of honor because it provided them with a measure of self-worth and, more importantly, allowed them to engage in economic transactions that depended on trust.[104] Serving as a godparent for someone of a lower class was viewed as an act of charity, generosity, and piety; thus, it exemplified virtuous behavior and conveyed honor.[105] Because most Puerto Ricans in the seventeenth century were illiterate, highly visible and public ceremonies like baptism took on symbolic meaning. Baptismal sponsorship provided soldiers with an opportunity to acquire honor by demonstrating virtuous behavior in a religious and social context. When they took on the responsibilities of godparenthood and effectively performed them, soldiers enhanced their reputation and standing in the community. In order to acquire and develop an honorable reputation in the city, Spanish soldiers welcomed the opportunity to serve as baptismal sponsors. This may be one reason why they were frequently selected. In the period 1672 to 1706, 225, or 23 percent, of the 997 men who served as godfathers were soldiers (table 7.2).

Table 7.2. Number of Times Soldiers Were Selected as Godfathers, 1672–1706

Number of Times an Individual Was Chosen	Baptisms in This Category	Total Baptisms
1	51	51
2	21	42
3	11	33
4	7	28
5	2	10
6	2	12
7	3	21
8	2	16
9	0	0
10	0	0
11	0	0
12	1	12
Totals	100	225

Source: Archivo Histórico Diocesano (hereafter AHD), Libro primero de bautismos para pardos y esclavos, 1672–1706.

Contemporary sources from the period suggest that Spanish soldiers often lived with and/or married women they met in Puerto Rico and formed families during their stay on the island. Many soldiers probably entered formal and informal unions and formed families with local free and unfree women. Because they were frequently rotated and sent from one military garrison to another throughout the Atlantic world, some soldiers probably were reluctant to formalize their union through marriage. However, they may have been selected as godparents because they were the infant's father, which could explain why some soldiers of low rank (artillery, privates, and corporals) were selected as godfathers. Not all low-ranking soldiers were the infant's father, which prompts the question of what resources would they have had to offer the child of a poor or enslaved parent. With limited access to cash, parents may have looked upon low-ranking soldiers and were thinking long term. Or perhaps these low-ranking soldiers and slaves, free Black people or people of mixed race socialized across racial lines, which may have led to their selection as godparents (table 3).

Over half of all godfathers selected (51 percent) were above the rank of second lieutenant, including Captain Antonio Carbajal y Benavides, who was selected three times as a godfather to enslaved infants.[106] As a high-ranking member of the military, Antonio had access to scarce specie and was connected to the upper echelons of local society. Enslaved mothers who selected a soldier as godparent likely acquired access to a social safety net that otherwise eluded them.

Table 7.3. Rank of Soldiers Selected as Godfathers, 1673–1706

Rank	Number	Percent
Artillery	5	5
Private	35	35
Squadron Commander	7	7
Corporal	2	2
2nd Lieutenant	26	26
Sergeant	12	12
Captain	13	13
Totals	100	100

Source: AHD, Libro primero de bautismos para pardos y esclavos, 1672–1706.

Because San Juan was cash-starved, many families in the late seventeenth and early eighteenth centuries had to find new ways of surviving. The priesthood provided a stable fixed income in an era of economic uncertainty. A career in the church also provided social prestige and created opportunities for individuals to expand social networks, especially for families of priests in the process of upward mobility or aspiring to this. This may explain why Juan Alonso González was willing to take on the responsibility of godfatherhood as he finished his studies for the priesthood. As mentioned previously, Juan was the son of Spanish soldier, Cristóbal González, and Catalina Ximénez de Hermosilla, a native of San Juan. No further information is known about Catalina's parents—Diego Fernández Sordis and Francisca Ortiz—but they were not slaveholders and do not appear in the 1673 San Juan census, which means that they were probably dead by then.[107] While it is impossible to know what was in the minds of Juan Alonso and his parents, the priesthood was a visible means of social mobility at a time when social and professional connections mattered very much.

Young men who were interested in the priesthood began preparing for their career at a young age. They began primary studies sometime between the ages of ten and thirteen. Following tonsuring, the adolescent also had to demonstrate his religious devotion or humility before he was conferred to one of the minor orders. Typically, this occurred during the early teen years, at age fourteen or fifteen, which coincided with the minimum age requirement for serving as a godfather. For the sons of lower- and middle-class families, serving as a godparent was a way to enhance their honor. This may explain the willingness of Juan Lorenzo de Matos, José Martínez de Quiñones, and Martín de Reyna to serve as godparents after they were tonsured.[108] Both Juan Lorenzo and José were from Ponce, located along the island's southern coast, and probably welcomed the opportunity to start building their reputation and expanding their social network in the city. It might have been the case with Martín, whose father Martín de Reyna was a Spanish soldier married to María Flores de Caldevilla.[109]

Because there was no seminary on the island and very few schools, future clergy were educated alongside future leaders of San Juan's society and government at the Colegio de Santo Tomas de Aquino (a convent school) in San Juan, which was operated by the Dominicans. This provided opportunities to form friendships and create networks that might prove advantageous in the future. Social and professional connections mattered very much in this period, and priests who were connected to the upper echelons of society tended to end up in more prestigious posts. Young men pursuing a career in the priesthood availed themselves of every opportunity to enhance their honor and expand social networks. Serving as a godparent for a child born to slave parents was one way to do so for someone of humble origins.

The Baptism of Adult Slaves

In areas where Catholicism was the officially recognized religion, slaves were often baptized forcibly. This was because one of the principal ideological justifications for enslavement was that African "pagans" would be converted to Christianity. Although owners were entrusted with this responsibility, the Church regulated the administration of baptism. Canon law in the diocese of Puerto Rico mandated that newly arrived Africans be baptized within six months if they were under the age of ten and within a year if they were adults.[110] Elsewhere in the Americas, the time frame varied; in Brazil, owners were required to see that slaves were baptized within three months after purchase.[111] However, while adults in Spanish and Portuguese America could not be baptized until they had successfully demonstrated their knowledge of the basic tenets of Catholicism, children under the age of six or seven were eligible for immediate baptism because they were thought to be under the age of reason.[112]

Apart from compliance with canon law, owners had their own reasons for ensuring that Africans and newborn infants were promptly baptized. First, at a time when most slaves in Puerto Rico were illegally acquired and few, if any, records of such transactions were kept, ownership was established when slaves were baptized, because parish records noted the legal status of the individual being baptized.[113] Second, some owners may have been inspired by the Church's teachings to take an interest in the spiritual welfare of their enslaved chattel and encouraged conversion, if not actively promoting it.[114] Whatever their motivation was for doing so, owners in San Juan ensured that their slaves were baptized.[115]

There were several reasons why adult slaves may have converted to Christianity and been baptized. Having been uprooted from family, friends, and community in Africa, and, for some, in the Americas also, they would have struggled to re-create their familial and community identity.[116] In the words of Joseph Miller, what slaves sought was "to find places of their own, to belong, somehow, somewhere."[117] For Africans, the severing of ties and alienation from family, friends, and community was tantamount in what Orlando Patterson calls "social death," but social well-being could be restored through the identification with and incorporation into a new family or community of fictive kin.[118] Africans also converted to Christianity as a means of acquiring protection from evil spirits. According to Monica Schuler, Central Africans in Jamaica believed that baptism conferred the protection of the Holy Spirit against injury or "abduction by spirits of the dead."[119] In such cases, slaves likely engaged in a process known as cultural synthesis whereby they converted to Christianity, but as James Sidbury notes, they used "the cultural vocabularies they brought from their old world" to interpret their new world.[120] Finally, some Africans, in particular those who were Kongo, embraced Christianity because they were familiar with Catholicism in their native country.[121]

The baptism of infants was another matter. Kathleen Higgins suggests that parents may have had their children baptized because they believed it conferred higher status on the children, which might result in better treatment for both themselves and the children who were baptized.[122] Likewise, some enslaved individuals probably baptized their children in the belief that cultural adaptation and/or assimilation was closely linked to participation in Hispanic society. It is impossible to discern whether conversion to Christianity and baptism were "imposed on slaves, adopted by them out of self-interest or conviction, or some combination of both," as Alejandro de la Fuente has observed.[123]

In communities with small African populations—as was the case with San Juan—enslaved newcomers were probably pressured to convert, or at least appear to have converted. This does not mean that slaves never retained characteristics of their previous religious or spiritual values, perhaps as a means of asserting or maintaining their African identity. However, as noted by Angel López Cantos, the retention of African religious beliefs and practices occurred less frequently than has been previously assumed.[124] It stands to reason that nearly all the city's enslaved population were, or eventually became, nominally Catholic. Slaves who lived in a society in which no other religion was officially tolerated probably had little choice but to outwardly comply with religious practices.

Turning our attention to the baptismal sponsorship of Africans in San Juan, a total of 182 children and adults (129 males and 53 females) were baptized from 1672 to 1706, resulting in the selection of 175 godfathers and 3 godmothers.[125] Similar patterns in the selection of godparents for African children and adults and native-born infants were observed. Members of the free and freed population were nearly always selected. The proportion of free (162 of 175, or 92.6 percent) and unfree godparents (13 of 175, or 7.4 percent) for African children and adults is nearly identical to the proportion of free godparents for the native-born infants baptized in San Juan (896 of 977, or 91.7 percent and 63 of 977, or 6.4 percent, respectively). This is different from what Kathleen Higgins observed among adult (African) slaves, especially males, who were baptized in Sabará (Minas Gerais, Brazil) during the 1730s. She found that enslaved godparents often sponsored unfree adult males.[126] Higgins attributes the frequent selection of enslaved godparents to the adult initiate having chosen their baptismal sponsor, as opposed to the owner.[127] This implies that owners rather than slaves were responsible for selecting godparents for African children and adults baptized in San Juan.

While owners did not sponsor their African slaves, they served as godfathers for Africans who belonged to others. For example, on April 29, 1692, Sergeant Francisco Arguelles sponsored sixteen-year-old Jacinto, a native of Loango who belonged to Captain Juan Caballero.[128] Likewise, on January 23, 1694, Juan de Almeida sponsored twenty-four-year-old Ana, a native of Angola, who belonged to Juan Felipe Cordero.[129] Soldiers were frequently called on to serve as sponsors for African slaves, with 38 of 159 or 23.9 percent of all godfathers serving in the military. Members of the clergy and individuals studying for the priesthood were also selected as godfathers for African slaves. A sacristan named Diego López sponsored three-year-old María, who belonged to Maria de Muriel, on November 17, 1689.[130] Few enslaved males and no enslaved females were selected as godparents for African children and adults imported to San Juan, and it is likely that adult slaves did not choose other slaves as godparents, in order to promote solidarity within the slave community. Instead, adult slaves chose free residents of San Juan to create ties of a patron-client nature.

A Multiethnic Community Is Formed

Ties of spiritual kinship were intended to serve a religious purpose, but in practice godparenthood often acquired a social character that it retains to this day. The selection of baptismal sponsors established a new set of fictive relationships between the godparents and the godchild (or the adult being baptized) that was known as *padrinazgo* (sponsorship). Between godparents and the parent or parents of the child being baptized, this relationship was known as *compadrazgo* (reciprocal relationship).[131] These relationships could be used to establish vertical ties with prominent or powerful members of the community, such as high-ranking members of the military or the clergy, or to reinforce horizontal relationships with persons of a similar legal or social status. Perhaps the scarcity of males in San Juan explains why soldiers were frequently selected. Nevertheless, the city's racial composition—nearly 63 percent of males were either enslaved, free Black people, or persons of mixed race—suggests some slaves established kinship ties with individuals who shared a similar racial and social background.

San Juan was undergoing important changes in the mid- to late seventeenth century. Sugar production declined in this period, as did the traffic of slaves from Africa to the Spanish Caribbean, especially Puerto Rico and to a lesser extent Santo Domingo. Because very few Africans were brought to San Juan through the slave trade during this period, the composition of the city's enslaved population transitioned from one that was predominantly African born to one that was native born. As the ratio of male to female slaves gradually equalized, demographic circumstances became more favorable to marriage and family life. By the 1690s, if not earlier, San Juan was exhibiting signs of natural growth. A total of 385 slaves were baptized in this decade; of these 49, or 12.7 percent, were African children and adults, and 336, or 87.3 percent, were native born infants.[132] As this process unfolded, the nature of race relations in both the city and on the island of Puerto Rico was transformed. A good deal of human interaction occurred in the workplace and in family, community, and religious contexts. Slaves had greater contact with members of the free population and were exposed to (and exchanged) elements of culture, including language and religion. As Angel Quintero Rivera has noted, such "*encuentros interétnicos*," or interethnic encounters, comprised the origins of a Caribbean culture.[133] The shared experiences of San Juan's impoverished inhabitants probably fostered a sense of nascent class solidarity. Frequent interaction among white, Black, and brown people blurred social distinctions and increased cultural exchanges. During this process, many residents of San Juan developed a common culture.

We need to pay more attention to interactions between free and unfree or white and nonwhite people and try to understand what those interactions meant to those who experienced them. In the absence of primary source material pertaining to the demographic behavior of enslaved and free populations in much of the Caribbean and throughout much of

Latin America, baptismal records provide a unique window on the past. Although baptismal records cannot tell us much about the baptized infant, his or her parent or parents and godparents, family reconstitution enables us to reconstruct some aspects of baptismal sponsorship. As Sherwin Bryant has noted, this information offers us a "momentary snapshot" of the intimate lives of an infant, his or her parent or parents and godparents, and the communities they lived in.[134] Baptismal records reveal much about how men and women who belonged to different communities and kinship networks used the selection of godparents to (re-)create and expand social networks and to reaffirm community solidarity. The range of identities of people selected as godparents in late-seventeenth and early-eighteenth-century San Juan—some were Black, some were white, some were free, and some were enslaved—suggests there was greater flexibility and openness regarding race relations. Africans and their descendants utilized the selection of godparents to (re-)create families and a sense of community in the Americas, whereas godparents (especially soldiers, priests, or males studying for the priesthood) may have agreed to serve in that capacity to publicly demonstrate their honor and enhance their reputation. In taking on religious and social responsibilities, godparents demonstrated themselves to be virtuous members of a multiethnic community.

Notes

I am very grateful to Else Zayas of the Archivo Arquidiocesano in San Juan for verifying the folios in the San Juan baptismal register and to Teresa de Castro who has provided advice, encouragement, and help over the years.

    1. Archivo Histórico Diocesano [hereafter AHD], Libro primero de bautismos para pardos y esclavos, 1672–1706, folio 27.

    2. AHD, Libro primero de bautismos para pardos y esclavos, 1672–1706, 142, 162, and 191v–92.

    3. AHD, Libro primero de bautismos para pardos y esclavos, 1672–1706, 195.

    4. AHD, Libro primero de bautismos para pardos y esclavos, 1672–1706, 167 and 194.

    5. Formerly, one entered the clergy by being appointed to discharge any of the functions reserved to ecclesiastics. Such functions were of two kinds. The liturgical ones constituted orders, though of a lower rank; by ordination the recipients of the minor orders received official authority to perform these functions. The other ecclesiastical functions were offices, entrusted to clerics, whether ordained or not. See www.newadvent.org, *Catholic Encyclopedia*, accessed February 6, 2020.

6. AHD, Libro primero de bautismos para pardos y esclavos, 1672–1706, 150.

7. For works that discuss godparent selection in the context of race and legal status in Colonial Latin America, see Stephen Gudeman and Stuart B. Schwartz, "Cleansing Original Sin: Godparenthood and the Baptism of Slaves in Eighteenth-Century Bahia," in *Kinship, Ideology, and Practice In Latin America*, edited by Raymond T. Smith (Chapel Hill: University of North Carolina Press, 1984), 35–38; Stuart B. Schwartz, *Sugar Plantations in the Formation of Brazilian Society: Bahia, 1550–1835* (Cambridge, UK: Cambridge University Press, 1986), 153–94; Stuart B. Schwartz, *Slaves, Peasants, and Rebels: Reconsidering Brazilian Slavery* (Urbana: University of Illinois Press, 1996), 137–60; Donald Ramos, "Community, Control and Acculturation: A Case Study of Slavery in Eighteenth-Century Brazil," *The Americas* 42 (April 1986): 419–51; José Roberto Góes, *O cattier imperfeito: Um estudo sobre a escravidão no Rio de Janeiro da primeira metade do século XIX* (Vitória-ES, Brazil: Lineart, 1993); Erika Pérez, "'Saludos from your Compadre': Compadrazgo as a Community Institution in Alta California, 1769–1860s," *California History* 88, no. 4 (2011): 47–73; David M. Stark, "Baptismal Sponsorship of Slaves in Eighteenth-Century Puerto Rico," *Slavery & Abolition* 36, no. 1 (2015): 84–110; David Wheat, *Atlantic Africa and the Spanish Caribbean, 1570–1640* (Chapel Hill: University of North Carolina Press, 2016); and Katherine Gerbner, *Christian Slavery: Conversion and Race in the Protestant Atlantic World* (Philadelphia: University of Pennsylvania Press, 2018).

8. Herman Bennett, *Colonial Blackness: A History of Afro-Mexico* (Bloomington: Indiana University Press, 2010), 10.

9. See David Wheat, *Atlantic Africa and the Spanish Caribbean, 1570–1640* (Chapel Hill: University of North Carolina Press, 2016), especially chapter 6; and David Wheat's "Biafadas in Havana: West African Antecedents for Caribbean Social Interactions," in *The Spanish Caribbean & the Atlantic World in the Long Sixteenth Century*, edited by Ida Altman and David Wheat (Lincoln: University of Nebraska Press, 2019), 163–86.

10. According to Gudeman and Schwartz, "Cleansing Original Sin," 42; Schwartz, *Slaves, Peasants, and Rebels*, 142; Higgins, *"Licentious Liberty" in a Brazilian Gold-Mining Region*, 131; Thomas N. Ingersoll, *Mammon and Manon in Early New Orleans: The First Slave Society in the Deep South, 1718–1819* (Knoxville: University of Tennessee Press, 1999), 113; and Sandra Lauderdale Graham, *Caetana Says No: Women's Stories from a Brazilian Slave Society* (Cambridge, UK: Cambridge University Press, 2002), 46, owners did not serve as godparents for their own slaves. In contrast, Alida Metcalf has observed that although owners did not sponsor their slaves at baptism, their unmarried children occasionally sponsored slave infants belonging to their parents; see Alida Metcalf, *Family and Frontier in Colonial Brazil: Santana de Parnaiba, 1550–1822* (Berkeley: University of California Press, 1992), 188. Cacilda Machado identified a similar phenomenon; see Cacilda Machado, "As muitas faces do compadrio de escravos: O Caso

da Freguesia de São José Dos Pinhais (PR), na passagem do século XVIII para o XIX," *Revista Brasileira de Historia* 26, no. 52 (2006): 68. In Spanish Florida and Louisiana, owners or members of their families commonly served as godparents for their slaves. See Kimberly J. Hanger, *Bounded Lives, Bounded Places: Free Black Society in Colonial New Orleans, 1769–1803* (Durham, NC: Duke University Press, 1997), 106; and Jane Landers, *Black Society in Spanish Florida* (Urbana: University of Illinois Press, 1999), 121.

11. Ana María Lugão Rios, "The Politics of Kinship: Compadrio among Slaves in Nineteenth-Century Brazil," *History of the Family* 5, no. 3 (2000): 292.

12. Lugão Rios, "The Politics of Kinship," 292.

13. Wheat, "Biafadas in Havana," 165.

14. Herman L. Bennett, *Africans in Colonial Mexico: Absolutism, Christianity, and Afro-Creole Consciousness, 1570–1640* (Bloomington: Indiana University Press, 2005), 152.

15. Katherine Gerbner, *Christian Slavery: Conversion and Race in the Protestant Atlantic World* (Philadelphia: University of Pennsylvania Press, 2018), 74.

16. The names of godparents were not legible for five infants and seven adults.

17. A total of 585 males were enumerated in the 1673 San Juan census. Of these 269, or 46.0 percent, were white; 218, or 37.3 percent, were enslaved persons; and 98, or 16.7 percent, were free Blacks and persons of mixed race. David M. Stark, "There Is No City Here, but a Desert": The Contours of City Life in 1673 San Juan," *Journal of Caribbean History* 42, no. 2 (2008): 262.

18. Scott K. Taylor, *Honor and Violence in Golden Age Spain* (New Haven, CT: Yale University Press, 2008), 229.

19. Few works focus on seventeenth-century Puerto Rico, and only a handful address slavery in this period. See Enriqueta Vila Vilar, *Historia de Puerto Rico (1600–1650)* (Seville, Spain: Escuela de Estudios Hispano-Americanos de Sevilla, 1974); Ángel López Cantos, *Historia de Puerto Rico (1650–1700)* (Seville, Spain: Escuela de Estudios Hispano-Americanos de Sevilla, 1975); Jalil Sued Badillo and Ángel López Cantos, *Puerto Rico negro* (Rio Piedras, PR: Editorial Cultural, 1986); and David M. Stark "Slavery and the Service Economy in 1673 San Juan," *Revista de Ciencias Sociales* 23, no. 2 (2010): 46–67. The number of studies on slavery in the seventeenth-century Caribbean is quite small and have focused almost exclusively on Havana (the largest city in the Hispanic Caribbean) and Bridgetown (the largest city in the non-Hispanic Caribbean), and to a lesser extent on Spanish Town (the former capital of Spanish Jamaica). See Alejandro de la Fuente and Cesar García del Pino, "Havana and the Fleet System: Trade and Growth in the Periphery of the Spanish Empire, 1550–1610," *Colonial Latin American Review* 5, no. 1 (1996); David Wheat, *Atlantic Africa and the Spanish Caribbean, 1570–1640* (Chapel Hill: University of North Carolina Press, 2016); Pedro L. V. Welch, *Slave Society in the City: Bridgetown, Barbados, 1680–1834* (Kingston, Jamaica: Ian Randle, 2003); James Robertson, *Gone Is the Ancient City: Spanish Town, Jamaica*

1534–2000 (Kingston, Jamaica: Ian Randle, 2005). Also see Bernard Moitt, *Women and Slavery in the French Antilles, 1635–1848* (Bloomington: Indiana University Press, 2001); and José Luis Sáez S. J., *Libro de bautismos de esclavos (1636–1670)* (Santo Domingo, Dominican Republic: Editora Buho, 2008).

20. See Article 1, The Sacrament of Baptism, in *Catechism of the Catholic Church*, accessed August 6, 2019, www.vatican.va/archive/ccc_css/archive/catechism/p2s2c1a1.htm.

21. Fernando Picó, *History of Puerto Rico: A Panorama of Its People* (Princeton, NJ: Markus Wiener, 2006), 43.

22. Stark, "There Is No City," 263–64.

23. All three owners owned an *ingenio* (sugar mill) in 1660 and likely grew sugar at the time of the census.

24. Picó, *History of Puerto Rico*, 75.

25. Joseph C. Dorsey, *Slave Traffic in the Age of Abolition: Puerto Rico, West Africa, and the Non-Hispanic Caribbean, 1815–1859* (Gainesville: University Press of Florida, 2003), 24.

26. Vicente Murga Sanz and Alvaro Huerga, *Episcopologio de Puerto Rico: De Francisco de Cabrera a Francisco de Padilla (1611–1695)*, vol. 3 (Ponce, PR: Universidad Católica de Puerto Rico, 1988), 274.

27. For information on informal communication networks that emerged during the eighteenth century, especially among people of African descent, see Julius Scott, *The Common Wind: Afro-American Currents in the Age of the Haitian Revolution* (New York: Verso, 2018).

28. David M. Stark, *Slave Families and the Hato Economy in Eighteenth-Century Puerto Rico* (Gainesville: University Press of Florida, 2017), 58–59.

29. De la Fuente and García del Pino, "Havana and the Fleet System," 103.

30. For instance, Manuel Nuñez Chaves and Pedro de Aranguren were reimbursed in September 1663, for work performed in the service of the Crown by their slaves as *aserradores*, or sawyers, and *hacheros*, or woodcutters. Archivo General de Indias [hereafter AGI], *Contaduria* 1078. Both individuals appear in the 1673 census as slaveholders, with ten and nine enslaved persons respectively, and likely continued hiring out slaves to the Crown, as work continued in various facets of military construction. David Stark and Teresa de Castro Sedgwick, "Padrón del año 1673 de las personas que hay en la ciudad de San Juan de Puerto Rico: Una transcripción con introducción y notas genealógicas," *Boletín de la Sociedad Puertorriqueña de Genealogía* 9, no. 3-4 (1997): 1–114, 48, 28.

31. Compiled from AGI, Escribanía de cámara 124A, pieza 25.

32. Welch, *Slave Society in the City*, 99.

33. See Arlette Gautier, Les soeurs de solitude: La condition femine dans l'esclavage aux Antilles du XVIIE au XIX siécle (Paris: Éditions Caribeénes, 1985), 31–32. Also see Moitt, *Women and Slavery*, 8.

34. AHD, Libro primero de bautismos para pardos y esclavos, 1672–1706.

35. Sáez, *Libro de bautismos de esclavos (1636–1670)*.

36. The *asiento* was the license issued by the Spanish crown, by which a set of merchants received the monopoly on a trade route or product. They were included in some peace treaties. An example of it was the payment of a fee, which granted legal permission to sell a fixed number of enslaved Africans in the Spanish colonies.

37. All parish registers in San Juan prior to 1625 were destroyed when the Dutch looted the city and laid waste to the island's capital. Lorraine de Castro transcribed a total of 666 baptismal entries from San Juan for the years 1625–1665, from photocopies of the originals made in 1944. A total of thirty-seven entries correspond to slaves: two adults and thirty-five infants. From June 1638 to March 1657, no slave baptisms were recorded in San Juan, but a separate register may have existed at this time for the entries for slaves and/or free persons of color. I am very grateful to Lorraine de Castro for bringing these baptismal entries to my attention.

38. Mary C. Karasch, "Central Africans in Central Brazil, 1780–1835," in *Central Africans and Cultural Transformations in the American Diaspora*, edited by Linda M. Heywood (Cambridge, UK: Cambridge University Press, 2002), 123; Matthew Restall, "Manuel's Worlds: Black Yucatan and the Colonial Caribbean," in *Slaves, Subjects, and Subversives: Blacks in Colonial Latin America*, edited by Jane G. Landers and Barry M. Robinson (Albuquerque: University of New Mexico Press, 2006), 147–74; and Matthew Restall, *The Black Middle: Africans, Mayans and Spaniards in Colonial Yucatan* (Stanford, CA: Stanford University Press, 2009).

39. *Slave Voyages: The Trans-Atlantic Slave Trade Database* (www.slavevoyages.org) is a database run by researchers at Emory University that aims to present all documentary material pertaining to the transatlantic slave trade.

40. Sáez, *Libro de bautismos de esclavos (1636–1670)*.

41. José Luis Sáez, *La iglesia y el negro esclavo en Santo Domingo: Una historia de tres siglos* (Santo Domingo, Dominican Republic: Amigo del Hogar, 1994), 81–82.

42. See António de Almeida Mendes, "The Foundation of the System: A Reassessment of the Slave Trade to the Spanish Americas in the Sixteenth and Seventeenth Centuries," in *Extending The Frontiers: Essays on the New Trans-Atlantic Slave Trade Database*, edited by David Eltis and David Richardson, 99 (New Haven, CT: Yale University Press, 2008).

43. For information on Tari, see Robin Law, "Problems of Plagiarism, Harmonization and Misunderstanding in Contemporary European Sources: Early (pre-1680) Sources for the 'Slave Coast' of West Africa," in *European Sources for Sub-Saharan Africa before 1900: Use and Abuse*, edited by Adam Jones and Beatrix Heinze (Stuttgart, Germany: Steiner, 1987), 351–52.

44. Bennett, *Colonial Blackness*, 63.

45. Gerbner, *Christian Slavery*, 20. Baptism was a requirement for marriage in the church (the only recognized union during slavery).

46. AHD, Libro primero de bautismos para pardos y esclavos, 1672–1706, 140 and 157.

47. Sued Badillo and López Cantos, *Puerto Rico negro*, 287.

48. Julian Pitt-Rivers, *The Fate of Shechem, or the Politics of Sex: Essays in the Anthropology of the Mediterranean* (Cambridge, UK: Cambridge University Press, 1977), 54.

49. Sydney W. Mintz and Eric R. Wolf, "An Analysis of Ritual Co-Parenthood (*Compadrazgo*)," *Southwestern Journal of Anthropology* 6 (Winter 1950): 341, 353.

50. Even in cases when an infant was baptized in *articulo mortis* at home, the ceremony was repeated at the parish church.

51. See Lieven A. Vandekerckhove, "The Role of Godparents: On the Integration of a Non-Familial Role in the Structure of the Kinship System," *Journal of Comparative Family Studies* 12 (Winter 1981): 148.

52. Pitt-Rivers, *The Fate of Shechem*, 54, 60–61; M. Bloch and S. Guggenheim, "*Compadrazgo*, Baptism and the Symbolism of a Second Birth," *Man* 16, no. 3 (1981): 378.

53. Pitt-Rivers, *The Fate of Shechem*, 61; Higgins, *"Licentious Liberty" in a Brazilian Gold-Mining Region*, 130.

54. Higgins, *"Licentious Liberty" in a Brazilian Gold-Mining Region*, 124.

55. AHD Libro primero de bautismos para pardos y esclavos, 1672–1706, 144v.

56. AHD, Libro primero de bautismos para pardos y esclavos, 1672–1706, 158.

57. During the period of observation (1672–1706), 489 Males and 45 females served as godparents in San Juan. The only census for San Juan conducted during this period was in 1673, when the community's population was 1,794. Males numbered 585, or 32.6 percent, and females numbered 1209, or 67.4 percent. Because the proportion of males was much lower than that of females and many more males were selected as godparents, I suspect that three-fourths of San Juan's male population sponsored a child at baptism.

58. Damián López de Haro, *Constituciones Sinodales de Puerto Rico, 1645*, edited by Álvaro Huerga (Ponce, PR: Universidad Católica de Puerto Rico, 1989), Constitución XXXIX, XLVI.

59. Schwartz, *Sugar Plantations*, 63.

60. Age at baptism was listed for 348 infants born to a slave parent in Arecibo in 1735–1772. Of these, 166 infants (48 percent) were baptized at the age of fifteen days. In addition, 246 (71 percent) of all such infants were baptized within fourteen to sixteen days of birth. The number of infants baptized between ten to twenty days of birth increases the total to 315 (91 percent). Although age at baptism for free and freed infants was not examined, they too were baptized

at the age of fifteen days. Stark, "Baptismal Sponsorship of Slaves," 106n26. Infants from other communities on the island were baptized at a similar age. For example, in Yauco, along the southern coast, a total of 238 (60 percent) of 395 infants born to a slave parent in the years 1751–1790 were baptized at the age of fifteen days. David M. Stark, "Creando su propia comunidad: La selección de padrinos y el compadrazgo entre la población esclava de Puerto Rico durante el Siglo XVIII," *La Revista del Centro de Estudios Avanzados de Puerto Rico y el Caribe* 19 (July–December 1994): 2–10.

61. Frank Proctor, "Gender and the Manumission of Slaves in New Spain," *Hispanic American Historical Review* 86, no. 2 (2006): 326.

62. Adám Szaszdi, "Los registros del siglo XVIII en la parroquia de San Germán," *Revista Historia* 1, no. 1 (1962): 62.

63. Robert Schneider, *Public Life in Toulouse, 1463–1789: From Municipal Republic to Cosmopolitan City* (Ithaca, NY: Cornell University Press, 1989), 247–48.

64. Pitt-Rivers, *The Fate of Shechem*, 58.

65. Higgins, *"Licentious Liberty" in a Brazilian Gold-Mining Region*, 132.

66. Five infants with no name were included in this study. Thus, there are 795 infants with slave parent(s).

67. The only other parish on the island with baptismal registers dating from the early eighteenth century is Coamo, where godmothers were present at the baptism of free and unfree infants in the years 1701–1722.

68. AHD, Libro primero de bautismos para pardos y esclavos, 1672–1706, 140.

69. Sáez, *Libro de bautismos de esclavos (1636–1670)*, 15.

70. Sole selection of godparents among whites in San Juan continued up through at least 1757–1771.

71. According to Ana María Lugão Rios's study of Cabo Frio (1795–1810 and 1870–1885), a rural parish outside Rio De Janeiro, 24 percent of infants (142 of 581) baptized in the latter period had female saints as godmothers. See Lugão Rios, "The Politics of Kinship Compadrio," 291.

72. The number of godmothers in San Juan decreased throughout the eighteenth century until 1771; after that, they were selected more frequently. I do not know why customs changed in this period.

73. The original baptismal record book exists but is badly deteriorated by moisture and insects. A copy of the original that was made at the end of the eighteenth century is still in good condition. However, in the transcription, eighteen of the godparent(s) names are illegible.

74. AHD, Libro primero de bautismos para pardos y esclavos, 1672–1706, 46.

75. AHD, Libro primero de matrimonios parroquia Nuestra Señora de los Remedios Santa Iglesia Catedral de San Juan, 1653–1725, 67.

76. AHD, Libro primero de bautismos para pardos y esclavos, 1672–1706, 136.

77. AGI, Santo Domingo 577, "Cartas y expedientes del cabildo eclesiástico y personas eclesiásticos de la Isla de Puerto Rico, 1700–1759," 427.

78. AHD, Libro primero de bautismos para pardos y esclavos, 1672–1706, 12.

79. AHD, Libro primero de matrimonios parroquia Nuestra Señora de los Remedios Santa Iglesia Catedral de San Juan, 1653–1725, 145.

80. AHD, Libro primero de bautismos para pardos y esclavos, 1672–1706, 61v.

81. AHD, Libro primero de bautismos para pardos y esclavos, 1672–1706, 145 and 149.

82. AHD, Libro primero de bautismos para pardos y esclavos, 1672–1706, 53.

83. AHD, Libro primero de bautismos para pardos y esclavos, 1672–1706, 99 and 100.

84. AHD, Libro primero de bautismos para pardos y esclavos, 1672–1706, 135.

85. AHD, Libro primero de bautismos para pardos y esclavos, 1672–1706, 54 and 163.

86. AHD, Libro primero de matrimonios parroquia Nuestra Señora de Los Remedios Santa Iglesia Catedral de San Juan, 1653–1725, 109v.

87. AHD, Libro primero de bautismos para pardos y esclavos, 1672–1706, 27 and 30.

88. AHD, Libro primero de matrimonios parroquia Nuestra Señora de Los Remedios Santa Iglesia Catedral de San Juan, 1653–1725, 134v.

89. AHD, Libro primero de bautismos para pardos y esclavos, 1672–1706, 68.

90. AHD, Libro primero de bautismos para pardos y esclavos, 1672–1706, 23v, 65, 28, and 28v.

91. Picó, *History of Puerto Rico*, 79–81.

92. Picó, *History of Puerto Rico*, 81–85, 88.

93. López Cantos, *Historia*, 230.

94. Isabelo Macías Domínguez, *Cuba en la primera mitad del siglo XVIII* (Seville, Spain: Escuela de Estudios Hispano-Americanos, 1978), 296.

95. By way of comparison, based on data for thirteen years during the same period I studied, López Cantos calculated troop strength to have averaged 228 soldiers, or fifty-seven percent of what it should have been. See López Cantos, *Historia* 230–31. López Cantos derived his figures from different sources than those I used. He draws primarily on reports that captains of the various companies wrote to various entities in Spain. My calculations for troop strength are lower than those of López Cantos. I suspect that this may be the result of the sources he used, which most likely exaggerated total troop strength. A similar situation probably prevailed in Havana, where there was a discrepancy between troop strength the governor reported and actual totals. See Macías Domínguez, *Cuba en la primera mitad del siglo XVIII*, 297. I relied on the *contaduria* (auditing) records that list the actual names of the soldiers who were paid in a particular year.

96. For example, in 1624, over 70 soldiers serving in Havana's military garrison were incapacitated to the point where they were unable to bear arms, and only about 250 out of 450 soldiers were in active service. Domínguez, *Cuba en la primera mitad del siglo XVIII*, 299.

97. It is not clear what type of malady struck the island, although documents referred to it as a *peste* (plague). The plague may have originated in San Martin and found its way to the island when troops from Puerto Rico attacked and destroyed the military fortress in the former in 1648. See Vila Vilar, *Historia de Puerto Rico, 1600-1650*, 29, 38. Similar maladies—possibly yellow fever—struck Havana and Cuba in 1649 and 1650, with equally devastating results. See De la Fuente and García del Pino, "Havana and the Fleet System," 27.

98. Quoted in Pío Medrano Herrero, *Don Damián López de Haro y Don Diego de Torres y Vargas: Dos figuras del Puerto Rico barroco* (San Juan, PR: Editorial Plaza Major, 1999), 273.

99. Manos de Oro might have been his nickname. AHD, Libro primero de matrimonios parroquia Nuestra Señora de los Remedios Santa Iglesia Catedral de San Juan, 1653-1725, 7.

100. Stark and Teresa de Castro Sedgwick, "Padrón del año 1673," 82.

101. López Cantos, *Historia de Puerto Rico*, 135-37. Funds were allocated for the upkeep of the permanent military garrison in San Juan, but rather than sending these from Seville, the Crown tapped the revenues generated by the silver mines of Mexico to provide a permanent subsidy for the garrison's salaries and other expenses.

102. López Cantos, *Historia de Puerto Rico*, 93, 127.

103. Sonya Lipsett-Rivera, *Gender and the Negotiation of Daily Life in Mexico, 1750-1856* (Lincoln: University of Nebraska Press, 2012), 17.

104. Peter Guardino, *The Dead March: A History of the Mexican American War* (Cambridge, MA: Harvard University Press, 2017), 59.

105. Elizabeth A. Foyster, *Manhood in Early Modern England: Honor, Sex, and Marriage* (London: Longman, 1999), 37.

106. AHD, Libro primero de bautismos para pardos y esclavos, 1672-1706, 65, 45, and 26v. For information on Spanish military ranks, see René Chartrand and Bill Younghusband, *Spanish Army of the Napoleonic War: 1793-1808* (Oxford, UK: Osprey Publishing, 1998), 19-20.

107. AHD, Libro primero de matrimonios parroquia Nuestra Señora de los Remedios Santa Iglesia Catedral de San Juan, 1653-1725, 67.

108. AHD, Libro primero de bautismos para pardos y esclavos, 1672-1706, 125, 56, and 88.

109. AHD, Libro primero de matrimonios parroquia Nuestra Señora de los Remedios Santa Iglesia Catedral de San Juan, 1653-1725, 4v.

110. Sued Badillo and López Cantos, *Puerto Rico negro*, 287.

111. See Donald Ramos, "Community, Control and Acculturation in Eighteenth-Century Brazil," *The Americas* 42 (April 1986): 441.

112. Children under the age of six were considered under the age of reason in Spanish Florida and were eligible for immediate baptism. See Landers, *Black Society in Spanish Florida*, 119. Canon law in the diocese of Puerto Rico mandated

that adults needed to know the following in order for them to be baptized: the Apostles Creed or the articles of faith, the Lord's Prayer, the Ten Commandments, and the seven sacraments. López de Haro, *Constituciones Sinodales de Puerto Rico, 1645*, XXXIV, 70.

113. Sued Badillo and López Cantos, *Puerto Rico negro*, 260. See also Fernando Picó, *Al filo del poder: Subalternos y dominantes en Puerto Rico, 1739–1910* (Río Piedras, PR: Editorial Universitaria, 1993), 100.

114. See David L. Chandler, "Family Bonds and the Bondsman: The Slave Family in Colonial Colombia," *Latin American Research Review* 16, no. 2 (1981): 109.

115. It is impossible to know if all owners in San Juan ensured that their slaves were baptized. There may have been owners who did not comply with the precepts of Catholicism and some were not Catholic. Perhaps they made it difficult for slaves to attend mass and/or to receive religious instruction by forcing them to work on Sundays and/or other major feast days of the Church. The time slaves spent in church or receiving religious instruction disrupted their work and limited their profitability. Sunday mass was followed by religious instruction for slaves, so much of the morning, if not the entire day, was taken up with fulfilling religious obligations. Some owners may have wished to avoid the expense associated with baptism and denied slaves the opportunity to participate in this sacrament. There are two ways to determine if owners baptized slaves. One is to examine death records from this period in San Juan, but they regrettably no longer exist. The other is to see if slaves were baptized in *articulo mortis*, or in danger of death. Among the 182 Africans baptized in San Juan, only one was baptized under these circumstances, which suggests that owners baptized their slaves.

116. See Barbara Bush, *Slave Women in Caribbean Society 1650–1838* (Bloomington: Indiana University Press, 1990), 105. Also, see Tânia Maria Gomez, Nery Kjerfve, and Silvia Maria Jardim Brügger, "Compadrio: relaçâo social e libertçâo espiritual em sociedades escavistas (Campos, 1754–1766)," *Estudos Afro-Asiáticos* 20 (June 1991): 229.

117. Joseph C. Miller, "Retention, Reinvention, and Remembering: Restoring Identities through Enslavement in Africa and under Slavery in Brazil," in *Enslaving Connections: Changing Cultures of Africa and Brazil during the Era of Slavery*, edited by José C. Curto and Paul E. Lovejoy (Amherst, NY: Humanity Books, 2004), 83.

118. See Orlando Patterson, *The Sociology of Slavery: An Analysis of the Origins, Development, and Structure of Negro Slavery in Jamaica* (London: MacGibbon & Kee, 1967); and Maureen Warner Lewis, *Central Africa in the Caribbean: Transcending Time, Transforming Cultures* (Kingston, Jamaica: University of the West Indies Press, 2003), 14, 39. See also Miller, "Retention, Reinvention, and Remembering," 84–88.

119. See Monica Schuler, *"Alas, Alas, Kongo": A Social History of Indentured African Immigration into Jamaica, 1841–1865* (Baltimore, MD: Johns Hopkins University Press, 1980), 86.

120. James Sidbury, *Ploughshares into Swords: Race, Rebellion, and Identity in Gabriel's Virginia, 1730–1810* (New York: Cambridge University Press, 1997), 5.

121. See John K. Thornton, "Religious and Ceremonial Life in the Kongo and Mbundu Areas," in *Central Africans and Cultural Transformations in the American Diaspora*, edited by Linda M. Heywood (Cambridge, UK: Cambridge University Press, 2002), 83.

122. See Higgins, *"Licentious Liberty" in a Brazilian Gold-Mining Region*, 137.

123. Alejandro de la Fuente, *Havana and the Atlantic in the Sixteenth Century* (Chapel Hill: University of North Carolina Press, 2008), 161.

124. Ángel López Cantos, *La religiosidad popular en Puerto Rico (Siglo XVIII)* (San Juan, PR: Centro de Estudios Avanzados de Puerto Rico y el Caribe, 1992), 11.

125. No godparent was listed for seven baptisms.

126. Higgins, *"Licentious Liberty" in a Brazilian Gold-Mining Region*, 141.

127. Higgins, *"Licentious Liberty" in a Brazilian Gold-Mining Region*, 142.

128. AHD, Libro primero de bautismos para pardos y esclavos, 1672–1706, 64.

129. Juan de Almeida owned Tomás, a mulatto slave, married to Francisca Barbosa, a free Black. Francisco de Argüeyes owned Lorenza, an adult African slave. AHD, Libro primero de bautismos para pardos y esclavos, 1672–1706, 76.

130. AHD, Libro primero de bautismos para pardos y esclavos, 1672–1706, 45.

131. Pitt-Rivers, *The Fate of Shechem*, 59.

132. Stark, *Slave Families and the Hato Economy*, 179.

133. Ángel G. Quintero Rivera, "Lo sagrado y lo profano," in *Vírgenes, magos y escapularios: Imaginería, etnicidad y religiosidad popular en Puerto Rico*, edited by Ángel G. Quintero (San Juan, PR: Fundación Puertorriqueña de las Humanidades, 1998), viii.

134. Sherwin Bryant, *Rivers of Gold, Lives of Bondage: Governing through Slavery in Colonial Quito* (Chapel Hill: University of North Carolina Press, 2014), 91.

Bibliography

Bennett, Herman. *Colonial Blackness: A History of Afro-Mexico*. Bloomington: Indiana University Press, 2010.

Bennett, Herman L. *Africans in Colonial Mexico: Absolutism, Christianity, and Afro-Creole Consciousness, 1570–1640*. Bloomington: Indiana University Press, 2005.

Bloch, M., and S. Guggenheim. "*Compadrazgo*, Baptism and the Symbolism of a Second Birth." *Man* 16, no. 3 (1981), 376–86.

Bryant, Sherwin. *Rivers of Gold, Lives of Bondage: Governing through Slavery in Colonial Quito*. Chapel Hill: University of North Carolina Press, 2014.

Bush, Barbara. *Slave Women in Caribbean Society 1650–1838*. Bloomington: Indiana University Press, 1990.

Chandler, David L. "Family Bonds and the Bondsman: The Slave Family in Colonial Colombia," *Latin American Research Review* 16, no. 2 (1981): 107–31.

Chartrand, René, and Bill Younghusband, *Spanish Army of the Napoleonic War: 1793–1808*. Oxford, UK: Osprey Publishing, 1998.

De Almeida Mendes, António. "The Foundation of the System: A Reassessment of the Slave Trade to the Spanish Americas in the Sixteenth and Seventeenth Centuries." In *Extending the Frontiers: Essays on the New Trans-Atlantic Slave Trade Database*, edited by David Eltis and David Richardson. New Haven, CT: Yale University Press, 2008, 63–94.

De la Fuente, Alejandro. *Havana and the Atlantic in the Sixteenth Century*. Chapel Hill: University of North Carolina Press, 2008.

De la Fuente, Alejandro, and Cesar García del Pino, "Havana and the Fleet System: Trade and Growth in the Periphery of the Spanish Empire, 1550–1610," *Colonial Latin American Review* 5, no. 1 (1996): 95–115.

Dorsey, Joseph C. *Slave Traffic in the Age of Abolition: Puerto Rico, West Africa, and the Non-Hispanic Caribbean, 1815–1859*. Gainesville: University Press of Florida, 2003.

Foyster, Elizabeth A. *Manhood in Early Modern England: Honor, Sex, and Marriage*. London: Longman, 1999.

Gautier, Arlette. *Les soeurs de solitude: La condition femine dans l'esclavage aux Antilles du XVIIE au XIX siécle*. Paris: Éditions Caribeénes, 1985.

Gerbner, Katherine. *Christian Slavery: Conversion and Race in the Protestant Atlantic World*. Philadelphia: University of Pennsylvania Press, 2018.

Góes, José Roberto. *O cattier imperfeito: Um estudo sobre a escravidão no Rio de Janeiro da primeira metade do século XIX*. Vitória-ES, Brazil: Lineart, 1993.

Gomez, Tânia Maria, Nery Kjerfve, and Silvia Maria Jardim Brügger, "Compadrio: relaçâo social e libertçâo espiritual em sociedades escavistas (Campos, 1754–1766)." *Estudos Afro-Asiáticos* 20 (June 1991): 101–19.

Guardino, Peter. *The Dead March: A History of the Mexican American War*. Cambridge, MA: Harvard University Press, 2017.

Gudeman, Stephen, and Stuart B. Schwartz, "Cleansing Original Sin: Godparenthood and the Baptism of Slaves in Eighteenth-Century Bahia." In *Kinship, Ideology, and Practice in Latin America*, edited by Raymond T. Smith, 35–58. Chapel Hill: University of North Carolina Press, 1984.

Hanger, Kimberly S. *Bounded Lives, Bounded Places. Free Black Society in Colonial New Orleans, 1769–1803*. Durham: Duke University Press, 1997.

Higgins, Kathleen J. *"Licentious Liberty" in a Brazilian Gold-Mining Region: Slavery, Gender, and Social Control in Eighteenth-Century Sabará, Minas Gerais*. University Park: Penn State University Press, 1999.

Ingersoll, Thomas N. *Mammon and Manon in Early New Orleans: The First Slave Society in the Deep South, 1718–1819*. Knoxville: University of Tennessee Press, 1999.

Karasch, Mary C. "Central Africans in Central Brazil, 1780–1835." In *Central Africans and Cultural Transformations in the American Diaspora*, edited by Linda M. Heywood. Cambridge, UK: Cambridge University Press, 2002.
Landers, Jane. *Black Society in Spanish Florida*. Urbana: University of Illinois Press, 1999.
Lauderdale Graham, Sandra. *Caetana Says No: Women's Stories from a Brazilian Slave Society*. Cambridge, UK: Cambridge University Press, 2002.
Law, Robin. "Problems of Plagiarism, Harmonization and Misunderstanding in Contemporary European Sources: Early (Pre-1680) Sources for the 'Slave Coast' of West Africa." In *European Sources for Sub-Saharan Africa before 1900: Use and Abuse*, edited by Adam Jones and Beatrix Heinze, 337–58. Stuttgart, Germany: Steiner, 1987.
Lipsett-Rivera, Sonya. *Gender and the Negotiation of Daily Life in Mexico, 1750–1856*. Lincoln: University of Nebraska Press, 2012.
López Cantos, Ángel. *La religiosidad popular en Puerto Rico (Siglo XVIII)*. San Juan, PR: Centro de Estudios Avanzados de Puerto Rico y el Caribe, 1992.
———. *Historia de Puerto Rico (1650–1700)*. Seville, Spain: Escuela de Estudios Hispano-Americanos de Sevilla, 1975.
López de Haro, Damián. *Constituciones Sinodales de Puerto Rico, 1645*, edited by Álvaro Huerga. Ponce, PR: Universidad Católica de Puerto Rico, 1989.
Lugão Rios, Ana María. "The Politics of Kinship: Compadrio among Slaves in Nineteenth-Century Brazil." *History of the Family* 5, no. 3 (2000): 287–98.
Machado, Cacilda. "As muitas faces do compadrio de escravos: O Caso da Freguesia de São José Dos Pinhais (PR), na passagem do século XVIII para o XIX." *Revista Brasileira de Historia* 26, no. 52 (2006): 49–77.
Macías Domínguez, Isabelo. *Cuba en la primera mitad del siglo XVIII*. Seville, Spain: Escuela de Estudios Hispano-Americanos, 1978.
Medrano Herrero, Pío. *Don Damián López de Haro y Don Diego de Torres y Vargas: Dos figuras del Puerto Rico barroco*. San Juan, PR: Editorial Plaza Major, 1999.
Metcalf, Alida. *Family and Frontier in Colonial Brazil: Santana de Parnaiba, 1550–1822*. Berkeley: University of California Press, 1992.
Miller, Joseph C. "Retention, Reinvention, and Remembering: Restoring Identities through Enslavement in Africa and under Slavery in Brazil." In *Enslaving Connections: Changing Cultures of Africa and Brazil during the Era of Slavery*, edited by José C. Curto and Paul E. Lovejoy, 81–124. Amherst, NY: Humanity Books, 2004.
Mintz, Sydney W., and Eric R. Wolf, "An Analysis of Ritual Co-Parenthood (*Compadrazgo*)," *Southwestern Journal of Anthropology* 6 (Winter 1950), 341–68.
Moitt, Bernard. *Women and Slavery in the French Antilles, 1635–1848*. Bloomington: Indiana University Press, 2001.

Murga Sanz, Vicente, and Alvaro Huerga, *Episcopologio de Puerto Rico: De Francisco de Cabrera a Francisco de Padilla (1611–1695)*, vol. 3. Ponce, PR: Universidad Católica de Puerto Rico, 1988.

Patterson, Orlando. *The Sociology of Slavery: An Analysis of the Origins, Development, and Structure of Negro Slavery in Jamaica*. London: MacGibbon & Kee, 1967.

Pérez, Erika. "'Saludos from Your Compadre': Compadrazgo as a Community Institution in Alta California, 1769–1860s." *California History* 88, no. 4 (2011), 47–73.

Picó, Fernando. *History of Puerto Rico: A Panorama of Its People*. Princeton, NJ: Markus Wiener, 2006.

Picó, Fernando. *Al filo del poder: Subalternos y dominantes en Puerto Rico, 1739–1910*. Río Piedras, PR: Editorial Universitaria, 1993.

Pitt-Rivers, Julian. *The Fate of Shechem, or the Politics of Sex: Essays in the Anthropology of the Mediterranean*. Cambridge, UK: Cambridge University Press, 1977.

Proctor, Frank. "Gender and the Manumission of Slaves in New Spain." *Hispanic American Historical Review* 86, no. 2 (2006): 309–36.

Quintero Rivera, Ángel G. "Lo sagrado y lo profano." In *Vírgenes, magos y escapularios: Imaginería, etnicidad y religiosidad popular en Puerto Rico*, edited by Ángel G. Quintero. San Juan, PR: Fundación Puertorriqueña de las Humanidades, 1998.

Ramos, Donald. "Community, Control and Acculturation: A Case Study of Slavery in Eighteenth-Century Brazil." *The Americas* 42 (April 1986), 419–51.

Restall, Matthew. *The Black Middle: Africans, Mayans and Spaniards in Colonial Yucatan*. Stanford, CA: Stanford University Press, 2009.

———. "Manuel's Worlds: Black Yucatan and the Colonial Caribbean." In *Slaves, Subjects, and Subversives: Blacks in Colonial Latin America*, edited by Jane G. Landers and Barry M. Robinson, 147–74. Albuquerque: University of New Mexico Press, 2006).

Robertson, James. *Gone Is the Ancient City: Spanish Town, Jamaica 1534–2000*. Kingston, Jamaica: Ian Randle, 2005.

The Sacrament of Baptism, in *Catechism of the Catholic Church*, www.vatican.va/archive/ccc_css/archive/catechism/p2s2c1a1.htm.

Sáez S. J., José Luis. *Libro de bautismos de esclavos (1636–1670)*. Santo Domingo, Dominican Republic: Editora Buho, 2008.

Sáez, S. J. José Luis. *La iglesia y el negro esclavo en Santo Domingo: Una historia de tres siglos*. Santo Domingo, Dominican Republic: Amigo del Hogar, 1994.

Schneider, Robert. *Public Life in Toulouse, 1463–1789: From Municipal Republic to Cosmopolitan City*. Ithaca, NY: Cornell University Press, 1989.

Schuler, Monica. *"Alas, Alas, Kongo": A Social History of Indentured African Immigration into Jamaica, 1841–1865*. Baltimore, MD: Johns Hopkins University Press, 1980.

Schwartz, Stuart B. *Slaves, Peasants, and Rebels: Reconsidering Brazilian Slavery.* Urbana: University of Illinois Press, 1996.

———. *Sugar Plantations in the Formation of Brazilian Society: Bahia, 1550–1835.* Cambridge, UK: Cambridge University Press, 1986.

Scott, Julius. *The Common Wind: Afro-American Currents in the Age of the Haitian Revolution.* New York: Verso, 2018.

Sidbury, James. *Ploughshares into Swords: Race, Rebellion, and Identity in Gabriel's Virginia, 1730–1810.* New York: Cambridge University Press, 1997.

Slave Voyages: The Trans-Atlantic Slave Trade Database, www.slavevoyages.org.

Stark, David M. *Slave Families and the Hato Economy in Eighteenth-Century Puerto Rico.* Gainesville: University Press of Florida, 2017.

———. "Baptismal Sponsorship of Slaves in Eighteenth-Century Puerto Rico," *Slavery & Abolition* 36, no. 1 (2015), 84–110.

———."Slavery and the Service Economy in 1673 San Juan." *Revista de Ciencias Sociales* 23, no. 2 (2010): 46–67.

———. "'There Is No City Here, But a Desert': The Contours of City Life in 1673 San Juan," *Journal of Caribbean History* 42, no. 2 (2008): 255–89.

———. "Creando su propia comunidad: La selección de padrinos y el compadrazgo entre la población esclava de Puerto Rico durante el Siglo XVIII." *La Revista del Centro de Estudios Avanzados de Puerto Rico y el Caribe* 19 (July–December 1994): 2–10.

Stark, David, and Teresa de Castro Sedgwick. "Padrón del año 1673 de las personas que hay en la ciudad de San Juan de Puerto Rico: Una transcripción con introducción y notas genealógicas." *Boletín de la Sociedad Puertorriqueña de Genealogía* 9, no. 3-4 (1997): 1–114.

Sued Badillo, Jalil, and Ángel López Cantos. *Puerto Rico negro.* Rio Piedras, PR: Editorial Cultural, 1986.

Szaszdi, Adám. "Los registros del siglo XVIII en la parroquia de San Germán," *Revista Historia* 1, no. 1 (1962): 51–63.

Thornton, John K. "Religious and Ceremonial Life in the Kongo and Mbundu Areas." In *Central Africans and Cultural Transformations in the American Diaspora,* edited by Linda M. Heywood. Cambridge, UK: Cambridge University Press, 2002.

Taylor, Scott K. *Honor and Violence in Golden Age Spain.* New Haven, CT: Yale University Press, 2008.

Vandekerckhove, Lieven A. "The Role of Godparents: On the Integration of a Non-Familial Role in the Structure of the Kinship System." *Journal of Comparative Family Studies* 12 (Winter 1981): 139–49.

Vila Vilar, Enriqueta. *Historia de Puerto Rico (1600–1650).* Seville, Spain: Escuela de Estudios Hispano-Americanos de Sevilla, 1974.

Warner Lewis, Maureen. *Central Africa in the Caribbean: Transcending Time, Transforming Cultures.* Kingston, Jamaica: University of the West Indies Press, 2003.

Welch, Pedro L. V. *Slave Society in the City: Bridgetown, Barbados, 1680-1834.* Kingston, Jamaica: Ian Randle, 2003.

Wheat, David. *Atlantic Africa and the Spanish Caribbean, 1570-1640.* Chapel Hill: University of North Carolina Press, 2016.

Chapter 8

A Tradition of Contraband

Secreting and Silencing the Illegal Importation
and Exploitation of Enslaved Africans in
Spanish Colonial Puerto Rico

JORGE L. CHINEA

In early February 1859, the Spanish authorities in Puerto Rico learned that a suspicious ship ran aground off the southeastern town of Humacao. Identified as the *Majesty*, the slaver was transporting hundreds of sick and emaciated young African captives.[1] Its presence contravened a string of treaties that Great Britain signed with such nations as Portugal, Spain, France, the Netherlands, and Brazil to ban the transatlantic importation of enslaved Africans to their respective colonial territories. The accords, which led to the establishment of international tribunals in Africa (Sierra Leone and Luanda), Brazil (Rio de Janeiro), the Caribbean (Jamaica, Cuba, and Surinam), and the United States (New York) charged with adjudicating cases of vessels suspected of partaking in the outlawed traffic, also called for freeing captives of condemned ships.[2] Governor Fernando Cotoner responded urgently to the unfolding humanitarian crisis and gave orders to have the 400-plus malnourished victims on board the stranded vessel transported to a makeshift *barracón*[3] across the bay of San Juan, where they received medical attention and food. Shortly thereafter, the authorities had them wear numbered metal identification tags and gave them new

(Spanish) names before transferring them to the *Casa de Beneficencia* as future apprentices for selective trustees. On paper, the private individuals who gained custody of the captives were expected to instruct them in the precepts of Roman Catholicism, satisfy their worldly needs, and train them in gainful occupations over the next five to seven years. In practice, as suggested below, the so-called guardians treated them as little more than slaves.

To our knowledge, the *Majesty* is the only known case of a slave ship confiscated by the Spanish government in Puerto Rico that resulted in the release of its involuntary passengers. The contrast with Cuba, where the Havana Anglo-Spanish Mixed Commission and the local authorities liberated over twenty-seven thousand Africans introduced illegally between 1824 and 1876, is striking but hardly surprising.[4] *Negreros* or slave traders had been supplying boatloads of captives to the territorially larger Spanish colony since at least the 1760s, triggering an unprecedented agricultural boom that accelerated following the destruction of the sugar and coffee plantations in nearby Saint-Domingue during the Haitian Revolution. According to the *Transatlantic Slave Trade Database*, an estimated 694,000 African captives were imported into Cuba between 1651 and 1850.[5] Recent research that tabulated direct shipments from Africa and from other sending areas has increased the figure to 803,283.[6] Cuba's extensive reliance on slave labor, especially after Spain agreed to cease its participation in the African slave trade effective beginning in 1820, made the island the main target of British and Spanish naval antitrade patrols in the region.

Just under twenty-seven thousand enslaved captives arrived in Puerto Rico during the same period, a figure that is but a fraction of the volume of the slave traffic in Cuba. However, it is likely that the former total does not include those who were disembarked on the island clandestinely, or those who government employees on the take or desperate to boost colonial revenues deliberately concealed or overlooked. Such schemes, which should have contributed to undercounting the enslaved African population, could also explain why one rarely sees contemporaneous images of Puerto Rico depicting busy harbors filled with large slave ships unloading their manacled victims, or of vast agricultural estates worked by large gangs of Black field hands. Despite a reported low level of transatlantic importations, African bonded labor was a significant factor in the post-1815 expansion of the Puerto Rican sugar industry. Considering this fact, the claim that the island "sits largely outside discussions of the African Diaspora and only peripherally enters discussions on the slave traffic itself" takes on a new meaning.⁷

In his seminal work on the history of the southern Puerto Rican plantation enclave of Ponce, historian Francisco Scarano explains that a veil of secrecy surrounds the island's involvement in the African slave trade. "On no other aspect of nineteenth-century Puerto Rican society," he maintains, "is the historian more likely to be misled than on the dimensions and timing of its participation in the African slave trade." As he explains, investigators seeking information on slave importations during the pre-1820 era, when the mercantile activity was "legal," are surprised by the lack of official documentation. The available source material on this form of human trafficking is both fragmented and sporadic, making it difficult to derive rough estimates or year-to-year counts. After 1820, and in response to the first of three Anglo-Spanish treaties that prohibited the importation of African captives to the Hispanic Caribbean, the author goes on, Iberian colonial functionaries began to "systematically conceal from metropolitan authorities the pervasiveness of the illegal traffic, which reached an all-time high in the decade following the ban." During this interval, Scarano concludes, "slaves continued to pour in, [but] official documentation indicated otherwise."⁸

Unlawful Commerce: Genesis of a Colonial Tradition

> Contraband commerce, by its very nature, is a subject that resides in the historical shadows.
>
> —Alan L. Karras, *Smuggling: Contraband and Corruption in World History*

The deliberate effort to hide or minimize the true scale of the importation and exploitation of enslaved African captives in Puerto Rico after 1820 fits squarely within a deeply entrenched tradition of contraband that, along with smuggling and related fraudulent economic undertakings, persisted over the entire Spanish colonial period.⁹ Historian Arturo Morales Carrión points this out when he writes that the quickness with which Governor Cotoner responded to the *Majesty* affair stemmed, in part, from his knowledge that the consuls of France and England were staking out the island's eastern coastline, "so conducive in the island's *historical tradition* [of participating in] . . . smuggling operations."[10] Fellow investigator Joseph C. Dorsey, who conducted the first systematic research on illegal slave trafficking in Puerto Rico between 1815 and 1859, could not agree more. He put it succinctly and to the point: "The origins of Puerto Rican participation in the clandestine slave trade are found in patterns established from the earliest years of Spanish settlement."[11] The underhanded mode of operation just described was not unique nor confined to the former Iberian colony, as attested by the Trinidadian historian Eric Williams, who declared that "West Indian history, conceived in monopoly, was reared in smuggling."[12]

Puerto Rico's lengthy apprenticeship in slave trading and slavery dates from the onset of the Spanish invasion of the Americas in the early 1500s, when the medieval-era European intruders began cloaking their illegal enslavement of Amerindians with a mantle of religious justifications. Obsessed with amassing wealth, avaricious Iberian conquistadors and their allies who found it expedient to "obey but not comply" with royal directives that did not suit their interests used various morally and legally indefensible mechanisms, such as the *requerimiento*, the self-serving pronouncement that they purportedly read aloud to the bewildered indigenous inhabitants before imposing their authority on them, peacefully or otherwise. "As Las Casas and others were quick to point out," writes the British historian J. H. Elliot, "the conquerors and first settlers made a mockery of the requerimiento, which in effect became a sanction for committing illegalities under the guise of legitimacy."[13] Another scheme, the *encomienda*, subjected the aborigines of the Greater Caribbean to slave-like living and working conditions in the farms, mines, cattle ranches, and other exploitative ventures that Europeans began setting up in the Americas. When Spain formally instituted legislation that banned the enslavement of the indigenous population, unscrupulous conquerors turned to another questionable justification, the concept of "just wars," to launch *cabalgadas*[14] against supposedly "belligerent" Indian villages inside Puerto Rico, where they committed numerous atrocities and took "prisoners of wars" that they later enslaved.[15] Slave-raiding expeditions camouflaged as punitive military campaigns were also deployed in the nearby islands and adjacent continental areas, and the Indian "enemies" seized in these mostly unprovoked onslaughts were subsequently brought involuntarily to Puerto Rico as slaves.

Not surprisingly, the shrinking pool of servile indigenous laborers hurt the embryonic colonial economy, of which the collapsing mining industry was its first major casualty. Colonists tried to salvage their decreasing fortunes by shifting to agriculture and animal husbandry, expecting to cash in on the favorable climatic conditions and the rapidly multiplying herds of wild animals transplanted from Europe. A handful of sugar growers had a promising start after the Crown awarded them generous concessions, including loans and tax exemptions, to help get their plantations off the ground. Some of the locally produced, commercially valuable staples, such as sugar, ginger, and hides, were exported to Spain.[16] Large quantities of corn, yucca, rice and a variety of edible fruits and vegetables, as well as horses, cattle, mules and pigs were shipped out with the Spanish expeditions that explored, conquered and colonized the surrounding continental territories.[17] Iberians who hoped to find greener pastures in *Tierra Firme* began leaving the islands, often without government authorization, taking along what was left of their worldly possessions and slaves. Although the Crown was aware that the exodus threatened to depopulate Puerto Rico, by about 1530 it began redirecting metropolitan immigration and trade to the mineral enclaves in Mesoamerica and the Andean region. As producers in Puerto Rico, Santo Domingo, and parts of central and eastern Cuba became increasingly cut off from the rest of the expanding Spanish-American empire, the Hispanic Caribbean became little more than way stations, underfunded military outposts, and penal colonies.

Sugar planters tried to fill the resulting labor vacuum with captive Africans, whom they considered to be better suited than Amerindians for the arduous work taking place in the fields and sugar mills. Like their encomendero forebears who ignored royal regulations designed to protect native laborers, *hacendados* who sidestepped the Justinian Codes to increase their profit margins exposed slaves to harsh living and working conditions in the sugar plantations, where they were frequently overworked, underfed, and physically punished, prompting those who did not succumb to the abuses to rebel or run away.[18] Consequently, plantations had to periodically restock their servile labor force with new replacements. *Hateros*, as the landowners devoted to pastoral pursuits on large open-range estates became known, fared better during the post–mining boom era. Unlike sugar planters, they relied on fewer slaves, mostly women and children, who performed work that was far less hazardous or strenuous than that which took place in the sun-baked fields, grinding mills, and boiling houses of the *trapiches*. Over the long run, their properties developed and sustained households of enslaved mates at a significantly higher rate than those of sugar plantations.[19]

However, the land barons could not afford the inflated price demanded by the *negreros* who Spain authorized to service the colony. For one thing, shipments were sporadic and often insufficient to meet local demand. The royal importation fees increased the expenses incurred by the cash-strapped prospective buyers. In keeping with Spain's monopolistic mercantile system, the port of San Juan managed all authorized import-export activity in Puerto Rico, including the traffic of enslaved Africans. This meant that residents of other towns and villages located at a significant distance from the walled city had to endure the long, dangerous, and costly trek to the capital to buy the incoming, pricier merchandise here and elsewhere or to ship out their own products.[20] Faced with such obstacles, colonists who felt that Spain had turned its back on them began to see contraband as a practical, and cheaper, alternative. Eventually, "the purchase of contraband goods [became] second nature to these overseas subjects of the King of Spain."[21]

An estimated fifty-one thousand enslaved Africans entered Spanish America between 1492 and 1595, "but the real numbers, swollen by a growing contraband trade, must have been substantially larger."[22] An unspecified number arrived with other undeclared (smuggled) goods brought from Spain. Ship captains often transported slaves disguised as stowaways or crews to sell in the Indies.[23] Different types of merchandise, including slaves, came aboard ships that allegedly made unplanned or unscheduled landings (*arribadas forzosas*) in Puerto Rico. By one account, 41 percent of the 6,661 bonded Africans introduced in Puerto Rico between 1540 and 1600 were acquired in that manner.[24] A recent study has found that just over 77 percent of the 5,213 slaves imported to the island during the period of 1580–1630 arrived in *navíos descaminados*, a Spanish expression for lost or misguided ships.[25] Portuguese negreros, merchants, financiers, seafarers, and allied personnel figured prominently in the unauthorized traffic.[26] Taken together, their illegal mercantile transatlantic activities literally transformed part of the archipelago under their economic sphere into a "Portuguese Caribbean."[27] As José Antonio Piqueras has noted, "early on the port of Puerto Rico had become the center of contraband between Brazil and the Windward islands."[28] In the 1540s, colonial officials in desperate need of scarce supplies and slaves for the haciendas and *hatos* (some of which they owned) or for completing crucial fortification or public works projects took a bolder step: they approved the capture of two Portuguese slavers sailing along the island's coastal waters on their way to Santo Domingo by claiming that they lacked the required clearance of the *Casa de Contratación* (House of Trade) or a license from the Spanish

Crown.²⁹ To their surprise, the *Real Audiencia* of Santo Domingo, which authorized the shipments, ruled against the confiscation of the vessels and their human cargoes. English corsairs who captured Portuguese slave ships often "dumped" captives they could not sell in Puerto Rico.³⁰

Toward the end of the sixteenth century, Philip II instituted the *carimbo*, the practice of branding imported slaves on their backs, shoulders, or face with a hot iron, to check smuggling. In theory, the government hoped that the draconian idea would make it easier for the local authorities to confiscate unfiscalized slaves and impose other sanctions against colonists who had not paid the *almorifazgo*, or the required custom tariffs. "This, like other measures," writes historian Luis M. Díaz Soler, "did not escape being circumvented by the smuggler, who on many occasions was helped by the royal officers themselves, who saw in the illicit trade one of the most effective means to foster the development of the economic life of the colonies."³¹ Another scholar, Francisco Moscoso, has identified two other modalities of contraband. An example of the first one occurred in 1574, when an unidentified royal accountant conspired with the slave dealer Jorge Díaz to allow him to import 100 African captives to Puerto Rico, a quantity that was double what the negrero's slave importation license allowed. Had the plot been a success, the monetary value of the uncollected duties and sale of the fifty smuggled slaves would have increased Díaz's profit margin. Moscoso illustrates the second approach by narrating the 1582 abduction of the governor of Puerto Rico, Francisco Ovando de Mejía, who was traveling to Santo Domingo to seek medical attention when French pirates took him hostage. The outlaws used the top official as a bargaining chip to force the Spaniards to barter sugar and hides for 100 slaves and textiles. Moscoso found that value-wise, the exchange favored the pirates, suggesting that the kidnapping for ransom deal became an economically viable opportunity to engage in contraband.³²

Historian David M. Stark points out that as commercial sugar cultivation declined during the early 1600s, so did the volume of legal slave imports, which dwindled significantly over the next decades. When the Portuguese *asiento* (or slave importation contract) ended in 1640, contraband trade expanded accordingly. Although the island had less use for slaves than in earlier times, there was enough demand for forced labor to keep the sourcing channels open. "Slaves began to arrive from diverse Caribbean locations, with the English—operating out of Jamaica and nearby Tortola—gradually assuming a more active role in the trafficking of Africans, as contraband." Spain sought to regain control of the supply pipeline by awarding an asiento to the Dutch in 1675, but "even then illegal trade continued unabated well into the eighteenth century."[33] Slaves sold by individual licensees and *asentistas* were simply more expensive than those available on the clandestine market. Since Spain lacked feitorias, or slave trading depots, in the west of coast of Africa, it relied extensively on subjects from other nations to procure the human cargoes. This subcontracting method increased the price of slaves which, as noted above, promoted their furtive introduction. "The only thing that facilitated the purchase of slaves at relatively low prices," Díaz Soler reiterates, "was contraband."[34] In her study of the British South Sea Company, which serviced a Spanish asiento starting in 1713, Victoria Gardner Sorsby found that its records for the last trading period (ca. 1728–1739) are incomplete because so many of the transactions were conducted "off the books," that is, via contraband. Although the British preferred to trade slaves for Spanish bullion, when the latter was unavailable, they welcomed other forms of payment. "In the case of Puerto Rico," she goes on, "the country was so poor that the governor authorized the exchange of mules and horses for slaves, even though it was against Spanish law."[35]

As the examples cited so far make patently clear, one of the ironies of the history of contraband in Puerto Rico is the complicity of colonial officials in the illegal activity. Intentionally or not, they emboldened civilians who relied on illegal slave traders because their human merchandise was not subject to the required royal importation fees and available at the number, price, quality, and sale terms that met their needs. "On many occasions the royal officials who knew the economic crisis affecting the island were indifferent to the violation of the royal laws."[36] Enriqueta Vila Vilar notes that between 1600 and 1650, the Spanish governors of Puerto Rico "who had been engaged in illicit businesses, had done so in a somewhat timid and moderate way. But from 1650 onwards, they threw themselves into it, not only by allowing all kinds of trade on the island, but by becoming smugglers themselves."[37] The historian Fernando Picó reports that by the 1700s, illegal trade implicated not only the governors, but also priests, soldiers, farmers, livestock raisers, and countless other islanders.[38] Curaçao played an active role in the illicit activity during the seventeenth and eighteenth centuries, when their ships hauled away sugar, indigo, cotton, tobacco, hides, and silver with the not-so-secret cooperation of the local authorities of Puerto Rico.[39]

Illegal trade was a complicated political, economic, and social problem that defied an easy solution. Since effective Iberian control in the

Hispanic Caribbean during the first two centuries of colonial rule seldom extended beyond the few existing urban settlements, such as San Juan and San Germán, developments taking place outside that limited sphere of influence, such as contraband, became much more difficult to control or eradicate. Runaway Indians and slaves, as well as their descendants inhabiting these remote, hard to reach areas, often eked out a living by hunting, lumbering, farming subsistence plots, or by plying the waters of the Atlantic world with minimal governmental knowledge or intervention.[40] This activity would have included smuggling. In the 1540s, the Crown tried to augment the colony's labor force and simultaneously check the potential security threat posed by maroons by offering to pardon those who returned voluntarily to their former masters. When the tactic failed to produce the desired results, it sought to bring them back to their reputed owners by force. Neither effort solved the persistent labor shortage problems of Puerto Rico.[41] The Spanish government had slightly better results with escaped slaves who fled to Puerto Rico from the nearby islands of the non-Hispanic Caribbean starting around the 1650s. It began freeing them but only after they worked for one year in the fortifications of San Juan. Thereafter, it settled them in the adjacent refugee town of San Mateo de Cangrejos, where they were expected to live a "civilized" life, provision the capital, and defend the island.[42]

Those regions that Spanish military and naval forces found difficult to guard or protect also enabled castaways, stowaways, pirates, fugitives, deserters, refugees, and illegal traders to slip into Puerto Rico and blend in with the surrounding communities where a variety of unregulated activities, including illicit trade, thrived. Even the asiento "was considered a vehicle for both contraband and clandestine migration."[43] It facilitated unauthorized immigration, especially of foreign smugglers. "Bootleggers" from the contiguous territories occupied by Spain's European rivals targeted these inaccessible or isolated sites for bartering a variety of industrial goods, especially farming tools, weapons, textiles, scarce foodstuff (e.g., flour, wines) and slaves for such local products as cured meats, hides, spices, tobacco, ginger, timber, and livestock. The intruders, as Spain labeled them, eventually began to move in to better manage their operations. In 1724, legal representatives of the South Sea Company discovered that one of its former subcontractors was running a slave-importation factory in Puerto Rico that he set up fraudulently under the British company's name in 1718. They alerted the governor of Puerto Rico, who refused to intervene. Eventually, they brought the matter to the attention of the Spanish Crown, which had the impostor put out of business.⁴⁴ In 1769, Governor Miguel de Muesas commissioned Juan González de Villafaña to find and apprehend contrabandists who had been active on the island's southern coast. Accordingly, Villafaña arrested and confiscated the boats, slaves, and other property of transgressors, but soon found himself in hot waters. Accused of torturing suspects and accepting bribes, the official was subsequently discharged. After dismissing the disgraced agent, the governor appointed Dr. Joseph Diepa, a judge of the Real Audiencia, to continue the mission. The findings uncovered during the investigation revealed that up to forty ships from the nearby non-Hispanic Caribbean visited Puerto Rico annually to conduct their illicit business. Their intermediaries collaborated closely with local contacts, which included Jewish, Corsican, Danish, Irish, or British smugglers stationed on the island, to expedite transactions with the civilians and town officials who enthusiastically welcomed them. One of the interlopers, the English Daniel Clos, set up a store that sold contraband wares, especially clothing and hats. He also shipped out cattle and timber to the nearby sugar islands and entrepôts and brought in slaves in return.⁴⁵ While touring the island in the 1770s, the Benedictine friar Iñigo Abbad y Lasierra noticed that contraband had become widespread. He found, for example, that it was the main way of life in the northwestern coast town of Aguadilla, whose residents "are in essence factors of the French in Guarico [northern Haiti], many of them foreigners."⁴⁶ The unlawful exchanges gradually evolved into a "subterranean economy."⁴⁷

Throughout the entire colonial period, the Crown continued to look for ways to deter or eliminate illegal trading in the Indies through the imposition of stiff fines, jail time, banishment, *indulto* (pardoning the offense upon payment of a tax), and/or confiscation of the unlawfully introduced products, including the slaves and ships of the offenders. From about 1675 Spain began taking a more forceful course of action against the foreign trespassers by granting *patentes de corso*, or letters of marque, to private ship owners, empowering them to attack the pirates, merchant vessels, and settlements of rival nations in the Caribbean.⁴⁸ Privateers from Puerto Rico were allowed to keep the impounded vessels, material possessions, and slaves as compensation for their unpaid services. Their critics regarded their sale as "legal" contraband. The eighteenth-century mulatto corsair Miguel Enríquez, who amassed a considerable fortune by capturing and confiscating countless ships and their cargoes, including slaves, was a frequent target of such accusations. The charge that privateers like him engaged in illicit trade is problematic because a legitimate desire to safeguard Spanish mercantile interests might have motivated commissioned pirates, while others simply plundered and pillaged for personal gain. "What is undeniable and evident," writes historian Ángel López Cantos, "is that contraband and privateering get mixed . . . [and] to distinguish one from the other is a very difficult task."[49] Under these ambiguous circumstances, it should come as no surprise that by 1719, Enríquez, a former shoemaker, accumulated personal assets—including dwelling units, warehouses, retail shops, a shipbuilding yard, haciendas, and other rural and urban property—valued as much as 150 thousand pesos. His 250 African captives, all acquired in the foregoing manner, easily qualified him as one the largest slave owners in Puerto Rico.[50]

The administration of Bourbon monarch Charles III took a series of bold steps designed to enhance Spain's global competitiveness, of which none seemed more important than regaining the economic edge that the Iberian power once enjoyed over its European rivals. This required tackling the corrosive effect that contraband, smuggling, fraud, and related unlawful commercial transactions were having on the imperial royal coffers. Historians Allan J. Kuethe and Kenneth J. Andrien point out that contraband reached alarming proportions after the War of the Spanish Succession (1702–1713). From that point onward, English, French, and Dutch illegal traders began taking an ever-growing share of the Spanish American market while also posing a threat to the Spanish ships hauling bullion and other resources back to Europe. "In essence," the authors state, "widespread contraband in the Pacific and the Caribbean threatened the very commercial lifeline of the monarchy."[51]

During the last third of the eighteenth century, Alejandro O'Reilly, Abbad y Lasierra, and other observers brought Puerto Rico's dismal contributions to the Spanish treasury and its vulnerability to foreign economic and territorial encroachments to the attention of the Iberian imperial planners.[52] Their reports persuaded metropolitan overseers to tighten up royal authority in the Spanish American colonial periphery and to recapture the wealth that illegal traders drained out of it. As a result, the fortifications of San Juan were upgraded; the local militias were reorganized into a disciplined military force; deserters, drifters, runaway slaves, and undocumented aliens were subjected to various measures of social and labor control; the dispersed rural inhabitants were increasingly congregated in new urban settlements, that is, in places where the colonial rulers would have a better chance of reforming their reputed antisocial ways. The Spanish Crown hoped to stamp out contraband by intensifying the exploitation of the human and natural resources of Puerto Rico and redirecting its marketable exports to the metropolis. To this end, landowning titles were issued to commercial farmers who previously had only usufruct rights to their parcels. Spain also strengthened mercantile ties to the island through the creation of chartered companies and the opening of more peninsular ports authorized to trade with the Hispanic Caribbean.

Although Spain promoted the importation of enslaved Africans to Puerto Rico to revive the large-scale cultivation of cash crops, such as sugar and coffee, a chronic shortage of capital prevented the financially strapped landowners from taking full advantage of the legal influx of bonded workers. As a result, they continued to rely on unlawful networks to market their products and to obtain slaves. Governor Muesas found this out in 1769, when he learned that most of the slaves toiling on the haciendas lacked the carimbo mark, a clear indication that they had not been cleared through customs.[53] A few years later, the iron rod mysteriously went missing![54] Some of the smugglers went as far as forging the dreaded branding tool to pass off their enslaved victims as legally introduced merchandise. Charles III abolished the inhumane practice in 1784, by which time annual revenues from legally imported slaves did not exceed one thousand pesos.[55] While the introduction of unregistered slaves, piecemeal or in small groups, went on unimpeded, Dutch smugglers operating out of St. Eustatius continued to siphon off copious quantities of Puerto Rican tobacco. According to the historian Birgit Sonesson, the volume of the illegally exported aromatic leaf surpassed the amount that the *Real Factoría de Tabacos*, another recently established Crown monopoly, had shipped to Amsterdam yearly between 1787 and 1792.[56]

Despite the unprecedented changes that Puerto Rico experienced during the last third of the eighteenth century—such as the restructuring of the local militias, the upgrading of San Juan's defensive infrastructure, population growth, increased urbanization, the liberalization of the slave trade, and the greater stress on commercial farming—the imperial overhaul did not improve economic conditions of eighteenth-century Puerto Rico measurably compared to the concurrent advances reported in several major mainland cities of the viceroyalties of New Spain, Peru, Rio de la Plata, and New Granada.[57] In 1775 more than 80 percent of the 1,612,248 acres of arable land in Puerto Rico was not devoted to agriculture. The following year, the volume of sugar produced amounted to a mere 136 metric tons.[58] Nevertheless, the revitalization program laid the groundwork for the post-1815 reemergence of the sugar industry. Within the Hispanic

Caribbean, only Cuba's western region, especially Havana, benefited from the commercial reform of 1765. For example, Havana received the bulk of Spanish imports destined to the Hispanic Caribbean and handled 97 percent of all exports shipped from the Spanish Antilles to Cadiz between 1778 and 1820.[59] Until the first decades of the nineteenth century, Puerto Rico had neither a stand-alone intendency nor a Sociedad Económica de Amigos del País, colonial institutions that helped to professionalize fiscal operations and promote economic growth, respectively, elsewhere in Spanish America.

The Importation of Enslaved African Captives in Puerto Rico during Spain's Second Empire: "Legalizing" the Illegal Traffic

When gauged by the increased level of exportation to Spain of a vast array of tropical commodities and minerals, especially gold and silver, Charles III's reorganization of the Hispanic American empire proved economically successful for the Bourbon ruler. On the other hand, as Kuethe and Andrien maintain, much of the royal revenue generated during that period was spent on quelling the anticolonial uprisings in Spanish America and in dealing with a series of costly wars in which Spanish interests were at stake, including the American and French Revolutions.[60] In short order, the solvency the Crown attained during the second half of the eighteenth century "dwindled and disappeared under the pressures of almost constant warfare in the years after 1790."[61] The Peninsular War (1807–1814) and the wars of Spanish American independence (ca. 1809–1825) became the proverbial last straws that broke the camel's back, by swelling even more the military outlays that the Iberian metropolis shelled out in a desperate attempt to suppress the violent contests that threatened its very existence as a world power.

The momentous events that shook the beleaguered metropolis during the first two decades of the nineteenth century further complicated Puerto Rico's deeply ingrained history of participation in illegal trading. In the first place, Iberian military and economic power would begin to shift from the mainland colonies to the Hispanic Caribbean, especially Puerto Rico and Cuba. Spain needed their financial and logistical support at first to fight off the French invaders and restore its independence and subsequently to support its military campaign against the rebellious colonies. Although peninsular forces and their allies failed to crush the

Latin American insurrectionary movements, in the long run the human and natural resources of both islands became indispensable to the future viability of Spain's restructured Second Empire.[62] Hence, as a reward for the loyalty shown by Creoles in Puerto Rico who did not join the anticolonial struggle, Ferdinand VII granted the island the 1815 *Cédula de Gracias*.[63] The decree sought to jumpstart the Puerto Rican economy, just as the Crown had tried to do after 1765, but this time around by allowing free foreign immigrants to relocate to the island with their capital, slaves and agricultural implements over the next fifteen years. As previously noted, the decision to double up on the importation of enslaved workers stemmed from the government's failure to transform Puerto Rico's peasants and urban workers into a tractable labor force, a process that began in the eighteenth century with the state's drive to congregate and control the recalcitrant rural population. Even the plebians who were landless and dispossessed preferred to engage in subsistence agriculture and other self-sufficient activities rather than to toil in the harsh, regimented atmosphere found on the plantations. Hence, they thwarted the antivagrancy statutes that sought to compel them to work on the sugar estates.[64] Proposals and other efforts to supplement the island's agricultural workers with European migrants, Canary Islanders, Chinese coolies, and free Africans went nowhere. As a result, the political influence of the *bando negro*, as the influential San Juan mayor Pedro Irizarry once called those who favored importing more enslaved Africans, became stronger thereafter.[65]

As Dorsey argues, the monarch issued the 1815 decree in anticipation of the date by which the first Anglo-Spanish treaty to end Spain's participation in the African slave trade was set to go into effect.[66] Hence, the Cédula shifted the responsibility for introducing slaves from the government, which was expected to cease their importation in the near future (1817), to the foreign immigrants. The specific articles of the Cédula pertaining to the introduction of slaves, Morales Carrión writes, reveal "an intention that's contrary to the provisions of the Anglo-Spanish Treaty of 1817 . . . [in that they encourage], by various means, the slave trade . . . [revealing] . . . a manifest incompatibility between this policy and the commitments contracted by Spain."[67] Negreros exploited this convenient loophole to create an alternate channel for supplying African captives to Puerto Rico under the guise, or protective cover, of the royal concession. From that point on, they were able to transport bozales to slave markets in the non-Hispanic Caribbean for subsequent transshipment to Puerto Rico.[68] Following the implementation of the royal order, slave ships began to show up across the island to disembark their human cargoes. Keenly aware that British suppression patrols would catch up with them sooner or later, the traffickers went to great lengths to disguise the true provenance and identity of the bozales by refitting their ships to look like passenger and merchant vessels, registering them in neutral countries, falsifying logbooks, shipping manifestoes, and sale receipts, and by bribing those who might stand in their way.[69] According to Julia Moreno García, Spanish liberals who gained political power between 1820 and 1823, the period known as the *Trienio Liberal*, did little to alter the status quo in the Iberian metropolis regarding the ongoing importation of African captives in the Hispanic Caribbean. Their unwillingness or inability to challenge the status quo that helped the slavocracy of Cuba and Puerto Rico to grow and flourish, she suggests, allowed the end of the legal trade to morph into its illegal continuation.[70]

In the 1820s, the British had enough. Naval commander Thomas Cochrane reported to the British Colonial Office that eight to ten slavers were arriving yearly in Puerto Rico. Unfazed by the potentially explosive allegation, Governor Miguel de la Torre, whom Morales Carrión calls "the master of evasion," dismissed the report and tried to attribute the introduction of slaves to the Cédula de Gracias. He also continued to hand out slave importation licenses to private parties who resumed bringing in captives from St. Bartholomew, Guadeloupe, St. Thomas, Curaçao, and other points in the Eastern Caribbean.[71] As Picó rightly observes, the traffic amounted to the smuggling of enslaved Africans under the auspices of the Spanish authorities in Puerto Rico, a pattern reminiscent of what countless Spanish governors had been accused of doing in the preceding three centuries.[72] In 1827, a French consul in Puerto Rico complained to his superiors that the colonial officials prevented him from boarding a slaver reputedly engaged in transporting African captives to Aguadilla. He suspected that corrupt local functionaries up and down the chain of command, from the port inspector to the regional military commander, were bribed to keep their mouths shut.[73]

Black slavery propped up the reemerging sugar industry, which became the colony's chief economic activity through at least the second half of the century, when coffee production became a major competitor for both land and servile labor. The sugar revolution gained momentum during the late 1820s, as shown by the establishment of an estimated 1,555 sugar estates, the largest of which controlled large numbers of slaves and were heavily clustered in the western and southern districts, especially around Ponce, Mayagüez, and Guayama.[74] As the number of haciendas multiplied, so did the need for slave labor. The sea captain George Coggeshall, who conducted business in Puerto Rico during the first third of the nineteenth century, reported that negreros dropped off three small cargoes of bonded Africans, numbering around 500 in total, near Mayagüez in early February 1831. He noted that slave traders eluded the suppression patrols by substituting their large vessels with "small, fast-sailing pilot-boat schooners . . . [that] carried from 150 to 200 of these poor creatures, and when chased by men-of-war, they crammed all of them below deck to avoid detection."[75] When he called on Ponce later on that month, he could not help but notice the extraordinary expansion of commercial agriculture in the district relative to 1815, when he last toured the island's southern coast. Back then, he pointed out, the area was sparsely populated, thinly cultivated, and had only a handful of low-producing sugar estates. Fourteen years later, he went on, it had "immense cane-fields, large sugar plantations, everything thriving, and the country comparatively rich and prosperous." He learned that the dramatic change was due to the liberal policies adopted by Spain to promote foreign immigration and the slave trade. During his stay, a large brig carrying 350 of the African captives arrived at a nearby port. They were "landed under the direction of . . . government officers," who collected the state's twenty-five pesos per head tax that buyers were required to pay.[76] After being told that a Guineaman, or slaver, disembarked seventy or eighty captives in San Juan in June 1831, the New Englander Edward Bliss Emerson, who had been staying in the island's capital at that time, declared that "the illicit trade is being connived at [here]."[77]

Clearly encouraged by the economic bonanza built on the backs of enslaved African men, women, and children, by the early 1830s the island's plantocracy worked intensely to maintain or expand sugar production. Metropolitan decision-makers, who hoped that an economically robust Puerto Rico would help Spain meet its own domestic and international financial obligations, acquiesced to it by extending the applicable slave acquisition clauses of the 1815 *Cédula*. In 1836, Spain authorized the importation of more slaves from the nearby French, Danish, and Dutch islands, as long as the captives were "hard-working, disciplined, healthy, from the countryside, and in no way African natives who could be even remotely included in the clauses of the treaty signed in 1835 with Great Britain."[78] Many of them came from St. Thomas, a colony that Coggeshall, who was very familiar with the Caribbean, described as "the very centre of the slave trade . . . [that distributed the human cargoes] among all the islands in the West Indies, but by far the greatest number are sold in Porto Rico and Cuba."[79] According to Henry Southern, British consul in Madrid, when the count of Toreno sent a copy of the 1835 Anglo-Spanish treaty to governor De la Torre, directing its due observance, he also enclosed a secret instruction to the official stating that Spain was forced to sign off on the accord, whose very intent went against its interests in the colony. Therefore, the dispatch authorized De la Torre to act in a manner most conducive to the welfare of the territory under his command.[80] Not surprisingly, between 1820 and 1834, the enslaved population in Puerto Rico, which was overwhelmingly comprised of Africans and their descendants, nearly doubled from just over 21,000 to 41,318.[81]

British documents show that Puerto Rico's participation in the slave trade continued over the next decade. On May 18, 1840, Richard Bartlett, British consul at Santa Cruz de Tenerife, reported that a Spanish ship brought 340 slaves from the coast of Africa to Puerto Rico.[82] The following year, British officials in Havana informed their superiors about the arrival of two Spanish slave-trading ships, the schooners *Constancia* and *Feliza*, which unloaded some of the slaves in Puerto Rico on their way to Cuba.[83] In a rare disclosure, the captaincy general acknowledged that seventy thousand slaves were imported to Puerto Rico from Africa or via the non-Hispanic Caribbean between 1815 and 1847.[84] Our research has accounted for some ten thousand approved petitions to import slaves from the "friendly colonies" of the Dutch, French and Danish West Indies between 1824 and 1847, most of them under the auspices of the Cédula de Gracias and generous slave importation licenses dispensed by such governors as Miguel de Torre, Santiago Méndez de Vigo, and Rafael Arístegui y Vélez. Hence, the revelation that an additional sixty thousand were also imported during the same period suggests that the paperwork documenting that influx has been lost, is yet to be uncovered, was never filed, or perhaps was purged from the records consulted.[85] Even though their introduction during this interval contravened the previously mentioned Anglo-Spanish accords, of which the last one was signed in 1845, officials in Puerto Rico derived tax revenues from the importation of smuggled slaves. "Only about a thousand slaves have arrived in this island this year [1837]," writes Charles Walker, a U.S. attorney who lived in Puerto Rico between 1835 and 1840. "It is contrary to express treaty and law," he added, "yet the Governor permits it & receives sixteen dollars a head & all the other officers in proportion—In all is paid $32 each."[86]

When compelled to address the slave importation duty, which had been in place through the early 1840s, metropolitan officials at the Ministries of Treasury and Maritime Affairs had no qualms with the idea of formalizing it as a means of raising colonial revenues. But the *Junta Consultiva de Ultramar*, which feared that England might get wind of the machination, ordered the colonial authorities in Puerto Rico to conceal or torch all files concerning illegally introduced slaves.[87] As the historians Enriqueta Vila Vilar and Jordi Maluquer de Motes have argued, a familiar silence dominated the political atmosphere surrounding the subject of slavery in the Spanish Antilles during the nineteenth century.[88]

The *Majesty* and Its Human Cargo: Exposing the Concealment of the African Slave Trade in Puerto Rico

As suggested by the *Majesty* case briefly referenced at the beginning of this chapter, smuggling in Puerto Rico did not cease entirely as the island entered the second half of the nineteenth century. Chronologically, the *Majesty* belongs to that phase of the human trafficking business that historian Michael Zeuske has aptly called the "forbidden and hidden Atlantic trade."[89] That time period, he reminds us, marks the emergence of a Second Slavery during the age of abolition, that is, after England ceased its participation in the international African slave trade and began pressuring its European competitors to do likewise.[90] From this point forward, the author added, the illegally introduced saltwater Africans were "written" into the system of slavery of the Hispanic Caribbean by notaries who invented or inscribed dubious versions of their names or identities on forged sales receipts, priests who reputedly baptized them, and a complicit colonial state that conveniently renamed them *emancipados*, a term that, contrary to its "freed" or "liberated" English-language translation, masked the servile condition under which many of them were held.[91] Those who were emancipated in Cuba and Puerto Rico were typically consigned to "trusted" *vecinos* (local citizens), most often planters who treated their wards as little more than slaves. Even the term *consignatario* given to the reputed trustees was a painful reminder of the commodification of the *libertos* and *libertas* (formerly enslaved Black people). The contemporaneous *Diccionario Nacional ó Gran Diccionario Clásico de la Lengua Española* (1848) defined the term, in part, as "He who has been entrusted with the cargo of a ship, or some portion of the merchandise that belongs to its commercial agent."[92]

In 1844, England set up a consulate in Puerto Rico, to prevent the unlawful importation of bozales into the Spanish Caribbean. However, as Dorsey has shown, the mission proved to be an ineffective deterrent.[93] The *Majesty* case further supports that conclusion. On the midnight of February 6, 1859, Manuel de Lara y Cárdenas, one of the sitting justices of the Real Audiencia Territorial de Puerto Rico, informed Governor Fernando Cotoner that a large slaver became stranded off the coast of Humacao, on the island's eastern coast. The following morning, the captain general held a court hearing that assigned a prosecutor and judge to launch an inquiry. Shortly after getting the initial report, Cotoner quickly realized that this was no ordinary maritime accident. Suspecting that it was a smuggling scheme, he dismissed and prosecuted the region's military commander. He also leveled charges against the chief judicial authority, a deputy administrator of the Spanish navy of Humacao, a former San Juan customhouse administrator, two lower-ranking naval employees, and a soldier for their alleged participation.[94] It was a swift and firm response, but not one primarily motivated by a humanitarian concern for the well-being of the African victims. Rather, as Morales Carrión has noted, the political repercussions of the case weighed heavily on the governor's mind. Given the presence of both the French and British consuls on the island, it became imperative to clear the colony and its upper bureaucracy of any wrongdoing by deflecting blame away from Puerto Rico. Hence, the official explanation underscored that the barque was heading to Cuba, and only stopped near Humacao when it ran aground. It also stressed that the government acted expeditiously and exercised due diligence by sheltering, feeding, clothing, and caring for the medical needs of the transportees, punishing culpable members of the *Majesty*'s crew, disciplining local functionaries for dereliction of duty, and by emancipating the Africans as required by the anti–slave-trading agreements.

The information that Cotoner initially received had the ship originating in Santiago de Cuba, from where it sailed off to New Orleans six months earlier, only to change course on the high seas and veer toward the west coast of Africa. The British and French consular representatives who responded to the scene of the real or staged shipwreck suspected that there was more than met the eye. To M. de Labordère, who served as secretary to the French consul in Puerto Rico, the *Majesty* incident had ties to the Fourcarde case, another plot hatched the previous year by a French planter in Cuba to recruit free Blacks in Puerto Rico to work in Martinique and Guadeloupe. Fourcade intended to pay an attractive commission to the captain and crew to reroute the ships to Cuba and sell off the unsuspecting workers there. Labordère also believed that the *Majesty* was a joint venture of merchants operating out of Cuba and Puerto Rico. The British agent Francis Ick had another take: he believed that the ship was of North American (U.S.) construction but outfitted in Cadiz and staffed by a Spanish crew. From there, it steered to the Congo River to pick up the human cargo. While Ick contended that Puerto Rico was its intended destination, his supervisor, George Samuel Lennon Hunt, maintained that the slaver made an unscheduled stop in Humacao when it ran out of supplies on his way to Cuba.[95]

While concrete information on the enterprise's financial backers is unknown, the evidence of U.S.-Cuban collaboration seems very persuasive. The Cuban historian José Luciano Franco noted that "Following the rigorous suppression measures taken by the British government, the slave trade [in the Caribbean] was carried out principally on U.S.-built ships, controlled by [North] Americans, and funded by [North] American capital under [North] American flag."[96] According to fellow researcher Craig Hollander, "by 1820 . . . [the United States'] transatlantic slave trade had already transitioned from a relatively open form of commerce into an underground smuggling operation." Those who partook in it "employed innovative techniques to mask their crimes, ensure their anonymity, and cover their tracks."[97] Vessels departing from such cities as Philadelphia, New York, or Charleston stocked up with tobacco and rum at Havana before setting off for the West African coast, where French, Brazilian, and Portuguese middlemen (known as *mongos*) provided the human merchandise.[98] By 1830, New York emerged as the chief North American base of operations of the profitable enterprise, which boasted strong ties with the Cuban slavocracy.[99] Two decades later, "New York and New Orleans . . . became key nodes in a new slaving nexus that stretched from Ouidah and Cabinda in Africa to Havana and Matanzas in Cuba . . . [becoming] . . . the slave trade's final triangle."[100] Another slaver that was launched from the United States surreptitiously, the *Batans* or *Brick Segundo*, ferried 700 mostly nonadult Congolese captives to eastern Cuba just four years prior to the *Majesty*.[101] Citing the *Transatlantic Slave Trade Database*, a recent study maintains that "the bulk of departures was from New York and New Orleans, which together accounted for more than 75 percent of all slaves disembarked [in the Americas but destined mostly to Cuba and Brazil] from vessels leaving North American ports between 1844 and the ending of the slave trade in 1867."[102]

The participation of United States merchants, capitalists, and shipbuilders in the nefarious business during the age of abolition is hardly surprising. "American" (U.S.) involvement in the slave trade was a significant part of the human trafficking business even before both Congress and England banned it 1807.[103] Prior to the Lincoln administration, U.S. law prevented British naval squadrons from searching "American" ships suspected of transporting enslaved Africans on the high seas, which in effect all but invalidated the aforementioned commitment to prohibit the traffic. Following the second Anglo-Spanish accord of 1835, when British suppression patrols stepped up the seizures of Spanish slavers, U.S. ships that had "become famous for their quality and capacities at sea" picked up the slack.[104] "In one specific area of the contraband slave trade," the historian Leonardo Marques writes, "the United States became unquestionably predominant: in the provision of ships." U.S. constructors eventually drove "numerous British shipbuilders to bankruptcy during the 1840s."[105] The U.S.-made vessels and allied financiers stocked the factories, or warehouses, on the African coast, and furnished the equipment, supplies and some of the crews manning the foreign-owned slave ships that ferried the captives across the Middle Passage. Moreover, U.S. merchants connected to the maritime ventures built lucrative trading companies in key areas of Cuba, often in partnership with business associates at home and abroad, to facilitate this transatlantic activity.[106] These firms, which inserted themselves strategically within the Cuban economy, extended credit to planters and exported tropical commodities, especially sugar, produced in the Spanish colony. Among the entrepreneurs were those who "invested in slave plantations on the island and became part of the two ends of the trading ties."[107]

To date, the exact number of captives transported aboard the *Majesty* or landed in Puerto Rico is still unclear. Early on Cotoner had learned that it originally carried between 1,000 and 2,000. Ick claimed that it was more like 1,050, of which planters hid between 800 and 850 in their haciendas before the governor intervened. The French vice-consular representative in Humacao, M. Sandoz, placed the number of slaves concealed in the district at 900. Lara y Cárdenas estimated the number of bozales on board the ship at 653, or about 150 to 250 fewer captives than what Ick and Sandoz had reported. According to Hunt no less than 338 bozales, a majority of whom were the young and robust who had survived the ill-fated voyage, suffered enslavement.[108] Cotoner later confirmed that his subordinates had deceived him and that in fact the number sold totaled 329. He knew the plantations where they were being held but either decided not to retrieve them or perhaps his hands were tied by article 9 of the 1845 law for the abolition of the slave trade, which forbade the colonial authorities from entering plantations to search for contraband slaves.[109] The Cuban historians María de los Ángeles Meriño Fuentes and Aismara Perera Díaz have noted that "by protecting the consumer market of slaves"—made up of planters for the most part—"the Penal Law of March 1845 became the greatest guarantee for the continuity of the [slave] trade."[110]

The Africans of the *Majesty* arrived in a deplorable mental and medical state of health, which contributed to a high mortality rate among the most vulnerable of them. Ick witnessed the landing of forty of the bozales, of whom about ten were near death and six had already perished. It was a heart-wrenching sight, the Englishman wrote to his immediate supervisor, a painful image he hoped never to see again. The terrible conditions under which they had been transported turned the cargo to "human pacotille."[111] "A long voyage and all of the horrors of thirst and hunger," Labordère explained, "have reduced them to the state of living skeletons."[112] Another contemporary report described the survivors huddled together, males and females, in a crowded palm-thatched hangar where adults and children afflicted by dysentery and leprosy were dying daily. Governor Cotoner had taken 392 of the Africans there around February 27. On April 2, the colonial administration also had 109 sick bozales who were being held in Humacao taken to the barracón that served as a detention and registration center. Ravaged by disease, malnourishment and exhaustion, many could not be saved, "despite the measures . . . both hygienic and curative that had been taken."[113] Besides those who expired during confinement, another 112 died at the haciendas to which the government had consigned them between early March and July of 1859.[114] It is not clear if the latter group were among the 114 Africans reported to have died in Humacao within two months of their arrival.[115] Altogether, at least 165 passed away between 1859 and 1864. Over 60 percent of the deaths occurred within one year of their forceful arrival.

On February 12, 1859, the local administration implemented a *Reglamento Provisional de Negros Emancipados* (Provisional Guidelines for the Emancipated Blacks). Six weeks later the *Ordenanza General de Emancipados* (General Regulations for Emancipated [or more accurately, apprenticed] Africans) superseded it. The latter instrument, which had been originally employed in Cuba, called for dividing the liberated Africans into two groups, emancipados and *colonos libres*.[116] Length of time on the island partially determined how the designations were to be assigned to the captives. The first category applied to the newly freed above the age of twenty. It called for placing them under government care for a five-year period.[117] The second applied to emancipados who completed the initial apprenticeship period. From the start, however, local planters treated the Africans as virtual agricultural workers. This becomes clear from Cotoner's decision, shortly after the case became public, to write to the island's municipal authorities requesting information on the number of hacendados and *estancieros* in their districts, the size of their properties, the amount of land devoted to sugar or coffee, their current workforce, and how many slaves they lost to the outbreak of cholera and smallpox that occurred in 1855–1856.[118] He subsequently used the information to split up the vast majority of the bozales among the landowners hardest hit by the infectious diseases.[119]

The colony's official newsletter, the *Gaceta Oficial*, published public notices of the impending distribution, as well as the results of the approved allocations. A *Junta Protectora de Emancipados* (Board for the Protection of the Emancipated [Africans]) managed the apportionments made to private parties and institutions. Bozales waiting to be distributed were moved to the Casa de Beneficencia, a one-stop correctional and labor recruitment agency that housed individuals who the authorities deemed dangerous, troublesome, or idle, as well as prostitutes, orphans, abused women, and slaves.[120] The establishment integrated the jobless and wards of the state into the colonial economy through supervised placement with private and public employers.

Each consignatario who was awarded emancipados posted a monetary deposit and three months' advanced wages to the *Casa* before receiving them.[121] The funds were not intended to compensate the bozales for their services. The Casa used the money to offset the costs incurred by the government in dealing with the liberated Africans. Up to 10 percent of the emancipados was set aside for beneficence agencies, widows, and orphans. It designated another two-thirds of the total for agriculture and the rest for industrial tasks.[122] Recipients of single emancipados were likely to be widows/widowers, pensioners, and retirees. Groups of emancipados were usually assigned to planters.[123] The "trustees" were expected to pay for their food, clothing, housing, and medical needs; to instruct them in the religious principles of Roman Catholicism in preparation for their subsequent baptism, and to train them in a useful skill, trade, or domestic occupation.[124] Much like slaves, emancipados who ran away could face confinement and various forms of corporal punishment.[125]

Planters hoped the emancipados would enable them to replenish their dwindling enslaved workforce following the previously mentioned epidemic eruptions, which claimed a staggering 25,000 lives, including 5,500 slaves.[126] Hence, "the human pacotille which the *Majesty* brought [to the island] was seen and sought out by the hacendados as a basic necessity."[127] Just eight days after the incident came to light, writes historian Gloria Tapia Ríos, sixty-five of the emancipados were taken to Joaquín Masfarré's plantation, known as Hacienda Luzanaris, located in Humacao. The *corregidor*, or local judicial officer, doubted the planter had the legal authorization to own them, and eventually forced him to give up fifty of them. Tapia Ríos found no paper trail to account for their whereabouts after the administrator removed them. Worse yet, she suspects there were more cases in which civil servants, consular representatives and other planters concealed and retained an undetermined number of *Majesty* slaves who were officially reported as having "disappeared."[128]

Forty-six consignatarios had 404, or 90 percent, of the total number of Africans under state custody. Close to 50 percent of them ended up in twelve haciendas located in fourteen towns. The economic activities of another thirteen consignatarios who had one of the 127 emancipados in their possession are not known, but it is likely that they too were landowners. It is also unclear where another 70 assigned to a partnership by the name of Srs. Gaveniz and Fern were placed, but the odds are they also worked on agricultural estates.[129] The harsh work of plantation agriculture took a toll on the emaciated Africans. The planter Luis Mariani claimed to have lost 33 of his 60 emancipados, and Cruziano Fantauzi alleged that 33 of the 50 sent to his estate had also died.[130] The frail mental and medical conditions of the captives, coupled with the added burden of plantation work, could well account for the high mortality rate; however, the possibility that some planters feigned the demise of emancipados whom they illegally retained in order to make up for losses sustained within their own servile workforce cannot be ruled out.[131]

Despite the overwhelming odds against them, documents of the era show that the bozales actively resisted their exploitation. Investigators have found evidence of Africans who ran away immediately upon landing on the island or from their reputed masters. Hunger caught up with one of the runaways captured while trying to feed himself inside the *bohío*, or hut, of a startled local couple. Two male escapees were found wearing women's clothes, presumably to pass off as local nonwhite females. The authorities apprehended a runaway found begging for food on a deserted road. Incidents involving emancipados who absconded were reported in the towns of Humacao, Yabucoa, Carolina, Trujillo Bajo, Maunabo, and Arecibo.[132] At least one emancipado filed a lawsuit against a planter for cruelty.[133] Some emancipados reached out to the British consul or sympathetic Spanish officials, refused to leave the *Casa* for their respective worksites, or were sent back after complaining of being sick. Others sought to confuse their tormentors by exploiting discrepancies over their imposed new names and numbered tin plates. Others complained of mistreatment at the hands of abusive trustees.[134]

The *colonos libres* designation aimed to preserve as much of the Africans' subordinate, servile laboring role as possible. Sugar and coffee planters who had long been complaining of the "shortage" of tractable workers decried the ineffectiveness of the forced labor *libreta* system that was instituted in 1849 to coerce the "vagrant" agregados and the "lazy" jornaleros to toil on the haciendas.[135] Hacendados and their supporters in the colonial administration were also painfully aware that their collective efforts to lure European *braceros* (field or manual workers) to Puerto Rico during much of the nineteenth century had failed to solve the island's labor "scarcity" problem.[136] Hence, just before the mandated five-year tutelage of the surviving Africans expired, Governor Félix María de Messina introduced a new *Reglamento* in 1864, requiring the surviving 165 *colonos* to "voluntarily" sign work contracts of up to six months in duration. The regulations spelled out the workers' length of service, salary, and hours of work, as well as the food rations, living arrangements, clothing, and medical aid available to them, while also pledging to keep their households together. Any amendments, including the transfer of colono contracts to third parties, needed the explicit approval of the workers.[137]

Díaz Soler seemed to have been favorably impressed with these and other protections.[138] But certain clauses contained in the new ordinance symbolically or expressly abridged the workers' other rights. For example, article 1 stipulated that the colonos' situation was akin to that of the *jornaleros*, which suggests that vagrancy laws applied to those who chose not to sign a contract or to hold a regular job. Article 12 allowed the colonos to wed if their *patronos* (employers) consented, a provision that gave planters control over the workers' decision to form church-sanctioned families. Article 49, which is certainly one of the more troublesome, gave patronos or their designees unprecedented disciplinary powers that should have fallen under the jurisdiction of the island's criminal justice system, such as the ability to punish colonos for a wide variety of infractions, including insubordination, refusal to work, drunkenness, running away, inflicting work-incapacitating injuries to peers, violating workplace rules, and engaging in indecent and malicious acts.[139]

The investigator Luis de la Rosa expressed reservations about the servile treatment of the Africans prescribed in the *Ordenanza General de Emancipados*. Nevertheless, he placed the controversial regulations in the context of the times. Most of the island's population, he pointed out, lived a wretched, oppressed life, especially "when measured by the libreta system."[140] When seen from that perspective, the author suggested, the idea of consigning the Africans to private parties who were expected to help integrate them into the economic and cultural-religious life of the island did not appear all that bad, at least on paper. Still, the incomplete and contradictory nature of much of the documentary evidence concerning the *Majesty* case troubled him: the number of bozales aboard the ship and those whom the government seized do not add up, even when those who were secreted in the local plantations are factored in; there is no record of the alleged deaths of the emancipados that occurred between their February 6, when they were first taken into custody, and their subsequent transportation to the detention and distribution center three weeks later; the numbered tin plates that had been created (453) exceeded the number of Africans (434) the government claimed to have taken into custody; and the number who allegedly died at the plantations (112) sounded disproportionately high. "Evidently," he concluded, "there was something shady in everything connected to the African survivors of the *Majesty*."[141] Regardless of how much we add or subtract, he went on, almost 500 of the original captives disappeared from the historical record, and we are unable to account for them.[142]

For the historian Teresita Martínez Vergne, the *Majesty* incident affords an opportunity to critically reassess the nature of slavery and race relations in the island within the context of the politics of Spanish liberalism. Although the liberated Africans were legally free, their integration into the colonial society suggested otherwise. Their mistreatment reinforced the existing stratified socio-racial order that had prevailed in Spanish America and persisted in one form or another after the region became independent. As such, it perpetuated the paternalistic attitudes of the well-off Iberian and

Creole guardians of the subordinated free Africans, who were coercively transformed into servile Black laborers. Several interrelated local developments contributed to the ambiguities and contradictions surrounding their subservient status: one, the captain generals' dictatorial grip over island affairs that effectively gave them unchecked control of the liberated Africans; two, the power wielded by the planter elite over the hapless victims; and three, the creation of so-called liberal institutions, such as the Casa de Beneficencia, that conveniently funneled the bozales to plantations and private homes, a "consignment system [that] also served to reinforce the unequal nature of social relations in the . . . colony."[143] After all, "Beneficence in the Caribbean and Latin America served as a . . . mechanism aimed at policing and controlling poor and colored people"—a common goal of both the upper classes and the colonial state.[144]

In short, in Martínez Vergne's judgment, the combination of these forces conferred a subordinate status on the liberated Africans at the hands of the interested imperial representatives and the trustees. And yet, as she and De la Rosa have noted, the bozales refused to fold under pressure. Against all odds, they asserted their humanity by engaging in a variety of day-to-day forms of resistance, such as running away, filing complaints, and refusing to work under onerous, servile conditions.[145]

Conclusion

Future research, particularly at a microhistorical level of analysis that considers how the enslavement of Africans evolved in the villages, towns, cities, and villas of Puerto Rico, might shed additional light on the true scale of the African slave trade in the Spanish Antillean colony. Given its furtiveness, the number of slaves imported to the island is not fully known. What seems certain, however, is that the introduction of enslaved Africans from other areas of the Caribbean across the entire Spanish colonial period oscillated according to shifting demand and supply factors and the changing state of inter-European relations, among other reasons. In this respect, there are parallels with pre-1800 Cuba. The historian Elena Schneider has found that most slaves brought to the territorially largest island of the Greater Antilles between 1640 and 1789 were conveyed there from non-African points of departure in the Americas. As in the case of Puerto Rico, the author notes that this traffic included both legal and illegal arrivals, including those who came as seaborne runaways or victims of inter-imperial conflicts, or were introduced against their will by unauthorized ships, pirates, kidnappers, and smugglers.[146]

Since smuggling cut into the royal revenues, the Spanish Crown clearly had a large stake in eliminating it. Nevertheless, the fraudulent practice was transplanted to the New World along with the other social, cultural, economic, and political mores and institutions rooted on the Iberian Peninsula. Contraband turned up in Spanish America from the initial period of Iberian settlement and expanded in the course of time. It seemed to have reached endemic proportions in the colonial periphery—that is, in those regions that were outside Spanish immigration and mercantile routes in the Indies. Starting around the middle of the sixteenth century, the colonial fringes included the territories that later became associated with the Hispanic Caribbean. In the absence of regular or consistent trade with the metropolis and/or its subcontracted agents, such as asentistas and chartered mercantile companies, the inhabitants of the archipelago and adjacent areas resorted to contraband to satisfy their daily needs for such items as food, wines, grains, textiles, household wares, candles, soap, weapons, and agricultural implements. Local officials who had the obligation to look after these territories participated in the illicit commercial activities out of necessity, but dishonest functionaries also did it for personal gain, unconcerned about the potential career-ending consequences of their corrupt practices. As the demand for cheap or tractable labor in the mining and agricultural sectors swelled after the abrupt decline of the indigenous population by about 1550, so did the need for enslaved Africans. However, the unaffordable prices and insufficient availability of the captives that were being supplied legally dashed the hopes of ambitious colonists, especially sugar producers, who managed to establish only a handful of estates. Other settlers turned increasingly to pastoral pursuits, which subsequently led to the formation of *hatos*, or open range ranches, that began to specialize in animal husbandry. These economic enterprises, and others that were set up thereafter, relied on slave labor that would have been secured in the main from smuggling channels that persisted to one degree or another until the late Spanish colonial period.

During the late Bourbon period, Spain sought to jump-start the stagnant economies of the Hispanic Caribbean as part of an imperial revitalization program aimed at restoring its global economic competitiveness. To this end, it liberalized the slave trade in the last third of the eighteenth century. But even during this "free" phase of the "odious commerce," which lasted until about 1820, Puerto Rico briefly became, for all purposes and effects, a slave depot.[147] For instance, the vast majority of slaves landed in San Juan by asentistas between 1766 and 1770 were reshipped to other Spanish American colonies because most landowners on the island could not afford their high sale price or lacked the capital with which to purchase them. Consequently, the financially strapped planters once again turned to smugglers with links to the non-Hispanic Caribbean to meet their needs by bartering local products for scarce commodities and slaves. Contraband, which by that time had become a time-honored tradition, intensified thereafter in response to the Spanish American wars of independence, when Spain sought to salvage the remainder of its shrunken empire by transforming Cuba and Puerto Rico into thriving sugar and coffee plantation producers. In this new context, the Iberian metropolis came to see the British campaign to end the slave trade as a self-serving tactic designed to squeeze Spain out of the international marketplace of tropical staples. Since the future of commercial agriculture in its two remaining insular territories seemed promising, due in part to favorable environmental conditions, the stimulating effects of the Caroline reforms and the destruction of the plantations of nearby Saint-Domingue in the aftermath of the Haitian Revolution, acquiescing to British abolitionist pressure amounted to an "econocidal" act for Spanish imperial interests. Consequently, Spain did everything within its power to avoid shooting itself on the foot. In practical terms, this meant deceiving England, whenever possible, about its role in the illegal importation of slaves and developing a new framework (the Cédula de Gracias) that would allow planters in Puerto Rico, especially sugar and coffee producers, to circumvent the Anglo-Spanish anti–slave-trading accords by importing slaves from the nearby colonies of the non-Hispanic Caribbean.

By then, a labor-hungry plantocracy in Puerto Rico and a revenue-short Iberian imperial state had all but joined hands to effectively legalize the illegal traffic. Insular colonial officials either profited from illegal slave trafficking, blindly adhered to a duplicitous governmental policy, or both. Since they had no real interest in preserving evidence of the clandestine introductions, the actual extent of the African influx became a closely guarded secret. The *Majesty* affair exposed the carefully orchestrated facade, leading to the confiscation of the ship and its involuntary passengers. Although the colonial administration conveniently repackaged the captives as *emancipados* and *colonos libres* to blunt any potential criticisms from British consular agents, the liberated Africans still toiled as servile workers. As late as 1866, a Spanish royal order reiterated the official prohibition against the introduction of enslaved Africans in Puerto Rico, where it continued at a reduced scale owing to the collusion of dishonest local authorities and unscrupulous United States skippers who were still involved in the illicit business.[148]

Notes

1. This chapter builds on an earlier attempt to address the *Majesty* from the broader perspective of the history of enslavement in Puerto Rico and what the incident reveals about the timing and composition of slave acquisitions, and the likely African origins and victimization of the young bonded captives. See Jorge L. Chinea, "Slavery and Child Trafficking in Puerto Rico at the Closing of the African Slave Trade: The Young Captives of the Slaver *Majesty*, 1859–1865," *Revista Brasileira do Caribe* 17, no. 32 (2016): 59–98.

2. Leslie Bethell, "The Mixed Commissions for the Suppression of the Transatlantic Slave Trade in the Nineteenth Century," *Journal of African History* 7, no. 1 (1966): 79.

3. Barracks used to confine slaves.

4. Inés Roldán de Montaud, "The Misfortune of Liberated Africans in Colonial Cuba, 1824–1876," in *Liberated Africans and the Abolition of the Slave Trade, 1807–1896*, ed. Richard Anderson and Henry B. Lovejoy (Rochester, NY: University of Rochester Press, 2020), 154.

5. http://www.slavevoyages.org/estimates/6nJYXq3d, accessed June 10, 2022.

6. See David Eltis and Jorge Felipe-Gonzalez, "The Rise and Fall of the Cuban Slave Market: New Data, New Paradigms," in *From the Galleons to the Highlands: Slave Trade Routes in the Spanish Americas*, ed. Alex Borucki, David Eltis, and David Wheat (Albuquerque: University of New Mexico Press, 2020), 204–5.

7. Ibrahim K. Sundiata, "Puerto Rico and Africa: The Ambiguity of Diaspora," *21st. Century Afro Review* 3, no. 1 (1997): 1–36.

8. Francisco A. Scarano, *Sugar and Slavery in Puerto Rico: The Plantation Economy of Ponce, 1800–1850* (Madison: University of Wisconsin Press, 1984), 121.

9. Lance R. Grahn presents a useful treatment of the various types of unlawful commercial activity under the general rubric of contraband in "Contraband (Spanish America)," *Encyclopedia of Latin American History and Culture, Encyclopedia.com* (August 16, 2001), https://www.encyclopedia.com/humanities/encyclopedias-almanacs-transcripts-and-maps/contraband-colonial-spanish-america.

10. Arturo Morales Carrión, *Auge y Decadencia de la Trata Negrera en Puerto Rico, 1820–1860* (San Juan, PR: Centro de Estudios Avanzados de Puerto

Rico y del Caribe/Instituto de Cultura Puertorriqueña, 1978), 217. I added the italics for emphasis.

11. Joseph C. Dorsey, *Slave Traffic in the Age of Abolition: Puerto Rico, West Africa, and the Non-Hispanic Caribbean, 1815-1859* (Gainesville: University Press of Florida, 2003), 23.

12. Eric Williams, *From Columbus to Castro: The History of the Caribbean, 1492-1969* (New York; Evanston, IL; San Francisco; and London: Harper & Row Publishers, 1970), 56.

13. J. H. Elliot, *Empires of the Atlantic World: Britain and Spain in the Americas, 1492-1830* (New Haven, CT: Yale University Press, 2006), 98.

14. Cavalry incursions into the villages of Amerindian communities led by Spanish conquistadors.

15. Miguel Rodríguez, "Entradas y Cabalgadas: 1511-1513; La Segunda o 'Postrera' Guerra contra los Indios Taínos de Boriquén," *Boletín del Museo del Hombre Dominicano* 35, no. 42 (2008): 147-56; Karen F. Anderson-Córdova, *Surviving Spanish Conquest: Indian Fight, Flight, and Cultural Transformation in Hispaniola and Puerto Rico* (Tuscaloosa: University of Alabama Press, 2017), 47-48.

16. Juana Gil-Bermejo García, *Panorama Histórico de la Agricultura en Puerto Rico* (Seville, Spain: Escuela de Estudios Hispano-Americanos, 1970), 99-102; 141-49; Elsa Gelpí Baíz, *Siglo en Blanco: Estudio de la Economía Azucarera en Puerto Rico, Siglo XVI (1540-1612)* (San Juan, PR: Editorial de la Universidad de Puerto Rico 2000), 84-93; Francisco Moscoso, *Agricultura y Sociedad en Puerto Rico, Siglos 16 al 18: un Acercamiento desde la Historia,* San Juan, PR: Instituto de Cultura Puertorriqueña, 2001), 64-75.

17. Frank Moya Pons, *Otras Miradas a la Historia Dominicana* (Santo Domingo, Dominican Republic: Librería La Trinitaria, 2017), 80-81; Gelpí Baíz, *Siglo en Blanco*, 97-98; Alfredo Castillero Calvo, "El Comercio Regional del Caribe: el Complejo Portuario Cartagena-Portobelo, Siglos XVI-XIX," in *Primer Congreso Internacional de Historia Económica y Social de la Cuenca del Caribe, 1763-1898,* ed. Ricardo S. Alegría (San Juan, PR: Centro de Estudios Avanzados de Puerto Rico y el Caribe, 1992), 293-311.

18. Gelpí Baíz, 54-60.

19. David M. Stark, *Slave Families and the Hato Economy in Puerto Rico* (Gainesville: University Press of Florida, 2015), 75, 50, 134.

20. Enriqueta Vila Vilar, *Historia de Puerto Rico, 1600-1650* (Seville, Spain: Escuela de Estudios Hispano-Americanos, 1974), 40-42.

21. Elliot, *Empires of the Atlantic World*, 317.

22. Elliot, 100.

23. Luis M. Díaz Soler, *Historia de la Esclavitud Negra en Puerto Rico*, 3rd ed. (San Juan, PR: Editorial de la Universidad de Puerto Rico, 2000), 67; David Wheat, *Atlantic Africa and the Spanish Caribbean, 1570-1640* (Chapel Hill: University of North Carolina Press, 2016), 123.

24. Gelpí Baíz, 232-34.

25. Jennifer Wolff, "*Emaranhado*: Puerto Rico y el Comercio Trasatlántico de Esclavos, 1580-1630," in *Sometidos a la Esclavitud: Los Africanos y sus Descendientes en el Caribe Hispano*, ed. Consuelo Naranjo Orovio (Santa Marta, Colombia: Editorial Unimagdalena, 2021), 125.

26. Wolff, "*Emaranhado*," 117-59.

27. Ignacio Chuecas Saldías, "El Caribe Portugués: Sobre Políticas Imperiales, Redes Planetarias y la Presencia de Portugueses en el Caribe durante el Gobierno de Felipe III (1598-1621)," *Iberoamérica Social: Revista-red de Estudios Sociales* 2 (2018): 27-45.

28. José A. Piqueras, *La Esclavitud en las Españas: Un Lazo Transatlántico* (Madrid, Spain: Los Libros de la Catarata, 2017), 56.

29. Díaz Soler, *Historia*, 62-63.

30. Gregory E. O'Malley, *Final Passages: The Intercolonial Slave Trade of British America, 1619-1807* (Chapel Hill: University of North Carolina Press, 2014), 87.

31. Díaz Soler, 78.

32. Francisco Moscoso, *El Hato: Latifundio Ganadero y Mercantilismo en Puerto Rico, Siglos 16 al 18* (Río Piedras. PR: Publicaciones Gaviota, 2020), 59-62.

33. David M. Stark, "A New Look at the African Slave Trade in Puerto Rico through the Use of Parish Registers: 1660-1815," *Slavery & Abolition* 30, no. 4 (2009): 496.

34. Díaz Soler, 50.

35. Victoria Gardner Sorsby, "The British Trade with Spanish America under the Asiento (1713-1740)" (PhD diss., University of London, 1975), 209.

36. Díaz Soler, 46.

37. Vila Vilar, *Historia*, 46.

38. Fernando Picó, *Historia General de Puerto Rico*, 1st ed. (Río Piedras, PR: Ediciones Huracán, 1986), 95.

39. Celestino Andrés Aráuz, "La Acción Ilegal de los Holandeses en el Caribe y su Impacto en las Antillas y Puerto Rico durante la Primera Mitad del Siglo XVIII," *Revista/Review Interamericana* 14, no. 1-4 (1984): 77-78.

40. Jalil Sued Badillo and Ángel López Cantos, *Puerto Rico Negro* (Río Piedras, PR: Editorial Cultural, 1986), 36-42.

41. Díaz Soler, 68-69.

42. Jorge L. Chinea, "A Quest for Freedom: The Immigration of Maritime Maroons into Puerto Rico, 1656-1800," *Journal of Caribbean History* 31, no. 1-2 (1997): 51-87.

43. Wheat, *Atlantic Africa*, 110.

44. O'Malley, *Final Passages*, 248-49.

45. Héctor Feliciano Ramos, "El Comercio de Contrabando en la Costa Sur de Puerto Rico, 1750-1778," *Revista/Review Interamericana* 14, no. 1-4 (1984): 80-99.

46. Fray Iñigo Abbad [y Lasierra], *Diario del Viaje a la América* (Caracas, Venezuela: Banco Nacional de Ahorro y Préstamo, 1974). Citation is from the section on Aguadilla, unpaginated. Additional details regarding this smuggling pipeline that extended from Puerto Rico to Santo Domingo and beyond, see Juan A. Giusti, "Sugar and Livestock: Contraband Networks in Hispaniola and the Continental Caribbean in the Eighteenth Century," *Revista Brasileira do Caribe* 15, no. 29 (2014): 13–41.

47. Ángel López Cantos, "Contrabando, Corso y Situado en el Siglo XVIII: Una Economía Subterránea," *Anales* 1–2 (1985): 31–61.

48. Luis González Vales, *Gabriel Gutiérrez de Riva, 'El Terrible': Albores del Siglo XVIII Puertorriqueño y otros Ensayos* (San Juan. PR: Centro de Estudios Avanzados de Puerto Rico y el Caribe/Recinto Metropolitano de la Universidad Interamericana de Puerto Rico, 1990), 112.

49. Ángel López Cantos, *Miguel Enríquez: Corsario Boricua del Siglo XVIII* (San Juan, PR: Ediciones Puerto, 1994), 183.

50. López Cantos, *Miguel Enríquez*, esp. chapters 2–5.

51. Allan J. Kuethe and Kenneth J. Andrien, *The Spanish Atlantic World in the Eighteenth Century: War and the Bourbon Reforms, 1713–1796* (New York: Cambridge University Press, 2014), 68–73; citation from p. 68.

52. "Memoria de D. Alejandro O'Reylly sobre la Isla de Puerto Rico" [1765], in Aida R. Caro Costas, *Antología de Lecturas de Historia de Puerto Rico (Siglos XV–XVIII)*, 2nd. ed. (San Juan, PR, 1980), 453–84; Fray Íñigo Abbad y Lasierra, *Historia Geográfica, Civil y Natural de la Isla de San Juan Bautista de Puerto Rico*, Anotada por José Julián Acosta y Calvo: Estudio introductorio por Gervasio L. García (Madrid, Spain: Ediciones Doce Calles/San Juan, PR: Historiador Oficial de Puerto Rico, 2002); see also, Fray Antonio Filangieri's 1791 report to the Spanish Crown: Archivo General de Indias, Santo Domingo (hereafter cited as "AGI-SD"), leg. 2370, Fray Antonio Filangieri to conde de Linai, June 24, 1791.

53. AGI-SD, leg. 2282, Gobernador Muesas to Madrid, November 28, 1769.

54. Altagracia Ortiz, *Eighteenth-Century Reforms in the Caribbean: Miguel de Muesas, Governor of Puerto Rico, 1769–76* (Rutherford, NJ: Farleigh Dickinson University Press, 1983), 151.

55. Díaz Soler, 183–84.

56. Birgit Sonesson, *Puerto Rico's Commerce, 1765–1865: From Regional to Worldwide Market Relations* (Los Angeles: UCLA Latin American Center Publications, 2002), 31–32.

57. Kuethe and Andrien, *The Spanish Atlantic*, 336–40; Elliot, 408.

58. Abbad y Lasierra, *Historia Geográfica*, 397.

59. John Fisher, "Imperial 'Free Trade' and the Hispanic Economy, 1778–1796," *Journal of Latin American Studies* 13, no. 1 (1981): 21–45 and by same

author, "Relaciones Comerciales entre España y la Cuenca del Caribe en la Época del 'Comercio Libre,' 1778-1820," in *Primer Congreso*, 220-24.

60. Kuethe and Andrien, 305.

61. Elliot, 408.

62. Christopher Schmidt-Nowara, *Empire and Antislavery: Spain, Cuba, and Puerto Rico, 1833-1874* (Pittsburgh, PA: University of Pittsburgh Press, 1999), 8.

63. Scarano, *Sugar and Slavery*, 103-4.

64. Francisco A. Scarano "Congregate and Control: The Peasantry and Labor Coercion in Puerto Rico before the Age of Sugar, 1750-1820," *New West Indian Guide* 63, no. 1-2 (1989): 23-24; Fernando Picó, *Libertad y Servidumbre en el Puerto Rico del Siglo XIX*, 2nd ed. (Río Piedras, PR: Ediciones Huracán, 1982).

65. "Informe de D. Pedro Irizarri, alcalde ordinario de San Juan, sobre las instrucciones que debían darse a don Ramón Power, diputado por Puerto Rico ante las cortes españolas para promover el adelanto económico de la isla: Año 1809," in *Crónicas de Puerto Rico: Desde la Conquista hasta Nuestros Días (1493-1955)*, ed. Eugenio Fernández Méndez (San Juan, PR: Editorial de la Universidad de Puerto Rico, 1973), 345-72.

66. Dorsey, *Slave Traffic*, 26.

67. Morales Carrión, *Auge y Decadencia*, 32-33.

68. Dorsey, esp. chapters 1-4, passim

69. Dorsey, chapter 4.

70. Julia Moreno García, "La Cuestión de la Trata en el Trienio Liberal (1820-1823)," *Cuadernos de Historia Contemporánea*, número extraordinario (2003): 162. The principal forces that favored or opposed slavery and abolitionism in the metropolis and its colonies are discussed in Josep M. Fradera and Christopher Schmidt-Nowara, *Slavery and Antislavery in Spain's Atlantic Empire* (New York: Berghahn Books, 2013).

71. Morales Carrión, 33-44.

72. Fernando Picó, *Ponce y los Rostros Rayados: Sociedad y Esclavitud, 1800-1830* (San Juan, PR: Ediciones Huracán, 2012), 162-63.

73. Dorsey, 49-50.

74. Jorge L. Chinea, "Confronting the Crisis of the Puerto Rican Plantation System: Bureaucratic Proposals for Agricultural Modernisation, Diversification, and Free Labour, 1846-1852," *Journal of Latin American Studies* 42, no. 1 (2010): 151.

75. Coggeshall, *Thirty-Six Voyages to various parts of the World Made between the Years 1799 and 1841* (New York: G. P. Putnam, 1858), 507-8.

76. Coggeshall, *Thirty-Six Voyages*, 512.

77. Frank Otto Gatell, "Puerto Rico in the 1830's: The Journal of Edward Bliss Emerson," *The Americas* 16, no. 1 (July 1959): 63-75. Edward was one of the younger brothers of the U.S. lecturer, poet, and essayist Ralph Waldo Emerson.

78. Chinea, "Confronting the Crisis": 142-44.

79. Coggeshall, 528.

80. Southern to Viscount Palmerston, Madrid, July 13, 1839, Great Britain, Foreign Office, *British and Foreign State Papers, 1839–1840*, Vol. XXVIII (London: Harrison and Sons, 1857), 20.

81. Sonesson, *Puerto Rico's Commerce*, 53.

82. Bartlett to the Right Hon. Viscount Palmerston, Santa Cruz [de Tenerife], May 10, 1840, in Great Britain, Foreign Office. Class A. *Correspondence with the British Commissioners at Sierra Leone, the Havana, Rio de Janeiro, and Surinam relating to the Slave Trade* [hereafter cited as "*Correspondence*"] (London: House of Parliament, 1841), 29–30.

83. J. Kennedy and Campbell J. Dalrymple to the Right Hon. Viscount Palmerston, Havana, July 18, 1840, in *Correspondence*, 278–79.

84. AGI-SD, leg. 2337, Capitanía General de la Isla de Puerto Rico a Antonio de Benavides, Secretario de Estado y del Despacho de la Gobernación del Reino, July 14, 1847.

85. Jorge L. Chinea, *Raza y Trabajo en el Caribe Hispánico: Los Inmigrantes de las Indias Occidentales en Puerto Rico durante el Ciclo Agro-Exportador, 1800–1850* (Seville, Spain: Escuela de Estudios Hispano-Americanos/Wayne State University/Oficina del Historiador Oficial de Puerto Rico/Asociación Cultural la Otra Andalucía, 2014), 159.

86. Kenneth Scott, ed., "Charles Walker's Letters from Puerto Rico, 1835–1837," *Caribbean Studies* 5, no. 1 (1965): 50.

87. AHN-Ultramar, leg. 1071, exp. 4: various communications between Intendente Del Valle, the Ministerio de Hacienda and Ministerio de Marina, de Comercio y Gobernación de Ultramar, and the Junta Consultiva de Ultramar, June 10, 1841–May 12, 1843.

88. Asunción del Pilar Pérez Marrero cites their respective works in her essay, "Aproximación al Estudio de la Esclavitud del Negro en las Antillas Españolas a través de la Prensa Tinerfeña en la Segunda Mitad del Siglo XIX," *Tibeto: Anuario del Archivo Histórico Insular de Fuerteventura* 5, no. 2 (1992): 224.

89. Michael Zeuske, "The Names of Slavery and Beyond: The Atlantic, the Americas and Cuba," in *The End of Slavery in Africa and the Americas: A Comparative Approach*, ed. Ulrike Schmieder, Katja Füllberg-Stolberg and Michael Zeuske (Berlin, Germany: Lit Verlag, 2011), 62–66.

90. Zeuske, "The Names of Slavery," 62–63.

91. Zeuske, 62–66.

92. Ramón Joaquín Domínguez, *Diccionario Nacional ó Gran Diccionario Clásico de la Lengua Española*, vol. 1, 3rd ed.(Madrid, Spain: Establecimiento Tipográfico de Mellado, 1848), 248.

93. Dorsey, 172–79.

94. Morales Carrión, 221; Luis R. Burset Flores, "El Contrabando de Esclavos frente a la Prohibición de la Trata: Los Africanos Emancipados del Barco Negrero *Majesty* en 1859," in *La Aportación de las Naciones Africanas a la Familia Puer-*

torriqueña, vol. III, Colección de Genealogía e Historia, ed. Elsa Gelpí Baíz (San Juan, PR: Sociedad Puertorriqueña de Genealogía, 2012), 88.

95. Morales Carrión, 220.

96. José Luciano Franco, "Contrabando y Trata Negrera en el Caribe," *Economía y Desarrollo* 25 (1974): 140.

97. Craig B. Hollander, "Underground on the High Seas: Commerce, Character, and Complicity in the Illegal Slave Trade," in *Capitalism by Gaslight: Illuminating the Economy of Nineteenth-Century America*, ed. Brian P. Luskey and Wendy A. Woloson (Philadelphia: University of Pennsylvania Press, 2015), 128.

98. Luciano Franco, "Contrabando": 144–153. The sociologist and historian William E. B. Du Bois made a similar claim in his 1896 study of the slave trade, as cited in Leonardo Marques, "The Contraband Slave Trade to Brazil and the Dynamics of U.S. Participation, 1831–1856," *Journal of Latin American Studies* 47, no. 4 (2015): 659–60.

99. Manuel Moreno Fraginals, *El Ingenio: Complejo Económico Social Cubano del Azúcar*, vol. I (Havana, Cuba: Editorial de Ciencias Sociales, 1978), 279–80.

100. John Harris, *The Last Slave Ships: New York and the End of the Middle Passage* (New Haven, CT, and London: Yale University Press, 2020), 3.

101. Arturo Arnalte, *Los Últimos Esclavos de Cuba: Los Niños Cautivos de la Goleta Batans* (Madrid, Spain: Alianza Editorial, 2001), 132.

102. Leonardo Marques, "Slave Trading in a New World: The Strategies of North American Slave Traders in the Age of Abolition," *Journal of the Early Republic* 32, no. 2 (2012): 257.

103. See Leonardo Marques, *The United States and the Transatlantic Slave Trade to the Americas, 1776–1867* (New Haven, CT, and London: Yale University Press, 2016), especially chapter 2.

104. Dale T. Graden, *Disease, Resistance, and Lies: The Demise of the Transatlantic Slave Trade to Brazil and Cuba* (Baton Rouge: Louisiana State University Press, 2014), 18.

105. Marques, *The United States*, 104.

106. Graden, *Disease*, 19–25.

107. Marques, *The United States*, 104–5.

108. Morales Carrión, 220.

109. Arthur F. Corwin, *Spain and the Abolition of Slavery in Cuba, 1817–1886* (Austin and London: University of Texas Press, 1967), 85–86.

110. María de los Ángeles Meriño Fuentes and Aismara Perera Díaz, *Contrabando de Bozales en Cuba: Perseguir el Tráfico y Mantener la Esclavitud: 1845–1866* (San José de las Lajas, Mayabeque, Cuba: Ediciones Montecallado, 2015), 92–93.

111. Pacotille is a French-derived term used to designate merchandise of little or no value that European traders exchanged for enslaved captives on the African coast.

112. Morales Carrión, 219.

113. Luis de la Rosa, "Los Negros del Brick-Barca Magesty: Prohibición del Tráfico de Esclavos," *Revista del Centro de Estudios Avanzados de Puerto Rico y el Caribe* 3 (1986): 48–52.

114. De la Rosa, "Los Negros," 48–52.

115. Burset Flores, "El Contrabando," 93.

116. The *Ordenanza General* went into effect on February 28, 1859, following its publication in the *Gaceta de Puerto Rico*. See the entire text in *Boletín Histórico de Puerto Rico* 9 (1922): 363–70.

117. The government reserved the right to lengthen the term of service or apprenticeship of bozales until they reached the age of twenty-five (Article 7:1). Consult the "Reglamento Provisional de 12 de Febrero de 1859, sobre Depósito y Entrega de Negros Emancipados," *Autos Acordados de la Real Audiencia de la Isla de Puerto-Rico y Reales Cédulas, Órdenes, Reglamentos, Decretos y Circulares desde el Año de 1858 hasta 1862 Inclusive*. San Juan, PR: J. González, Imprenta de la Real Audiencia, 1863), 47.

118. De la Rosa, 51.

119. Morales Carrión, 220.

120. Teresita Martínez Vergne, "The Allocation of Liberated African Labour through the Casa de Beneficencia: San Juan, Puerto Rico, 1859–1864," *Slavery and Abolition* 12, no. 3 (1991): 200–16.

121. Except for Rosa Mandriz, who received two emancipados, most trustees listed on the documentation consulted had male names.

122. "Reglamento Provisional de 12 de Febrero," Article 7:6 (pg. 47).

123. Burset Flores, 91.

124. "Reglamento Provisional de 12 de Febrero," Article 7:9 (pg. 47).

125. "Reglamento Provisional de 12 de Febrero," Article 7:7–8 (pg. 47) and Article 15 (pg. 49).

126. For the casualty figures see Ángel de Barrios Román, *Antropología Socioeconómica en el Caribe: Puerto Rico-Mayagüez 1840-75* (Santo Domingo, Dominican Republic: Editora Cultural Dominicana, 1974), 288–91; see also Ricardo R. Camuñas Madera, "Desarrollo Económico, Cambio Ambiental y Cólera Morbo en el Puerto Rico del Siglo XIX," *Revista Universidad de América* 6, no. 2 (1994): 49–53; and Ramonita Vega Lugo, "Epidemia y Sociedad. Efectos del Cólera Morbo en Puerto Rico y en Costa Rica a Mediados del Siglo XIX," *Diálogos: Revista electrónica de Historia*. 9º Congreso Centroamericano de Historia, Universidad de Costa Rica, 2008, 219–42.

127. De la Rosa, 50.

128. Gloria Tapia Ríos, *La Central Lafayette: Riqueza, Desarrollo y Política en el Sureste de Puerto Rico* (San Juan, PR: Ediciones Magna Cultura/Oficina del Historiador Oficial de Puerto Rico, 2014), 132–34.

129. Burset Flores, 91.

130. De la Rosa, 52.

131. See David R. Murray, *Odious Commerce: Britain, Spain and the Abolition of the Cuban Slave Trade* (Cambridge, UK: Cambridge University Press, 2002), 295.

132. De la Rosa, 53–54.

133. Dorsey, 180.

134. Martínez Vergne, "The Allocation," 206–7.

135. In 1849 the colonial administration required all able-bodied day laborers to carry a *libreta*, or passbook, to record their working hours. Those lacking evidence of regular employment could face vagrancy charges. See Fernando Picó, *Libertad y Servidumbre en el Puerto Rico del Siglo XIX*, 2nd ed. (Río Piedras, PR: Ediciones Huracán, 1982).

136. Chinea, *Raza y Trabajo*, 42; 173–87.

137. "Reglamento Provisional para el Régimen de los Negros Africanos Emancipados que existe[n] hoy en la Isla, Procedentes de la 'Barca Magesty' Apresada en Humacao en el Año 1859," October 21, 1864, in Joaquín Rodríguez San Pedro, *Legislación Ultramarina Concordada y Anotada*, vol. 10 (Madrid, Spain: Imprenta de Manuel Minuesa, 1868).

138. Díaz Soler, 239.

139. "Reglamento Provisional para el Régimen."

140. De la Rosa, 51–52.

141. De la Rosa, 53.

142. De la Rosa, 53.

143. Martínez Vergne, 202–5; citation belongs to p. 205.

144. Félix V. Matos Rodríguez, *Women and Urban Change in San Juan, Puerto Rico, 1820–1868* (Gainesville: University Press of Florida, 1999), 4.

145. For examples of emancipado acts of defiance see: De la Rosa, 53–54; Martínez Vergne, 207; and Miguel Correa, *Presencia Africana en Humacao: 1859* (Humacao, PR, 2011), 34.

146. Elena A. Schneider, "Routes into Eighteenth-Century Cuban Slavery: African Diaspora and Geopolitics," in *From the Galleons to the Highlands*, 249–51.

147. I borrowed the phrase "odious commerce" from the title of David R. Murray's book, *Odious Commerce*.

148. Lidio Cruz Monclova, *Historia de Puerto Rico (Siglo XIX)*, vol. I, 5th ed. (Río Piedras, PR: Editorial Universitaria, 1965), 471.

Bibliography

Archival/Digital Collections

Archivo Histórico Nacional [Madrid, Spain], Ultramar, *legajo* 1071.

Archivo General de Indias [Seville, Spain], Santo Domingo, *legajos* 2282, 2337, and 2370.

The Transatlantic Slave Trade Database (https://www.slavevoyages.org/).

Secondary Sources

Abbad [y Lasierra], Fray Iñigo. *Diario del Viaje a la América*. Caracas, Venezuela: Banco Nacional de Ahorro y Préstamo, 1974.

———. *Historia Geográfica, Civil y Natural de la Isla de San Juan Bautista de Puerto Rico*. Annotated by José Julián Acosta y Calvo. Introduction by Gervasio L. García. Madrid, Spain: Ediciones Doce Calles/San Juan: Historiador Oficial de Puerto Rico, 2002.

Anderson-Córdova, Karen F. *Surviving Spanish Conquest: Indian Fight, Flight, and Cultural Transformation in Hispaniola and Puerto Rico*. Tuscaloosa: University of Alabama Press, 2017.

Aráuz, Celestino Andrés. "La Acción Ilegal de los Holandeses en el Caribe y su Impacto en las Antillas y Puerto Rico durante la Primera Mitad del Siglo XVIII." *Revista/Review Interamericana* 14, no. 1–4 (1984): 67–79.

Arnalte, Arturo. *Los Últimos Esclavos de Cuba: Los Niños Cautivos de la Goleta Batans*. Madrid, Spain: Alianza Editorial, 2001.

Bethell, Leslie. "The Mixed Commissions for the Suppression of the Transatlantic Slave Trade in the Nineteenth Century." *Journal of African History* 7, no. 1 (1966): 79–83.

Burset Flores, Luis R. "El Contrabando de Esclavos frente a la Prohibición de la Trata: Los Africanos Emancipados del Barco Negrero Majesty en 1859." In *La Aportación de las Naciones Africanas a la Familia Puertorriqueña*, vol. III, Colección de Genealogía e Historia, edited by Elsa Gelpí Baíz, 81–104. San Juan, PR: Sociedad Puertorriqueña de Genealogía, 2012.

Camuñas Madera, Ricardo R. "Desarrollo Económico, Cambio Ambiental y Cólera Morbo en el Puerto Rico del Siglo XIX." *Revista Universidad de América* 6, no. 2 (1994): 49–53.

Castillero Calvo, Alfredo. "El Comercio Regional del Caribe: el Complejo Portuario Cartagena-Portobelo, siglos XVI–XIX." In *Primer Congreso Internacional de Historia Económica y Social de la Cuenca del Caribe, 1763–1898*, edited by Ricardo S. Alegría, 293–373. San Juan, PR: Centro de Estudios Avanzados de Puerto Rico y el Caribe, 1992.

Chinea, Jorge L. "A Quest for Freedom: The Immigration of Maritime Maroons into Puerto Rico, 1656–1800," *Journal of Caribbean History* 31, no. 1–2 (1997): 51–87.

———. "Confronting the Crisis of the Puerto Rican Plantation System: Bureaucratic Proposals for Agricultural Modernisation, Diversification, and Free Labour, 1846–1852." *Journal of Latin American Studies* 42, no. 1 (2010): 121–54.

———. *Raza y Trabajo en el Caribe Hispánico: Los Inmigrantes de las Indias Occidentales en Puerto Rico durante el Ciclo Agro-Exportador, 1800–1850*. Seville, Spain: Escuela de Estudios Hispano-Americanos/Wayne State University/Oficina del Historiador Oficial de Puerto Rico/Asociación Cultural la Otra Andalucía, 2014.

———. "Slavery and Child Trafficking in Puerto Rico at the Closing of the African Slave Trade: The Young Captives of the Slaver *Majesty*, 1859–1865." *Revista Brasileira do Caribe* 17, no. 32 (2016): 59–98.

Chuecas Saldías, Ignacio. "El Caribe Portugués: Sobre Políticas Imperiales, Redes Planetarias y la Presencia de Portugueses en el Caribe durante el Gobierno de Felipe III (1598–1621)." *Iberoamérica Social: Revista-red de Estudios Sociales* 2 (2018): 27–45.

Coggeshall, George. *Thirty-Six Voyages to Various Parts of the World Made between the Years 1799 and 1841*. New York: G. P. Putnam, 1858.

Correa, Miguel. *Presencia Africana en Humacao: 1859*. Humacao, PR, 2011.

Corwin, Arthur F. *Spain and the Abolition of Slavery in Cuba, 1817–1886*. Austin and London: University of Texas Press, 1967.

Cruz Monclova, Lidio. *Historia de Puerto Rico (siglo XIX)*, vol. I, 5th ed. Río Piedras, PR: Editorial Universitaria, 1965.

De Barrios Román, Ángel. *Antropología Socioeconómica en el Caribe: Puerto Rico-Mayagüez, 1840–75*. Santo Domingo, Dominican Republic: Editora Cultural Dominicana, 1974.

De la Rosa, Luis. "Los Negros del Brick-Barca Magesty: Prohibición del Tráfico de Esclavos," *Revista del Centro de Estudios Avanzados de Puerto Rico y el Caribe* 3 (1986): 45–57.

Díaz Soler, Luis M. *Historia de la esclavitud Negra en Puerto Rico*, 3rd ed. San Juan, PR: Editorial de la Universidad de Puerto Rico, 2000.

Domínguez, Ramón J. *Diccionario Nacional ó Gran Diccionario Clásico de la Lengua Española*, 3rd ed., vol. I. Madrid, Spain: Establecimiento Tipográfico de Mellado, 1848.

Dorsey, Joseph C. *Slave Traffic in the Age of Abolition: Puerto Rico, West Africa, and the Non-Hispanic Caribbean, 1815–1859*. Gainesville: University Press of Florida, 2003.

Elliot, J. H. *Empires of the Atlantic World: Britain and Spain in the Americas, 1492–1830*. New Haven, CT: Yale University Press, 2006.

Eltis, David, and Jorge Felipe-Gonzalez. "The Rise and Fall of the Cuban Slave Market: New Data, New Paradigms." In *From the Galleons to the Highlands: Slave Trade Routes in the Spanish Americas*, edited by Alex Borucki, David Eltis, and David Wheat, 201–22. Albuquerque: University of New Mexico Press, 2020.

Feliciano Ramos, Héctor. "El Comercio de Contrabando en la Costa Sur de Puerto Rico, 1750–1778," *Revista/Review Interamericana* 14, no. 1–4 (1984): 80–99.

Fisher, John. "Imperial 'Free Trade' and the Hispanic Economy, 1778–1796," *Journal of Latin American Studies* 13, no. 1 (1981): 21–56.

———. "Relaciones Comerciales entre España y la Cuenca del Caribe en la Época del 'Comercio Libre,' 1778–1820." In *Primer Congreso Internacional de Historia Económica y Social de la Cuenca del Caribe, 1763–1898*, edited by Ricardo S. Alegría, 209–58. San Juan, PR: Centro de Estudios Avanzados de Puerto Rico y el Caribe, 1992.

Fradera, Josep M., and Christopher Schmidt-Nowara, ed. *Slavery and Antislavery in Spain's Atlantic Empire*. New York: Berghahn Books, 2013.

Franco, José Luciano. "Contrabando y Trata Negrera en el Caribe," *Economía y Desarrollo* 25 (1974): 139–53.

Gardner Sorsby, Victoria. "The British Trade with Spanish America under the Asiento (1713–1740)." PhD diss., University of London, 1975.

Gelpí Baíz, Elsa. *Siglo en Blanco: Estudio de la Economía Azucarera en Puerto Rico, Siglo XVI (1540–1612)*. San Juan, PR: Editorial de la Universidad de Puerto Rico, 2000.

Gil-Bermejo García, Juana. *Panorama Histórico de la Agricultura en Puerto Rico*. Seville, Spain: Escuela de Estudios Hispano-Americanos, 1970.

Giusti, Juan A. "Sugar and Livestock: Contraband Networks in Hispaniola and the Continental Caribbean in the Eighteenth Century." *Revista Brasileira do Caribe* 15, no. 29 (2014): 13–41.

González Vales, Luis. *Gabriel Gutiérrez de Riva, 'El Terrible': Albores del Siglo XVIII Puertorriqueño y otros Ensayos*. San Juan, PR: Centro de Estudios Avanzados de Puerto Rico y el Caribe/Recinto Metropolitano de la Universidad Interamericana de Puerto Rico, 1990.

Graden, Dale T. *Disease, Resistance, and Lies: The Demise of the Transatlantic Slave Trade to Brazil and Cuba*. Baton Rouge: Louisiana State University Press, 2014.

Grahn, Lance R. "Contraband (Spanish America)," *Encyclopedia of Latin American History and Culture. Encyclopedia.com* (August 16, 2021). https://www.encyclopedia.com/humanities/encyclopedias-almanacs-transcripts-and-maps/contraband-colonial-spanish-america.

Great Britain, Foreign Office. *British and Foreign State Papers, 1839–1840*, vol. XXVIII. London: Harrison and Sons, 1857.

Great Britain, Foreign Office. Class A. *Correspondence with the British Commissioners at Sierra Leone, the Havana, Rio de Janeiro, and Surinam relating to the Slave Trade*. London: House of Parliament, 1841.

Harris, John. *The Last Slave Ships: New York and the End of the Middle Passage*. New Haven. CT, and London: Yale University Press, 2020.

Hollander, Craig B. "Underground on the High Seas: Commerce, Character, and Complicity in the Illegal Slave Trade." In *Capitalism by Gaslight: Illuminating the Economy of Nineteenth-Century America*, edited by Brian P. Luskey and Wendy A. Woloson, 127–49. Philadelphia: University of Pennsylvania Press, 2015.

"Informe de D. Pedro Irizarri, alcalde ordinario de San Juan, sobre las instrucciones que debían darse a don Ramón Power, diputado por Puerto Rico ante las cortes españolas para promover el adelanto económico de la isla:

Año 1809." In *Crónicas de Puerto Rico: Desde la Conquista hasta Nuestros Días (1493-1955)*, edited by Eugenio Fernández Méndez, 345-72. San Juan, PR: Editorial de la Universidad de Puerto Rico, 1973.

Karras, Alan L. *Smuggling: Contraband and Corruption in World History*. Lanham, MD: Rowman & Littlefield, 2010.

Kuethe, Allan J., and Kenneth J. Andrien. *The Spanish Atlantic World in the Eighteenth Century: War and the Bourbon Reforms, 1713-1796*. New York: Cambridge University Press, 2014.

López Cantos, Ángel. "Contrabando, Corso y Situado en el Siglo XVIII: Una Economía Subterránea." *Anales* 1-2 (1985): 31-61.

———. *Miguel Enríquez: Corsario Boricua del Siglo XVIII*. San Juan, PR: Ediciones Puerto, 1994.

Marques, Leonardo. "Slave Trading in a New World: The Strategies of North American Slave Traders in the Age of Abolition." *Journal of the Early Republic* 32, no. 2 (2012): 233-60.

———. "The Contraband Slave Trade to Brazil and the Dynamics of US Participation, 1831-1856." *Journal of Latin American Studies* 47, no. 4 (2015): 659-84.

———. *The United States and the Transatlantic Slave Trade to the Americas, 1776-1867*. New Haven, CT, and London: Yale University Press, 2016.

Martínez Vergne, Teresita. "The Allocation of Liberated African Labour through the Casa de Beneficencia: San Juan, Puerto Rico, 1859-1864," *Slavery and Abolition* 12, no. 3 (1991): 200-16.

Matos Rodríguez, Félix V. *Women and Urban Change in San Juan, Puerto Rico, 1820-1868*. Gainesville: University Press of Florida, 1999.

"Memoria de D. Alejandro O'Reylly sobre la Isla de Puerto Rico." 1765. In *Antología de Lecturas de Historia de Puerto Rico (Siglos XV-XVIII)*, 2nd. ed., edited by Aida R. Caro Costas, 453-84. San Juan, PR: n.p., 1980.

Meriño Fuentes, María de los Ángeles, and Aismara Perera Díaz. *Contrabando de Bozales en Cuba: Perseguir el Tráfico y Mantener la Esclavitud: 1845-1866*. San José de las Lajas, Mayabeque, Cuba: Ediciones Montecallado, 2015.

Morales Carrión, Arturo. *Auge y Decadencia de la Trata Negrera en Puerto Rico (1820-1860)*. San Juan, PR: Centro de Estudios Avanzados de Puerto Rico y del Caribe/Instituto de Cultura Puertorriqueña, 1978.

Moreno Fraginals, Manuel. *El Ingenio: Complejo Económico Social Cubano del Azúcar*. 3 vols. Havana, Cuba: Editorial de Ciencias Sociales, 1978.

Moreno García, Julia. "La Cuestión de la Trata en el Trienio Liberal (1820-1823)." *Cuadernos de Historia Contemporánea*, número extraordinario (2003): 157-67.

Moscoso, Francisco. *Agricultura y Sociedad en Puerto Rico, Siglos 16 al 18: Un Acercamiento desde la Historia*. San Juan, PR: Instituto de Cultura Puertorriqueña, 2001.

———. *El Hato: Latifundio Ganadero y Mercantilismo en Puerto Rico, Siglos 16 al 18*. Río Piedras, PR: Publicaciones Gaviota, 2020.

Moya Pons, Frank. *Otras Miradas a la Historia Dominicana*. Santo Domingo, Dominican Republic: Librería La Trinitaria, 2017.
Murray, David R. *Odious Commerce: Britain, Spain and the Abolition of the Cuban Slave Trade*. Cambridge, UK: Cambridge University Press, 2002.
O'Malley, Gregory E. *Final Passages: The Intercolonial Slave Trade of British America, 1619-1807*. Chapel Hill: University of North Carolina Press, 2014.
"Ordenanza General de Emancipados." *Boletín Histórico de Puerto Rico* 9 (1922): 363-70.
Ortiz, Altagracia. *Eighteenth-Century Reforms in the Caribbean: Miguel de Muesas, Governor of Puerto Rico, 1769-76*. Rutherford, NJ: Farleigh Dickinson University Press, 1983.
Otto Gatell, Frank (ed.). "Puerto Rico in the 1830's: The Journal of Edward Bliss Emerson," *The Americas* 16, no. 1 (1959): 63-75.
Pérez Marrero, Asunción del Pilar. "Aproximación al Estudio de la Esclavitud del Negro en las Antillas Españolas a través de la Prensa Tinerfeña en la Segunda Mitad del Siglo XIX." *Tibeto: Anuario del Archivo Histórico Insular de Fuerteventura* 5, no. 2 (1992): 219-76.
Picó, Fernando. *Libertad y Servidumbre en el Puerto Rico del Siglo XIX*. 2nd ed. Río Piedras, PR: Ediciones Huracán, 1982.
———. *Historia General de Puerto Rico*. 1st ed. Río Piedras, PR: Ediciones Huracán, 1986.
———. *Ponce y los Rostros Rayados: Sociedad y Esclavitud, 1800-1830*. San Juan, PR: Ediciones Huracán, 2012.
Piqueras, José A. *La Esclavitud en las Españas: Un Lazo Transatlántico*. Madrid, Spain: Los Libros de la Catarata, 2017.
"Reglamento Provisional de 12 de febrero de 1859, sobre Depósito y Entrega de Negros Emancipados." In *Autos Acordados de la Real Audiencia de la Isla de Puerto-Rico y Reales Cédulas, Órdenes, Reglamentos, Decretos y Circulares desde el Año de 1858 hasta 1862 Inclusive*, 45-52. PR: J. González, Imprenta de la Real Audiencia, 1863.
"Reglamento Provisional para el Régimen de los Negros Africanos Emancipados que existe[n] hoy en la Isla, Procedentes de la 'Barca Magesty' Apresada en Humacao en el Año 1859" October 21, 1864. In *Legislación Ultramarina Concordada y Anotada*, compiled by Joaquín Rodríguez San Pedro, vol. 10. Madrid, Spain: Imprenta de Manuel Minuesa, 1868.
Rodríguez, Miguel. "Entradas y Cabalgadas: 1511-1513; La Segunda o 'Postrera' Guerra contra los Indios Taínos de Boriquén," *Boletín del Museo del Hombre Dominicano* 35, no. 42 (2008): 147-56.
Roldán de Montaud, Inés. "The Misfortune of Liberated Africans in Colonial Cuba, 1824-1876." In *Liberated Africans and the Abolition of the Slave Trade, 1807-1896*, edited by Richard Anderson and Henry B. Lovejoy, 153-73. Rochester, NY: University of Rochester Press, 2020.

Scarano, Francisco A. *Sugar and Slavery in Puerto Rico: The Plantation Economy of Ponce, 1800–1850*. Madison: University of Wisconsin Press, 1984.

———. "Congregate and Control: The Peasantry and Labor Coercion in Puerto Rico before the Age of Sugar, 1750–1820," *New West Indian Guide* 63, no. 1–2 (1989): 23–40.

Schmidt-Nowara, Christopher. *Empire and Antislavery: Spain, Cuba, and Puerto Rico, 1833–1874*. Pittsburgh, PA: University of Pittsburgh Press, 1999.

Schneider, Elena A. "Routes into Eighteenth-Century Cuban Slavery: African Diaspora and Geopolitics." In *From the Galleons to the Highlands: Slave Trade Routes in the Spanish Americas*, edited by Alex Borucki, David Eltis, and David Wheat, 249–74. Albuquerque: University of New Mexico Press, 2020.

Scott, Kenneth (ed.). "Charles Walker's Letters from Puerto Rico, 1835–1837," *Caribbean Studies* 5, no. 1 (1965): 37–50.

Sonesson, Birgit. *Puerto Rico's Commerce, 1765–1865: From Regional to Worldwide Market Relations*. Los Angeles, CA: UCLA Latin American Center Publications, 2002.

Stark, David M. Slave *Families and the Hato Economy in Puerto Rico*. Gainesville: University Press of Florida, 2014.

———. "A New Look at the African Slave Trade in Puerto Rico through the Use of Parish Registers: 1660–1815," *Slavery & Abolition* 30, no. 4 (2009): 491–20.

Sued Badillo, Jalil, and Ángel López Cantos. *Puerto Rico Negro*. Río Piedras, PR: Editorial Cultural, 1986.

Sundiata, Ibrahim K. "Puerto Rico and Africa: The Ambiguity of Diaspora," *21st Century Afro Review* 3, no. 1 (1997): 1–36.

Tapia Ríos, Gloria. *La Central Lafayette: Riqueza, Desarrollo y Política en el Sureste de Puerto Rico*. San Juan, PR: Ediciones Magna Cultura/Oficina del Historiador Oficial de Puerto Rico, 2014.

Vega Lugo, Ramonita. "Epidemia y Sociedad. Efectos del Cólera Morbo en Puerto Rico y en Costa Rica a Mediados del Siglo XIX." *Diálogos: Revista electrónica de Historia: 9º Congreso Centroamericano de Historia*, Universidad de Costa Rica 9 (2008): 219–42.

Vila Vilar, Enriqueta. *Historia de Puerto Rico, 1600–1650*. Seville, Spain: Escuela de Estudios Hispano-Americanos, 1974.

Wheat, David. *Atlantic Africa and the Spanish Caribbean, 1570–1640*. Chapel Hill: University of North Carolina Press, 2016.

Williams, Eric. *From Columbus to Castro: The History of the Caribbean, 1492–1969*. New York; Evanston, IL; San Francisco; and London: Harper & Row, 1970.

Wolff, Jennifer. "*Emaranhado*: Puerto Rico y el Comercio Trasatlántico de Esclavos, 1580–1630." In *Sometidos a la Esclavitud: Los Africanos y sus Descendientes en el Caribe Hispano*, edited by Consuelo Naranjo Orovio, 117–59. Santa Marta, Colombia: Editorial Unimagdalena, 2021.

Zeuske, Michael. "The Names of Slavery and Beyond: The Atlantic, the Americas and Cuba." In *The End of Slavery in Africa and the Americas: A Comparative Approach*, edited by Ulrike Schmieder, Katja Füllberg-Stolberg, and Michael Zeuske, 51–80. Berlin, Germany: Lit Verlag, 2011.

Contributors

Jorge L. Chinea was born in Puerto Rico and raised in Spanish Harlem, New York City. A Distinguished Service Professor of History at Wayne State University, he holds a PhD in history from the University of Minnesota. His research has been supported by fellowships and grants from the National Endowment for the Humanities, the Andrew W. Mellon Foundation, and the Society for Irish Latin American Studies. His first monograph, *Race and Labor in the Hispanic Caribbean: The West Indian Worker Experience in Puerto Rico, 1800–1850*, was published in 2005. An augmented and revised Spanish-language edition of it came out in 2014. Along with J. Raúl Navarro García, he recently coedited the book *Esclavos, Penados y Exiliados en Puerto Rico, Siglo XIX: Cambios y Continuidades en una Sociedad en Transformación*.

Lissette Acosta Corniel is an assistant professor in the Department of Ethnic and Race Studies at the Borough of Manhattan Community College, CUNY. She writes about gender, race, and slavery in colonial Hispaniola. Her articles have been published in *Estudios Sociales*, *Perspectivas Afro*, and *Women, Gender, and Families of Color*. She was the research associate for the database *First Blacks in the Americas* (www.firstblacks.org).

Jacqueline Jiménez Polanco is an associate professor in the Social Science Department at Bronx Community College. The author holds a PhD in political science and sociology, as well as a JD. She has published extensively on her areas of expertise, which include gender studies, politics, political parties and elections, corruption, immigration, and LGBTIQ studies. Selected publications include *Dominican Politics in the Twenty First Century: Continuity and Change*, principal editor (2023); "The Odebrecht

Fraud: An Analysis of Corruptive Practices in the PLD's Cartel Politics," in *Dominican Politics in the Twenty First Century: Continuity and Change*, edited by Jacqueline Jiménez Polanco and Ernesto Sagás (2023); "The Dominican LGBTIQ Movement and Asylum Claims in the United States," in *Migrant Marginality: A Transnational Perspective*, edited by Philip Kretsedemas, Jorge Capetillo, and Glenn Jacobs (2013); and "Women's Quotas in the Dominican Republic: Advances and Detractions," in *Diffusion of Gender Quotas in Latin America and Beyond: Advances and Setbacks in the Last Two Decades*, edited by Adriana Piatti-Crocker (2011).

Aurelia Martín Casares is a professor of historic anthropology at the University of Málaga, Spain. She has a PhD in history and civilization from the École des Hautes Études en Sciences Sociales, Paris. Her areas of interest include slavery and abolition in the Hispanic World and the Western Mediterranean, and her methodological perspectives involve historical anthropology and gender studies. She has held research residencies at internationally renowned centers (Universities of Toulouse-Le Mirail, British Columbia in Vancouver, University of Cairo, EHESS-Paris, and Queen Mary-University of London). Martín Casares is the director of I+D Research Projects, funded by the Spanish Ministry of Science, the Agency for International Cooperation (Spain), and the Junta de Andalucía (Regional Government), and she is a research collaborator in projects funded by the European Union. She is the author of books and chapters in books by various presses and has published articles in international peer-reviewed journals, as well as lectured at international universities (Oxford, Palermo, Lisbon, Nice, Tunisia, New York, and London).

Rocío Periáñez Gómez holds a BA in liberal arts with a specialty in modern history and a PhD from the University of Extremadura. Her research focuses on slavery in the Extremadura region of Spain, and has appeared in several magazines and book anthologies. She is the author of *Negros, mulatos y blancos: los esclavos en Extremadura durante la Edad Moderna, 1600–1800* (*Blacks, Mulatos and Whites: Slaves in Extremadura during the Modern Era, 1600–1800*) (2010).

David Stark was a historian of colonial Latin America, particularly interested in enslaved populations of the Spanish Caribbean. His work focuses on the demography and family life of slaves in eighteenth-century Puerto Rico, and draws on parish baptismal, marriage, and death registers. He is the author of *Slave Families and the Hato Economy in Eighteenth-Century Puerto Rico* (2015), and select articles include "A New Look at the African Slave Trade in Puerto Rico through the Use of Parish Registers: 1660 to 1815," *Slavery & Abolition* 30, no. 4 (2009): 491–520, and "Slavery and the Service Economy in 1673 San Juan," *Revista de Ciencias Sociales* 23, no. 2 (2010): 46–67.

Anthony R. Stevens-Acevedo is an independent scholar of colonial Santo Domingo. His selected publications include *Juan Rodríguez and the Beginnings of New York City* (2013), coauthored with Tom Weterings and Leonor Alvarez Francés, and *The Santo Domingo Slave Revolt of 1521 and the Slave Laws of 1522* (2019). He is the developer of the Spanish Paleography Digital Teaching & Learning Tool supported by the NEH (http://spanishpaleographytool.org) and is the creator of the database *First Blacks in the Americas*, www.firstblacks.org.

Richard Lee Turits is a historian of the Caribbean and Latin America, particularly the Hispanic Caribbean and Haiti. A graduate of Brown University, he received an MA from Yale University and a PhD from the University of Chicago. His research and teaching have focused on histories of race, slavery, violence, peasantries, nondemocratic regimes, and US Empire. He is the author of *Foundations of Despotism: Peasants, the Trujillo Regime, and Modernity in Dominican History* (2003), which received the John Edwin Fagg prize of the American Historical Association and the Bolton-Johnson Prize of the Conference on Latin American History, and was named a Choice Outstanding Academic Title. His latest book, coauthored with Laurent Dubois, is *Freedom Roots: Histories from the Caribbean* (2019).

Index

Abbad y Lasierra, Iñigo, 238–39
Acosta Corniel, Lissette, 62
Adoration of Christ by the Three Kings, 37
Afro-Iberians, 2
"Afro-Spain," 2
Aguero, Gerónimo de, 196
Al-Andalus, 30
Albornoz, Bartolomé de, 34
Alcantara Serrano, Pedro, 200
Alemán Iglesias, Javier, 15n32
Alfonso X "the Wise" (*el Sabio*), 30, 166
Almeida, Juan de, 211
Alonso, Cortés, 14n21
Alonso, Francisco, 187, 189–90, 202
Altman, Aida, 141, 143
Alvarez, Francisco, 197–98
Amerindians, the, 232–33
Amezquita, Juan de, 191–93
Andrien, Kenneth J., 239, 241
Antillón, Isidoro de, 40
Antonio Piqueras, José, 234
Arab-Moslem authorities, 34
Arabs
  Arab-Muslim slavery, 32
  in Muslim Spain, 30
  of North Africa, 29
Arana, Barbola de, 144
Aranguren, Pedro de, 201

Arguelles, Francisco, 211
Arístegui y Vélez, Rafael, 245
Aristotle, 30–31, 40
Asiento (Legalization of slavery), 6, 37, 194, 217n36, 235–37
Austrias Carmine (Latino), 28
Atlantic studies, 1–2
Austria, Don Juan de, 28
Avellaneda Farfan, Alonso de, 144–45
Ayala, Cepeda de, 79
Ayala, Sebastiana de, 202

Barrera, Juan de la, 76, 78
Baralt, Guillermo, 21n58
Bardecí, Captain Agüero, 5
Bartlett, Richard, 245
Battle of the Number, 17n36
Battle of Palo Hincado, 16n36
Bennett, Herman, 188, 196
"Biafara," 5, 10
Black *horro*, 154–55
Blacks in Spain
  diasporic experience of, 2
  fictional representations of, 3–4, 28–29
  historiography of, 2
Black women
  as active agents in Santo Domingo, 143, 145–49, 151–57
  arrival in the Americas, 147–49

Black women *(continued)*
    as bait to preserve enslaved communities, 138
    foundational role in Americas, 138, 157
    free black women, 13n2, 141–49, 152, 155
    intercolonial migration by, 145
    participation in Hispaniola economy, 151–57
    as property owners, 143
    role in Santo Domingo's enslaved African society, 142
    role in slave uprisings, 139
    role in sugar production, 140–42, 151, 156
    travel by, 143–47
Blumenthal, Debra, 83, 94n36
Boca de Nigua (sugar mill), 142
Bolivar, Simon, 16n36
Boyer, Jean Pierre, 8, 16n36
Bran, Catalina, 150, 161n54
"Bran" (ethnic group), 5
Braudel, Fernand, 74
Bravo, Francisco, 149
Brougham, Henry, 7
Brown, George W., 7
Bryant, Sherwin, 213

Caballero, Álvaro, 142
Caballero, Juan, 211
"Caçanga," 5
Cáceres 1569 (ordinance), 51
Calderon de la Barca, Francisco, 188, 192, 195, 202
Campoamor, Clara, 40
Carabalí, 5
Carbajal y Benavides, Antonio, 207
Carcel Real in Manatí, 11
Caribbean, the, 194, 203, 229, 237, 239, 240–41
    abolition of slavery in, 27
    aborigines of, 232
    colonization of, 9
    demographics of, 194, 212–13
    illegal trade by, 236–38
    neglect by scholars, 8, 74
    plantation economy of, 85
    plantation/provision division of labor, 8
    slave trade with Africa, 77, 80–82
    slave trade involving PR, 195–96, 235, 238, 242–43, 255, 257
    slave trade involving Santo Domingo, 78, 104
    and Spanish colonialism, 74
    See also Spanish Caribbean
Carleval, Ana de, 38
Carlos II, 148
Carlos III, 148–49, 179, 183n22
Carlos V, 41
Carpentier, Alejo, 147
Carrasquillo, Ana de, 196, 202
Carrión, Morales, 247
Casa de Beneficencia, 230, 251, 255
Casa de Contratación (House of Trade), 234
Casare, Martín, 14n21
Casas, Bartolomé de las, 36–37
Castelar, Emilio, 40
Castilla, Fernando, 187
Castilian Crown, 108
Catholic Spain, 11
Cauallero, Constanzo Don Fernando y Ramires, 168
Cédula de Gracias, the, 243, 245, 257
Cervantes Saavedra, Miguel de, 3
Charles II, 20
Charles III, 239–41
Charles IV, 11
Charter of the Rights of Man, 42
Chávez Mujica, María de, 202
Chilean War, the, 36
Chinea, Jorge L., 9–10

Christophe, Henri, 16n36
Cipriano de Utrera, Fray, 149, 155–56
Clifford, George, 203
Clos, Daniel, 238
Cochrane, Thomas, 243
Código Negro Carolino, 32, 106, 129n13
Código Negro Francés, 32
Coggeshall, George, 244–46
Colegio de Santo Tomas de Aquino, 208
Columbus, Christopher, 88n4, 93, 138, 143, 157
Compañía de Guinea de Francia, 31
Compañía del Asiento de Inglaterra, 31
Compañía Real de Guinea, 37
Company of England, 37
Concepción, Nicolás de la, 176
Constancia (slave ship), 245
Contaduría, 193
Cordero, Giusti, 8
Corral, Bartolomé, 75
Cortés, José Luis, 58
Cortés, Vicenta, 2
Cortijo, Sebastián, 200–1, 203
Cota, María de, 144–46, 152
Cotoner, Fernando, 229, 231, 247, 249–51
Council of Trent, the, 166–67
creoles, 141, 242, 254
Crown of Castile, 50
Cuba, 146–47
  abolition of slavery in, 40–41, 230
  antiblack racism in, 121
  Black women in, 143
  Cuban *son*, 147
  free blacks in, 251
  isolation from Spanish-American empire, 233
  and the *Majesty* affair, 247–48
  slavery in, 39, 105, 188–89, 192–93, 230, 243, 245

Spanish imports to, 240
Spanish soldiers in, 203–5
and U.S. slave merchants, 249
sugar production in, 257
CUNY Dominican Studies Institute, 13n2

Deive, Carlos Esteban, 106
Dessalines, Jean Jacques, 16n36
Días, Domingo, 157
Díaz, Andrea, 165–67, 176–78, 180–81.
Díaz, Alonso, 76
Díaz, Jorge, 235
Díaz Soler, Luis M., 235–36
Diccionario Nacional ó Gran Diccionario Clásico de la Lengua Española, 246–47
Diepa, Joseph, 238
Domínguez, Luisa, 144
Domínguez Ortiz, Antonio, 2, 64n8
Dominican Republic, 8, 17n36
Dorsey, Joseph, 192, 232, 242
Drake, Sir Francis, 203
Draque, Francis, 148
Dubois, Laurent, 8

Eguiluz, Paula de, 144
"El Celoso extremeño" (Saavedra), 3
El ingenioso hidalgo don Quijote de la Mancha (Cervantes), 28
encomienda (entrustment) system, 77, 232
Eller, Anne, 8
Elliot, J. H., 232
Emerson, Edward Bliss, 244
Enríquez, Melchor, 202
Enríquez, Miguel, 202, 238–39
Enslaved Blacks, 2–4
  activities forbidden to, 55–59, 61–62, 69n40
  allies of, 11–12

Enslaved Blacks (continued)
  arrival in Americas, 1, 9, 38
  in the Americas, 9, 10, 36–38, 74, 77–78
  conversion to Christianity, 209–10
  death by illness, 10
  dehumanization of (see also slaves, punishment of), 4, 29–30, 62, 74, 78, 120, 127, 152, 157, 230, 233, 235, 240, 250
  desperation of, 141
  entrepreneurship among, 12
  experience of, 2, 4, 7–8, 11, 13, 14n18, 29, 51–52, 104, 137, 157, 158n9, 189, 193, 212
  French transport of, 7
  godparents of, 187–91, 197–203, 206–11, 213
  as godparents, 188–89, 198, 202
  in the Indies, 4–5, 14n18
  jobs/tasks imposed upon, 10, 84, 114, 192–93, 232
  legislation regarding, 11, 36, 38, 40–42, 73, 78, 80, 94n36, 104–128, 139, 151, 250–51
  newspaper reports on, 29
  in Portuguese Brazil, 27
  ransoming of, 34
  recreation among, 55
  in Spanish America, 234
  in the Spanish colonies, 37–38, 83
  trafficking of, 6, 10–11, 50–51, 195, 212, 229–235, 241–243, 246, 249, 255–258
Escaño, María, 168–69
escapees, 141
  of the Carcel Real in Manatí, 11
  control over, 126–27, 139
  from Extremadura, 11, 57–58, 146
  fear of slaves' escaping, 54, 57–58, 124
  "grace period" for, 109
  in the Hispanic Caribbean, 237
  ingenuity of, 253
  from La Española, 105, 107
  laws and ordinances regarding, 12, 56–57, 122–24
  means of escape, 57–58, 85, 122, 125, 252–53
  from the non-Hispanic Caribbean, 237
  penalties for helping, 122–23, 125–27
  police reports on, 127
  population of, 85
  and Prince Phillip, 120–21
  from Puerto Rico, 11, 233
  in Puerto Rico, 237, 252–53
  punishment of, 109–11, 122, 132n22, 252
  recapture of, 86, 108–9, 111–12, 120, 124, 127, 237, 253
  from Santo Domingo, 5, 85–87, 108–110, 122, 125–27, 129n10
esclavos cortados (cut slaves), 38
Espinosa, Ana de, 201

Falcon, María, 202
Fantauzi, Cruziano, 252
Felipe Cordero, Juan, 211
Felipe, Don, 39
Felipe, Jacinto, 202
Felipe III, 38
Feliza (slave ship), 245
female slaves
  absence of in in colonial documents about S.D., 141
  laws regarding, 53–55, 113, 116–17, 119–20, 123, 126
  in Puerto Rico, 192–93, 207, 212, 233
  in Santo Domingo, 140–41, 149–52, 156–57
Ferdinand VII, 242

Fernández de Oviedo, Gonzalo, 106
Fernández Sordis, Diego, 208
Fernández, Vicente, 82
Fonseca, Francisco de, 176
Fuente, Alejandro de la, 210
Fuente García, Alejandro de la, 105, 121, 192–93
Figueroa, Luis A., 9
Flores de Caldevilla, María, 208
Fourcarde case, 247–48
Franklin Franco, 16n36
free Blacks, 116, 242
  acquisition of freedom, 1, 75, 81–84, 86, 105, 143–44, 151–52, 230
  and the Catholic Church, 197
  cooperation with enslaved Blacks, 113, 122
  discrimination against, 121, 125–27
  in Dutch and British colonies, 36
  experience of, 10–12, 212
  free Black women, 116
  judicial documents regarding, 149–50
  liberation of, 49–50
  license requests by, 1
  in Puerto Rico, 10, 11, 13, 15n32, 41, 191, 193, 201–2, 207, 211–13, 248, 250–55
  reenslavement of, 80–81
  research on, 1, 10, 50
  in Santo Domingo, 11–13, 16n36, 73–75, 80–83, 86–87, 108–9, 113, 114, 116, 121–22, 124, 137, 141–47, 155–57
  in Spain, 13, 35
  and Spanish law, 82–83, 86–87
Fregenal de la Sierra statutes, 56
Fuero juzgo, 30

Gaceta Oficial, 251
Galiano, Bernaldino de, 82
ganadoras, 151–52
García de Loyola, Governor Martín, 36
García, Julia Moreno, 243
Garrigus, John D., 155
Gaveniz and Fern (PR partnership), 252
Gautier, Arlette, 194
Gelofa Pelona, Juana, 150
Gerbner, Katherine, 189
Gil, Juan, 156–57
Ginés, Micaela, 146–47
Ginés, Teodora, 146–47
Golden Age, the, 28, 55
Gómez de Avellaneda, Gertrudis, 40
González, Adriano, 198
González Arévalo, Raúl, 4
González, Cristóbal, 75, 81, 83, 201, 207
Gonzalez, Juan Alonso, 188–89, 200–1, 203, 208
González Manos de Oro, Pedro, 205
González, Raymundo, 121
Gorgoran Castilla, Antonio de, 202
Gorrevod, Lorenzo de, 77
Gorjón, Hernando, 141
Gould, Alice, 157
"Graciana," 187, 189, 196, 199
Guardino, Peter, 206
Gutierrez, Lazaro, 145

Haiti, 5–6, 8, 238
  annexation of Santo Domingo, 87
  as desirable destination for PR slaves, 11
  free Blacks in, 16n36
  Haitian Invasion, 16n36
  Haitian Revolution, 230, 257, 16n36
  history of, 16–17n36
  research on, 7
Hall, Gwendolyn Midlo, 6
Hardwick, Julie, 167

Harris, Richard, 156
Havana Anglo-Spanish Mixed
    Commission, the, 230
*Havana and the Atlantic in the
    Sixteenth Century* (de la Fuente
    García), 105
Heraclitus, 30
Hernández, Andrés, 152
Hernández, Catalina, 143, 146
Higgins, Kathleen, 197, 210–11
Hispaniola (*see* Santo Domingo)
Historia: Militar de Santo Domingo
    (Utrera), 122
Hollander, Craig, 248
"Hordenanças de la horden que se a
    de tener en el tratamiento con
    los negros," 122
Hunt, Samuel Lennon. 248–50

Iberian Studies, 2
Ick, Francis, 248–50
Indians, 167
    enslaved Indians, 35–36, 78, 80,
        83–84, 88, 114, 123, 232–33
    and escaped Black slaves, 122
    escaped Indian slaves, 237
    Indian rebels, 85
Indigenous Canarians (aka Guanches),
    2
*Ingenious Gentleman, Don Quixote
    Quixote la Mancha* (Saavedra), 3
*Inquiry into the Colonial Policy
    of the European Powers*, An
    (Brougham), 7
Introduction to Dominican Blackness
    (Torres-Saillant), 128
Irizarry, Pedro, 242

Jaca, Francisco José de, 41
"Jealous Extremaduran, The"
    (Saavedra), 3
Jelofa, Ana, 150

Jelofes, 5, 10
José, Juan, 187, 189
Journal of Negro History, The, 7–8
Juan Bautista Muñoz collection of
    colonial documents, 140
Juan Latino, 38
Justinian Codes, 233

Karasch, Mary, 194
Karras, Alan L., 231
King Balthazar, 37
King Felipe, 36
King Felipe II, 31
King Felipe V, 37
King Recesvinto, 30
Kuethe, Allan J., 239, 241

Labordère, M. de, 247–48, 250
Labra, Rafael María de, 40
La Comedia Famosa de Juan Latino
    (de Enciso), 28
La Concepción de Nuestra Señora
    (sugar mill), 142, 151
Ladina, Ana, 150
La Española, 13
LaFleur, Greta, 166–67, 182n5
la Isla Española (Spanish Island), 76
*La mala vida: delincuencia y picaresca
    en la colonia española de Santo
    Domingo* (Deive), 158n2
Lamb, Ursula, 137
Lara y Cárdenas, Manuel de, 247, 249
Las Siete Partidas, 48, 78, 166, 179
Latino, Juan, 3–4, 28–29, 42n1-2
Lavrin, Asunción, 166, 181, 183n12
Law, Robin, 6
Lazarillo de Tormes, 3
León, Rodrigo de, 73, 76, 8
Lepanto, battle of, 28
Ley Moret, 40
Leyes de Burgos, 32
Leyes de Toro, 31

Leyes Nuevas, 41
Liber Iudiciorum (King Recesvinto), 30
Lister, Elissa L., 15n36
López, Antón, 75–76
López Cantos, Ángel, 205, 239
López, Catalina, 75, 81–82, 84
López, Diego, 144, 157, 211
López, José Cortés, 2, 14n21
López, Rodrigo, 12, 73–77, 79, 80–84, 86–88n5
López, Ruy, 74–75, 77, 82
López, Sebastián, 168–71, 174–75, 179
Lorenza, Isabel, 165–76, 178–81
Lorenzo, Rodríguez, 148–49
Louverture, Toussaint, 8, 16n36
Lozano, Phelipe, 176
Luciano Franco, José, 248
Luis, Alferez Joseph, 176
"Luisica," 150

Magdalena, María, 165–70, 172–76, 178–81, 183n22
Majesty, the, 11, 229–32, 246–50, 252, 254, 257–58n1
Malave, Catalina, 201
Maluquer de Motes, Jordi, 246
Mandinka, 3, 5, 10
María, Juana, 187, 189
María, Manuela, 156–57
Mariana of Austria, 204
Mariani, Luis, 252
Marmolejo, González, 180–81
maroons
  escapees, 237
  maroon slave squads, 112
  punishment of, 120–21
  in San Lorenzo de los Minas, 6
  in/near Santo Domingo, 5, 105
  security threat posed by, 237
Márquez, Juan, 41
Marques, Leonardo, 249
Marques, Manuel, 168–70

Marte, Roberto, 140
Martinez-Alier, Verena, 180
Martínez de Quiñones, José, 208
Martínez, Joana, 145
Martínez Vergne, Teresita, 254–55
Martyr, Peter, 15–16n36
Masfarré, Joaquín, 252
Masso, Calixto C., 28–29
Matías, Joseph, 29
Matos, Juan Lorenzo de, 208
Melinton, Andrés, 11
Méndez de Vigo, Santiago, 245
Mercado, Tomás de, 33–34, 41
Mercedarians, 34–35
Meriño Fuentes, María de los Ángeles, 250
Messina, Félix María de, 253
mestizos, 140
Mexia, Andrea, 201
Miller, Joseph, 209–10
"Minas," 5–6
Mintz, Sidney, 9
mixed race people, 190–91, 193, 196 198, 207, 212, 215n17
Moirans, Epifanio de, 41
Moors, 4–5, 14n21, 29, 34
Morales Carrión, Arturo, 231–32, 242–43
Morel, Rodríguez, 142
morenas, 143
Moreno, Domingo, 176
Moret, Benjamin Nistal, 11
Morgan, Jennifer, 156
Morisco people, 31–32
Moscoso, Francisco, 235
Moya, Silverio de, 187, 189–90
Muesas, Miguel de, 238, 240
Mujica, Ana, 199
mulattos, 143, 152–55, 238–39
  in Puerto Rico, 10
  in Santo Domingo, 166–81
  as slave owners, 156

Muñoz, Francisco de, 188
Muriel, Maria de, 211
Muslims, 79
  Arab-Muslim slavery, 32
  capture of Christian Spanish women, 29
  clashes with Spaniards, 32
  hostility toward, 5
  in Iberia, 83
  Muslim slaves, 36
  Muslim Spain, 30
  Sharia law, 30

New World slavery, 1
Nieves, María de las, 165–71, 173–75, 178–81
Novísima Recopilación de Leyes, 31, 48
Nueva Recopilación, 49
Nueva Recopilación de Leyes del Reino, 31
Nuevas Leyes, 32.

Ordenamiento de Montalvo, 31
Ordenanza General de Emancipados, 250–51, 254, 265n116
O'Reilly, Alejandro, 239
"Origins of Abolition in Santo Domingo, The," 7–8
Ortiz, Francisca, 208
Osorio, Antonio de, 152, 155
Ovando de Mejía, Francisco, 235
Ovando, Nicolás de, 137–38, 140, 147, 149
O y de Moya, María de la, 168–69

Padilla, Christoval, 168–69
Padilla, Pedro, 168–69
Pantoja, Victoria, 202
Panza, Sancho (fictional character), 3
Patterson, Orlando, 210
Peninsular War, the, 241
Perera Díaz, Aismara, 250

Periañez Gómez, Rocio, 146
Petion, Alexander, 16n36
Philip II, 235
Picó, Fernando, 236, 243
Pineda, Juan de, 170, 172
Pino, García del, 192–93
Pons, Moya, 167
Pragmática y declaración sobre los moriscos esclavos que fueron tomados en el reyno de Granada, 31
Prince Phillip (of Spain), 120–21
Proctor, Frank, 198
Puerto Rico, 1, 11
  arrival of slaves in, 6–7, 9, 12, 39, 194–96, 212, 229–32, 234–35, 237, 240, 245
  baptism in, 187–91, 194–202, 206, 209–13, 252
  Catholicism in, 196
  and the *Cédula de Gracias*, 242–45
  child/infant slaves in, 187–90, 194–203, 207, 209–13
  contraband slaves in, 192, 195, 231–32, 234–41
  and enslaved Blacks/Africans, 6–7, 9–11, 13, 39, 41, 187–203, 207–13, 229–31, 233–53, 256–58
  escaped slaves in, 237
  emancipados in, 250–54, 257–58
  house slaves in, 10
  laws regarding slavery, 11, 21n58, 27
  liberalization of slave trade, 240
  prohibition of slavery in, 40–41, 242
  role of slavery in economy, 10
  scholarship on, 7, 9, 11, 205–6, 231–32, 235, 242–43, 247, 249–50, 254–56
  skin shades of population, 9, 190
  slave trade in, 12, 195–96

slave demographics of, 12, 191–95, 212, 215n17, 230, 234
slave trade post-1815, 241–58
slave traffic with Spain, 234
Spanish soldiers in, 203–7, 239
sugar production in, 9–10, 191, 193–94, 212, 230, 233, 240, 242–44, 251, 253, 256–57
whites in, 10

Quakers, 40
Queen Anne Stuart, 37
Queen Isabel I, 36–37, 40
Quintero Rivera, Angel, 212
"Quot servi, tot hostes" (So Many Servants, So Many Enemies) (Seneca), 30

Ramírez, Dixa, 7
Ramírez Fuenleal, Sebastián, 107, 111–13, 118, 120, 122
Real Cédula, 11, 106, 242, 244
Real Factoría de Tabacos, the, 240
Recopilación de Leyes de Indias, 32
Relaciones históricas de Santo Domingo (Demorizi), 155–56
Resolución sobre la libertad de los negros (de Jaca), 41
Restall, Matthew, 194
Reyna, Martín de, 208
Ribera, Carvajal y, 148
Rios, Ana María Lugão, 188
Rios, María de los, 191, 193
Robles, Antonio de, 192, 197–98
Rodríguez, Ana, 168–69
Rodríguez Demorizi, Emilio, 155
Rodríguez, Fabiana, 168–69
Roig de Leuchsenring, Emilio, 105
Romero Martín, Victor José, 4
Roman Empire, the, 78
Roman Hispania, 11, 29–30
Rosa, Jacinto de la, 187

Rosa, Luis de la, 253–55
Rosario, Francisca del, 201
Royal Archives of Higüey, 178
Royal Prison (*Cárcel Real*), 170
Russell-Wood, A. J. R., 79

Sáez, José Luis, 141, 199–200
Saint Ambrose, 30
Saint Augustine, 30
Saint Domingue
  French colonization of, 8, 13n1
  scholarship on, 8
  as a Spanish colony, 8
Salazar, López de, 150
Samudio, Edda O., 167
Sandoval, Alonso de, 36, 41
Sandoz, M., 249
San Juan, Juan de, 200–3
San Lorenzo de los Minas, 5–6
Sanmillán, Inés de, 205
Santana, Pedro, 17n36
Santo Domingo (i.e., Hispaniola), 1, 8, 121
  annexation of, 87
  arrival of slaves in, 11, 15n35, 73, 76–80, 137–38, 151
  Audiencia of, 73, 81, 106–7, 109, 120, 123, 129n10, 180, 235, 238
  Black ladinos in, 127
  Black population of, 103, 107, 114–128, 140–41
  Black women in, 137–157
  bozales in, 110–11, 127, 138, 141, 158n5, 242, 243, 247, 249–52, 254–55
  control over sexual/ private lives in, 167
  as desirable destination for slaves, 11, 138
  enslaved Blacks in, 6–8, 10–13n1, 14n18, 73–78, 104–128, 138–140, 144, 152–54, 179

Santo Domingo *(continued)*
  as first slave society, 11–12, 103–4
  as "hub" of African-Atlantic slave trade, 77
  indigenous American slaves in, 77
  interethnic/racial/ class marriages in, 180
  ladinos in, 110–11
  naming of, 13n1
  neglect by scholars, 8, 11
  plantation division of labor, 8
  racialization of slavery in, 80, 121–23
  scholarship on, 7–10, 15n34
  slave laws of, 11–12, 54, 79
  slave population of, 84–86, 141, 152, 155
  slave rebellions in, 12, 85–86, 106–7, 119–20, 122, 138, 150, 233
  Spanish women in, 141
  sugar production in, 10–11, 74, 76–77, 81, 84–86, 95n43, 103, 118, 124, 140–42, 151, 156, 230
Scarano, Francisco, 231
Schneider, Elena, 255
Schuler, Monica, 210
Seneca from Córdoba, 30
Serafina, Francisca, 187, 189, 202–3
Shepherd, Verene A., 11
Sidbury, James, 210
Siervos libres o justa defensa de la libertad natural de los esclavos (de Moirans), 41
Siete Partidas, 30–32
Silva Campo, Ana María, 144, 168, 174
slavery, 1, 6, 34–35, 6, 78
  in Africa, 27, 34
  in the Arab and Asian world, 27
  in Chile, 39
  in Colombia, 36
  concealment of, 231
  concept of, 2, 121–23, 179
  contemporary forms of, 41
  in fiction, 28–29
  fiscal/ commercial aspects of, 32, 38–40, 74, 80–81, 83–84
  growth/expansion of, 50–51, 74, 84
  in Guatemala, 39
  in Guinea, 34
  in Honduras, 39
  inhumanity of, 38, 84
  in Isla Española, 39
  justifications for, 32–34, 36, 38, 232
  laws/ legislation regarding, 30–32, 34–35, 37–38, 43n8, 48–62, 63n5, 64n10, 80–84, 104–128, 139, 179–80, 229–31, 250–51
  main "focus" of, 10–11
  in the Mediterranean, 32, 34–35, 79
  from the Middle East, 4
  modern forms of, 41–42
  of Morisco people, 31
  neglect of by scholars, 7, 49, 104–5, 107, 114–15, 128–9n7, 137, 140, 149, 157, 188, 190
  in Portugal, 79–80
  in Portuguese Brazil, 27
  prohibitions on, 32, 40–42, 84, 87, 242, 247–48, 258
  in Puerto Rico, 6–7, 39, 194–96, 212, 229–58
  reasons for, 2, 32–32
  role of wars in slave trade, 78
  as social condition or status, 122
  in Southern Europe, 78–79
  in Spanish America, 78
  and the United States, 40, 248–49
Slavery without Sugar: Diversity in Caribbean Economy and Society since the 17th Century (Shepherd), 11

slaves
  Animist slaves, 30
  baptism of, 187–91, 194–203, 206, 209–13, 222n115, 246
  in the Canary Islands, 2
  child/ infant slaves, 187–90, 194–203, 207, 209–13, 233
  Christian slaves, 30–31, 36, 78–79, 124, 187–91, 194–202, 206, 209–13
  as contraband, 12, 77, 195, 229–250, 256–57
  defects/vices attributed to, 57–60, 62, 118–19, 122, 124
  European population of, 84
  fear of, 51–52
  financial agreements with masters, 116
  in the Iberian Peninsula, 27, 29–31
  illegal reenslavement of, 80–81
  godparents to, 187–91, 197–203, 206–11, 213
  kidnapping of, 80, 83
  kinship networks among, 188–90, 198–99, 211–13
  lack of legal representation, 188
  lodgings for, 118
  in the Middle East, 2
  Native American slaves, 32, 35–36, 40–41
  perception of, 50
  population of, 5, 50, 53–54, 86, 94n39
  punishment of, 38, 50–51, 53–54, 56, 58–62, 69n40, 75–76, 105–14, 118–23, 126–127, 132n21, 139–40, 150–51, 166, 233, 252, 254
  religious conversion/indoctrination of, 36, 123–25
  resistance by, 85–87, 103–4, 120, 125–27, 140

social networks among, 188–92, 205, 208–10, 213
uprisings/rebellions by, 32, 38, 54, 85–86, 106–7, 112, 122, 139, 233
"white" slaves, 79, 90n16, 129n12
Smuggling: Contraband and Corruption in World History (Karras), 231
Sociedad Económica de Amigos del País, 241
Soler, Díaz, 253
Sombrero, Juan, 75, 81, 83
Sonesson, Birgit, 240
Sorsby, Victoria Gardner, 236
Soto, Luis de, 143
South Sea Company, 237
Spain, 7
  annexation of Dominican Republic, 8
  Black people in, 2–3, 7
  colonies of, 11, 73, 76–78
  colonization of Americas, 2
  Consejo de Indias, 81
  economic competitiveness of, 238–40, 256
  historical amnesia in, 27–29
  ignorance of slavery in, 11
  and illegal trade, 233–34, 238–39
  laws banning slavery, 229–30, 232, 242
  manipulation of African people, 33
  modern slavery in, 41
  Muslim rule of, 3
  use of San Juan as military outpost, 203–4
  slavery/enslavement in, 2–3, 7, 43n14, 79–80, 86–87
  and slave trade, 6, 232, 235–38, 239, 241–46
Toro Laws of, 179
trade with Spanish Caribbean, 192
use of slaves in its colonies, 6

"Son de Ma' Teodora" (song), 147
Southern, Henry, 245
Spanish American War, 7
Spanish Black Code, 151–52
Spanish Caribbean, 233, 256
   and Black identities/ societies, 1
   Black people in, 2
   slaves' social ties in, 188, 191
   slave trade and, 5–6, 8–10, 27, 77, 85, 104, 212, 232, 246
   study of, 1–2, 6–7, 188
   trade with Spain, 192
Spanish Crown, the, 240
   enslavement of Moriscos, 31
   and free Blacks, 1, 36, 38, 41, 74–75
   fiscal struggles of, 31, 239–41
   and Indigenous Canarians, 2
   and indigenous laborers, 77, 80
   and indigenous slaves, 83, 232
   legalization of slavery (*Asiento*), 6, 76, 106
   licenses granted by, 36, 76–77, 79, 234–35
   and Moors, 5, 29
   policy re black marriage, 138–38
   and Puerto Rico, 203, 233, 237–42, 244
   recapture of escaped slaves, 237
   regulation of Blacks in Spanish empire, 108
   religious indoctrination of slaves, 123
   requests made of, 138
   Royal Provision of, 41
   and slave ordinances, 107
   and slave smuggling, 256
   and slaves in Cuba, 193, 230
   and slaves in Puerto Rico, 194
   and slaves' resistance, 120
Spanish Christians, 32, 35, 79, 139
Spanish Inquisition, 144, 180

Spanish Renaissance, 3, 28, 30–31, 37
Spanish Royal Court, 33, 35, 173
Sperling, Jutta, 166
Stark, David M., 235
St. Méry, Moreau de, 84
Stone, Lawrence, 166
sub-Saharan Africans
   conflicts among, 33–34
   enslavement of, 1, 31, 33, 51, 79
   free status of, 1, 83
   importing of into Spain, 28
   names given to, 37
   in literature, 29
Suma de Tratos y Contratos (de Mercado), 33–34
Szaszdi, Adám, 198

Taino Arawaks, 13
Taino Indigenous population, 6–7, 15–16n36
Tannenbaum, Frank, 7
Tapia Ríos, Gloria, 252
Taylor, Scott, 190
Terrazas-Williams, Daniel, 143
Ticknor, George, 28
Tinoco, Catalina de, 149–50
Tormes, Lázaro de (fictional character), 27–28
Torre, Miguel de la, 243, 245
Torres, Constanza de, 191, 193
Torquemada, Miguel de, 143
Torres-Saillant, Silvio, 128
Transatlantic Bondage (Corniel), 1–2, 13, 15n34
Transatlantic Slave Trade Database, the, 230, 248
Traspuesto, Catalina, 187
Trinitarians, 34–35
Trujillo, Rafael Leonidas, 7
Turdetani Iberians, 29–30
Turits, Richard Lee, 8, 12, 121

University of Granada, the, 4, 28

Valdés, Luisa, 202–3
Valera, Juan, 168–70
Valverde de Llerena statutes, 56
Verlinden, Charles, 17n40
Villafaña, Juan González de, 238
Villalobos, Enrique, 41 Vilar
Villasante, Juana, 10
Vila Vilar, Enriqueta, 236, 246
Visigothic Hispania, 11, 30
Viveros, María de, 202
von Germeten, Nicole, 143
Voyages: The Trans-Atlantic Slave Trade Database, 194

Walker, Charles, 245
War of the Spanish Succession, 239
Welch, Pedro, 193
Wheat, David, 9, 103, 129n7, 133n40, 143, 155, 188
Whites, 92n24
  assistance to Blacks, 11–12, 122

  as godparents to slaves, 188, 190, 213
  marriage to free slaves, 38
  in Puerto Rico, 10, 188, 190–91, 193, 201, 212
  role in racial hierarchy, 122–23
  in Santo Domingo, 12, 86, 103, 155
  "white" slaves, 78, 109
Williams, Eric, 232
Wolofs, 5

Xavier, Francisco, 187
Ximénez de Enciso, Diego, 28
Ximénes de Hermosilla, Catalina, 201, 207
Ximenez, Juan, 168–69

Zafra, 54–56, 60–61
Zafra 1528 (ordinance), 51–52
"Zape," 5, 10
Zayas, Martín, 79
Zeuske, Michael, 246
Zuazo, Alonso, 138–40

www.ingramcontent.com/pod-product-compliance
Lightning Source LLC
Chambersburg PA
CBHW030526230426
43665CB00010B/780